The Amethyst Light

Messages for the New Millennium
from the Ascended Master Djwhal Khul

through Violet Starre

Light Technology Publishing

Cover art by Delmary

ISBN 1-891824-41-4

 Published by
Light Technology Publishing
PO Box 3540
Flagstaff, AZ 86003
(800) 450-0985

Printed by

Contents

Foreword

Ascended Master
Djwhal Khul

A scended Master Djwhal Khul (pronounced jwäl kool) was one of the group known as the Mahatmas, who worked with the Theosophical Society and Madame Blavatsky in the 1870s and onward. The Mahatmas were supposedly a brotherhood who lived in the foothills of the Himalayas and had miraculous powers.

Master Djwhal Khul became better known for his work with Alice A. Bailey from 1919 to the end of the 1940s, when he was a lama in a monastery on the border of Tibet and Bhutan. During that time, Mrs. Bailey channeled and wrote twenty-six books and founded the Lucis Trust and the Arcane School. Later Djwhal Khul worked with Janet McClure and her Tibetan Foundation. A number of working channels emerged out of this organization and started ashrams within the continental United States. At that time, the Master was residing in a higher dimension.

A number of people currently channel Djwhal Khul, including Dr. David Joshua Stone, Reverend Terri Newlon, Moriah Marston, Kathlyn Kingdom, Wistancia Stone and Violet Starre. This is the second collaboration with Violet Starre to produce a contemporary update on conditions on the planet and within the spiritual hierarchy on the inner planes.

1

The Seven Rays as Fields of Endeavor

G reetings! I am the Ascended Master Djwhal Khul. Spiritual truth is like a running river of clear water the individual can drink from by meditating and performing guided visualizations. Inner work leads to that pristine source of wisdom available to all. Books and spiritual teachers are but signposts that point to that inner source. I hope to be a signpost, pointing the way to the living waters within all of you.

First of all, or right off the bat, I would like to clarify that I am not a "spirit" in the sense that you imagine that I am intangible, or made of light, or haunting your world as an insubstantial being. I exist as a solid being within a different dimension. I am in a specific dimension, but there are many other dimensions of the Earth and the universe. The planet in other dimensions is not formless or pure light; rather, it is the same as in your dimension in that there are mountains, hills, valleys, oceans and cities. The higher dimensions differ from yours in that there is no death, sickness, hunger, cold or a need to earn money or to eat.

I am one of a group of individuals who have a certain amount of responsibility toward the spiritual development of humanity within the third dimension. I live within a city within a higher dimension that has beautiful buildings, which serve as libraries and art galleries, places of worship and colleges of science. It is possible to gain access to these buildings from your physical plane through guided visualizations. My work as part of the Council of Twelve is with the seven teaching masters of the rays and the five other spiritual beings who form the Planetary Hierarchy. As the spiritual ruling council of the planet, we meet at regular intervals to discuss our progress.

Sanat Kumara, known to many as Vywamus, is the being also generally known as "God." He is the higher consciousness of all life forms of this planet; as the higher self of humanity, he is relevant to all of us here. He appears as a youth with platinum colored hair.

Second to Sanat is Maitreya, which is the name given to the soul who was the Buddha and who over-lighted the Master Jesus. Maitreya is the Planetary Christ, which is an office that beings hold for a term of service.

Mary is one of the names of the third spiritual being who is a part of the Council of Twelve. Known by many names in many lands, she is also the Mother Earth consciousness. She is the compassionate female principle that over-lights the physical planet.

Then come the masters of the rays and their closest students. Many individuals known to you as saints throughout history or as celebrities of great character are close to the masters and their work. There are many more students, who appear in the third dimension as the most humble and ordinary people.

I am a master of the rays, which means that I am an entry point for a certain cosmic energy to enter the planet. I am something like a crystal. You know that the first radios used crystal quartz to receive transmissions of sound. I receive transmissions of love combined with wisdom. It is a teaching impulse; it comes from one of the signs of the zodiac and is amplified by some of the planets. I anchor this vibration on the inner planes, and it spreads through me to all the members of my inner planes ashram and to all the souls of humanity who vibrate on that ray. The energy is stepped down as it moves away from me. You might imagine me as being at the center of a vast crowd.

The Second Ray

Individuals who are affected by the vibration of this ray feel inwardly compelled to take up occupations and hobbies that the love-wisdom teaching energy encompasses. This ray includes healers of all kinds, from medical doctors to practitioners of all kinds of counterculture methods of healing, such as chiropractors, acupuncturists, massage therapists and spirit healers. People on this ray often have an interest in diet and nutrition as they relate to health. They are also interested in exercise such as tai chi and other moving meditation methods. The ray includes healing of the mental and emotional states and motivates counselors and therapists. It also is related to the collective unconscious mind and creative writing. Books of channeled wisdom and techniques of guided visualization are connected to this ray and this ashram.

I spend most of my time working with my students. There are the students who exist in my dimension because they are between lifetimes, and there are the students who come into my dimension during their sleep cycle. I lecture on spiritual topics and lead meditations and visualizations; I give personal readings in person. My main task is to organize the teachers who channel and the souls who teach.

My personal teacher, the Ascended Master Kuthumi, is also a master of the second ray of love-wisdom, and he works with large groups and full-moon meditations. He was formerly Saint Francis of Assisi, and so some of his keynotes and hallmarks are of such harmlessness that wild animals approach closely. If you frequently experience birds and animals coming unusually close to you, then you may be a student of Master Kuthumi; you are certainly developing a peaceful aura.

The second-ray ashram, which Master Kuthumi presides over, has two masters, because he has his focus in love and I have my focus in wisdom; the activities of both of us result in the ashram of love-wisdom. My interests include, and are not limited to, Chinese medicine, meditation, Reiki, astrology, the martial arts, psychosynthesis, psychotherapy, astrophysics, physics, chemistry, health and wellness, yoga, creative writing and storytelling, screenwriting, mythology and the collective unconscious. Therefore, many of the students I work with have a focus on one or many of these interests. Some of the occupations of this ashram include teaching, but also helping individuals discover the purpose of their incarnation and their occupation. It includes psychologists, therapists and counselors, but also astrologers, health practitioners and writers of fiction for children and for the movies. I work with those writers who tap into the collective unconscious mind. In fact, the more of these interests students of mine have, the better the rapport they have with me.

The work of Master Kuthumi involves channeling the ancient wisdom teachings, promoting good relationships among nations and encouraging peace in the world. Both of us are focusing on encouraging large groups of people to meditate for world peace at the same time, at the time of the full moon.

The energy of the second ray pertains more to the astral plane, the fourth dimension and the collective unconscious than to the other dimensions. Therefore, it is connected to astrology, psychotherapy, career counseling and discovering the purpose of the incarnation. Occupations for second-ray students are psychology, psychotherapy, screenwriting, creative writing, children's literature, channeling and teaching the ancient wisdom. (At the time of Atlantis, the students of the order of the second ray were trained in symbology and dream analysis, astrology, visualization, the science of the chakras; their work was to help individuals find their purpose for incarnating.)

The second ray is connected to the archetype of the goddess and the energies of the Moon — and to Neptune, the planetary ruler of Pisces, who is conceptualized as the archetypal figure of sea god. So the energies of the second ray enter the planet from Pisces. When the Sun is in Pisces, she acts similarly to a lens that magnifies the energy. At the time of the full moon, the Moon acts similarly to an additional lens that magnifies the energy of the sign opposite the Sun. Throughout the year, the seven rays are transmitted steadily and continuously from the twelve directions of the zodiac, but the movements of the Sun and planets magnify or diminish their effectiveness. These energies are coming to humanity through the astral plane, and they are coming to the astral bodies of humanity as well as to the mental and causal levels.

The First Ray

The first ray is the first impulse within the primal ocean of oneness, tranquillity and harmony for the formless to express itself in form. It is as a deep desire that arises from the depths of the Creator, who encompasses all that is to have another to love, to be separated into individual selves who might express divine traits, because without the many, divine traits are meaningless. What use is love if there is no one to love? What use is forgiveness if there is no one to forgive? So the first impulse is for separation within unity and the creation and maintenance of the forms that create the many lower worlds. So the first ray of will to good, or intent, is that of conceptualizing the forms of manifestation before they are manifest and conceptualizing the rules or laws of physics and chemistry.

With the conceptualization of the first ray come all of the souls who will be working on that ray, both human and devic. All of these beings will be builders and maintainers of the form side of life. Within the Hindu religion, this corresponds to the concept of Shiva the creator, and this links back to the Atlantean teachings that exist within the Hindu tradition.

The impetus of this ray is related to the concept of the protection of the weak from being oppressed and abused by the strong. So this ray relates to laws, codes, fines and punishments — to deterrents in general that prevent beings with physical strength and weapons from terrorizing smaller, weaker, younger beings.

This ray is associated with the archetype of the father. Divinity expresses itself in the form of an authoritative male who protects the child from others and who plans and provides. So I might digress by adding that the tendency of Judeo-Christian religions to personify God as a male father figure is a remnant memory of the ancient

Atlantean religion of the seven rays. This ray is also associated with the archetype of the warrior king.

The first ray relates to building and sustaining the forms of creation, protecting the most delicate of them and planning the patterns for civilizations. Contained within this stream of divine energy are such patterns as sacred geometry and such concepts as the flower of life, structure, patterns, blueprints, plans, codes and laws especially pertaining to the third dimension, although pertinent to all dimensions. Because sacred geometry is a first-ray phenomenon, the first ray is connected to mystery schools and schools of initiation that teach sacred geometry.

This ray pertains to occupations that are related to planning civilizations and the relationships between nations. Under the umbrella of this ray fall lawyers, architects, city planners, police, military, politicians, diplomats and all occupations that specifically build societal structures and enforce laws to protect the citizenry of that society. It also pertains to the interactions between civilizations, nations and states.

At this time, of course, the United Nations is the major force in the world for embodiment of first-ray energy. However, any structure that higher powers can use as a force for good in the world can also be subverted as a tool for ill. The United Nations is not necessarily inherently positive, but it can be used to further the divine plan of All That Is.

So individuals who are part of the ashram of the Master Morya and who anchor the energy of the first ray on the planet are in the world at this time. There are also first-ray individuals with much lower consciousnesses, who are affected by the energies of the zodiac coming through the astral plane focused through the astral lord of the first ray.

The astral lord of the first ray takes the archetypal form of an emperor or warrior and transmits energy from the constellations Aries and Sagittarius to humanity on an emotional level. The archetypes on the astral plane have the most effect on those who embody the archetype in the third-dimensional reality. The astral lord of the first ray has the most effect on soldiers, police, politicians, heads of state and so on. In the negative, this lower expression of first-ray energy can take the form of aggression, hatred and violence; in the positive, it can take the form of courage and love. This energy sweeps through the astral plane, or fourth dimension, like a great wind that affects the astral body of individuals just as physical wind chills people.

In reverse, events in the third-dimension reality that are communicated by the media generate emotions in large numbers of people, who then create a large mass of energy on the astral plane that rises up like a cloud. You might conceptualize it as a crowd of people with the individuals giving off colored smoke that rises up above their heads. The astral emotional smoke from each individual forms one great, colored cloud. The cloud might be a brownish red for anger, a murky gray for fear or other dismal colors. These clouds generated by emotion do not just go away, however. They can erupt as physical conditions such as hurricanes or storms or other disasters, depending on what emotion generated them.

The energies affecting humanity at any given time are a blending of the emotional responses to mass events by large groups of people with low levels of consciousness, the energies of the rays entering the planet through the zodiac signs on the astral plane (affecting the collective subconscious mind of humanity) and the rays transmitted through the masters and their ashrams from the higher dimensions, bypassing the astral plane and going to the etheric.

What is important to understand at this time is that the balance is shifting slowly so that the energy generated by a low-consciousness humanity is diminishing, and the energy from the masters and their lightworkers is increasing. The balance is tipping toward a greater spirituality expressing itself on the planet. This is the result of a greater number of souls within the ashrams coming into the third dimension and of those times when the planets are positively aspected to the zodiac and focusing the positive aspects of first-ray energy through the astral plane.

For those individuals who are on the first ray — and they are often those born under the signs of Aries and Sagittarius or whose occupations are in politics or law enforcement — the color of light to meditate on is a pale rose pink. The student should suffuse him- or herself with that rose pink, which is the expression of the highest love for humanity. This pink color is traditionally associated with femininity, girlishness and being effeminate, and it is frequently eschewed by those extremely masculine men who follow a career with the army or police. Such an aversion to pink brutalizes the individual and makes him or her insensitive to the sufferings of others. Therefore, it is highly necessary to meditate on the color of pink light to overcome the brutalizing, desensitizing effect of dark reds in the personal aura.

Those souls who have come in with a first-ray mission to fulfill will have specific negative traits that they need to balance and transmute, such as rashness, impulsiveness, domineering qualities, inability to listen and absorb new information, tendency to violent rage, desire to do things their way, a love of giving orders but not of following orders, a lack of sensitivity to the feelings of others and a very strong sexual drive. A positive first-ray type who has worked on these negative tendencies in this life or another will be a natural leader, who inspires people to cooperate to work for a common goal and who draws inspiration from listening to the many suggestions of many people. This person will be fired with contagious enthusiasm toward positive goals that inspire participation. The focus will always be on a better future for all.

The Third Ray

From the second ray we went to the first ray, and we now come to the third ray of active intelligence, which encompasses the remaining four rays much as a school of science might encompass physics, chemistry and biology. The third ray corresponds to the energy of the archetypal son. The union of the father and mother produces the son, and the activity of the first ray and the second ray produces the energy of the third ray, which is intelligence in action in the physical world.

The third ray corresponds to the color yellow in the spectrum and the concrete mental plane. It is a ray of intellectuals and thinkers who conceptualize patterns for society and those who teach. It is the ashram for those who are active in the world in founding groups and societies that have a purpose in furthering the future of the human race and the planet. The energy of this ray relates to technology and communications and comes in through Gemini and Aquarius. An example of this energy at work might be the Internet and all the individuals who participate in it. Occupations that relate to this ashram include inventors, scientists, researchers, activists, astronauts, aviators, electricians.

The Fourth Ray

The energy of the fourth ray relates to that of the arts

and healing, and the unifying principle between art and healing is color. The fourth ray is the middle ray of the seven; it is represented by the color green, which is a healing and balancing color, the color of nature. The science of the fourth ray is the study of light, color and form in relationship to healing and balancing individuals. The energy of the fourth ray comes from Taurus and Libra. Activities related to the fourth ray are the study of the medicinal attributes of plants, which of course are green, as well as traditional medicine and other forms of medicine.

This ray is connected to the heart center and the abstract mental plane as well as abstractions of form and color. People on this ray often express themselves as artists, doctors, nurses, craftspeople, gardeners, herbalists, pharmacists, research scientists or chemists and in similar occupations. People who are concerned with healing the planet are also on this ray. Healing is viewed from the point of view of attaining and maintaining balance, which means to never go too far to one extreme in any behavior and keeping the body system in homeostasis.

People who work extensively and deeply with this energy are sensitive and empathetic to others, and their presence is healing. They exude a healing force that helps those who are suffering from an emotional, mental or physical imbalance to feel more balanced around them. They are the nurses who walk into a room and immediately make the patient feel better. Sometimes they actually exude tangible heat through their hands.

The Fifth Ray

The fifth ray is related to harmony through conflict, which expresses itself as mathematics and music, and as the concept of the resolution of disharmony into harmony. This concept can be illustrated in a number of ways, but the underlying principle might best be described by iron filings that are all shaped into a pattern by a magnet. It is the principle of many diverse individuals forming a larger body, like the many cells of an organism such as a plant or animal. It is a ray that also relates to wave forms and frequencies that express themselves as sound.

Souls who are working within this ashram express themselves as musicians, poets, composers. songwriters and mathematicians. This ray is related to the causal, or soul, plane of the inner planes. Issues of the ray relate to cycles and karma. This is the ray that produces charisma in an individual, as the individual is the force that bends all others to his or her will. The charismatic individual sounds a note that produces a resonance in others and a response.

The Sixth Ray

The energy of the sixth ray is the energy of devotion and relates to the color indigo blue. It is the path of viewing the divine as a lover or the beloved and seeing the handiwork of the beloved within everything in nature. This is the ray of monks and nuns of all denominations, who view themselves as married to the divine, and it is also the ray of contemplation and meditation.

This ashram relates specifically to religious practice and the process of bringing together all of the world religions so that they support one another as pathways to the divine. It encompasses everything the Master Jesus was able to perform as a miracle. It is the ray of psychics and magicians; it is the ray of the opened third eye and communication with the spirit world.

The Seventh Ray

The energy of the seventh ray has been called that of

ceremonial magic, which of course means the invocation of the natural forces of the inner planes for the purpose of manifesting some specific event on the third-dimensional reality. It is the final ray as the individual soul — having moved through and learned from all of the rays — finally comes into his or her own on this last ray and may act as the magus and command the forces to obey his or her will.

The seventh-ray ashram has involved itself with all magical and secret orders, such as Masons and covens. It is also related to the founding of the New World as an expression of creating heaven on Earth according to principles of pursuing happiness and living in freedom. People on this ray are usually members of some specific order even if it is only the local Shriners or Elks Club.

Now, there is not anything especially new or astonishing about this information on the rays and the ashrams, as it has all been written before. However, what we expect to see in the future is greater organization and structure to the externalization of the ashrams in the world. The ashrams exist on the inner planes as the halls of learning. In the future, there will be more organizations on the outer world that will seek to express the higher purpose of these ashrams. There are certain spiritual truths that we adhere to that are not represented by any particular religion on Earth. All the religions of Earth are distorted — and were distorted — by individuals who wanted power over others. All of the expressions of the rays that we teach encompass these spiritual principles. That means that they are embedded truths within fiction, drama and the movies.

They are embedded truths within politics and planetary development. They are embedded truths within churches and movements.

All groups who have as their mission and direction the sacredness of human life, the sacredness of the planet and the belief in the possibility of a better future for all, are in alignment with the ashrams of the masters. Activist groups and environmental groups are an expression of the third ray of active intelligence, whereas those who seek to heal the Earth through prayer and meditation are fourth-ray ashram groups. Those groups who seek to bring together many religions are sixth-ray ashram groups.

We live in a time where first-ray impetus has taken over the total direction of politics in the USA and Britain. The other rays have taken a back seat, and many consider this impulse to be "materialistic" and the opposite of spiritual; many pray for peace. However, in all situations there needs to be discernment. First-ray activity at its height may appear to some who are firmly planted on some other ray, such as the second, third, fourth or sixth ray, as totally "evil," because it is foreign to their nature. We are not suggesting that the planetary hierarchy of ascended masters directed the USA toward war during the beginning of the twenty-first century, but that sometimes war is the only means to clearing the way for a better future.

Some first-ray souls feel themselves inwardly to be like archangels who are fighting a battle in heaven against some demonic hordes. They truly see their enemies as purely possessed by evil and behaving as demons, and they feel empowered by God to stop the evil. When first-ray souls find themselves in positions of power, they reason that they were put there to do some particular mission that corresponds to their nature. They fight for a world free of a certain type of evil, whereas others view their fight as evil. They may be entirely wrong in this supposition. However, make no mistake, you have come into a world that is under the thrall of darkness and ignorance, and you are here to battle for light and knowledge. This battle may not take the form of warfare, but of establishing a better way.

2

The Evolution of a World Forum

So there are seven orders within another dimension that work with souls who have incarnated on Earth. One might think of these souls as being on a gradient scale of more or less evolved, based on reincarnation and the number of lifetimes they have experienced on Earth. The most advanced souls are generally older souls who have been on Earth and stayed here without moving on to advance further on other planets.

The more advanced souls form the ashrams of the masters. These are individuals who are actively involved in such areas as politics, the military, economics, the media, healing, medicine, science, writing, drama, the movies, art, music, the church and all religions and cults as well as activist groups; they are people who

hold to ethical and moral principles in alignment with
the masters. Generally speaking, they work for the
greatest good of the greatest number of people. They
are to be found in all countries.

Independent Nations in a World Forum Are the Goal

The goal is to have a planet where all countries are
independent and send representatives to a world council and where a world force composed of soldiers from
all nations maintains peace. I can imagine that there are
readers within America who are instinctively opposed to
such an idea as undermining the role of the USA as the
major power in the world, policing the world.

Many readers might also be unaware of the relentless
changes in the past 120 years or so that have inevitably
brought about the independence of many nations that
were once in thrall of foreign powers. The twentieth
century has seen the collapse of the British Empire, the
French Empire, the Dutch Empire; and all of the countries with holdings in Africa and the Far East were
forced to let them go. It has been divine will that
nations should be independent. It follows logically that
there should be a planetary organization with representatives from every nation.

Is it unreasonable to consider that all the varied and
different national cultures of the world should rule
themselves and be policed by a representative army that
has the best interests of the entire planet at heart?
Should not all nations be accountable to a world forum,
and should not all nations be required to provide the
basics of food and shelter for the people residing within their boundaries? In that sense, the Old World
Order has passed away and we no longer have empires;
we have a forum of nations.

So we call the period after World War II an era of reconstruction, and now we are within the era of the New World Order. It is a term that simply reflects that the era of the British Empire and other European colonial powers is over and we have a world of sovereign nation states. Now it is necessary to have a world forum or parliament where representatives of every nation can speak.

The Master Morya, who works primarily with national leaders and politicians on the inner dimensions, is leading the training of individuals who will have a vision of what the planet could be and of the role of a world forum in bringing it to pass. The goal is for individual sovereign nations to maintain their ethnic culture and individuality, their national boundaries and their armies within the structure of a peaceful world where every government has the responsibility to prevent starvation and homelessness.

A New Approach to Teaching Moves the Energy from the Intellect to the Heart

However, from the point of view of the divine plan and my work, the past fifty years or more were a period of assimilating and integrating the ancient wisdom teachings on a planetary basis. During many years of many groups meditating and visualizing an etheric web was formed, which has made it possible for higher energies to be focused on the planet. During that time frame, the late Janet McClure founded the Tibetan Foundation, which continued the work of Alice A. Bailey but with a focus on teaching students how to channel telepathically — as Alice A. Bailey did — and also by trance. This important facet of the work was missing from the Arcane School. The vision was that from this time on aspiring students would contact their teacher within and avoid the pitfalls of joining dubious groups and following dubious teachers. To do this with safety, students had to learn the protecting techniques and about the potential dangers. The Tibetan Foundation also produced a number of individuals who learned to give personal readings and teachings to students.

So as we stand perched on the verge of a new millennium, we may look back on the vista spread behind us, whereby we laid our preparations for great wars against the forces of evil as they expressed themselves in the form of fascism and totalitarianism. The wars are won and some of the evil is driven forth from the world. We can see distinct periods and distinct groups involved in specific work. The millennium marker indicates the beginning of a new era after the period of reconstruction, which will be largely characterized by the energies of Aquarius overriding the period of Pisces mixed with Aquarius that characterized the past century. The turmoil is almost over.

Now, a lot of the Alice A. Bailey teachings focus on the externalization of the planetary hierarchy that exists on the inner planes or in remote places on the physical plane onto the world stage, and on the appearance of the world teacher who will unite all religions.

Well, you know, so many aspiring students read these thoughts and it creates an expectation that someone external will come along and sort out the mess that the world is in and solve all of the problems. However, if a group of supermen who are experts in all fields of endeavor took over the planet and created utopian societies, then the bulk of humans would miss out on many opportunities to learn and grow and develop their spiritual muscles. It is humans themselves who must come up to the level of consciousness of the ascended masters — not the ascended masters coming out onto the world stage to help humans! The masters work with the most gifted members of humanity on the inner planes while they sleep.

What will be happening is that various locations on the planet will become centers attracting students and experts in particular focuses that correspond to the ancient orders of Atlantis. Points of focus will include patterns for future civilizations, legislation and political science; psychology and mythology; science and technology; the visual arts and healing; all work with color, light and frequency; music, mathematics and correspondences; meditation, religion, contemplation and prayer; and ritual invocation. There may be many large centers that incorporate all aspects.

An example of such a center might be a grouping of residences and businesses, churches and schools, forming a small community of people who pioneer new forms of living together in harmony that incorporate daily meditations; organic farming; daily occupations and group expressions in music, dance and drama incorporating light, sound and color for the purposes of healing and enlightening. The new technologies will be included within this structure, because they are part of the Aquarian impulse. So there would be computers, web pages, video cameras, recording studios and televisions in evidence as part of the community. Such centers might pop up all over the world as avant-garde kibbutzim in Israel, communal farms in Eastern Europe or areas in the USA.

There may be blatantly new age centers with channels, which publish New Age books, or there may be centers of science and technology that do not incorporate other aspects such as meditation, but focus solely on science or education. As the planet develops greater organization according to the seven rays, young people will get a better sense of where they belong and what they should be doing with their lives — and then doing it. All of these centers will be inspired and directed by the group of masters on the inner planes, or fifth dimension.

Also, a large group of souls, who began to incarnate after World War II, has come to this planet with a mission to form anchors for a lightbody for the planet. The Cosmic Christ, a being of love and wisdom, might then work through this lightbody to raise the atomic frequency (the speed at which electrons move around the nucleus) of the planet. As the planet becomes over-lighted by the presence of the Cosmic Christ, it becomes one of the sacred planets.

We anticipate that there may be skeptics who read this material and object, saying that anyone could easily detect that this material does not have the tone and voice of the real Tibetan as presented by Alice A. Bailey. We anticipate that some will argue that the material presented is in direct conflict with the Alice A. Bailey teachings. We, in our collaboration, are in no way attempting to duplicate the tone and tenor of the Alice A. Bailey collaboration.

In its own time, the strong intellectual component provided mental sustenance for those attracted to the paranormal who were too intellectual to be satisfied by such movements as the Spiritualists or other groups who proliferated at the end of the nineteenth century. In fact, the work we produced repelled those who were not intellectually inclined. In other words, we deliberately strategized that we wished to produce a certain caliber of material and attract a certain caliber of student. The purpose was to engage intellectually inclined students into the meditation-focused Arcane School. We wished to move the energy from the intellect to the heart.

However, we also wish for the esoteric student to learn discrimination and to measure the written word against the truth of the heart. There is much within the Alice A. Bailey teachings that is now untrue or inaccurate, and some of this was intentional. We do not desire to see individuals treat the written word as sacrosanct, absolute truth written in stone. Some inaccuracies may be deliberately written into this book; this is intentional to protect the truth from those who would misuse and abuse it.

However, as we stand perched on the brink of the new millennium, it is not our intention to promote a highly complicated, intellectually oriented series of books that are difficult for the average reader to follow. Instead, we want to generate books that are simple and compelling and meet the need of the incoming generation for some explanation of the world they find themselves in.

For those who have some sense of some mysterious explanation to reality that is a hidden secret that may be sought for and discovered, we wish to offer some theories that may slake their thirst for knowledge. There is more, however, than meeting the intellectual curiosity of those who sense some secret meaning or purpose beyond the obvious order of things; there is also training individuals to be more receptive to the impulses of their own higher selves, their inner teachers and guides.

I am undertaking another phase of my work, which involves the externalization of the second-ray ashram of love and wisdom and is building up a body of light-workers who will be my students as well as teachers of the ancient mysteries. Some of these students will channel general information such as this book; others will work with small groups of students in informal classes; and yet others of my students will be more in the nature of counselors who will work one-on-one with individuals on a variety of related abilities such as healing, clearing blockages in the chakras and relaying information from me and other guides and angelic hosts.

This externalization of my ashram will not be located in one spot, but will be scattered all over the planet. I will be working simultaneously with my best students all over the planet. I will not necessarily tell one student what the others are doing. There will be students who work directly with me, and there will be students who work with a host of other entities as part of my ashram, which is based on the theme of dispensing love-wisdom or the teachings into the world and organizing large group meditations around the times of the full moon.

This book is the second work Violet Starre and I have collaborated on. If possible, *The Diamond Light* should be read first, as this book is a progression from some of the concepts expressed in our first work. I recommend that all of my personal students examine these works using due discrimination and bearing in mind that all of my teachings are deliberately flawed — much in the fashion of oriental rug-makers who deliberately weave an imperfection into their design. Pure truth, absolute truth, can only be found from within, and books should never be treated as absolute authorities, as they only can reflect the level of consciousness of humanity at that stage in time when the book was written.

Vision Held by Bulk of Humanity Becomes the Future

The media has presented a less than hopeful vision of the future. You are being told that there will be more people than the planet can support; you are being told that we have reached six billion people, that in a short time, there will be ten billion people and there will not be enough food to feed the population. You are being told that as humans expand across the planet, many species are becoming extinct, ecosystems are being destroyed and pollution is destroying the natural environment. On top of this you can add the hole in the ozone layer, global warming and the melting of the polar icecaps — truly an alarming vision of the future.

As I have taught before, it is the vision held by the bulk of humanity that creates the future. On the one hand, by painting a gloomy picture of an undesirable future, the media may succeed in motivating the masses to act to stop unwelcome developments; however, too much of such information only serves to make the younger generation feel angry, hopeless and betrayed. It is my hope in writing these thoughts to turn the tide of the massive wave of depression that sweeps across many young people who completely believe the gloomy prognosis for the future of the planet and humanity. If the bulk of humanity feels hopeless about the future, it will actually be hopeless, even though this is not necessary. I am going to attempt to paint a positive vision of the future in the hope that I can assist in turning the tide.

So for centuries the church in the West has held the vision out to humanity that the planet will end in destruction and disaster. Much of this has been based on the psychic predictions of seers such as John the Divine in the Book of Revelations, Nostradamus or, in more recent times, of men like Edgar Cayce. But who has seen a future with prosperity, harmony and peace?

Now, when you come to accept a concept along the lines that you create your own reality and that the mass reality is created by consensus, then you can see that holding out negative images of the future for thousands of years simply becomes a self-fulfilling prophecy of endless decades of human atrocities. *Whatever you allow yourself to buy into will become yours.* How is it even possible for humanity to create a positive future when there are so many images of disaster within the collective consciousness of the race?

So the starting point I desire you to consider is that any and all sources who predict terrible futures are to be discarded as dangerously untrue — no matter how well-intentioned they are — because *the future is unformed and it will be the result of your imagination, creativity and intent.* I would say that this is the core of my message to humanity at this time. This is more important to grasp than any abstruse concepts about planetary or personal initiations or ascensions, although the ideas are related.

When scientists suggest that the planet is on a course toward destruction, this information is only useful if a remedy is also suggested. Filling people's minds with fear of the future feeds into planetary evil. This is because fear is a tangible substance on the inner dimensions. It is something that can be seen and touched; it is something that can be utilized. So there is an evil intention to create fear in the minds of the masses, with the desired outcome that negative probabilities will become realities. I would like to focus some energy on all of the exciting prospects for the future.

Exciting Prospects for the Future

You may have heard that the Earth is on a collision course with a comet. In response to this I would like you to close your eyes and imagine the enormous darkness of interstellar space, perhaps with areas of colored gas as shown in the photographs taken by large telescopes. Picture the solar system as a very small object, moving through space in a curve. Picture a star the size of an orange and an object the size of a pea, spinning and whizzing around the orange. (You know that the relationship between the real Sun and Earth is quite different — that the Sun is bigger and the distance between them is quite vast.) Imagine these objects moving quite fast. Now try to imagine shooting the Earth (the pea) with a BB gun and hitting it. If you are performing this exercise correctly, you should be having a hard time hitting the Earth with a pellet.

You can see that the vastness of space, the relentless movement of the solar system and the comparative sizes would make it very hard for an object to hit the Earth. The solar system would have to move through a field of static objects. (Now, I am sure that the cleverest readers can raise some objection to the guided imagery, but it still is unlikely that an object would hit the Earth, even if magnetism from the Sun were pulling it toward the Sun. Jupiter serves to draw many objects toward itself and captures them as moons.) You are still accustomed to thinking of the planet as they thought of it in the Dark Ages: as the center of the universe.

Those of you who believe in New Age philosophies can no longer sit on the fence. If you truly believe in reincarnation, in karma and that thoughts shape your reality, then you will not be afraid of death and dying, and you will know that you create your own health through your lifestyle. If you consider that death is but a transition into another reality, then all of the tragedy and horror are removed from life on Earth. This does not mean that laws are not important or that there is no real harm done if one human kills another. It does mean that if you claim to have a spiritual inclination, you will have an unshakable certainty in the unseen; the horror show enacted before you on the world stage will appear as a tragic production, but you will be aware that it is in reality an illusion. This certainty will keep you strong through many dark days to come.

What I would like lightworkers to hold in the forefront of their minds is the concept that we are leaving the Age of Pisces and entering the new age of Aquarius, which heralds a wonderful future for all of the inhabitants of the planet. The Age of Pisces has just passed away, and it was characterized by rigid hierarchical, institutional structures; class systems; inequality; emotional and devotional thinking; many holy orders shut away from the world; and visionary and healing powers — two thousand years of a very mystical and technologically primitive world culture, with a great deal of exploration and discovery; an era of sailing the oceans in ships; an era of fishermen and carpenters.

The Aquarian Age is already well under way, but it will not come completely into its own for a few hundred more years. In the transition, everything that was Piscean is crumbling and falling away, which is not necessarily a pleasant sensation. Structures are falling down. The Aquarian Age brings a different type of politics that is not from the top down, but from the roots up. One might imagine that the references in the Bible to an old world being destroyed refer to the Age of Pisces and not the total destruction of the planet; "A new heaven and a new Earth" refers to the new era.

3

The Planetary Chakras and the Angelic Beings

The seven sacred planets are referred to as conscious beings within differing streams of thought. Western astrology has the planets identified with the Roman gods. The Judaic tradition has the archangels identified as having archetypal functions and roles such as healing or protecting, and so they might be referred to as the warrior, the healer, the teacher, the judge, the messenger, the artist, the musician and so on. Many people at this time are confused into relating to both angels and planets.

So we might come to think of the planetary beings as great archangels who over-light the planets. We might recognize that there are even more vast beings, who over-light entire constellations of the zodiac, and that these vast beings receive and transmit the energy of the seven rays to our solar system. The rays are received by the vast planetary angels who transmit them to our planet and to the masters of the rays.

Earth's Holy Sites Are Her Chakras

The masters and their ashrams receive the oncoming ray energies and anchor them in the physical planet at sacred sites all around the planet. The Earth has chakras just as people do, and they are considered to be holy sites, depending on the type of energy anchored at them. The planet has forty-nine chakras, organized into groups of three, which usually occur within either mountains or man-made mounds all around the planet. The type of energy that is anchored at a particular site affects the nation of people who live at that site. It is important to have groups of people meditating and anchoring the energies at that site.

For an example, ancient Greece with its many differing city states was an expression of first-ray energy, and the ancient Greeks embodied first-ray traits. The Greek developed a mighty empire based on city planning, politics and organizations of law. This was energy that came through Mars from Aries and Sagittarius. The archetypal energy of the first ray was connected to the warrior-ruler, or emperor, as depicted within the tarot cards.

Tibet is an anchor point for love-wisdom energy, and Tibetan Buddhism has been forced out of Tibet to find homes all around the planet. This energy is connected to Pisces and Neptune. The Buddhist people of Tibet express a great deal of wisdom, especially through the Dalai Lama. The Dalai Lama brings Tibetan wisdom to the West, especially in the form of psychological exercises for peace of mind. The Dalai Lama is considered to be an incarnation of the Buddha, so it makes sense that he would be reincarnated in Tibet.

The energy of the second ray is connected to the collective unconscious, which may be presented symbolically as a vast ocean of unconsciousness. The second ray connects to the second plane, level, dimension up, or the fourth dimension or astral plane. Whatever you call it, it is an ocean of collective awareness that is mainly unconscious. The main ruler of the collective unconscious is the Moon as Isis, the priestess archetype who is easily confused with Neptune, as they enjoy a close relationsip. The energy of the second ray is more properly focused through the Moon, but the Moon is the ruler of Cancer the crab, which relates more to the home than the collective unconscious and the astral plane within astrology. Nevertheless, second-ray energy is more properly connected to Isis, the Moon Priestess, and Cancer.

America, surprisingly enough, anchors the third ray of active intelligence and activist groups who promote enlightened commerce and enlightened politics. However, there are powerful sites within America that are not third ray, which is connected to the archetype of the messenger and teacher. Sedona and Mount Shasta are second-ray expressions.

The British Isles anchor the fourth-ray energy that comes through the heart chakra. It is an energy of healing through color, sound and art. The British people are very much affected by the energy of the fourth ray, which comes from Taurus and Libra through Venus. The archetype for this ray is that of the healer. The energy is anchored at Glastonbury and at several other famous sites.

India has a strong sixth-ray expression and has been an ancient seat of spirituality, temples and many orders of priests and priestesses, monks and nuns. This ray has the archetype of the spiritual teacher. The energy of the sixth ray of devotion comes from Pisces and is amplified by the planet Neptune, which acts something like a lens to enhance it. The Piscean era of 2000, which has just gone by, is symbolized by the sign of the two fish, but it is also ruled by Neptune, who is presented as the archetype of a sea God.

There are sites all over the planet, in such varying places as Hawaii, the Bahamas, Australia, India, Israel, Egypt, Mexico, Peru and many more; sites are also in any pyramids and some ancient temples or stone circles. Some of these sites are considered to be portals to other dimensions, and the significance of this is that it is easier to visualize and enter the inner planes at some of these sites. In the past, religious movements have been anchored at these sites.

I would like to take a mild digression at this point, to note that within the Celtic tradition, certain special individuals were lured by white deer or other sacred animals into secret entrances to an "other world," which was sometimes underground or within mounds and hills. It is within this ancient tradition of the goddess that Alice in Wonderland begins, with Alice following a white rabbit down a hole into an underworld called Wonderland. Many people assume that this children's tale was the result of some strong hallucinogenic drug such as an opium derivative or absinthe, but as is the case with many scholars at Oxford or Cambridge, it was the result of a brain over-stimulated from reading too many ancient texts — Lewis Carroll (AKA Dodson) was a theology student who was steeped in the ancient Celtic lore and much poetry. There is much embedded wisdom within the Alice tales that is derived from Celtic magical practices, such as going through a magic mirror into a reverse-polarity world; Celtic Wiccans practiced mentally going through mirrors into the reverse world within them to astrally project themselves into the other dimensions of reality, beyond the third dimension.

Wherever there are sacred sites there are inner-dimensional temples that may be entered by those who meditate and perform visualizations at the site. These temples are places of healing and learning. While within the site, the meditator may be healed physically, emotionally and mentally; transmit healing to others; and receive messages and impressions, teachings and spiritual truths. These physical sites will begin to accelerate in the process of anchoring the temples that exist within the inner dimensions into the third dimension. Organizations of all kinds will be based at these sites, and individuals will be inspired to do certain work there.

There are angels who over-light these sites. They are connected to the temples. The angels correspond to planets and dimensions and entry points for cosmic ray energies into the planet. Individual members of the ashrams of the ascended masters anchor high levels of these ray energies on the physical-plane third dimension. Such individuals are drawn to live at sacred sites.

Spiritually Inclined People Respect All Human Life

So although the world may be full of politicians, psychologists, counselors, doctors, nurses, artists, musicians, monks, nuns, priests, writers, scientists and inventors, only those who are in alignment with spiritual principles are working with the planetary spiritual government — either awake or asleep. The hallmark of those individuals who espouse spiritual principles is a respect for all human life. The planet may be becoming very crowded and cities may be becoming very large, but each individual is a divine spark of God.

There is no person — no matter how ignorant, vulgar, addicted, criminal, violent or unbalanced — who is not a spark of God. Humans are a work in progress, and each of us somewhere in our lengthy history was a person of no consequence or status to others, including even the ascended masters. We have all been poor, powerless, oppressed and without money or power, forced to live a life that violated our deepest truths.

Spiritually directed individuals believe in the other dimensions and an afterlife after death, but they respect life. Such beings are always against senseless killing for its own sake; they seek negotiation to prevent war where possible and punishment over the death sentence. Spiritually inclined individuals are concerned about the issues of environment and pollution; they are for regulating businesses to reduce pollutants and for limiting the exploitation of animals — fish and mammals — to extinction.

The hallmark of spiritual persons is that they are galactic citizens rather than identifying themselves with one country; they find patriotism very uncomfortable and reminiscent of Nazi propaganda. They have a vision of one healed planet of planetary citizens living in peace and prosperity; each nation in this vision is a unique people that rules itself.

The student of the ascended master may not be an outwardly religious person, but he or she will be involved with work that furthers the aims of the Planetary Hierarchy within the seven fields of endeavor. The major endeavor the spiritual hierarchy is attempting to promote with its most gifted students is a world religion that encompasses the best and most positive of all religions. This is a most difficult task, which failed in the twentieth century when the Theosophical Society tried to prepare several candidates to be over-lighted by the Ascended Master Maitreya with the idea that this being would be recognized by many religions as the Second Coming of Christ, as the Iman Mahdi, as the return of Krishna and the Buddha.

At this time, the world is somewhat in chaos with warring religious factions who believe that they serve the true God. There are no soldiers on Earth who think of themselves as serving evil, darkness or the devil. All who fight think that they are earning themselves a place in a warrior's heaven for ridding the planet of great evil. That is what they all think. They acknowledge that the dispute might be over territory, but they think that they serve a higher power.

As meditating groups of all faiths and denominations pray, worship, meditate and contemplate, they create the spiritual grid of the planet, which can be seen on the inner dimensions as a lacy web of light all over the planet. The energy of constant prayer and meditation is accelerating the atomic frequency of the planet, bringing it to the high end of the third dimension and the threshold of the fourth. The energy coming in through the planetary chakras that is being anchored by these meditating groups is facilitating the planetary ascension.

The various planetary archangels, of which there are seven, receive and transmit the energy of the seven rays to the sacred centers of the planet through the masters and their meditating students. There are times when these planets form interesting relationships to one another and the planet, as in the Harmonic Convergence and the Harmonic Concordance. At these times, the angelic beings stand in unison to transmit the energy of the rays. This has a powerful effect on the consciousnesses of humanity. The ascended masters accept the energy from the archangels, and students accept the energy from their teachers.

4

The World Economy as a Reflection of Human Values and Creativity

These are difficult and dangerous times that you find yourselves living in on the material plane, the third dimension. Many of you are baffled and puzzled by the extreme discomfort during a time that is supposed to herald a new age, a better time, a future of prosperity. Some of you may feel that these are the end times and that we are witnessing the dissolution and destruction of the planet.

The problems that face you at this time are many. There is a worldwide sluggish economy with massive job losses. The extreme numbers of layoffs and the disappearance of many jobs are creating massive pain and discomfort. This process has a domino effect, whereby those who have lost their jobs and have either no income or reduced income are not spending as much, and so the economy begins to falter and the production of goods and services is reduced. Much of this general pain is caused by short-sighted politicians who cannot see the economy as a whole and in its entirety. It is your responsibility as enlightened voters to recognize those politicians running for office who bear the hallmarks of enlightened beings.

The economy is also shaped by the feelings that the great masses of people have about the economy. If people are fearful and hoarding their money for the bad times they expect in the future, then the decline in spending will cause a downturn. Much of the problem is that economics is so complicated and involves so many variables that it is hard for any trained individual to comprehend what is going on. However, money trends reflect spiritual trends. When the people are optimistic and enthusiastic, the economy fares well; but when the people are depressed and in debt, the economy fares badly.

What Is Money?

There is much dispute as to what money actually is. Some people have currency confused with precious and rare items such as gold and diamonds, and they feel that going off the gold standard caused problems, because now money is worthless paper and not valuable metal. When you consider a situation such as pre-World War II Germany, where a wheelbarrow full of paper currency might buy one loaf of bread, one can see how this confusion might occur. However, currency represents the inventiveness, skill, creativity, effort and ingenuity of humanity, of which it is an abstraction. Currency is also a unit of measure for comparing goods and services against each other. Currency could be summed up by the word "value" of an object or operation. Currency represents the value of individual effort.

The purpose of using gold in ages past, when the population was small, was that it was part of the barter system. Gold was another object of barter. There were problems inherent in the barter system in that food items did not keep and were not useful for the future. Transactions could not be made at the same time — I might want to repay your service to me with fruit grown in the summer or with some other seasonal item. Gold coins were the most useful objects of barter, because they were close to indestructible, lasted over a long period of time and could be made into measurable units. However, it was not only the rarity and indestructibility of the gold, but the units of measure that gave it value in transactions. When populations were small, kingdoms could set up systems of currency issued by the king or emperor mainly to the troops, who circulated amongst the people of the kingdom.

As populations grow, there is a need for the currency to grow with the expanding populations. But there is also a need for the majority of people to be employed in using their skills and creativity to generate products. As the population grows in relationship to the amount of gold in circulation, the value of the currency must go down, since it is split more ways, like a pie cut into more slices. If there are more people not creating anything as either a service or a product, then new services and products need to be invented and markets need to be created for them. These are industries.

If, for example, people stopped going to the movies or renting them, there would be no more movies and there would be a whole industry of unemployed people numbering in the thousands. There is a very large movie industry in America, which also has worldwide sales, but many other countries have only a small movie industry and produce only a few films a year.

The USA has a large population who supports this industry, and it can also make sales in other English-speaking countries. Industries are supported by large groups of people using their goods and services frequently and paying for them. When those large groups of people stop using these industries, they start to fail and economies fall into tailspins.

So to increase a failing national economy requires many variables to be at play at once. Individual members of society need to be given whatever it takes to create goods or services. This can take the form of more training and higher skills, or they can create their own small business. It can take the form of incentives to people with capital to start new industries that might employ a large number of people.

Currency is something that is created by national governments according to their formulas, but obviously, as the population grows, the currency that is issued must grow to match the gross national product, every service offered or every item manufactured within a year. So money — currency, wealth — is not something limited, rare or static, but rather a unit of measure that matches the collective entrepreneurial spirit of a nation. When a nation is very inventive and creative and presents a great variety of goods and services, it creates wealth.

What I am attempting to convey here is that the basis of wealth is a creative and inventive spirit that comes up with an idea for some sort of service or product that is useful to others. It starts with a good idea. If you lack good ideas, you can pray and ask the divine power for a good idea. If you have a business that is struggling, you can also pray and ask for some good ideas to help your business.

There Is Plenty for Everybody

There are roughly six billion people in the world today. Some are very old and some are very young, and some are so poor that they are starving. This image of starving people creates the notion of limitation. There is no good reason for there to be any starving people in the world today. The poor people of the world are the responsibility of the government of the country they reside in. It is the responsibility of other nations to pressure the nations that have large populations of homeless, jobless and starving people to provide a social system to help and support them. The governments need to generate currencies and invest money in projects that create industries, in housing projects and in a safety net. The planet is generating enough food to feed the entire population, and with methods of preserving food that has been produced, such as canning, freezing or dehydrating, it has become possible to use more food with less going to waste. The more people there are, the more need there is for products and services.

So if you have a business that is not generating a great deal of income, perhaps because people in general seem to be cutting down their spending to essentials, then you might need to reach out to new markets; advertise farther away using newspapers, the radio or television; employ the Internet; or generally cast out a wider net to reach more people.

Economics is such a complicated and intricate field of study, containing so many variables at play, that it is difficult to make any predictions about outcomes. However, once there are very wealthy people with large amounts of money living within one particular country, there is some moral burden upon them to invest their money in their country. It is not imperative, because the other institutions that invest in countries are the banks. Then, of course, you have the World Bank, which lends money to countries.

Many people realize that there is something inherently wrong or odd about the banking system. People put their money in a bank to keep it safe from robbers, but then the banks themselves take the money and use it to lend to other people and they charge money to do this. They are brokering a commodity that is not theirs in the first place.

Even worse than banks are credit cards, which are revolving loans of other people's money. Because credit cards come with high interest rates and late fees, they can easily balloon out of proportion to the original loan, and then all of the disposable income earned by workers goes to debt instead of goods and services. When you have a nation that consists of families working to pay off their debts, then the result is going to be a recession, because they have no money available for goods and services. A healthy economy depends on a large mass of people with money to spend on goods and services. If people are given a big tax refund and they need to use it to pay off their credit cards, it is not doing the economy a great deal of good.

Much that develops within the world economy is the result of decisions made by the World Bank, which can be a force of evil or good but is, to a large degree, driven by the profit motive. The wealthiest people in all of the countries of the world keep their money mainly in Swiss banks, and a group of Swiss banks decides what countries to invest in.

On Comparative Economies

The largest problem with the USA is that it is at the top of the economic tree, along with some other countries, which means that the exchange rate for the dollar is such that if you compare what a dollar will buy within the USA to what it will exchange for in other countries, it will usually buy more foreign goods. That means that Americans going out of the USA with a set amount of dollars can afford more foreign goods than the natives if they are paid the same amount of money.

However, that creates an illusion. The individuals within another country may be paid in euros or yen and not dollars, but their comparative expenses may be lower. They might earn less money, pay less in expenses and be better off than an American in the same profession. This is referred to as standard of living.

Comparative economies result in that it is best to earn an income in America and live somewhere else where the cost of living expenses are lower. However, what has happened is that banks and wealthy people have invested in manufacturing companies in countries that have a comparative economy that is much lower than the American one and that export to the American market. Ultimately, eroding the manufacturing base within America and establishing the production of much needed goods outside the country means that the mass of American workers must become more skilled or more involved in small businesses and industries such as health care, which are focused on services to people. The result may be periods of transition where large numbers of unemployed people seek training or change occupations.

So from the spiritual perspective, organizations such as the World Bank and governments play a major role in directing the global economy, and the more spiritually aware and enlightened members of these organizations are, the better life is for the ordinary individual.

When such institutions are in the hands of the selfish, greedy and short-sighted, then massive suffering is created. However, individuals who are working on developing their spirituality will have access to the creativity that springs from All That Is.

For a brief example, let me mention the author of the Harry Potter books, who, as everyone knows, was an impoverished teacher with an infant child who wrote the first book during many visits to a tea room in Edinburgh. There are many instances of someone taking an idea and creating wealth out of almost thin air, as in the case of writing. On the other hand, it is of no use to tell every impoverished woman with an infant that she also has the power to become rich by writing. Even someone who might have the general idea of a story such as the Harry Potter series might not have the experience and talents that led to the creation of this book, as the author has a special way with words, which captures children's attention. The author has the talent, but the inspiration comes from the divine.

So I use this example to illustrate that economies at the top of the world finance tree move away from their original manufacturing base of working with raw products like cotton, steel and wood, toward more of what we call "luxury" items, inasmuch as they are not necessary for survival but provide entertainment, which has stress-reduction value.

So having moved away from the nuts and bolts of manufacturing to entertainment industries, First-World countries are more involved in writing fiction and producing music, music videos, movies and television programs. There is a huge and booming entertainment industry anchored in America, which is possible due to a large population with disposable income.

Growing Industries Are Those
Aimed at an Aging Population

In the recent past, the largest demographic group with available income to spend was teenagers, but now we are moving to a period where the baby boom generation — mainly those born after World War II up until 1963 — is generally in their fifties. Most of their children have grown up, and they are dealing with more available wealth — if they are employed or on early retirement. Some will be spending money on their grandchildren and others will spend it on leisure, self-improvement workshops and travel. These are the industries that will grow. For the next thirty years, the economy will be directed by services, products and leisure activities aimed at an aging generation. Products that maintain health and youthfulness will be in extreme demand.

From approximately 2030 onward, the bulk of the baby boomers will be leaving the planetary world stage. Since this group comprises such a large segment of the population, their departure will produce significant changes in the economy. By 2050 the majority of the baby boomers will be gone. This will be a worldwide phenomenon, but it is easiest to predict the changes in the Western world.

In the USA, many homes will be coming onto the market and there will be more homes than buyers. The value of houses may come down. A house that is currently worth 140,000 dollars may go down to about 80,000 dollars. Certain rural areas may become depopulated, and there may be many abandoned old houses. There may be a great demand for skilled and educated workers, as there may be more job vacancies than employees. Wages may be high to attract skilled workers. There may be the need for major adjustments in many areas of life to compensate for the gradual loss of population.

There Will Be a Decrease in Population

I would make a guess that while the current population of the USA is roughly 300 million, by the year 2050 it may have come down to roughly between 200 and 250 million. I would qualify this prediction by stating that this is the most prevalent probable reality and that the depopulation trend will be worldwide. If you are wondering how such an idea is possible, consider that during the 20th century, there was a major adjustment in lifespan with the advances in medical technology; at the beginning of the 20th century, the average age at death was in the 50s and now, a hundred years later, it is in the 90s. Since people are hanging around twice as long, the population becomes exponentially more than twice as large, and for a while the birth rate exceeds the death rate. However, soon the death rate will exceed the birth rate. With advances in medicine there is the possibility that at the close of the century, people will be living well into their hundreds, and a child born today might live to be one hundred and fifty and live to see his great-great-great-great-grandchildren.

The question at this time is that if life can clearly be extended, can youthfulness be extended also? This will come down to lifestyle, and while growing up, the average person will be taught the ingredients for a healthy lifestyle repeatedly in school. By following a simple regimen of healthy diet, regular exercise and avoiding unhealthy habits such as overeating, undereating, smoking or drinking alcohol, youthfulness will be extended. What cannot be accomplished by lifestyle will be accomplished by surgery and medications.

Technology Changes How
Ancestors Are Viewed

The times you live in are astonishing times, and future generations will look back at this point in history with awe. They will study the twentieth and twenty-first centuries in history classes, and it will all be the more vivid because there will be movies and music preserved for them and people will be able to look at their family trees for many generations back on web pages. Can you imagine your personal story becoming legend within your family? Can you imagine that within a few hundred years, you will have thousands of direct descendants, all of whom will have learned about you from the family records on the Internet? The actions that you take right now will become part of your family legend. While this has always been true, the boost in technology will make it possible for your descendants hundreds of years from now to study photographs and biographies of some of you stored on computer diskettes. You have lived through the beginning of the great technological age, and a thousand years from now people will still listen to the music of this era and watch the movies made in this era; they will laugh and sigh over heartthrob actors and actresses who will have been dead for hundreds of years.

What will become manifestly clear to future generations as they study their family histories is that each individual is descended from millions and billions of direct ancestors, and each generation backwards becomes somewhat like a net that encompasses more and more individuals. This is not a simple concept to grasp when many of you have been educated to think of the family tree in limited terms.

Each generation back doubles in quantity, hence from two parents we move to four grandparents, eight great-grandparents, sixteen great-great grandparents, and then the numbers rapidly increase from thirty-two to sixty-four to over a hundred. As the individual travels back through the family tree, the numbers of direct ancestors keep growing larger and larger, until eventually they encompass all of humanity, and then there are more theoretical ancestors than there were people alive on the planet. However, the quantity doubles with each generation back, and the only way to explain a smaller population is that each individual is counted two or three times over.

Well, the development of this technology of the Internet and maintaining family records will gradually change the way people in the future think about one another, and there will be a greater interconnectedness and sense of human family. So even as the population of the planet may be the greatest that it has ever been, the sense of relatedness will be far greater than it has ever been. The average person will be able to read the biographies and study the photographs of thousands of highly diverse direct ancestors, many of whom will not resemble him or her in any fashion and may include diverse ethnic groups.

So we are looking at the possibility that within this century, there will be a dramatic decrease in population and that wealth will be passed on from the parent generation to those who follow, resulting in a reduction in the numbers of the poor and homeless. This will occur on a planetary level.

From the point of view of history, it will be seen that there was a generation who fought in World War II and saved the planet from the darkness of fascism. It will be seen that they ushered in a generation who changed the world and then left, leaving a legacy of music, movies and other forms of media.

The rapid decline in population when this large group leaves the planet will have a substantial effect on the consequent unfoldment of the future. The rapid rise in technology will mean that when the baby boomer generation leaves, the nature of everyday reality will have been totally transformed, in ways that we cannot yet predict.

For example, what kind of transportation can we expect to see perhaps fifty years from now? Fifty years back in time, there were clumsy automobiles. Fifty years prior to that were the horse and carriage. Fifty years from now, will there still be automobiles — or will the era of the automobile pass and the memory of it fade away due to lack of fuel supplies? Will automobiles run on electricity or some other form of power, such as anti-gravity? Perhaps there will be hovercrafts? We cannot say for sure, but we know that the development of technology is speeding up, and every decade presents us with new gifts to make our everyday lives easier. We have within our grasp the means to solve all of the problems that beset the planet.

We Are Entering More Fully into the Age of Aquarius

What is significant about this point in time at the beginning of the twenty-first century is that we are entering more fully into the Age of Aquarius. The energies that are influencing this era are precisely related to new forms of energy, such as electricity and others that have yet to be discovered, as well as advances in technology.

On the one hand, the new influences of Aquarius are related to science, technology, energy and air travel and everything that we have witnessed in the cusp period of the twentieth century, as well as brotherhood, equality and leveling people so that all share health, wealth and prosperity. We have seen, with vaccinations and inoculations, the beginnings of equalizing the potential to avoid the suffering from terrible diseases such as polio, small pox, diphtheria and so on, and a whole arena of human misery has been eliminated.

More changes are to come in keeping with the energies of Aquarius. The influence of Pisces is phasing out, and Pisces is very much related to bureaucracy and structure in its twelfth-House aspect. Therefore, the past has been shaped by large, structured organizations with a distinct hierarchical pattern of rulers on top and followers on the bottom. In particular, the Christian Church has emerged during the past two thousand years out of this Piscean energy stream, and so it reflects this rigidity. Nations have evolved along this pattern. The pattern for the future will be based on concepts of equality, shared input and a totally different paradigm. Perhaps the concept of the round table, where all who sit at it are equals, best represents the paradigm for Aquarian organizational structures.

So the future does not so much hold the prospect of a new age as that of an Aquarian age with Aquarian characteristics — a planetary-wide movement into a more advanced technology utilizing new forms of energy; new structures of government, religion and schooling; and a greater spirit of brotherhood within humanity.

5
Replacing the Word "Love" with "Kindness"

Many people feel less safe in the world today, after the terrorist events of September 11, 2001, even after the launching of the war on terrorism. This sense of danger has been heightened by the modern technology that made it possible for people all over the planet to watch the two World Trade Center towers come crumbling down. Many people have experienced mild posttraumatic stress syndrome, which is the same condition that was called shell shock in World War I.

The fact of the matter is that none of you is or ever has been safe in the world. Any one of you could be taken at any minute. In some sense, the citizens of the USA have been lucky in that they have not experienced the high level of terrorism that has been prevalent in Europe or in other areas of the world. There has been an unusual era of peace and prosperity in the USA from the 1950s to 2001, which was only marred by the Vietnam War in the late 1960s. In fact, what has been unusual in the history of life on the planet has been the relative peace and safety enjoyed by the population of the USA during the latter part of the twentieth century.

Every day thousands of people die and thousands of babies are born. Many individuals die peacefully of old age, but thousands more die as a result of natural disasters, accidents or acts of extreme violence. Your sojourn on the planet is but a brief episode that may come to a close at any time, without any warning. Your sense of safety is and always has been an illusion.

To Be Kind Is to Be Loving

Many sources at this time are instructing students to choose love and not fear and not to promote fear. I would like to say that the idea of "love" has become somewhat meaningless and distorted, into a form of sentimentalized affection by the overuse of the word to promote a variety of items, especially in music.

If the word "love" is replaced with "kindness," then there is a different spin on the issue. It is not kindness to chide those who experience or express fear. If one is mindful to be kind in all situations, including when writing letters and email, then one cannot stray from the path of love. There cannot be any possibility of being unkind to someone as an act of love for his or her own good. Such a concept is contradictory. To be unkind is to be unloving.

There is certainly some confusion amongst those treading the spiritual path that it is possible to be unkind directly to people in the name of love, for their own good, to give them a better understanding of their errors. Worse yet, there are those attempting to open their psychic powers who may give unkind messages from the "spirits." Such messages come from one source alone, and that is the lower mind, the lower ego, which delights in feeling superior and separate from others.

True love is an overwhelming kindness, and those who are steadfastly kind are remembered by all they contact for their kindness. Kindness embraces a number of worthy attributes, and the hallmark of the ascended master and other advanced beings on the path is their kindness. Some of the attributes of a kindly nature is having time for people and their problems; always speaking to them in a respectful manner; never chiding or criticizing, which is the reflection of a judgmental nature.

When we talk of the need for love in the world, what we mean is really an abundance of kindness. There is a very definite distinction between love and kindness, because love can simply be a feeling that is not actually manifested as any outward action, whereas kindness is not defined as a feeling; kindness is expressed in actions. Kindness is a smile to someone who needs one. Kindness is a small action of helping someone in small ways. Kindness is expressed in giving gifts of time, money, thoughtful presents, positive feedback, appreciation, compliments and gratitude. Standing up for another person who is under attack or protecting someone when there is no gain for the self is an act of kindness. Useful advice may be an act of kindness. If all people expressed themselves in acts of kindness, the world would be a happier place.

Kindness Is Not Weakness

People become cruel by forming judgments of others and then acting on these judgments to punish and hurt the people whom they judge. They imagine that their behavior is justifiable. They think of themselves as good people.

The first step on the spiritual path is to work on becoming a kind person in the face of every obstacle. Being a kind person also involves speaking kindly of people when they are not present.

There is a tendency in some circles to consider kind people as being weak and fearful, as performing acts of kindness out of fear that others may harm them if they do not. This is a misconception. There is that kindness that requires courage in standing up and speaking up for others. It takes making a decision to remain kind when one feels angry, frustrated or overtired. It is very much easier to be unkind. However, being a good and a kind person does not in any way guarantee safety in the third dimension, and very often it seems as if the kindest people suffer the worst fates. Many who were considered to be theosophical disciples and initiates experienced great difficulties in their lives.

I would like to dispense with such a system of rigid labels and have all interested in my teachings consider themselves to be along the lines of lightworkers. Conceptualizing esoteric students in various ranks and grades serves only to maintain the negative ego, which delights in feeling superior to others and serves to prevent many worthy students from making the leap in consciousness required to attain the third initiation (gaining enlightenment) — that of the realization of the oneness of all life. When individuals think of themselves as disciples and initiates, they lose sight of the fact that they are completely enlightened beings who are attempting to express through the third-dimensional density.

Opening to Psychic Abilities
Is Not Possession

At the beginning of the twentieth century, when the theosophists and occultists were very active, creating lectures and meditations for the public, they were in competition with the extremely popular spiritualist organizations in both Britain and the United States. There was some rivalry between the two groups and even animosity, although the hierarchy of the planet was working through both groups. Due to the rivalry and animosity between spiritualism and occultism in the Western world at the beginning of the twentieth century, there was a certain degree of confusion and resistance that set back those souls looking for guidance on their spiritual quest.

There was much in the early occult teachings warning about the dangers of possession, the dangers of attempting to open to psychic powers without the instruction of a master and also about how remote and unattainable the masters were. Much of these warnings came out of the rivalry between the two groups. Ironically, the pivotal individuals in both groups, such as Helena Blavatsky, Alice A. Bailey, Edgar Cayce, Sir Arthur Conan Doyle, were all highly advanced souls from the temples of Atlantis who reincarnated to help bring spirituality to the masses.

Psychics are given images and thoughts to communicate, which come to them consciously. Channels go into very light trance states where they are aware of everything that is going on, and they receive an inflow of thoughts through the higher self and into their subconscious minds, which they clothe in words. In both cases, beings in another dimension give thoughts in the form of visual images and symbols and meanings to the psychic or channel. These beings do not take control of the bodies of the sensitives.

The points to consider about opening to channel or psychic information at this time is that it is not developing the connection to the fifth dimension that causes possession, but it is substance abuse that does. It is that simple. Much of the crime on the planet at this time is the result of minor possession by individuals who are under the influence of drugs or alcohol.

So let me again emphasize that it is not the attempt to develop psychic abilities or siddhis that forms a problem, but rather getting enmeshed in alcohol, which is a very popular and socially acceptable legal drug. I might also add that marijuana, which in the form of hashish gave rise to the name "Assassins" (a cult of people who smoked hashish and then executed people), is another substance dangerous to those attempting to open themselves psychically.

The Planetary Hierarchy Is Always Accessible to Humans

So on to the next point, which is the accessibility of the Planetary Hierarchy to any human in the third dimension. Not only is the Hierarchy accessible, but so are the archangels and angels, and we are all becoming increasingly more so. You may call upon any one of us at any time and we will respond to you. It may come in the form of direct transmission or, if you are block-ing direct channeling, in form of a dream or a coinci-dence or assistance from another person. Besides the angelic kingdom are the guides who planned your incarnation with you, who are available to work with you and help you. There are also members of the faerie kingdom and animal totems.

As I have mentioned before, the future is not fixed and there are probable futures in the fourth dimension that become actual futures in the third dimension. Each soul creates a plan for his or her incarnation with goals for the development of talents and gifts that will serve humanity. If a soul plans to become some famous celebrity in some particular field, for example, then that outcome might be called that soul's destiny. A team would work with the soul to promote this outcome, and the incarnate soul and the team of guides would meet on the inner planes during dreamtime to discuss the means of attaining the goals. Goals may change.

So it is true for any one of you that at all times you are surrounded by a team of guides who have been assigned to you through their great love for you and who are there to help you, but you are required to ask them to help and to give them your permission. These uncertain times that contain a lot of fear of danger demand a greater involvement with the spiritual levels. As you feel fear and uncertainty, turn to the angels and ask them for their protection for you, your loved ones, your nation, your planet.

Join a Group

So I would advise you to join meditation groups and psychic development groups that use guided visualizations and send out healing. When you join such a group, you become a part of the network of light on the planet. Such a group is not very difficult to form. Any group of dedicated and spiritually inclined friends who make a commitment to meet at the same time every week can do this work. There should be an opening prayer asking for protection, a visualization, a time of quiet to receive impression and a time for healing. Some time might be given to opening and clearing the chakras. The group should finish with a closing prayer. By joining a group that is a part of the network of light, the individual worker is helping in the process of accelerating the frequency of the planet and making it a safer place.

The souls of humanity who are coming into incarnation at this time and who are now referred to as the Indigo children are the forerunners of an advanced humanity who evolved beyond life on Earth during the time of Atlantis, because those of the Order of Melchizedek spent hundreds of years accelerating their evolution through the process known as initiation. These beings have been in other dimensions on other planets, but they are coming back. They will be the Aquarian souls. They have planned their destiny as a large group with many guides to bring about a transformation of the planet.

The Aquarian approach is currently being expressed through the channeled messages of many: *You are all masters having a human experience.* Now, while on the one hand you — all of you — are divine in essence, which means that you are eternal and part of one greater consciousness, the distinction lies in the extent to which you have control over your three-fold personality vehicle. So you are a master within my dimension of existence, but not in the three-dimensional world that you reside in; there, you are in the process of attaining mastery.

So those of you who have come in together on a special mission are referred to simply as lightworkers. You are a vast, interplanetary, interdimensional team of souls who have come here on a special mission. Many of you have come here from other planets in other star systems. So not only have you come into incarnation, but many of you are now in your fifties, and some of you are discouraged and disappointed with life on this planet. You have forgotten what it was that you came here to do. Well, I hope to remind you.

6

You Came to Earth
on a Mission

There is an infinite number of stars in the universe, and the majority of these stars have planets, just as atoms have electrons. Many of these planets are inhabited by intelligent life forms. This is a fairly new concept, because in times past the people of Earth did not know what the stars were and that there was a solar system. Humanity has contemplated the existence of myriad stars formed into myriad galaxies with infinite planets during the latter part of the twentieth century.

You must take my word, because I do not have evidence, that there are inhabited planets and that there are also more inhabited planets within the higher dimensions. Souls move in large groups through planetary rounds. Souls come to Earth to learn the lessons Earth has to offer.

A Hard Life Offers Useful Experience

You should be cheered to know that an extremely hard life offers a great deal of useful experience, and when that lifetime is over and behind you, it does not seem as if it was even hard enough. I know, because this particular channel laments somewhat that a difficult lifetime with little obvious support seems too hard to bear or understand.

If you could actually see all of the loving beings who surround each and every one of you; even though there are six billion of you, there are one hundred billion of us, here to assist. There are nymphs, gnomes, faeries, sylphs and devas, who are all part of the elemental kingdom. They build and maintain the dimensions. They help and protect those who are victimized. There are relatives and ancestors; there are friends and family from previous lifetimes; there are angels. If you are struggling with little or no income and no work, then ask these beings to help you.

When your lifetime is over and you review it, you will be shown all of the times that you were given help or a prayer was answered, and you will see that you were always watched over. You will see the teachings you were given, which were so true that you forgot about and ignored them. In the blink of an eye from birth to death, you find yourself back in the familiarity of the fourth dimension and the fifth dimension, and you are exasperated to find that you did not grow enough and beg to be given the opportunity of a much harder lifetime. You can measure your growth by the brightness of the light that you emanate.

Once your life is over, you will wish that you had always been cheerful and kind. You will be mortified to view yourself as depressed and unkind, even in the worst situations. You goal is to be a light to others.

When you leave this planetary round and go to evolve on another planet, you will bring everything you learned on Earth with you, especially skills and talents.

At this time, there are infinite planets with human-type life forms on them. Some of these planets have been claimed by the light, and others are under the thrall of darkness. You came to this planet, because it is time to liberate it from the darkness. This planet is in a state of battle. You experience suffering, because this is still a planet in darkness. When this becomes a planet of light, there will be no more suffering. It will no longer exist in the third-dimensional frequency, but in the fourth dimension. When you leave this planet to go to other worlds, you will either experience the wondrous love of a light planet or the suffering and oppression of a dark planet. You will choose. The advantage to helping those suffering on a dark planet is that you will grow in the process.

In order to grow, you must encompass greater compassion, kindness and understanding. You must do frequent group and individual meditation work. You must attempt to be moral, ethical and honorable.

There Are Two Types of People in the World Today

In the next decade, the baby boomer generation will consist mainly of people in their fifties and forties who will have a lot of their time and energy freed as their children grow up and leave home. They will also be assisting with grandchildren. Large numbers of these baby boomers will undergo the various procedures to become certified as ministers within progressive or spiritualist churches. By becoming a minister, in undertaking to minister to those who need assistance, an individual changes his or her relationship to the divine. The individual who assumes the mantle of holy orders is under stricter karma and more likely to suffer immediate consequences from failing his or her flock.

There are, in fact, two types of people in the world today: the conscious lightworkers and the unconscious remainder of humanity. The conscious lightworker is one who meditates daily as a point of entry for light onto the planet; acts on the hunches, intuitions and directions from the higher self; studies the ancient wisdom teachings in some form or another; and has an orientation of selflessness and service. The remainder of humanity varies, from those who have some appreciation of the wisdom teachings but who have not made a serious commitment to selflessness or meditation, to those who are intensely selfish and self-motivated. Who do you think you came here to serve?

A Special Team Came to Halt Earth's Descent

I must explain that for a variety of reasons, the humans who inhabited the planet for most of the twentieth century and thousands of years prior to that were the laggard souls of the human round, and true humanity had gone on to better things. You might say that the laggard souls were the special education class of planet Earth or those who failed to graduate. However you explain them or their origins, they are a portion of humanity who not only became trapped in endless cycles of rebirths on the planet, but there also was a danger that the planet would sink deeper and deeper in density, into matter, on account of the group selfishness of these souls.

You might imagine a diver descending to the ocean floor in a diving suit, and the deeper he goes, the greater the pressure of the water is upon him and the darker it is. Well, the laggard souls of humanity and the planet were descending on a runaway course, deeper and deeper, and without some higher intervention, the planet would have spun out of control, deeper, until it would have been impossible to go any deeper and all life on the planet would have been lost.

So a special team was assembled of mainly — but not totally — human souls who had been spending their time on other planets within higher dimensions, who would make the dangerous descent into a third-dimensional reality as a very large team of lightworkers for the purpose of stopping the descent — and beginning the ascension!

So in your mental imagery, your mental model, you do not need to conceptualize a conflict between the forces of light and the forces of darkness, but rather picture the forces of sinking versus the forces of rising! Mentally see the little blue planet spinning down into deeper density, and then imagine a net of light being cast around it and see it coming upward along the path of return.

In order to save this planet from extinction, the cries of a suffering humanity attracted the attention of All That Is to send the Cosmic Christ in the form of millions of fourth-degree initiates and higher humans on a mission to save the planet. The Cosmic Christ is a great mystery. The Cosmic Christ is both a consciousness and a being and also the sum total of many saintly individuals. There is also a Planetary Christ, which is a different entity! The Planetary Christ, of course, is a part of the Cosmic Christ. There is also a Solar Christ. So the work of reclaiming the planet appears to be very difficult and requires a Cosmic Christ to do it! That is the reason why souls who have spent their time on other planets are coming in great numbers to this planet. They are members of the Order of Melchizedek and part of the body of the Cosmic Christ.

So not only is there a body of lightworkers on the planet working to anchor higher energies from the Cosmic Christ, there is also a task force of alien souls on the inner dimensions. The entire group of aliens from other planetary rounds and human souls who have been sojourning on other planets can be thought of as the family of light, the Order of Melchizedek and the White Brotherhood and Sisterhood. It incorporates the Ashtar Command, the Planetary Hierarchy, the Council of Twelve and also the angels and archangels!

Well, if only you could see the assembled masses within the fifth dimension or the abstract mental plane! There is a tremendous gathering of souls who were not present a few decades ago! This vast conclave of lightbeings is gathering around the masters in their ashrams according to the seven rays, and they greatly augment the power of the masters to transmit the seven rays to humanity.

I should explain that all of humanity is to be found on one of the seven rays, but only those who have reached a certain level of understanding in the physical dimension are within the ashram of a master. So we are dispensing with the Piscean terms such as aspirant or probationer on the path and are simply calling the members of the ashrams the lightworkers. The qualifications for being within an ashram if you are an incarnated being are daily meditation, familiarity with the wisdom teachings and a commitment to selfless service. There are also those within the ashrams who are geniuses in their field of endeavor within the physical world but who have little or no interest in the ancient wisdom teachings in their conscious daily lives.

Selfless Is Doing What Is Right

I would like to share a few thoughts on the concept of selfless service, because there is opportunity within this notion for the gullible and idealistic to be exploited. The ascended masters of this planet in no way, shape or form support the exploitation of individuals in the name of selfless service. Giving unstintingly to some particular group or cause in the form of volunteer work or gifts is not exactly what is meant by selfless service.

There are many groups that exhort their membership to practice the art of selfless service by giving their all to the group. We view this as a form of stealing and we hold the perpetrators of such exploitation accountable for their actions. Selfless service is a permanent orientation toward doing whatever is right without thought for oneself. It is not, however, performing services without due recompense. It is a very subtle concept, because if an individual wishes to give a gift or perform a free service, that is one thing — and it is selfless service. But when another tells individuals that they must give their services for the good of the planet, it is often spiritual exploitation. We do not wish to see individuals who own nothing and who become a burden and a liability to others because they gave a large portion of their services as volunteers. Much of the work of the hierarchy today is being performed by wealthy philanthropists who have earned or inherited vast sums of wealth.

Younger Generations Are More Advanced Souls

So a great many events are transpiring simultaneously at this point in time, which include the efforts of the family of light and the Cosmic Christ to accelerate the planet along the arc of return from extremely dense matter to a higher frequency of matter, which is the planetary ascension process.

Then there is the Age of Aquarius, or the New Age, which is a two-thousand-year cycle under the auspices of the constellation Aquarius, a mental sign of increased advanced technology and the utilization of new forms of energy as well as themes of brotherhood.

So what is also transpiring is that the laggard souls are leaving the planet and are being replaced by humans who have been biding their time on other planets, within other dimensions. The laggard souls are on the seven rays but outside the ashrams of the masters, and the more advanced souls coming in are within the ashrams of the masters. So the younger generations coming in are in reality more advanced souls than the elderly individuals who are about to leave the planet. We are right in the middle of this process at this time, and there is a mixture of laggard souls and advanced souls on the planet. This is a very difficult time to be alive and it will be much easier in the future.

The density of the planet has caused both forgetfulness of past incarnations and the interim as well as separation from the will of God within humanity. This has been a painful experiment. As all of you and the planet are accelerated up the frequency spectrum, you will regain your inner contact to the will of God, which is another way of saying that you will rejoin your angelic brothers and sisters who have never known separation from the will of God.

Those of you who are the lightworkers may have felt a lifelong sense of confusion about the humans who surround you, including members of your own family. Their greed, stupidity and self-centeredness at times may bewilder you. You may feel that you belong with a different sort of humans, with those who are truly loving and generous. This feeling of alienation may indicate that you are part of an alien nation!

This Is the Time of Separating the Sheep from the Goats

This is the time mentioned in the Bible of separating the sheep from the goats. One set of human souls will not be reincarnating back onto the planet; they will be going to a new planet. The other group of souls will be reclaiming the planet. Those souls who are to be considered goats, who will be leaving, are those who are not under the control of their own soul or higher self. These are the times where, by a massive effort, such souls might be able to make a leap in consciousness and attain the higher levels. (During World Wars I and II, many souls had the opportunity to perform acts of great courage and unselfishness and therefore made the transition to a higher state.)

Personalities who are not under the control of the higher self are characterized by their lack of soul traits, which are intelligence, humor, tolerance, kindness, flexibility and creativity. So by definition, they are stupid, dull, humorless, unkind, intolerant, judgmental, inflexible and uncreative.

This may not be the type of thinking you expect from an ascended master. You might imagine that we see the Christ in everyone and by focusing on the good, draw it out. After all, everyone is a divine spark in incarnation. Well, from our perspective, it is not always quite like that. Sometimes it is appropriate to see the good in others and draw it out.

We look at some humans and we can see the true self that is the Christ self or higher self shining through, and we look at other humans and we see that there is no one home — the true self has failed to form the bridge to the personality and all that is operating is the earth elemental, which rules the body; the water elemental, which rules the emotions; and the air elemental, which rules the mind. Without the over-lighting presence of the higher self, the personality vehicle is but a shell, endlessly repeating habitual behavior. As such individuals age without the connecting bridge to the higher self within, the personality shows signs of disintegration such as memory loss, poor judgment and confusion.

It is these unconnected beings who are bound for some other planet after they die. The higher self resides within them as a silent observer and witness, a prisoner. However, it is still possible, even now, for them to change their lifestyle and form the bridge to the higher self.

The Aquarian souls who are coming onto the planet will be highly intelligent and creative as long as they do not become mired in drugs and alcohol, as this is where we lose many higher souls. Alcohol and drugs are two of the most serious problems of the planet at this time, as many who would have been lightworkers become alcoholics or drug addicts instead.

It is quite amazing to see how organizations such as AA and NA have become a spiritual path in their own right, and many souls have taken a detour into substance abuse and recovery to find their spirituality. However, we would much rather that lightworkers avoided the entire experience. The addiction of humanity to chemical substances has been a stumbling block in the reclamation mission that is under way.

In a sense, the desire for drugs and alcohol is the result of the conditions of the third dimension in which the ego is isolated and feels pain and confusion while yearning to feel euphoria. As the planet rises in frequency and humanity moves toward what is currently being called unity consciousness, humans will experience an end to the desire for chemical substances that produce euphoria, because they will experience true joy and fulfillment.

So when you are surrounded by individuals who display characteristics such as stupidity, intolerance, animal cunning, greed, selfishness and spite, remember that at this point in time it might be the last chance for these people to make the leap in consciousness required for them to continue on with the humanity on planet Earth. There is going to be a separation of the ways and it is going to be painful, because soul families will be split up. It may be that these individuals have been thrown across your path because you have an opportunity to help them redeem themselves. This is their last chance. So if you have difficult parents or children or both, it may be that you chose to come into incarnation specifically to work with having some enlightening impact on these souls.

This is not to say that the planet they are going to is going to be an unpleasant experience, and many more advanced souls will opt to go with them to act as teachers and guides, but it will be a division. That will be painful.

You will help these people, not by imposing your beliefs upon them, but by loving and accepting them, no matter how unlovable they are. This is a part of your mission at this time. You as lightworkers may have a few difficult laggard souls in your lives who you must hold in love and acceptance. Your love helps them to love themselves.

You may not see any observable effect, but you are having an effect. Because you are a lightworker — and you have been lightworkers since before you were born — your energy levels are much higher than those of the humans around you who you are here to love. When things are looking ugly and people are becoming threatening, hold them all in your love. (You might need to run for your life in some situations, so use common sense!) If you are reading this book, you are most likely a lightworker and not a laggard soul.

So this leads to the question, "Besides reading this book, how do I know that I am a lightworker?" You may have experienced some indications in your lifetime, and now you are beginning to get a growing sense of who you really are. It is time to meditate daily as a point of entry for light energies onto the planet and to stand with all the other lightworkers as a part of the body of the Cosmic Christ.

7
Meditations

So I would like to share some basic guided meditations to be used by individuals and groups that are relevant to the work that is being carried out on the planet at this time. All group guided meditation work should begin with an invocation to the Mother/Father God, Infinite Intelligence, to create a safe place protected by the divine white light, where only the highest energies can come in. Such an invocation might be stated as follows:

Mother/Father God, we invite your presence here tonight, and we ask you to envelop us in radiant white light that enters through the crown chakra at the top of our heads and moves down through our bodies, through our arms and legs, into the ground. We also ask that the

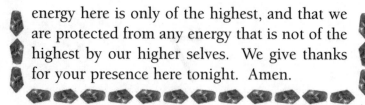

energy here is only of the highest, and that we are protected from any energy that is not of the highest by our higher selves. We give thanks for your presence here tonight. Amen.

I am going to give you a classic guided visualization, similar to many that are in use today. These visualizations are being given in order of progression and should be followed in this order.

The Temple of the Element of Earth

You are out in nature on a beautiful fall day. The sun is out, the sky is blue, and there is a slight breeze. It is warm out but not too hot. The leaves are beginning to appear on the trees. They are pale green. You are walking along a path through the woods. You are walking along the banks of a small stream of clear water that is running over multi-colored stones. It is not very deep. You are walking uphill. You emerge from the woods at the base of a hill. There are steps carved into the hillside, and they lead up to a Grecian-style temple. You can see a circle of white pillars holding up a domed crystal roof. You ascend the stairs easily and enter the temple. It is a temple of healing and knowledge.

As you pass through the pillars, you enter a large, brightly lit sacred space. A huge, multifaceted, blue diamond is suspended in the center of the circular room. It turns slowly and emits brilliant, blue-white light. You absorb the light from the diamond.

You have the opportunity to meet with loved ones and guides. Teachers may come to teach you. There is a circle of plush armchairs around the room. You sit in an armchair with your loved ones beside you. They take this time to give you messages and healing. [There follow about thirty minutes of silence.]

*Now you bid your friends goodbye and leave the temple.
You go down the steps in the side of the hill. You are back
in your chair. You are now aware of the room. Bring yourself back and slowly open your eyes.*

If the lights had been turned off, you may now turn
them back on. This first temple is the temple of the element of earth. There are many temples of earth, in
many forms. Some you enter by going through a door
into a hillside or a mountain. This temple is the most
exalted temple of earth. It contains the diamond, which
is the highest representation of third-dimension physi-
cality for organic life forms.

Diamonds embedded in the planet's mantle that have
yet to be mined are the remnants of ancient forests that
have been compressed into the ground. Diamond is
superior to quartz in its molecular structure and is
quite rare. It takes millions of years to pass for a forest
to become a bed of diamonds.

Before the group disbands, you need to say a few
words of thanks in the form of a short prayer and also
express the desire to be protected by angels until you
meet again.

The next meditation in the series might be like this:

The Temple of the Element of Water

*You are out in nature on a beautiful fall day. The sun is
out, the sky is blue, and there is a slight breeze. It is warm
out but not too hot. The trees are the bright, deep green of
mid-summer. You are walking along a path through the
woods. You are walking along the banks of a small stream
of clear water that is running over multicolored stones. It
is not very deep. You are walking uphill. You emerge from
the woods at the base of a hill. There are steps carved into
the hillside, and they lead up to a Grecian-style temple.
You can see a circle of white pillars holding up a domed*

crystal roof. You ascend the stairs easily and enter the temple. It is a temple of healing and knowledge.

As you pass through the pillars, you enter a large, brightly lit sacred space. There is a beautiful pool with green and blue mosaic tiles sunken into the floor. Steps descend slowly deeper into the water. You descend the steps into the water and swim across the width of the pool. You ascend the steps at the other side. You are handed a towel and you mentally dry yourself.

You have the opportunity to meet with loved ones and guides. There is a circle of plush armchairs around the room. You sit in an armchair with your loved ones beside you. They take this time to give you messages and healing. [There follow about thirty minutes of silence.]

Now you bid your friends goodbye and leave the temple. You go down the steps in the side of the hill. You are back in your chair. You are now aware of the room. Bring yourself back and slowly open your eyes.

This second meditation is almost the same as the first, except that the temple is a temple of the element of water. It is a temple of healing the emotions and feelings.

The third meditation is also almost the same, but inside the temple, a beam of light descends from a hole in the roof. This is the temple of mental healing.

The Temple of Mental Healing

You are out in nature on a beautiful fall day. The sun is out, the sky is blue, and there is a slight breeze. It is warm out but not too hot. The trees are the bright, deep green of mid-summer. You are walking along a path through the woods. You are walking along the banks of a small stream of clear water that is running over multicolored stones. It is not very deep. You are walking uphill. You emerge from the woods at the base of a hill. There are steps carved into the hillside, and they lead up to a Grecian-style temple.

You can see a circle of white pillars holding up a domed crystal roof. You ascend the stairs easily and enter the temple. It is a temple of healing and knowledge.

As you pass through the pillars, you enter a large, brightly lit sacred space. The light is coming down from a hole in the ceiling. As you look up, you can see the night sky filled with stars, and a full moon is directly overhead. The brilliant white light of the moon is descending. You bathe in the moonlight.

You have the opportunity to meet with loved ones and guides. There is a circle of plush armchairs around the room. You sit in an armchair with your loved ones beside you. They take this time to give you messages and healing. [There follow about thirty minutes of silence.]

Now you bid your friends goodbye and leave the temple. You go down the steps in the side of the hill. You are back in your chair. You are now aware of the room. Bring yourself back and slowly open your eyes.

The final meditation, of course, is a temple of the element of fire.

The Temple of the Element of Fire

You are out in nature on a beautiful fall day. The sun is out, the sky is blue, and there is a slight breeze. It is warm out but not too hot. The trees are beginning to lose their leaves. You are walking along a path through the woods. You are walking along the banks of a small stream of clear water that is running over multicolored stones. It is not very deep. You are walking uphill. You emerge from the woods at the base of a hill. There are steps carved into the hillside, and they lead up to a Grecian-style temple. You can see a circle of white pillars holding up a domed crystal roof. You ascend the stairs easily and enter the temple. It is a temple of healing and knowledge. As you pass through the pillars, you enter a large, brightly lit sacred space. In the center of the space is a large flame spurting from the floor.

You may stand in the flame without being burned or harmed. It is the flame of purification. It begins as a bright red and purifies your base chakra located at the base of your spine. It turns orange and purifies your sacral chakra. Then the flame becomes yellow and purifies your solar plexus chakra. Then the flame becomes green and purifies your heart chakra. Then the flame becomes blue and purifies your throat chakra. Then the flame becomes indigo and purifies your third-eye chakra. Finally, you are enveloped in violet light and this violet light purifies your crown chakra. You stand in violet flames. Then all of your purified chakras give a burst of colored light and you stand within a pure white flame, unharmed.

You have the opportunity to meet with loved ones and guides. There is a circle of plush armchairs around the room. You sit in an armchair with your loved ones beside you. They take this time to give you messages and healing. [There follow about thirty minutes of silence.]

Now you bid your friends goodbye and leave the temple. You go down the steps in the side of the hill. You are back in your chair. You are now aware of the room. Bring yourself back and slowly open your eyes.

I wish to impart some information on the directions that are associated with the elements. Each of the four compass directions is associated with an archangel and qualities with the European tradition of magic. The north is associated with the Archangel Michael and the element of earth, especially as a storehouse of food and general wealth. The east is associated with the element of air and Uriel. The south is associated with the element of fire and Raphael. The west is associated with the element of water and Gabriel. (In the North American shamanistic tradition, the directions play a very important part and are associated with elemental attributes also; these different traditions emerged out of the one tradition of ancient Atlantis and evolved differently over time.)

To these four elemental directions we might also add the directions of up, down and center, which represent the elements of the higher planes and the higher triad, the Monadic triad of Monadic, Atmic and Buddhic levels. The Monad is the divine spark of consciousness who separated from All That Is. Atmic and Buddhic are slightly denser sheaths that surround the Monad and give it consciousness on denser levels or dimensions. The Buddhic level is generally called the causal body or causal level, and this is the first level of self-awareness that never dies. It is permanent. The memory of all past lives and experiences are housed there.

There are also archangels who are connected to the elements of Buddhi, Atman and Monad, as well as the directions of up, down and center. The directions of north, east, south and west are all related to the lower vehicles of the personality composed of a body, emotions and two levels of mind — the lower concrete mind represented by air and the higher fiery mind represented by fire.

So on performing these four guided meditations it is possible that one might encounter the archangelic beings who are related to the elements and the sites and the ascended masters associated with the rays. These are meditations that are mainly connected to the personality vehicle and getting it under the control of the higher vehicle.

There are more temples that relate to the higher levels of consciousness, but it is not necessary at this point to consider them. Working as an individual or a group, making a recording of the narrative with music or speaking it aloud and working several times with each image should have a gradual healing and strengthening effect. The four lower chakras should become stronger and purified. Possible health problems should be eliminated while they are in the aura and before they become manifest.

This does not sound like extraordinary work, but millions of people are struggling with damaged emotions from traumatic experiences that affect the dietary and appetite systems. Feelings of massive emptiness, loneliness, worthlessness create hungers and cravings or the reverse, a distorted self-image. Much of this has to do with the sacral chakra and the color orange. When this chakra is in balance, the chakras above and below it are in better balance. When the four lower chakras are healed and in balance, the higher chakras may be better employed for spiritual work. The first steps are establishing a healthy physical body that is neither too fat nor too thin, healthy emotions and the healing of emotional damage caused in the past, and a healthy mind healed from mental damage inflicted in the past. Guides and teachers may give much in the way of instruction during these visualizations. This is a means to tap directly into one's own inner spiritual fount of knowledge.

8

Giving Personal Channeled or Psychic Readings

This is a thorny issue, because there are many individuals who give personal psychic readings, and some people give readings from the Ascended Master Djwhal Khul! My philosophy is that you live in a consensus reality and that what you buy into becomes yours. Your beliefs about your future are going to shape your future, although the shape of history is going to be determined by group thought. The small individual who is hoping for a happy future may be swept away by group realities that are not so pleasant.

So when a psychic or a channel tells an individual what his or her future is going to be, this prediction has no power in or by itself until the individual chooses to believe in it and thus irradiates it with power. If a psychic gives an individual a time limit, it is the belief of the individual that makes something come about at that time. If an individual comes for a reading looking to strengthen his or her belief in things unseen, which is looking for evidence, then a good reading may be helpful. However, people posing as psychics may take many cues from asking innocent questions or standard questions that give them a lot of information. If one desperately wants to believe, many vague and sketchy statements can be expanded upon by the inquirer.

However, the spirit guides who are assigned to each individual when he or she is born enjoy trying to work on giving some evidence, and this may come with reoccurring themes. There may be a song, an animal, a bird, a flower, a place that has special meaning to the querier, and spirit guides will work to repeat this theme over and over. A psychic may tap into the theme and mention it.

The person who is in the driver's seat is the individual coming for the reading, and the spirit guides, teachers and masters may not do anything without invitation and consent, so readings given that suggest that the spirit guides desire the inquirer to perform various tasks or do things a particular way should not be considered as directives, but as suggestions that might bring about improvements. If individuals pray regularly that outcomes might be for their highest good or for the safety of their loved ones, then a seemingly negative turn of events might be the removal of an individual from a situation in order for some other, better outcome to occur. When a medium or psychic says that the guides are doing something deliberately, such as stopping a project, it would only be within the parameters of a request already made. In other words, dead relatives, guides, teachers and masters do not have the right to intervene and stop or interfere with an individual's will for the future. However, the individual may have made some blanket agreement in the sleep state or before embarking on the incarnation.

So in the same vein, guides, teachers and former relatives are not empowered to make critical judgments about the personality of the inquirer or suggestions for improvement. Anything coming through a psychic that has a very judgmental ring to it is not coming from true spirit guides, but from the lower mind of the psychic. In order to be a good psychic channel, it is necessary to have done some work on the lower mind and to be operating from the higher mind, the illuminated mind. This is a problem right here, because many who undertake to develop their psychic abilities by joining psychic development groups do not do the necessary work to clear through the lower mind to the higher mind.

In the past, priests and priestesses of ancient cults and temples went through a training process and a purification process before they could awaken the third eye and the power that comes with it. Many of the people alive today with an extraordinary psychic ability of great accuracy reached the higher initiations that awakened the psychic powers in a past lifetime and carried them through many lifetimes. Many psychics alive today trained either in ancient Atlantis or in ancient Egypt. The most prevalent group trained in ancient Egypt.

Of course, it is difficult to generalize about the temple training, because it occurred over a long period of time and therefore, there were changes. Additionally, the Egyptian temple training differed slightly in quality from the Atlantean, because the highest teachers were on the inner dimensional planes and not on the outer plane.

Temple Training Activated the Chakras One by One

We are discussing the training in a time period of roughly 10,000 to 5,000 B.C. Basically speaking, though, the candidates for entering the temple system were taken in childhood, and they began training at age seven.

From seven to fourteen, they were trained in sports and dance, and so they had forms that were like a cross between ballet dancing and belly dancing, wrestling, kick-boxing and yoga postures. The purpose of this training was to ground them in the physical body and to activate the root chakra in a healthy fashion. (It is still a practice today to teach young children dance and the martial arts, and this is a good means of opening the first chakra at the base of the spine.) Just like in elementary schools today, they were trained in a variety of disciplines from an early age. They were taught to read and write in hieroglyphs. They were taught basic mathematics and geometry. They learned the basics of astronomy and astrology. They were taught art and sculpture. They learned architecture and masonry. By about the age of fourteen, it generally became clear as to what an individual's specialty might be for that life.

The second chakra work was related to the control of emotions, which ties in to the digestive system and the thyroid gland. (It is clear in the modern world that people who feel emotionally empty feel compelled to eat, and often a sluggish thyroid results in becoming severely overweight. There is a clear relationship between control of the emotions and the digestive system.) From fourteen to twenty-one, there was a focus on being tested for positive emotions. Initiates were taught the virtues of compassion, selflessness, non-attachment, generosity and also how to integrate the correspondingly large shadow self created by empha-sizing one pole of a duality. Opportunities were creat-ed for them to feel jealousy, competitiveness, selfish-ness, anger and greed on a daily basis until they tran-scended these feelings. They also had wise teachers counseling them on methods of overcoming these impulses and better ways to think about reality.

From twenty-one to twenty-eight, they were involved in creating a factual mental database about the world around them — in chemistry, physics, biology, astrolo-gy, counseling theory and psychology, music and math-ematics. The work at this stage was to develop the ana-lytical mind into a fine tool. It was also to overcome the false ego that was created.

The activated third chakra creates a very intellectually gifted person. Having developed the intellect, it is also important to gain "enlightenment" and overcome the ego.

To Move Onward and Upward, You Must Control Your Lower Ego

Now I wish to pause a moment and have you consid-er that in many cultures, in many lands, the ordinary people did not experience anything like this — they were born, worked hard in the field or in factories, had children and died. In the modern world in Western cultures, there has been a revival of the temple system in the form of school as mandatory for all citizens of a certain age. We are now so used to school as a part of reality that it is hard to imagine a time when everyone was illiterate except for a handful of scholars. It is hard to imagine that subjects such as biology were taught only to those who had taken spiritual vows to particu-lar gods and goddesses. In general, it is hard to imag-ine all of the centuries that have transpired with the majority of humanity in darkness, their chakras barely open or under control. What is also hard to imagine is that souls who seem to have a quick understanding of the subjects taught in schools are reviewing topics that they are already familiar with.

A massive number of souls in the Western culture are going through the process of having their root chakras brought under control with organized sports and dance; their emotional chakras balanced through religious and moral training; and their solar plexus chakras activated in schools, colleges and universities. However, often they are left without enlightenment and their lower ego is running rampant. This is a major problem in modern society. The majority of people in Western cultures are left at this point and are looking for something more, something that has been missing. They seek enlightenment and spiritual teaching. They are ready to complete the initiation of the solar plexus and move up to the initiation of the heart chakra. They are often stopped by their lower ego.

Without due work on the lower ego, it is potentially dangerous to attempt to open the higher chakras. This stage must be completed before moving onward and upward. The main developmental technique is self-observation of negative mental chattering and noticing trends of thought and detaching the self from them. Control of the lower ego begins with the realization that "I am not my thoughts." When the realization is made that there are thoughts and an observer observing the thoughts, the beginning of overcoming the ego is under way.

Meditation on the concept of one universal intelligence pervading all of creation as the awareness "I Am" is the second step.

Awareness of the nature of the lower ego and how it attempts to gain control of the self represent the next level of learning. The lower ego begins as a contradictory form of self-expression. When another individual states something, the lower ego contradicts. I do not mean correcting false information, but a mental stance of opposing others as a matter of course. With this opposition also come deriding, demeaning, criticizing in a very negative fashion; judging in a cruel fashion; and the desire to inflict pain on others emotionally and mentally.

People who are controlled by their lower ego as opposed to their higher self cannot see the higher self in others and cannot give due credit to others for their attainments. When the lower ego is out of control, the majority of other people are perceived as insane, unbalanced, immoral, stupid and lazy, with the growing sense that they should be punished merely for existing. This is convenient, as then only the lower self itself is perceived as sane, balanced, moral, intelligent and industrious — and deserving.

So for those attempting to gain control over their lower egos, they should vigilantly observe their thinking processes and consider the mind to be like a wild horse that needs to be tamed. Some effort should be made to correct negative and judgmental thoughts about others. Another technique is replacing a thought with its opposite and considering how accurate it is. Taking some time to give acknowledgment to the good in others and their accomplishments is yet another important technique.

The key to success is viewing the vanquishment of the lower ego as of supreme importance toward gaining enlightenment and spiritual progress. This is symbolized as the knight killing the dragon. The knight represents the higher self, being a warrior of light who protects the weak and the innocent, as well as beautiful women, from suffering and harm. The knight is the higher self or soul. The qualities of selfless love of others is the embodiment of the knight and the higher self.

I want to add that modern societies are not arranged to train the majority of people in overcoming their negative lower egos, but rather the lower ego is being constantly fed like a hungry dragon on a chain. Also, the training system that has come down through the eons from the most ancient days of Egypt to Greece and Rome, then to Europe, to the modern world, has worked on the root chakra and the solar plexus chakra; it skipped over the second chakra, leaving it underdeveloped, and the third chakra is not totally under the control of the soul.

So the way that society has been set up in the present time is not in accordance with the Melchizedek training system of developing the chakras one at a time, over time, in their proper order. This system has been brought to the planet by wise spiritual teachers and continues in an unbalanced fashion within the lower worlds. The majority of modern people have imbalances within their lower chakras, unless they seek out a system that will train and balance them, such as a yoga system or a Buddhist path or some form of advanced psychotherapy such as psychosynthesis.

However, when the individual who is seeking to embody a loving consciousness is surrounded by others who are driven by the lower ego, it is like being in shark-infested waters, metaphorically speaking. In the home, the workplace and in social settings, the individual is constantly at the mercy of others driven by their lower ego to acts of unkindness, cruelty and selfishness.

This is particularly true in Western cultures and not necessarily true in other cultures where the belief system differs. For example, in the Middle East there are teachings about treating strangers and outsiders with great kindness. Some cultures place a greater degree of emphasis on treating others with kindness.

This, of course, was the absolute core value of original Christianity, which took some attempt to train the individual to overcome the lower ego and awaken the heart chakra. However, the church was changed from the early teachings and today remains rather far from the original teachings that were heavily derived from the Egyptian temple training.

Everything that the master teacher Jesus ever said that was recorded and written down at some later time, had something to do with raising the consciousness above that of the lower ego, to the level of the higher self, which is loving and compassionate. All of the little parables that he told describe some situation where someone acts from the level of the soul and not the lower ego. Out of the teachings of Jesus emerged many religious institutions, but the most faithful to the spirit of Jesus were perhaps the tradition of the Knight Errant and also the Franciscan monks.

The Temple Training Continues

However, in the Atlantean and Egyptian temple training systems, candidates did conquer their lower ego and move on to the next level of development, which was activating the heart chakra. (The numbers of years become less clear. Once we are past the solar plexus chakra, development becomes very individualistic. Although all humans have some control of the lower chakras, very few have actually activated the heart chakra properly. The heart chakra might be activated at any point between twenty-eight and never! Well, I joke, but it might be not at all in a particular incarnation. The mass majority of individuals have stopped development at the level of the mind, and even within the temple training system, the numbers of trainees have become less and less as they progress through the chakras. So there are some who have returned who had made it to the level of the activated heart chakra in a past temple training and will therefore reawaken it in a present incarnation, and then there are many who will not.)

In the Western world, in the modern day, the heart is associated with pure love of others — and this is a very curious notion that is taken for granted, because the heart is a muscle that acts as a pump and pumps blood around the body, and there is no apparent reason to associate it with the feeling of love. Now, the majority of the feelings and emotions are related to the second chakra. These would include feelings like happiness, sadness, loneliness, jealousy and so on, but love is not on that level. It relates to the fourth chakra and healing, so the power of healing is effected by holding a consciousness of perfect love. Psychically, this is observed as a clear, green energy that flows through the heart chakra. What this energy does is align the inter-dimensional bodies together so that the physical body more closely matches the body on the lighter levels, which are perfect. It also works to balance the chakras and open blockages.

The master teacher Jesus had an open heart chakra that channeled a tremendous amount of green healing energy, and he was able to heal the sick and even raise the dead. This was very common amongst the high priests and priestesses of Atlantis and Egypt in the earliest days after the flood. Fourth-level priests and priestesses could heal the sick and raise the dead simply with the energy that flowed through them. (However, this thought should not inhibit any of those who wish to make themselves a channel for healing energy, as the practice of meditating, praying and asking to be a channel of healing energy will develop the heart chakra. For some the heart chakra was developed in past lives, and for others this is a new experience.)

For those who had successfully established the power to heal, the next step was to work on the fifth chakra from age thirty-five to forty-two. This chakra related to the throat and communication and the power of the voice. This chakra related to trance mediums and channels. Those who had opened this chakra were able to form a connection to an over-lighting teacher. This is not to suggest that younger people or more intellectually oriented people cannot form such a connection, but this was the stage in the development within the ancient temple system.

The sixth chakra developed between forty-two and forty-nine and was the third eye, which made clairvoyance possible. With the opened third eye the candidate could see the spirits of the dead who surrounded individuals, and something of the future. Candidates were often trained to see the future in broad, sweeping eras; the rise and fall of nations; and the rise and fall of technologies.

The final chakra was the crown chakra, or the thousand-petaled lotus as it was known in the East, and this was symbolized in art as the halo around the head. When the crown chakra was activated, there was a general knowing about everything, as the individual was connected to the cosmic intelligence pervading all the universes. One could ask a priest or priestess who had attained this level a question about anything and he or she could answer accurately.

So within this system, which was like a complicated university where the priests and priestesses dressed in clothes with colors and jewelry that denoted their rank and status, it was possible to get stuck at any stage and remain on that level for that lifetime and just develop on that level. For example, certain youths never really transcended the martial arts and dance. Others became experts in martial arts and dance but went on to a level of science, specializing in physics, chemistry, biology and medicine. They ended their lives exploring this level and being very intellectual and concrete. Others, who passed through these levels with proficiency, became healers or seers. They would, of course, tend to be either older people or older souls.

Of course, it bears mentioning that in the early days of the Egyptian society this was very evolved and complex, and over time it declined. The cause of this decline had something to do with the planet being on the arc of descent, which meant that it was moving into a state of greater density and more fully into the third dimension, away from the fourth dimension. (And we have just turned the corner and are returning to a higher density. The many effects of greater density are forgetfulness of the past, disconnection from the soul level and inability to hear the spirits who guide on the inner planes, or higher dimensions. The world becomes more materialistic and violent as the illusion seems more real.) So over time, the essence of the teachings became lost and confused and there was greater tendency toward money and power as the motivating factors.

The True Story of Moses' Task

The Egyptian Empire might even exist today if it had not been for Moses, a prince and high priest. A group, who had retained spacecraft, directed him to steal some of the Atlantean devices and a large group of Semitic slaves and take them out of Egypt. The story that Moses told and passed on to the Semitic people makes it appear that his job was to free them from slavery in Egypt, but actually he was being directed to create a new country and organize the people around protecting the Atlantean objects.

Obviously, one of the items that he stole was a dangerous weapon that could have wreaked mass destruction, and the Egyptians were no longer of a high enough consciousness to have such a thing. Moses had the task of instructing the Semitic people to be of a high enough consciousness to protect these artifacts. (Clearly, there is some reference in the Bible to these weapons: Joshua using such a device to make the walls of Jericho fall down or God destroying Sodom and Gomorrah.)

Moses also took the kabbalah system out of Egypt, which was the study of the tree of life and the various spheres on the tree. These spheres and pathways were created by the Atlanteans on the inner planes. By this time, the significance was beginning to be lost on the materialistic Egyptian descendants of the Atlanteans. However, the people who Moses led out of Egypt to start a new society and guard the Atlantean devices were part Chaldean and part Egyptian. The spiritual teachings of the kabbalah were given to the priesthood to study.

If the story of the flight from Egypt is studied from the point of view that they were not performing miracles but that they had a variety of scientific and advanced technology devices, it can be seen that some of the plagues or the work of the "Angel of Death" were the result of test-tube viruses and germ warfare. We take it for granted today that "God" unleashed plagues on the enemies of his chosen people, but it certainly sounds like the biological warfare that is being contemplated today.

Clearly, Moses had plenty of devices and tricks and was able to manufacture food out of nothing and keep the people alive in the desert for forty years. Finally, when the Egyptians had failed to find them, had died trying and had forgotten all about them, they were able to build the country of Israel. By this time, Moses had shaped them for their future with his teachings. Once in Israel, they built a large temple and developed a priesthood who was to guard the Arc of the Covenant with force, if necessary. Some of the priests knew how to use some of the devices, but there were objects that needed fuel or electricity to function.

Over several thousand years, the tiny state of Israel fought off many invaders, from Persians to Philistines, and in the process the devices, which might have protected Israel from the Greek Empire and the Roman Empire, were taken and the people came to depend on prophecies that a Messiah would come and save them. The ancient Jewish people existed to protect the world from the ancient Egyptians, who could have used the devices in the Arc of the Covenant to destroy the planet. (The Germans in World War II are thought to have believed in advanced technological devices, and they were searching for them.)

There is no reason for such a scenario to reoccur. Modern science today is beginning to outstrip the inventions of Atlantis. The third-ray temple has reestablished itself and will continue to do so under the auspices of the Age of Aquarius, which rules the third-ray temple. There will be many new inventions and new forms of energy in the next two thousand years of Earth history. People of all races, types and colors will emerge as geniuses as they are offered the means to express themselves.

So these terrible ancient weapons are lost, and many souls incarnating today were trained in the ancient temple systems of Egypt, India, Britain and Scandinavia. Those souls who have been through these ancient training programs give good psychic readings based on using the ancient principles and on having already gained control over their lower mind.

There are those souls who give psychic readings who have contact only on a fairly low level and are unaware of higher levels. Their contacts reflect their character and their spiritual level — they either did not participate in the temple training system or they backslid to a lower level in subsequent lifetimes. The ideal channeled or psychic reading that the masters desire to give to individuals would be suggestions for increased health on all levels, greater wisdom and understanding, greater alignment to the plan that the individual created before incarnating and greater expression of talents and abilities that may serve the greater good.

If an individual is an artist, musician, poet, writer, dancer, actor, teacher, instructor, singer, scientist, healer, psychic or has one or more of many other unlisted talents, then the masters will not desire to see such individuals slaving away at MacDonald's to earn a living. If you have a talent, then you are working on developing that talent over many lifetimes and are in the third dimension to express it. You may need a day job, but the guides wish to see your talents expressed.

9

Astrology Works through the Collective Unconscious Mind

Carl Jung was one of the first psychologists to conceptualize the idea of a collective unconscious mind, which he theorized as a genetically encoded set of symbols, meanings and archetypes that communicated to individuals during their sleep state. His concept of the collective unconscious was something like a computer program that was written into each human being at a mental level. It was something like a primitive language that was mainly visual. He came to his theory by trying to explain certain anomalies of the human psyche, such as similar symbols being found in varied cultures existing at differing times, and mentally ill patients having knowledge of things that they could not know by rational means.

I am presenting a differing definition of the collective unconscious mind — that it is a place that is very subjective and different from third-dimensional reality that you may enter during the sleep state. It is known in esoteric and occult circles as the astral plane; I call it the fourth dimension. It is the frequency range directly above the third dimension, and it is the realm of feeling and emotion.

I have stated elsewhere that there are seven subplanes to the astral plane, but there are also infinite locations. The astral plane is almost limitless. There are levels that exactly mirror your world; there are astral hells and astral heavens — but none of it is really real. It is more malleable and plastic than your reality; thoughts may instantly shape themselves into things and you may experience strong emotions of great fear, hate or love.

Some of the books in the Bailey series contain great emphasis that the astral plane is an illusion. I do not desire to continue that emphasis. The astral plane must be respected for what it is: a highly subjective reality where it is possible to encounter real other people or thought forms of other people. It is a realm of embodiment that is very close to the Earth plane. It is very easy to slip into it. It is the first destination that the dead encounter.

Many of you do not remember their dreams or have only scrambled impressions, because the process of returning to the sleeping human body and activating the sleeping brain quickly destroys the memories of the experiences that you have in your sleep. You may catch a few memories as you awake. You may have spent the night hanging out with your friends or in an astral temple of learning, but when you wake up, your brain will only present you with confusing, scrambled memories. It takes some effort to bring back clear memories.

So the collective unconscious is a location where all of humanity journeys to during the sleep cycle. There are seven major levels, and so humanity is divided into seven major groups who each gravitates to its own level — and the majority, of course, is in the middle levels. You might call this level Middle Earth. (Or you might not.) However, it is very appropriate at this time that the trilogy of the Lord of the Rings movies has been released, that it represents the collective unconscious of humanity and most especially of Westerners and Europeans of the Celtic, Scandinavian and Mediterranean traditions. A great battle is being fought within Middle Earth; it has been fought all during the twentieth century and is still being fought.

Ensouled Planets Affect Humans

My original point, which I am moving slowly toward, is that great planetary rocks moving through space obviously would not on their own influence and affect individual humans, but these planets are ensouled by consciousnesses of great angelic beings who emit energies and emotions on the astral plane, in astral locations.

There are twelve locations on the astral plane that represent the Houses of the zodiac. These locations are filled with the colors, sounds, symbols, elements, animals and archetypal beings associated with each sign. The Houses are populated by the planetary beings who are moving through that sign.

For example, in the House of Aries, it is a Nordic country in the spring. Trees are coming into leaf. Spring flowers are coming out. Lambs are frisking about in fields with large rams and ewes. There is a castle with burning braziers and torches where an emperor is sitting on a throne. The emperor is looking at blueprints and plans. There are guards and soldiers around him.

In the House of Taurus, it is a Nordic country in later spring, with differing flowers. There is a crafts fair with many craftspeople selling their wares. Calves and bulls are penned in a field; there are large tables of food and drink and merchants selling fabrics, housewares and cosmetics. There are musicians and singers performing in one area and comedians in another. A beautiful queen is presiding over the events.

So each sign of the zodiac is represented by a location. The various planetary rulers enter as archetypal figures with a lot of pomp and ceremony as might befit royalty.

The Seven Orders

Now, as humans move through these twelve locations in the sleep state, they are progressing through the initiations of the chakras. The first, the base chakra, is associated with the first ray and the sign of Aries. Individual souls also move through the seven orders, or ashrams, which were established by the Melchizedek priesthood who came to Atlantis in the middle period and began the schools of initiation. They are now the ashrams headed by the masters. Souls working within the orders have been doing so for hundreds and thousands of years. The orders used to be physical and in the world, and now they are hidden and within the collective unconscious mind.

The First Ray Order was that of the Warrior King, and out of it came an organization that had some resemblance to the masons, yet only inasmuch as masonry and building with stone were incorporated into this temple. This was a temple of the mysteries, and the mysteries of pattern, order, sacred geometry, form, building, the flower of life design and the pentagram were associated with it, as was the color red. The element associated with this order was that of earth and the third dimension along with the five-pointed flower of life as the pentagram. This temple was an expression of the mysteries of building — building universes, buildings, civilizations. It included an understanding of physics and chemistry as the building blocks of the universe, as well as the study of atoms and geometry. The work of Pythagoras was the remnant of this order in Greece.

The energy of this order was embodied in the gold coin, the diamond, the pentagram, and symbols associated with it are of being in caves under the ground. This was the Order of the First Ray and the element of earth. A symbolic initiation into having gained control over the element of earth as in the form of control over the physical body and its many appetites was that of having climbed a high mountain and entered a cave or having descended into the depths of the Earth.

Within the Atlantean system, there was a space on the astral plane, or fourth dimension, that the candidate for initiation, for the first initiation, might enter and experience this descent into the Earth. On the journey, there would be various entities along the way who would try to impede his or her progress or who would allow him or her to pass by. The successful completion of this journey on the astral plane would mark the completion of the first initiation. The energy of the kundalini, which is coiled at the base of the spine, would have been anchored at the base chakra. In future incarnations, whether male or female, this individual would have control over the physical appetites and the physical body, keeping it fit and healthy.

Now, as was mentioned before, the children entering the temple system were trained in martial arts and dance forms during the ages of seven to fourteen, and this fell under the aegis of the First Ray Order, being an order that trained policing forces and taught law as well as architecture and had a focus on physical activity. However, every order and temple had some form of physical expression that it developed extensively, so one order might have a dance form and another might have yoga asanas. The First Ray Order offered everything. It would be similar to going to the local YMCA and finding classes in many disciplines.

(At this time, all of the ancient forms are being redeveloped and offered in local workshops. Every soul who ever was trained in a temple order has some memory of the discipline and is remembering it, which might come as an impulse to take up belly dancing, ballet, tai chi chuan, tae kwon do, yoga or whatever else might involve physical activity.)

So some souls would stay within an order and develop the physical dance, martial art or meditation form through deeper levels and become an expert in a form. These individuals would have been great athletes within the first lifetimes within the temple system. A soul would spend that incarnation developing a physical form to its highest level.

The next levels within the First Ray Order would be the study of subjects such as law and justice, geometry and architectural design. From this level, a soul might spend a lifetime as a city planner or part of a justice system.

Having spent lifetimes as an athlete, a warrior, a police officer of the ancient world, a military general, an architect, the higher roles were that of politician and military leader of a nation. It might take ten or more lifetimes for a soul to rise to the level of a local or national leader. The royal family of local areas of Atlantis or Egypt were trained within the First Ray Order. The order was like a combination of a school, a YMCA and a university, offering a progression of related themes under a teacher. Instead of a final exam, there was an initiation, which was an inner planes journey and encounter with many strange entities who were friends and foes.

The Second Ray Order, that of the Empress Queen, focused on the mysteries related to the unconscious mind and the study of astrology, the tarot, the tree of life, archetypes and the element of water. It also related to storytelling, mythology, fairy tales, the story of the hero's quest, the element of water and the sphere of the Moon.

This was the order of counselors and psychotherapists working with guided meditations, visualizations, archetypal figures and subpersonalities. Souls moving through the various levels in this order lifetime after lifetime would begin with a dance form and progress to studying astrology, tarot and kabbalah and the unconscious mind. They would assume the role of storyteller, mythmaker or counselor and therapist.

The initiation connected to this order had to do with water and crossing a body of water. With a bit of luck, Anubis the ferryman might row the candidate over in a boat. He would also bring him or her back again.

The Third Ray Order was a temple of science that studied medicine, anatomy, biology, physics and chemistry. The god of this order was a fount of knowledge or a messenger. The priests in this order had completed lifetimes in the previous orders. They were fluent in criminal justice and psychology and the other related topics, and now they were developing the intellect.

The initiation for this order was that of the element of air. Of course, this initiation was carried out on the inner planes and involved having a helper fly the candidate to a place where he or she was shown many strange things. In such a case an angel was necessary, or a winged god or goddess.

The Fourth Ray Order had a focus on healing through the laying on of hands and prayer. The heart chakra was the point where the kundalini fire was anchored. The initiation at this level involved the element of fire or possibly an encounter with a lion. The goddess of this order was a goddess of love and motherhood.

The Fifth Ray Order related to music, mathematics, harmonies, spatial relationships, vibrations, sonics, frequencies, transmissions, crystals, poetry and songs. The students of this order developed the power of the voice and learned to play musical instruments.

The Sixth Ray Order related to the power of the third eye, seership, clairvoyance, predicting the future. The priests and priestesses of this order had been through the other orders in previous lifetimes and had attained this level of psychic ability.

The Seventh Ray Order was that of the Magus, or the individual who had attained all of the orders and become a magician, capable of invoking the powers of the inner planes to his bidding and performing miracles.

You may observe that an individual who has had many lives within the system of development will have many strings to his or her bow, so to speak, and will have developed several aspects of the various orders. So these orders that were once physical are now hidden within the astral plane, and every human soul is within one of them, where more advanced beings act as teachers and instructors. Spirit guides are assigned from the order to which an individual soul belongs.

Planetary Beings Appear in Different Roles

At this point, you should be wondering what the mechanism would be that would make physical events happen as a result of symbolic events within astral astrological locations. Well, one aspect is that individuals are affected by archetypal planetary beings entering their birth House or Sun sign or aspecting it positively or negatively. These beings appear in a variety of roles.

Saturn brings limitations and acts as a teacher or tester, creating trials and tests to be overcome. He is the ruler of the ray of harmony through conflict, or that of vibrations and harmonies. He works in octaves, or higher turns of the spiral. He returns with similar but harder tests. He appears as a hermit figure in a deep but bright blue robe, sometimes carrying a lantern or a scythe. He is also called Father Time. He is the prime Lord of Karma, as he brings the harvest of what seeds you have sown. However, that is only one of many roles that he has within the parameters that define him. An individual may be taken over by Saturn as an archetype and seek a profession that relates to that archetype, as a teacher or in corrections. He may, as an entity, visit you and thousands of other souls on the astral plane at the same time and adjust your energy so that you attract certain events. These beings affect the energies in your aura coming through your chakras. Saturn affects the energies of the throat chakra and the blue energy in your aura.

Jupiter, by contrast, is jovial, effusive, expansive, warm and a bringer of opportunities and rewards. He appears as a white-bearded old man, like a traditional wizard, and he is the wizard of all wizards. He has a purple-violet robe and a matching hat. He affects the crown chakra and when that, the last chakra, is functioning, the energy changes to pure white. He is the second Lord of Karma. He affects the energies of the crown chakra. The energies of the crown chakra turn thought forms into realities. Once initiates have reached this level, they are safe enough that their thoughts can create reality. It would be a very unsafe place in the world if everyone could create his or her own reality. Enemies would be dropping like flies and everyone would win the lottery!

Pluto is an especially interesting figure, because he is the Lord of Hades, the King of the Underworld, and he brings what is hidden down in the depths of darkness into the light. This is often interesting in world politics. He reveals secrets and he brings skeletons out of the closet. He brings elements of the past into the present. He is dressed in a dark midnight blue robe. He is the third Lord of Karma. He affects the third eye and seership. He makes the hidden visible to the inner eye. He affects the energy of the brow chakra and the emotions going through it. The emotions going through this chakra affected by the movements of Pluto are often secret infatuations or obsessions. He also affects terrorists and fanatics when negatively aspected.

Mars affects the base chakra according to how he is aspected in the natal horoscope. He may affect the base chakra to create a personality that is filled with rage, lust and anger, or with enthusiasm and leadership abilities. People who are negatively aspected by Mars may be very active in the world in the role of starting fights or warfare. He appears as a traditional war lord dressed in a red robe.

The Sun, or Apollo, the Solar Logos, affects the sacral chakra, whereas the sign he rules, Leo, affects the heart chakra and so there is a link there. Apollo represents the true self, or the higher self. Movements of the Sun affect the emotional life and the sense of self-esteem. He is the inner child, filled with enthusiasm for life.

The lady Venus is dressed in a green gown that is embroidered in gold thread with all the animals, crops, birds, fish and humans of the Earth. She brings energy to the heart chakra and both healing powers and artistic sensibilities, which are united into a sense of perfect form. There is a perfect archetype for every being and thing that is the most beautiful version of that thing, and the energies of Venus restore physical objects to a greater correspondence to the original blueprint. She represents truth, beauty, justice and the realm of perfect blueprints. She brings justice into the life, and balance and order.

The lady Moon may appear as Isis or Mary, as a lady dressed in a bright blue gown with a hood over a white dress. She may be accompanied by a dove, which represents the presence of divine spirit of wisdom. The Moon represents the anima or animus — the unconscious opposite gender aspect of the self. The House she is placed in will be the House of the potential partner.

Mercury may appear as the traditional trickster, a changer of shapes and a liar, or a teacher who instructs in medicine and the sciences. His energy affects the solar plexus chakra and the ability to read if others are truthful or not. He affects mental energies and intellectual prowess, or the lack of such energy. He appears with winged boots and a winged helmet.

Uranus is the most eccentric of the planetary rulers. He causes sudden changes, unexpected changes. He and Neptune, who appears as a sea god complete with trident, will rule the Age of Aquarius.

So those souls who have not worked on their chakras through the means of meditation, prayer, visualization and visiting powerful sites that anchor higher energies from the rays, are open to being affected by the energies impacting their chakras through the inner planes and in relation to their natal chart. Those who are working on their chakras are freeing themselves from the influences of astrology.

For example, the planet Mars, who represents masculine energy, can express through the root chakra as either enthusiasm, energy, motivation, action, effort and leadership or, conversely, as aggression, rage, hostility, the tendency to bully and start fights. If it is badly aspected in the natal horoscope, the individuals will be born with aggressive tendencies that they may need to work on.

As the planets move in relationship to the Houses, signs and one another, the root chakras of certain people may become flooded with either enthusiastic or aggressive energy that floods their auric field. They may experience particular antagonism to the auras of certain other people whose auric fields are being flooded with energies through other chakras.

My last thought on the matter of astrology is to mention that the astral plane is causal in relationship to the physical plane, and that events that happen in the physical world begin as events in the astral plane. That means that events can be prevented from happening. It also means that success or failure in the material world is determined by events in the astral world. This is how karma is played out.

10
Reflections on the Immediate Future

As I have stated, the astral plane, or fourth dimension, is causal to your world, and so the near future may be found unfolding on the astral plane. There are many probable futures within the fourth dimension, or astral plane; there are personal futures and group futures. The astral plane, besides being causal to your reality, is also the collective unconscious, and all the plans and aspirations of humanity take shape here.

If I wanted to predict events on the world stage in the next five years, I could study the astrological aspects and make comparison charts for the major countries and charts for the leaders of those countries. It would be a lot of work, even within this dimension. I could travel down a 90-percent probable timeline and see what unfolds within that timeline. Some psychics, when giving indi-

vidual readings, can see a little way into the most probable timelines; they are the most probable, because they
are related to what the subject dwells on most often.

However, there are all these interactive variables
affecting one another simultaneously, and the best pre-
dictor for the best outcome is the greatest number of
people attaining a higher level of consciousness. The
best means to do this is to daily meditate briefly to
anchor light on the planet and to mentally link up to
others doing this work. It would also be helpful if the
greater number of people focused their imagination on
a better future for all, with peaceful coexistence, an end
to world hunger and poverty and all the peoples of the
Earth having the opportunities to earn their livelihood
in a pleasant and productive fashion.

It is much easier to look at the problems of humanity that need to be solved than to look at the possible
events within the next five years. I find it interesting to
make predictions about the future, because reality is
always much stranger than fiction or the strangest predictions. However, so much is happening simultaneously that it is very difficult to predict.

My major prediction is that there will be several
events within world politics that will be so startling that
no one could have predicted them. The next thirty
years are going to be driven by the baby boomers entering their declining years or late adulthood. Those who
have been working under the direction of a master in a
field that the master teaches will now have more time
and money available than ever before to engage in projects for the benefit of humanity as a whole.

Working On Goals in Several Areas

The ashrams will be working on goals in several areas:
They will be working on the project of a world gov-

ernment where each sovereign nation has a voice within a forum, and on efforts to make Third-World nations more equal with First-World nations. They will come up with a definition of the role of government on a national level and on an international level. The progress of this work may be either enhanced or impeded.

The second area will be a focus on bridging the gaps between religions and on emphasizing what they have in common. Much of the work in this field will be to bring groups of differing religions together to work on some project that will break down the barriers of the prejudices that maintain hate.

A third area of focus in the future will be all green and activist groups who campaign for the environment. Only greed, stupidity and selfishness would would cause any group of humans not to be concerned for the environment. There will be more work with international codes and agreements restricting the use of environmentally unfriendly and hazardous chemicals.

A fourth area will be within the arts and entertainment and using the medium of the movie to portray embedded truths about the nature of reality and esoteric teachings. There may be only a few movies produced in any given decade that teach spiritual truth to the masses, but there will be some. When those movies are successful, it will create a demand for more. Within the field of music and entertainment, there will be songs that teach the young people values. Of course, there will still be a lot of corrupt music, encouraging a violent and materialistic lifestyle that disrespects women and children.

There will be advances in science, medicine and technology, especially in regards to forms of energy and communication. The process of breaking down the barriers between people will continue.

It Is Possible to Gain Sweeping
Psychic Visions of the Future

It is possible to gain sweeping psychic visions of the future. One might see vistas of wars played out, followed by an era of peace, and technological breakthroughs. However, what might be a compelling psychic vision might not ever actually come to pass. There are higher and lower visions of probable futures, and as humans raise their consciousness, so do the levels of the psychic visions shift and better futures come to pass.

All of the forces at work — the lightbeings converging in the fifth dimension, the birth of the group of lightworkers after World War II, the etheric web raising the frequency of the planet — are likely to succeed. The Earth will be birthed into a new age and a positive future. The work undertaken in the early years of the twenty-first century to eliminate terrorist groups and training camps is very important to the future of the planet.

Then there are the young people who are in their twenties who were the Indigo children. These are the individuals who have the color indigo strongly in their auras and who often suffered from attention deficit disorders and were put on medication. These individuals have the capacity to see with the opened third eye. They will get inspiration from the angelic kingdoms in whatever occupations they follow.

What I find most interesting is that following the amount of research on the paranormal performed in the former Soviet Union and the corresponding research performed within the American military, much of what was learned will become mainstreamed in the future, and the spiritually most resistant people will become exposed to concepts such as the chakras and energy centers of the planet.

Many young people will be fluent in the concepts of astrology, which are fairly complex. They will be familiar with the functions of the Houses, the roles of the planets and the meanings of the signs of the zodiac. The aura will be viewed through the use of Kirlian photography and so there will be no doubt that it exists. Most importantly, as the frequency of the planet rises and the density lessens, the barrier to the astral plane will be weakened and more serious and useful information from the ashrams and the angelic kingdom will be transmitted directly to individuals. (If you have problems channeling information or getting psychic visions, you can request that information be given to you in the sleep state, just before you wake up. You can choose a master, ask him or her a question and see what thought pops into your head first thing on waking in the morning.)

Feng shui will be more commonly accepted as a means of organizing the environment. It works on the basis of programming the collective unconscious mind by placing symbolic objects that carry a specific meaning at specific sites, which speaks to the symbolic language of the unconscious mind.

There will be a greater mainstreaming of these more esoteric, New Age and unconventional modes and thinking and being, because as the manufacturing base of America shifts — or has shifted — to the Far East, there will be a need for new industries to employ Americans, and the focus will be services that emphasize leisure, entertainment, relaxation, healing and rejuvenation. In other words, people will need to invent entire new industries to generate wealth. This fortunately coincides with the largest number of consumers requiring healing and rejuvenation. There will be a rise in the use of vitamins, skin creams, plastic surgery, health drinks, spas and cruise trips. In particular, cruise trips that feature self-improvement workshops will be on the increase.

We might see increases in the formation of small colleges that teach New Age skills such as psychic development, healing through the laying on of hands, giving readings, feng shui, yoga, Reiki, Qui Gong and massage therapy. Graduates from these institutions will go into private practice. There will be a revitalization of spiritualism in the coming decades as more people experience having loved ones who have passed over and as more people need spirit healing.

I have to say that I expect a resistance movement to the progress of the forces of light, as well as events that impede the progress of the work of the lightworkers. The hallmarks of those who work for the forces of darkness and ignorance will be their elitism and their contempt for the poor, ignorant and underdeveloped masses. They will work to serve their elite group at the expense of the greatest numbers of humanity. At their very worst expression, they seek to eliminate those whom they consider defective. They seek to remove the safety nets that prevent unfortunate souls from falling into destitution, and they seek to create destitution. Driven by greed and self-interest, they seek election by bribing the electorate with promises of tax cuts and the elimination of programs that serve the needy. This is quite obviously wrong.

The Concept of Karma Is Often Misunderstood

Having established that the Christian concept of hell is not totally accurate, what retribution is there for souls who are evil? Well, the lower astral hells are temporary states created by the imaginings of those who have recently passed over to the astral plane. However, those who have lived lives of great evil are confined in them according to the vibratory rates of their auras. The slow, dense, dark vibrations of resentment, envy, prejudice, suspicion, unforgiveness, cruelty, jealousy, vindictiveness correspond to low and dense astral frequencies.

If individuals have lived a life filled with behavior that is vindictive and low, they will have to purify themselves by spending a term of time on the level that corresponds to their frequency. This may be a long or a short term, depending on their ability to be capable of feelings of remorse or sorrow. When they have cleared through these dense and dark feelings, they might come to the next astral level. They might clear through by passing a test on the astral plane where they do not respond to a situation in a vindictive fashion. These low levels of the astral plane are in some cases bleak, cold and wintry, or in other cases hot hells.

There is some confusion with the popularity of the Eastern concept of karma, which has been introduced to the West through many means, that there are no hells and that punishment must be worked through within the lifetime. Generally, the doctrine of karma has had some unfortunate results, in that one of the greatest faults within the mentality of those on the Indian subcontinent is an attitude of apathy and an unwillingness to change the conditions of those who suffer at the lowest levels of society. The philosophy that those who are poor, uneducated and jobless, who are suffering in terrible conditions with terrible ill health somehow deserve to be suffering is a similar Western development of apathy and lack of compassion. There is no progress on the spiritual path without love of humanity.

There has even developed within some levels of society a love of the planet and the animals and the endangered species, which has produced a negative attitude in people who view them as infesting the planet instead of inhabiting it and as having a desire to see a massive reduction of population in humans. This will come naturally as a planet that is out of balance comes into balance.

So the doctrine of karma is often much misunderstood, and when people complain of their experiences, those who think they believe in karma lack compassion and sympathy, since they view such experiences as receiving some punishment from God. This is not something that we wish to see. There are small enclaves of New Age devotees who espouse doctrines that lack compassion, kindness and warmth, which gives the New Age teachings and the ancient wisdom a bad reputation. Not only do they lend a bad reputation, but they create apathetic and smug individuals who are held back in their spiritual progress.

It is my intention with this book that just a few people may read it and become inspired to do something specific through their own meditations, guidance and understanding that will further the progress of the planet. I hope that some people will grasp a vision of the future and see something akin to Abraham Maslow's hierarchy of needs in relation to planetary industry; that they will see that the countries at the very bottom of the economic totem pole, such as China, can produce basic items for sale in America that meet the basic needs for clothing, decoration of the home and simple requirements, while in America industries develop that serve the spiritual, health and rejuvenation needs of the populace. There will be major growth in taking care of the elderly in their own homes, but this should not be abused into keeping people whose time has come alive by extraordinary measures. At this point in time, there is a discrepancy between longevity and maintaining youthfulness, and in the future the elderly will be very youthful and healthy.

11

A Word on the Great Invocation

During the past seventy years or so, many thousands of people have used the great invocation as a means to send out thoughts of love, light and healing all around the planet. There have been groups like the Lucis Trust Triangles groups that have used it, and large groups have used it at full-moon meditations. However, as we move away from Piscean attitudes and into an Aquarian era, there are many people who experience problems with the wording of the great invocation.

Some of you reading this might have no idea what the great invocation is, so I will remind you:

From the point of light within the mind of God
Let light stream forth into the minds of men.
Let light return on Earth.

From the point of love within the heart of God
Let love stream forth into the hearts of men.
May Christ return to Earth.

From the center where the will of God is known
Let purpose guide the little wills of men,
The purpose which the masters know and serve.

From the center that we call the race of men
Let the plan of love and light work out.
May it seal the door where evil dwells.
Let love and light and power restore the plan on Earth.

There are instructions within Mrs. Bailey's books that the wording must not be changed, because it is very important to the integrity of the invocation that the ancient phrases be spoken as they are written. (The Lucis Trust has come to reconsider that position.) This contention that the words should not be changed cannot be true, of course, because the invocation originally was not o written in English but in an ancient tongue that is older than Sanskrit. However, the fact that it has been used by thousands of people daily for many years in the form that it is in has given that form tremendous power.

Various individuals have come up with corrected versions of the great invocation, and I would say that what is truly important are the intention and thought behind the invocation. However, what does it actually mean?

After having collaborated on dozens of tomes that never once refer to a being called "God" but rather discuss the nature of the Planetary Logos in the form of Sanat Kumara or the Solar Logos and the stellar logoi, suddenly there is reference to "God." Surely, this would strike a somewhat jarring note in all of those students who had become familiar with the concept of planetary and stellar consciousnesses. Can "God" be anthropomorphized into having a mind and a heart?

Well, of course, the idea was that the great invocation would not alienate those who were not arcane students. If the first line had been, "From the point of light within the mind of the Solar Logos," people would probably have been repulsed by it.

But there are many in this age who find the idea of "God" too sexist and would prefer a reference to a Father/Mother God or an Infinite Spirit. While it is debatable whether the term "God" is too sexist, there is no doubt that the references to "men" in each stanza certainly are. Clearly, what is meant is "humanity," but when this was written, "men" popularly meant "mankind."

So a concept that I would like you to attempt to imagine is a three-star One who is the Sun existing on three levels — physical, emotional and mental — as does each of you. The point of love, light and power is the physical Sun, the Solar Logos, the star of your solar system. You are invoking a desire that humanity should become aligned with the Solar Logos and the divine plan.

There is also controversy about the name "Christ," since many religions do not acknowledge Christ, who is thought to be Jesus Christ of the Christians. The Christ referred to is a being who holds the office of Christ and who over-lights the personality of the Master Jesus. We are looking to the eventual return of the Planetary Christ and have taught through Mrs. Bailey that the return would be threefold in that it would involve the over-lighting of many advanced souls, the anchoring of Christ energy on the planet and the physical appearance of the man.

The point of the reappearance of the man is that all people will know him and recognize him as the head of their religion; those thoughts that he will teach will make sense to everyone. When all religions become unified, there will be an end to most of the wars. You are all quite aware that the wars are caused by economic issues and the control of raw materials in the ground such as oil, gold, diamonds and various metals and minerals, or by issues over self-government. However, ordinary people are motivated to fight fanatically on behalf of some group on the basis of religious conditioning. When the religions are unified, the masses will not be mobilized against one another. The reappearance of the Christ will unite humanity.

Now, there is going to be some speculation and doubt about "sealing the door where evil dwells" and this, of course, is within the hearts of humanity. This is a reference to the endeavor of each person using the invocation to seal his or her own door to evil, which is the door in the heart that allows the self to brood on hateful and selfish themes, and to seal the collective human door.

From my point of view, I feel that it is more important that the great invocation is understood than that the words should be preserved in a certain format. If the current version is highly offensive to certain people, then it should be reworked into an inoffensive form. I would suggest that there might be several reworked versions that are all acceptable. I find that the briefest version is more powerful than four stanzas of verse. It is adequate to state:

From the point of light within the mind of infinite intelligence,

From the point of love within the heart of infinite love,

From the point of power within the will of infinite wisdom,
May love and light and power restore the plan within humanity on Earth.

If you wish to keep the stanzas but change some of the words, that will work also. (I understand that there already is a revised version in circulation.) Notice that there is no reference to a coming One, and it is not the purpose of the great invocation to make the Christ return to Earth. He has never left it; he is here, in a different dimension; he is a powerful presence; he is an eternal spirit; he is part of the planetary council on the fifth dimension. It is probably more important that the mass majority of humans exercise their conscious free-will choice to align themselves to the light, love and power of the divine will, wisdom and love.

But, as I have remarked before, the purpose of the Earth experiment is to see what the kingdom of human souls would do with free will. Fortunately, the third-dimensional experience is not really real and no real harm has been done. More lightworkers are teaching and working to reveal the ancient truths, and many souls caught in the lies of existing religion will come to see the truth. Those limiting thoughts about themselves that have kept them back are released, and more people work within their ray for the improvement of life in the third dimension.

12

Links to the Stars

A gain I wish to say that I offer these insights with a grain of salt, to be considered as possibilities and not as absolute truths. Up until now you have been raised and educated to consider the development of humanity as that of ignorant cave people who slowly developed greater and greater intelligence until the modern-day pinnacle of success. The development of humanity has been presented as a straight line slanting upward.

I am suggesting the alarming possibility that humanity has been recovering from a major technological disaster for about eleven thousand years, a disaster that threw people back into the Stone Age. Over time people have become so primitive that the descriptions of technological devices sound merely fanciful. That is my first suggestion for consideration.

My second proposal for your consideration is that a group of aliens called the Melchizedek Priesthood colonized the planet about fifteen thousand years ago with benevolent intentions, and that their DNA has been evenly distributed throughout the population of the planet over fifteen thousand years to even the most remote Aborigines. Although it might not be obvious, it is there.

My third proposal is that these alien colonists brought with them universal educational and spiritual systems through which they progressed millions of human souls and which continued until roughly five thousand years ago, when the density of the planet had become too low to continue.

So now the question must arise as to what happened to the souls who had attained a certain level within the Melchizedek system but were unable to complete their training. Well, of course, one answer is that there were secret organizations such as the Freemasons and Rosicrucians that arose at various points in time and were organized by the family of light. Another answer is that many of these souls incarnated into heretic groups such as the Albigenses or Cathars, or just into ordinary people, and were persecuted by the Catholic Church in Europe through witch hunts. (Many of the witches were individuals who had been born with the higher chakras activated and with psychic gifts. These individuals were strenuously hunted down and eliminated by the church groups. Their gifts were attributed to the forces of evil.) Many souls incarnating now have a personal history of many lifetimes in prehistoric Egypt or the East and of lives of persecution in the Dark Ages, where they were able to heal and prophesy and were tried and killed in the Dark Ages.

So at this time there is a group in incarnation referred to as the Starseed children. This is a group of souls who have come into incarnation to affect a change in the social structure and to transform the planet from a Piscean planet to an Aquarian planet. A typical Starseed might be that geeky guy who develops personal computers and becomes a millionaire, thus bringing the planet into the twenty-first century and changing the way everything is performed.

The Starseeds are a group of human souls who assist in planetary transitions. They are a group of human souls within the Melchizedek Order who have not completed their seven initiations but are close to completion. This group includes the much talked about Indigo children. These are children who often suffer from attention deficits and hyperactivity but who are also very creative. Psychics have noted that they see the color indigo in these children's auras, which is a rather unusual color.

Well, these are souls who suffered the fate of having been drowned or burned as witches in past lives and who had attained the level of having an activated third-eye chakra, which gave them psychic awareness. They are coming back as a large soul group, to complete their process and open the crown chakra. The average age of the Indigo is roughly twenty-six, with a ten-year span of thirty-six to sixteen.

There are also Blue children and Green children, who are a little unusual in that they have evolved beyond a high intellect, toward altruistic occupations and healing techniques and channeling the ancient wisdom teachings. As children they are somewhat precocious.

What we are also moving toward is that the souls who left the planet and went to the next level of the Melchizedek Order are coming back. They have attained all the levels and are masters. They will definitely transform the planet and bring about a new age or era.

However, as I have mentioned before, the real work of transforming the planet is occurring with an energy grid established all around the planet, with groups meditating at the vortexes of light. On the inner planes in the fifth and sixth dimensions there has been a massive influx of Pleiadian and Sirian beings to assist in this acceleration. They are here because they have a karmic connection to the planet. This cannot be done without lightworkers in the field anchoring the energy in the third dimension.

Now, there is some other conclusion that might be formed from this entire line of thought, which is that there is a Pleiadian home world from which the ancient aliens came from. If one were to journey to this world, one could see familiar elements in the civilizations established there. For a start, the Pleiadians physically appear the same as humans. They had advanced technology already fifteen thousand years ago, so their technology is even more advanced now. While Earth regressed into the Stone Age, their civilization has continued to advance. However, they have learned a great deal from the people of Earth, and they are interested to see if we can ever establish a planet of peace, prosperity and equality with a powerful push from the spirit worlds and the acceleration of the planetary frequencies.

Many spiritually inclined people today are interested in the humanistic traditions of the Native American people. The ancient teachings of the Atlanteans are also within the Native traditions of spirituality. The Native Americans place a great deal of emphasis on the four directions, which are also emphasized within European magical traditions such as the Golden Dawn. There are rituals and concepts around the four directions within the Atlantean teachings, and they even emerge in Christianity as the cross of matter upon which we are all crucified. The four directions represent four of the seven rays, which become complete with center, up and down to make seven directions — and seven rays.

So in conclusion, there is much wisdom embedded within the diversity of teachings around the world. There is wisdom to be garnered from the Native Americans, the Australian Aborigines, the Tibetan teachings, the ancient Egyptians, mystical Judaism, the Spiritualists, Celtic Wicca, Scandinavian runes, Hinduism, the New Age books, the Golden Dawn and many diverse sources. The archangels draw in closer, and so there is much available describing them. The totem animals also draw closer as the frequencies of the planet accelerate.

So as you meditate and hold your focus on love and see love as a beautiful, clear pink energy like rose quartz, hold your focus on kindness and charitable thoughts. Picture the future. Hold the image of the planet in the future, surrounded in the Christ white light and the pink light of love. You never know who is being influenced by ascended masters and the guardians of the rays to do group healing work for the planet. You may find the signature keynote in the strangest places.

I end with blessings to you all. Namasté, Djwhal Khul.

THE DIAMOND LIGHT

The purpose of this book is to present esoteric teachings similar to those given to Alice A. Bailey during the period between the two great world wars and offer them to the public in an updated form that is short, concise and simple. The original teachings from the Master Djwhal Khul were presented in lengthy volumes that were somewhat difficult to understand without a thorough background in the religion known as Theosophy, founded by Madame Blavatsky in the late 19th century. It is the Master's current wish that he contribute a short book to the world that is simple and clear to the general New Age reader.

The Master is one member of a planetary council of spiritual beings who exist within another dimension and who guide the spiritual destiny of this planet and the life forms on it. Although a spiritual government exists, it does not interfere with the free will of humanity but occasionally sends teachers to guide us.

The Master would like to convey the concept that he is accessible to average mortals and does not reserve his communication only for the most well-read and well-known advanced souls. Rather, he is available for those who most desperately need him, who feel as if they are struggling to survive in the modern world without a message of hope.

ISBN 1-891824-25-2 $14.95

TOPICS INCLUDE -
- TOWARD A COSMIC PSYCHOLOGY OF BEING
- THE SEVEN RAYS
- TIME AND PROBABILITY
- ATLANTIS
- DEALING WITH DAILY LIFE

- THOUGHTS ON LOVE, SEX AND RELATIONSHIPS
- SHAPING YOUR FUTURE
- THE LANGUAGE OF MYTHOLOGY
- THE ASCENSION PROCESS
- INTO THE MILLENNIUM AND BEYOND
- INHABITANTS OF THE FOURTH DIMENSION
- THE ETHERIC LEVELS
- CREATING PROSPERITY
- THE ARTHURIAN LEGEND
- KARMA, REINCARNATION AND MORALITY
- THE CHRIST

LIGHT
TECHNOLOGY
PUBLISHING

Call us at
1-800-450-0985
or log on
www.lighttechnology.com

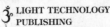

SHAMANIC SECRETS for PHYSICAL MASTERY

The purpose of this book is to allow you to understand the sacred nature of your own physical body and some of the magnificent gifts it offers you. When you work with your physical body in these new ways, you will discover not only its sacredness, but how it is compatible with Mother Earth, the animals, the plants, even the nearby planets, all of which you now recognize as being sacred in nature. It is important to feel the value of oneself physically before one can have any lasting physical impact on the world. The less you think of yourself physically, the less likely your physical impact on the world will be sustained by Mother Earth. If a physical energy does not feel good about itself, it will usually be resolved; other physical or spiritual energies will dissolve it because it is unnatural. The better you feel about your physical self when you do the work in the previous book as well as this one and the one to follow, the greater and more lasting will be the benevolent effect on your life, on the lives of those around you and ultimately on your planet and universe. SOFTCOVER 600P.

$19⁹⁵ ISBN 1-891824-29-5

Chapter Titles:

- Cellular Clearing of Traumas, Unresolved Events
- Cellular Memory
- Identifying Your Body's Fear Message
- The Heart Heat Exercise
- Learn Hand Gestures
  —Remove Self-Doubt
  —Release Pain or Hate
  —Clear the Adrenals or Kidneys
  —Resolve Sexual Dysfunction
- Learning the Card Technique for Clarifying Body Message
- Seeing Life as a Gift
- Relationship of the Soul to Personality
- The New Generation of Children
- The Creator and Religions
- Food, Love & Addictions

- Communication of the Heart
- Dreams & Their Significance
- The Living Prayer/Good Life
- Life Force and Life Purpose
- Physical Mastery
- His Life/ Mandate for His Ancestors/ Importance of Animals/ Emissaries
- Physical Mastery
- Talking to Rain/ Bear Claw Story
- Disentanglement
- Grief Culture
- Closing Comments

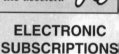

Charlie Kray was t'... Ronnie and Reggie, who ... years in 1969 for two murders. Both a... ... died from heart failure in April 2000, while serving ... ve years for drug offences.

Robin McGibbon first met Charlie Kray in 1975 when, as managing director of Everest Books, he published the first edition of this autobiography. Since then, he has worked as a sub-editor on the *Daily Express* and written and co-written ten books, including the autobiographies of Christopher Lambrianou, who got caught up in the Kray madness, Barbara Windsor and Eamonn Andrews.

McGibbon, who has also produced a Talking Book of his conversations with all three Kray brothers, lives in Kent with his second wife, Sue.

CHARLIE KRAY
with ROBIN McGIBBON

Me and My Brothers

HARPER PERENNIAL

London, New York, Toronto, Sydney and New Delhi

Charlie dedicated this book to his parents,
who were forever in his thoughts

Harper Perennial
An imprint of HarperCollins*Publishers*
77–85 Fulham Palace Road, Hammersmith, London W6 8JB

www.harperperennial.co.uk
Visit our authors' blog at www.fifthestate.co.uk

This Harper Perennial edition published 2008
1

First published in Great Britain by Grafton, an imprint of
HarperCollins*Publishers*, in 1988. Reissued by HarperCollins in 1997 and 2005.

Copyright © Charles Kray 1988, 1997
This Perennial edition © Charles Kray and Robin McGibbon 2008

Robin McGibbon asserts the moral right to be identified as the author of this work

A catalogue record for this book is available from the British Library

ISBN 978-0-00-727581-6

Typeset in Times by
Rowland Phototypesetting Ltd, Bury St Edmunds, Suffolk

Printed and bound in Great Britain by Clays Ltd, St Ives plc

Mixed Sources
Product group from well-managed
forests and other controlled sources
www.fsc.org Cert no. SW-COC-1806
© 1996 Forest Stewardship Council

FSC is a non-profit international organisation established to promote the
responsible management of the world's forests. Products carrying the FSC
label are independently certified to assure consumers that they come
from forests that are managed to meet the social, economic and
ecological needs of present and future generations.

Find out more about HarperCollins and the environment at
www.harpercollins.co.uk/green

Author's Note

The first edition of *Me and My Brothers*, which my company Everest Books published in 1975, made little impact. Charlie knew he had an interesting story to tell but was broke, and more eager to cash in on the notoriety of the Kray name than to write a no-holds-barred blockbuster.

Ronnie and Reggie hated the book. So did Charlie. Like many things done for the wrong reasons, it lacked emotion, conviction – and honesty. The murder of Jack 'The Hat' McVitie had destroyed Charlie's life, but, in 1975, neither twin had admitted their roles in the killing, so family loyalty prevented him disclosing how or why.

In 1988, HarperCollins gave Charlie a second bite at the cherry – a chance to reveal what he didn't, or couldn't, say before. Then, when he was convicted on a drugs charge nine years later, Charlie was given an opportunity to further update his story.

For the 1997 edition, I would like to thank Melvyn Howe, courts' correspondent of The Press Association, for offering help with the trial copy, and his then boss, Mike Parry, for supplying it.

For their help in ensuring that this final edition of Charlie's life story is accurate, I must thank Charlie's best friend Wilf Pine and his wife, Ros, Maureen Flanagan, Les Martin, Steve Wraith, Albert Chapman, Trish Ellis, of the *Sunday Telegraph*, Jonathan Goldberg QC, David Martin-Sperry and Ronnie Field.

I would also like to thank my dear friend Mike Harris for all the fact-checking research at the British Library –

and, of course, my wife, Sue, for all the donkey work that goes into writing a book.

But special thanks must go to Dave Courtney, who was always there when I needed him. Thanks, Poppet.

Robin McGibbon
Bickley, Kent
March 2008

Prologue

My name is Kray. But I'm not a gangster; never was, never wanted to be.

And I don't want a gangster's funeral.

I don't want to be remembered as a gangster, just because I had twin brothers, Ronnie and Reggie, who got a kick out of violence and a thrill out of murder.

I was never like the twins. And I don't want people thinking I was. Even when I'm dead.

I could throw a punch, too, and have boxing trophies to prove it.

But I'd rather throw a party. That's why people called me Champagne Charlie. And that's how I'd like to be remembered.

I spent my life trying to distance myself from the twins' way of life, and a gangster's funeral would associate me with all they stood for. And that wouldn't be right.

When my time comes, I want to be carried to the flat I shared with the woman I adored, then be buried the next day, with the minimum of fuss – and certainly no TV cameras – next to my lovely son who died tragically young.

Reggie will want to stage a showy spectacular, like the one he laid on for Ronnie that brought the East End to a standstill.

But I don't want that and I'm sure that, despite the differences we've had all our lives, Reggie will respect my wishes.

Chapter One

The ringing of the phone brought me out of a deep sleep. Through half-closed eyes I squinted at my watch on the bedside table: 5.15 A.M. I took the phone from its cradle. 'Hello,' I muttered, husky from tiredness. An unfamiliar woman's voice apologized for waking me, then spoke quietly in an abrupt, businesslike manner. I heard what she said, but I couldn't take it in. Didn't want to. I thought I must be still asleep. Numb with shock, I passed the phone to Diana, lying next to me. She listened for a few moments, thanked the caller, then stretched past me to put the phone down. She looked at me and shook her head, sadly. 'I'm afraid it's true, Charlie.'

In a daze, I got out of bed and shuffled, zombie-like, downstairs into the lounge. I took a bottle of Remy Martin from the cocktail cabinet and filled a long tumbler, then I gulped the brandy fast, again and again, until it was gone. Diana came into the room in her dressing gown. We stared at each other in shock. I went to say something but no words came out. And then she moved towards me and put her arms round me and I started to sob.

That morning at my home in South-East London was the worst moment of my life. Worse than the day I was jailed for ten years for a crime I didn't commit. Worse than being charged with a murder I knew nothing about. But my tears that morning of 5 August 1982 were not only for myself; they were for my twin brothers, Ronnie and Reggie, too. And for our old man.

How on earth were they going to take it when I told

1

them that the woman we all worshipped, the lovely lady we thought would live for ever, was dead?

She had gone into hospital just three days earlier. We all thought it was just a check-up for pneumonia: a week or two and she'd be out as fit as ever. I'd gone in to see her that day. She was the same old Mum, bright and cheerful, full of life. She wasn't in two minutes and the nurses loved her. It was coming up to her birthday and she had all her cards by her bedside. She looked as good as gold.

Then she had the test she had gone in for and when I went in the next day she was hot and flustered. I'd never seen her like that before. She said she could never have anything like that again. I think the test embarrassed her, apart from the pain.

The next day she was lying there, her eyes closed. She wouldn't open them; perhaps she couldn't. Softly, I told her I was there. She didn't answer. One of the old ladies in another bed, who had made friends with Mum, called me over and said there was something wrong: Mum hadn't been at all well. I went back to Mum and spoke to her again and she answered me. She was hot. I put a damp cloth on her forehead. But she began to get delirious. I called a nurse who said Mum had pneumonia. I didn't believe her; she had been all right the day before. But the nurse shook her head. Then she said the doctor wanted to see me.

He broke the news as gently as he could. Mum *did* have pneumonia. But she had cancer, too. Bad. He wanted to operate, but he needed to clear the pneumonia first.

Hearing the dreaded word 'cancer' knocked me bandy. I'd thought we'd get over the pneumonia, then take her away somewhere nice to get well again. She had many years to live yet. All her family lived on: she had a brother

2

of 88, an aunt of 102. My mum was one of the fittest. She was going to live for ever.

I gave the doctor my phone number 'in case of an emergency'. I didn't expect it to come to anything. Then Diana and I left the hospital. I was in a daze.

Early the next morning, that phone call came. The cancer had taken my mum on her seventy-third birthday.

The brandy must have done me good. I didn't feel it at the time, but it must have helped me pull myself together, helped me to be strong. I had no choice. There would be a lot to do, and with my brothers in prison and our father ill I was the only one to do it. To begin with, they each had to be told. But who first? As usual, I found myself in the middle. From the moment the twins were born, they had dominated the household and, eventually, my whole life. But on that August morning they came second. It would break him, I knew, but my old man had to be the first to know.

An hour or so later, at about seven o'clock, Diana and I arrived at Braithwaite House, my parents' council flat in Bunhill Row, in the City of London.

'What's going on at this time in the morning?' the old man wanted to know.

I'd decided there was no point in mucking about. I told him to sit down, then I took a deep breath and said, 'Unfortunately, she's just died.'

Almost before I'd got the words out he began to scream. I'd never seen him show so much emotion. It just knocked him over. He was very ill and after those first shock waves, he found it difficult to breathe. He kept panting, saying, 'I can't believe it. How can she die before me? I won't be long. It's just a matter of time. I'm waiting for it now.'

My old man, bless him, didn't have to wait long to join

3

his beloved Violet. That morning he lost the will to live and was dead eight months later.

I decided to tell Ronnie next. Wednesday was not a normal visiting day at Broadmoor, but I could be there in little over an hour if I was allowed to see him; the train – boat – taxi journey to Reggie on the Isle of Wight would take about five. Broadmoor's director told me to come immediately and agreed to say nothing to Ron. But I wasn't thinking straight when I asked Parkhurst to keep the news from Reggie until I got there the next day.

'That's not going to be easy, Charlie,' said a prison officer I knew from previous visits. 'He's got his radio in his cell. We can't take that away. Anyway, someone else will hear.'

I didn't say anything. The thought hadn't occurred to me.

'Charlie,' the welfare officer said, 'if you can trust me . . . I've been with Reggie for years. I'll take him somewhere quietly and tell him myself.'

I thought hard. I knew the officer quite well; I felt I *could* trust him. He was right. If Reggie heard on the radio . . .

'Would you do that for me, please?' I said.

Diana and I got to Broadmoor at about eleven o'clock. The authorities were very kind: they took us into the hospital wing, where visitors aren't usually allowed. They had got a little room for us. A few moments later Ronnie came in, looking concerned. He said later he thought it was odd, us being in that room. When he sat down I looked at him and said gently, 'Ron, our mother's passed away.'

He just broke down, as I knew he would. He leaned forward, put his head in his hands and burst out crying.

4

I'd had a bit of time to get over the shock, but Ronnie started me off again.

Finally he said in his quiet voice, 'I thought you were going to say our father had died.' Then a few moments later: 'We expected that. But never in a million years, Mum. Why did it happen to her?'

The three of us sat there for about an hour, remembering how lovely she had been, and then I said I had to go; I had a lot to do. As we got up Ronnie said, 'Could you ask them if I can stay here a bit? I want to be on my own.'

The nurses were very kind. 'Don't worry, Charlie,' they said. 'He won't be disturbed. We'll leave him.'

Ronnie stayed in that little room for four hours.

That afternoon the welfare officer at Parkhurst rang me to say he'd broken the news to Reggie.

'How is he?' I asked.

'Better now,' the officer said. 'He broke down. But I told him you'll be here tomorrow and he's waiting to see you. He'll feel better when you're here.'

Someone else telling him was not the same as me, though. When Diana and I met him in a private room at the prison, Reggie broke his heart. And, of course, it started Di and me off again.

Tragedy always brings people closer together and I don't think I've ever been closer to my brothers than those two days when we shared the same grief.

We didn't want a circus. We wanted a funeral our Mum would have been proud of, a funeral people would remember. George English, an undertaker from Hoxton, had buried my grandparents and I knew he would do things the way we wanted. Ronnie and Reggie were given permission to attend the funeral at Chingford Mount in

Essex. It would be the first time they had seen the outside world in fourteen years.

Crowds packed the streets from my mother's flat through the East End. The media brought out many out of curiosity, I suppose, but hundreds came out of respect; not only for my mother, but for the family as a whole. The number of wreaths amazed us: they filled eight cars. So many friends were there: from people my mum had known all her life, to some she had met through her sons in recent years. Diana Dors was there with her husband, dear Alan Lake, and Andrew Ray, the actor.

And so, of course, were the police. I don't know what they thought was going to happen, but for a couple of hours that afternoon of 24 August the village of Chingford looked like a setting for a war movie. Police on foot and on motorbikes lined the main street. A helicopter circled noisily overhead. There were even two officers in trees with walkie-talkies.

When we were all assembled in the tiny church of St John's, Ronnie was brought in, then Reggie, each handcuffed to a giant policeman. The one escorting Reggie was no less than six feet seven! I had reserved the front row to the right of the nave for the twins, just in front of my old man, Diana, myself and Gary. But Ronnie was led to the front row on the left. He listened to the service for his dead mother out of sight and touch of his family. Reggie sat in front of us.

After the service, the twins were led out swiftly and taken to Chingford Mount police station. While their mother was being lowered into her grave, the twins sat in a room, surrounded by fifty coppers.

The old man was marvellous that day. He was desperately ill, but he managed to stand up in the church and at the graveside. He was very proud; if anyone tried to help him, he'd pull his arm away. He wanted to do things by

6

himself, even though he wasn't strong enough. How he managed to get through it all, I don't know.

He was terribly upset by all the police fuss; he knew it was all unnecessary. I tried to convince him everything had gone well, that Mum would have been pleased, but he felt it was too much like a circus. As we left the graveside he said firmly, 'If anything happens to me, I don't want all this.'

The twins made sure that request was granted. When the old man went the following April each one decided independently not to go to the funeral. They wanted to, of course, but they didn't want a repeat performance. At the time, officials at Broadmoor and Parkhurst rang me to say that permission would be given. I told them the twins wouldn't be going and it threw them back a bit. They didn't expect that.

But then they didn't understand the twins. They still don't. If anyone in authority had the slightest clue what my brothers are about, our mother's funeral would have been handled differently and given the dignity and respect that she deserved and we all wanted.

How daft and unnecessary to separate the twins from each other and their family, and to handcuff them to strangers throughout the most harrowing ordeal of their lives. How irresponsible and wasteful to employ enough men to control a football match. And how crazy and insensitive to banish the twins from the graveside and guard them with *fifty* men in a police station while their mother was being buried.

The government and its servants were more concerned that August day with a massive, well-orchestrated propaganda exercise; a show of strength to the nation for reasons known only to themselves. I don't know how much the whole business cost the taxpayer: £30,000 has been mentioned. But what I do know – and what the

7

authorities themselves should have known if they truly believe in penal reform – is that Messrs Ronald and Reginald Kray could have been trusted to go to that funeral on their own. And to return afterwards.

They respected and adored their mother too much even to consider doing anything else.

Chapter Two

Respect was something Mum had always commanded. She had a wonderfully sunny attitude to life, always laughing, always happy. I never once heard her criticize anybody or complain. As a woman she was immensely popular: always upbeat and chatty, but never gossipy. As a mother she was unbeatable, simply the tops. And I have her to thank for giving me a wonderful, happy and secure childhood in an East End that suffered as much as anywhere from the Depression that bit in to Britain in the late twenties and thirties. Hungry children roamed around Hackney in rags, stealing food from barrows and shops. But I was always well fed and dressed in smart, clean clothes; one vivid memory is of being taken for a walk in a strikingly fashionable sailor suit and noticing other children with holes in their trousers.

Millions throughout the country were penniless, but my old man made sure there was always money in our home in Gorsuch Street, off Hackney Road. He was a dealer who called on houses buying up gold and silver – anything of value, in fact. 'On the knocker' it was called. And he was good at it. The job meant he was away from home a lot; when he wasn't 'on the knocker' he was selling the goods on the street stalls that had been in his family for fifty years. And even when he was at home he went down the pub nearly every night, like most men at that time. It didn't bother Mum; she seemed happy to stay at home looking after me and go out with him just once or twice a month.

The old man was sport-mad and was chuffed when I

was picked to play football for Laburnum Street School. He always made sure I had the right gear, and when he came to watch I'm sure he took an extra pride in seeing that his kid was one of the best-dressed players on the pitch. Boxing was his passion, though, and when he wasn't in the pub he would go to professional contests at nearby Hoxton Baths, or other venues. Sometimes, he would take me. I can remember sitting in the crowd in my sailor suit, entranced by the sight of giants thumping hell out of each other.

The old man's father, who ran a stall in Hoxton, could handle himself. He was known as 'Big' Jimmy Kray and was afraid of nobody. I used to sit on his knee at home as he told me thrilling stories of famous boxers he had known, including Hoxton's own hero, Ted 'Kid' Lewis, who became world lightweight champion. Often I'd go to bed, my six-year-old head filled both with these stories and with the real thing I'd seen with Dad, and I would dream of standing in a ring, the treasured Lonsdale belt round my middle, as the cheering crowd hailed me Champion of the World.

The brutality of East End life, where most disputes were settled with fists, rubbed off on the children: it was not uncommon for two tiny tearaways to slug it out with the venom of the fighters I'd seen in the ring. I was one of them. I didn't get involved too often but I quickly learned how to handle myself. Mum didn't approve of fighting, however, and wasn't too impressed that I'd inherited Grandad's natural boxing ability. Whenever I had a scrap at school I made sure I tidied myself up before going home.

In 1932, we moved to Stean Street, the other side of Kingsland Street. Just along from our new home was a stable yard, and the old man who looked after it let us kids play there. It was an exciting place and I spent a lot

10

of time sitting on a wall, watching the man mucking out and grooming the horses when they came in after hauling the delivery carts. I would go home smelling of manure and with muddy shoes. Mum would tell me off, but in a nice way. She never screamed and yelled like other women in that street . . .

One day a year later, when I was seven, I was encouraged to go out and play and not come back until called. Curious, and not a little put out, I watched the house from my wall for most of the day. There was a lot of coming and going and then, in the early evening, I was told I could go in. I went up to my mum's bedroom and there they were.

'Where did they come from?' I asked.

'I bought them,' my mum replied.

'But, Mum,' I said. 'Why did you buy two?'

She laughed.

It was a little after eight o'clock on 24 October 1933. My twin brothers had arrived.

Suddenly my aunts May and Rose started coming round to the house more than usual. They adored the twins and begged Mum to let them take them for walks in their brand-new pram. Mum usually agreed and May and Rose would fuss over them like mother hens with their chicks. When Mum was busy I would take them out too, and, like my aunts, I would feel a surge of pride when neighbours stopped to lean over the pram, enthusing about how gorgeous they were. The twins, of course, lapped it up. It did not take long for them to expect to be the centre of attention all the time. And to show their displeasure when they weren't.

The Kray family was already well known. Big Jimmy Kray, and Mum's dad, Jimmy Lee, worked for themselves, and their independence was envied by less ambitious people who were forced to do what they were told.

Jimmy Lee was a legend in his own time. He had been a bare-knuckle fighter with the nickname 'Cannonball' and he later became a showman and entrepreneur. In an area where competition was tough he was an outstanding personality. He was teetotal, which meant he didn't hit it off with the old man, but he was very fond of me and the twins. He loved entertaining us: his favourite trick involved a white-hot poker which he would lick without burning his tongue. He gave us a scientific explanation – something about the saliva making contact with the hot metal – but it went over our heads. To us it was just pure magic.

He'd always been an amazing athlete. Once, one of his sons – my Uncle Johnnie – drove a coach party forty-two miles to Southend for the day. As he was preparing to bring them back again, Grandfather Lee turned up – on his bike. He'd cycled there just for the fun of it and was eager to do the return journey, until Uncle Johnnie insisted he took the coach. Grandfather Lee was seventy-five years young at the time.

In those early thirties, the Kray family had a sort of local fame. And in their own way the beautifully dressed, scrubbed-clean twins, sitting up in their big double pram, beaming into the faces of all their admirers, were just as famous as their grandfathers.

I was thrust into the background but I didn't resent my brothers. If anything I was pleased, because Mum was obviously overjoyed at having them. At night I shared the same upstairs room with them, because Mum's brother and his family were living downstairs. But neither twin cried much at night and they never disturbed my sleep. When they were put in their cots I would stare at them, trying in vain to tell which was which. Sometimes they

12

looked up at me in a strange, adult sort of way, and I'd have this weird feeling that they knew all about me and what was going on around them. Their dark eyes seemed to lack that childlike innocence. It was as if each boy knew more than he ought to.

The mental and physical relationship between them was intense. Nobody was more aware of it than Mum – the only person who could tell them apart – and she demonstrated this when Reggie became ill at the age of two. Whenever he got excited his face would turn blue and sometimes he would fall down, screaming in pain. The doctor diagnosed a double hernia and sent Reggie into hospital for an operation. It wasn't long before Ronnie started to get ill himself at being separated from his twin. And when Reggie failed to improve after the operation, Mum took matters into her own hands. One day she marched into the hospital and announced she was taking Reggie home. Shocked doctors and nurses told her he was not ready to be discharged and insisted he would be better off in trained care. But Mum was adamant; she said quietly but firmly that the child needed to be with his mother and twin brother and that was that. She was proved right. Within days of being reunited, both boys were back to normal.

While my brothers were toddling about that house in Stean Street I spent most of my spare time running. Like Grandfather Lee I was sport-crazy and as well as soccer I was involved in athletics then boxing. At my senior school in Scawfell Street, off Hackney Road, I was a tiddler in a big pond, but a marvellous all-rounder called Gregory helped me achieve a sporting triumph I'll never forget. He was the school goalkeeper and wicketkeeper, and it was largely due to him that I got in the school football team that won the district finals. Gregory boxed well, too, and gave me tips on how to improve my ring-craft.

13

In the East End in those days, violence was never far below the surface; settling a disagreement with fists was the accepted thing. I forget the name of the boy I swapped punches with in my first serious street fight, but I do remember a crowd of adults loved every bruising minute of it. They formed a circle and watched us slug it out for nearly an hour. Afterwards they made us shake hands, as though we'd been fighting purely for their entertainment.

There was a wood yard in Hackney Wick where local villains settled disputes between rival gangs. Sometimes the punch-ups would not take place and the gangs would drift off to a pub together. Often, though, a chance remark would upset somebody and fighting would break out. Razors and broken glasses would be used as weapons and blood would flow.

That was the way of East End life in 1938 as we began to hear stories of a little thin-faced German madman with a moustache who wanted to conquer the world.

The old man's business boomed at that time. The factories and docks took thousands off the dole queues and there was more money about. Cash registers sang in the pubs as people talked over their pints about the prospect of war. And householders eagerly chucked out their old gear to make way for the new.

Oswald Mosley's fanatical Blackshirt mob marched noisily through Mile End and Whitechapel, striking terror into the Jews. But for me football, as usual, was far more important. One day the old man came home with a new pair of football boots for me; they were the latest style and very expensive. We had a game at the local recreation ground that afternoon and I couldn't wait to try them out. I trotted off excitedly, the boots dangling by the laces over one shoulder. Suddenly, as I walked under a railway arch, three kids grabbed the boots and ran off. I sprinted after them, shouting as loudly as I could. They dodged round corners, clambered over walls, crossed roads, but I kept after them. It was worth it: first, they dropped my socks, which had been inside the boots, then the boots themselves. I picked them up then dashed back to the park, making it in time for the game.

When I got home, I told the old man what had happened. He listened intently, then patted me affectionately on the shoulder. 'You're a real trier, son,' he said. 'A real trier.' At that moment, I'd never felt closer to him.

Don't get me wrong. Although the old man was away a lot, he was a good father. He loved the booze, but he never put that before his wife and kids. Unlike many East End wives Mum never had to go out to work, which meant that the twins and I were never left to roam the streets like other children.

I can remember only one time when she had the hump with me. I came running along the courtyard where we lived and crashed through the front swing door frightening the life out of her. I was twelve at the time and thought it was a funny practical joke. But Mum was angrier than I'd ever seen her. Her blue eyes hardened and she shouted, 'I'm going to whack you for that, Charlie!'

This terrified me because Mum always spoke in a soft, calm voice. But she didn't hit me; she would not have known how to. The old man handed out a few whacks, but I was a bit of a mummy's boy and she would always step in and put it right for me.

Mum had great will-power. Once she had set her heart on getting something she would persevere until she got it. She had no ambition in life but to bring up her children as well as possible, and she placed a lot of importance on having her own house, with a back garden and a front door that wasn't shared. One day, Aunt Rose came round excitedly, saying her next-door neighbours were leaving.

Something in Mum's reaction told me we would soon be on the move ourselves – to that house. I was not mistaken.

Vallance Road runs between Whitechapel Road and Bethnal Green Road for about half a mile and is roughly parallel to Commercial Street, which lies to the west. Number 178 was a terraced house with two rooms, a kitchen and a scullery downstairs, and an outside loo. Upstairs there were three rooms and out of two of them we could see the trains thundering along a raised track between Liverpool Street and Bethnal Green stations. When we moved in late that summer of 1939 it was just a humble East End house. But it was not long before Mum made it into a warm, happy and secure home.

With the excitement of moving, the outbreak of war meant little to the twins and me. We'd been told that enemy planes would be dropping bombs on to our home, but all we could see around us were sandbags being packed around public buildings, gas masks being handed out, and men in makeshift uniforms dashing about. When I wasn't at school, I was playing football, running or boxing. The twins, coming up to their sixth birthday, spent their time either with Aunts May and Rose, Grandpa and Grandma Lee, nearby, or in Uncle Johnnie's cafe across the street. If it was time to eat, they would be at home. They loved Mum's cooking.

The twins were fascinated by Grandfather Lee's stories of when he fought bare-knuckle in Victoria Park for a few shillings on Sunday mornings and whenever I knelt down to spar with them they shaped up like miniature prize-fighters. Even at six, they were tough and incredibly fearless, and sometimes they would catch me with a punch that surprised me with its speed, accuracy and power.

When the bombs began to fall and the anti-aircraft guns opened up, the twins showed no fear. They had always been content in each other's company and in the Blitz

16

that contentment deepened into security. While other kids cried in terror as the shells dropped, the twins just clung on to each other's clothes and shut their eyes. And when Mum said she was taking us to the shelter under the railway arches they would toddle along unconcernedly, hand in hand, more excited than afraid.

But the East End in the Blitz was no place for kids, and soon someone somewhere decided women and children should go away until it was all over. Mum didn't fancy the idea much; she had only just moved into her long-sought-after house. But as usual the twins and I came first, and she prepared for our evacuation. The old man wasn't coming. His business was still booming and he needed to stay in London. He would be recruited into the Army, of course. But he had other plans for when his call-up papers arrived.

We had no idea where we were going. All we were told was that we would be living in a house in a country village, fifty miles further east of London. To many, the massive exodus from Liverpool Street Station that January in 1940, was The Evacuation. But to the twins and I, who had seldom left the narrow, crowded streets of Bethnal Green, it was An Adventure.

The village was Hadleigh, in Suffolk, and the house was a huge Victorian building belonging to a widow called Mrs Styles. After the cramped terraced house in Vallance Road it was a palace, and Mrs Styles went out of her way to help us adapt to the traumatic change in our lives.

I quickly got a job in the local fish-and-chip shop and later worked full-time as a tea boy in a factory making mattresses. The people there were friendly, but we didn't have much in common and I missed the East End, particularly my football and boxing. The twins, though, were happier than ever. In fine weather they would spend

17

hours scouring the fields and woods for miles around, revelling in the fresh air and boundless freedom of country life. When the snow came, Mrs Styles's nephew lent me his sledge and I'd take the twins to the nearest hill. I'd lay full-length on the sledge with the twins on my back and push off. We nearly always ended up in a heap of tangled arms and legs, laughing. It was great fun.

Mum, however, was not enjoying being away from her family and friends. She never complained, but I sensed her unhappiness, especially when the old man visited us. He was popular in the local pub, with his news of what was going on in London, but he was always keen to get back after a day or two.

We'd been in Hadleigh for about a year when rumours of a German invasion on the east coast started sweeping the village. Mum got more and more worried until one day she announced that she was taking us back to London.

Mrs Styles tried to dissuade her, but Mum said she had given it a lot of thought and her mind was made up. Later, it was found that the rumours were unfounded, but by then it was too late: Mum and I and the twins were back in Vallance Road. I was pleased; I couldn't wait to see my mates and take up boxing again. But the twins were not. They had fallen in love with the countryside and preferred green fields and animals to teeming streets and noisy traffic.

The old man's call-up papers finally arrived. He'd made up his mind that he wasn't going to serve, and promptly went on what was called the 'trot'. He reasoned that he didn't start the war, so why should he help finish it? The police called at the house from time to time looking for him, but the twins and I had been told to say nothing. Lying for the old man didn't bother me; he was my dad and he'd done his best for all of us all his life. Now I was

18

in a position to do my best for him, and I lied without so much as a blush.

It did affect the twins, though. Soon they started seeing the coppers' uniform as The Enemy. Aunt Rose didn't help: if she was around, she'd have a right go at the officers, four-letter words and all. If the twins were there, they would stand side by side, gravely taking it all in. Whatever they thought, they kept to themselves, but I had a feeling then, even though they were just eight, that they were beginning to distrust uniformed authority.

With so many men in the Army there were plenty of jobs, and I became a messenger boy at Lloyd's in the City, within walking distance of Vallance Road. For five and a half days a week, I was general dogsbody for eighteen bob. In the old man's absence, I wanted to do my bit as the man of the house, so every Friday night I proudly gave Mum my wages. She didn't need the money, but she took it to make me feel good. Needless to say, I got most of it back during the week, one way and another.

Boxing now dominated my spare time. I went to the local institute for training three nights a week and Grandfather Lee fixed up a punchbag in the top back room of our house. The twins would watch me hammering away, and now and then I'd stand them on a chair so they could have a go. Mum wasn't that keen on the preoccupation with boxing; she probably remembered her dad coming home from Victoria Park, looking the worse for wear after his bare-knuckle scraps. But when I told her amateur boxing was safe and the gloves were like feather pillows, she seemed satisfied. Anyway, she didn't put up much of a fight. I suppose she thought boxing was the lesser of two evils: if I wasn't down the institute, I'd more than likely get into bad company – or worse, start showing an interest in girls. Both had their dangers: if boys of my age weren't breaking into shops or factories, they were going too far with girls and walking down the aisle almost before they'd drawn their first pay packet. I think Mum was secretly pleased that my only passion at that time was not for kissing the opposite sex but for belting the daylights out of the boy in the opposite corner.

I had not touched alcohol or smoked a cigarette. I was as fit as a fifteen-year-old can be. And then suddenly I was whipped into hospital with a mystery illness that was to terrify me so much I thought of killing myself.

It started with a sore throat. Gargling with salt water did no good, so Mum took me to hospital where doctors wasted no time taking me in. I was put in a bed and told to do nothing but lie still; I wasn't even allowed to get up to go to the toilet. The illness was diagnosed as rheumatic fever and it kept me in that hospital for four weeks. The enforced idleness was maddening and I counted the minutes and hours between the visits of Mum, my aunts and my friends. Lying on my back helpless for a few weeks was one thing, but then I learned that I might become a permanent invalid with a heart condition. I was terrified. For someone so energetic the thought was too much to bear and it was then that I seriously thought about doing myself in.

In the end, the Germans saved my life. They scored a direct hit on the hospital and in the pandemonium I walked, unsteadily and unnoticed, out of the ward and down the stairs. In view of the things I'd heard, I expected to drop dead any minute, but nothing happened and the next day Mum took me home. For the next week or so the old man – still 'on the trot' – took a risk and stayed with me day and night. And then, one morning, I felt well enough to get up. Touch wood, I've been as right as ninepence ever since – a walking miracle, according to the doctors.

Before I was taken ill, I'd graduated from the Coronet

junior club to Crown and Manor youth club in Hoxton, and as soon as I'd recovered from the rheumatic fever I took up boxing again. I also joined the naval cadets at Hackney Wick, where the training facilities were good, and it wasn't long before I started taking the sport very seriously. I'd been a very useful welterweight, and the idea of turning pro appealed to me: a good crowd-pleaser could earn as much as ten quid for four three-minute rounds. There was also the handy bonus of 'nobbins' – coins thrown into the ring by satisfied customers – although boxers often came off second best to their helpers. Try picking up a handful of coins wearing boxing gloves and you'll see what I mean.

When the twins saw some of the cutlery, glassware and trophies I won as an amateur they felt boxing might be for them, too, and they joined me in my early-morning road running, copying my side-stepping and shadow-boxing in the streets around Vallance Road. They were so enthusiastic that I turned an upstairs room into a sort of gym, with a speedball, punchbag, skipping ropes and weights. I found some boxing gloves to fit the twins and started to teach them. We were at it every day. It used to drive them mad, I suppose: keep that guard up, shoot out that left, duck, weave, watch that guard now, keep the left going . . . Ronnie was a southpaw; he led with his right. I corrected this by tying his right arm down, so that he couldn't move it.

The twins loved that little gym and it wasn't long before they started inviting their mates round for some sparring. I'd come home in the evenings to find the room full of kids, all waiting for me to get them organized. After a while, I started arranging contests and bought books and things to give the winners as prizes. The kids adored it. That gym was like their own little club.

Mum made sure all our gear was the cleanest by

21

washing it every day, and the old man even cleaned and ironed the laces on our boxing boots. Mum didn't come upstairs much, except to bring the boys tea and sandwiches. But as long as no one was getting hurt she didn't mind all the noise and running around. She loved having kids in the house and the Kray home got a reputation for always being full up.

A year later the twins showed so much promise that I took them to the Robert Browning Institute in Walworth, near the Elephant and Castle in South London. One of the resident trainers watched them in the ring, a look of amazement on his face. 'How old did you say they were, Charlie?' he asked.

'Ten,' I said.

'Are you sure they haven't been in the ring before?'

'Absolutely,' I replied proudly.

'They're amazing,' the trainer said. 'Bloody amazing.'

'So you want them in the club?'

'Definitely.'

And so the short-lived but sensational career of the young Kray twins was born.

My own career in the ring was about to take off, too – courtesy of the Royal Navy. I decided to volunteer for the Navy before being called up and sent into the Army, which I didn't fancy. I joined towards the end of the war, but my boxing reputation preceded me, and I spent most of my active service representing the Navy as a welterweight against the Army and Air Force.

After the war, contests were arranged to keep the men entertained while they waited to be demobbed. I found myself boxing roughly twice a week in various parts of the country. Whether it was the pressure of these fights or the legacy of my rheumatic fever I don't know, but I suddenly developed chronic migraine and was discharged from the Navy on health grounds.

I was thrilled to return home to find that my little twin brothers had become quite famous locally with their spectacular triumphs in the ring. They had fought locally and nationally with outstanding success. In the prestigious London Schools competition they got to the final three years running and had to fight each other.

I shall never forget the third encounter at York Hall in Bethnal Green; it was a classic. I went in the dressing room beforehand and told them to take it easy and put on a good show. Ronnie was as calm as ever, but Reggie was extra keyed up. He had lost the previous two fights and I sensed he'd made up his mind he was going to win this one.

The announcements ended. The bell rang. And to the deafening roar of a thousand or so school kids the tenacious thirteen-year-old twins came out of their corners to do battle: Reggie the skilful boxer, Ronnie the fighter, who never knew when he was beaten. For three two-minute rounds they were totally absorbed, both committed to winning. They were belting each other so hard and so often that Mum and the old man wanted to get in the ring and stop it and it was all I could do to restrain them, although the battle got so bloody in the final round that I nearly shouted 'Stop!' myself.

The judges found it difficult telling the twins apart in the first part of the fight but they had no trouble towards the end: Ronnie's face was a mess and Reggie got a unanimous verdict.

Afterwards, in the dressing room, Mum laid into them. She was horrified at the sight of her two babies knocking the daylights out of each other and told them in no uncertain terms that they would never appear together in a ring again as long as she was alive.

23

The twins burst into tears. But they never did fight each other again.

Back in civvy street again, I teamed up with the old man on the knocker, and dedicated myself to boxing. The Kray fame began to spread. Three brothers – two of them identical twins – chalking up one victory after another was hot local news, and suddenly our photographs were all over the *East London Advertiser*, with reports of our fights.

Mum hated boxing, but she always came to our fights with her sisters; she felt she had a duty to be there. We used to laugh at her because she admitted that half the time she didn't look. She tried to talk us out of it, saying, 'Do you really want to end up disfigured?' And if one of us got hurt, she'd say, 'You've got to stop – it's no good for you.' But in the end she gave up because she realized we loved the sport.

As boxers, the twins were quite different from each other: Reggie was the cool, cautious one, with all the skills of a potential champion and, importantly, he always listened to advice. Ronnie was a good boxer too, and very brave. But he never listened to advice. He was a very determined boy with a mind of his own. If he made up his mind to do something, he'd do it, no matter what, and unlike Reggie he would never hold back. He would go on and on until he dropped.

A trainer told me, 'I know Ronnie doesn't listen half the time. But he's got so much determination that he'd knock a wall down if I told him to.'

Once, at Lime Grove Baths in West London, Ronnie was fighting a boy Reggie had knocked out a few months before. In the dressing room, I warned Ronnie, 'This lad can punch. If he catches you, you'll be over, I promise.'

Ronnie nodded. But I sensed he wasn't listening.

24

In the first round, his opponent threw a huge overhead punch. Everyone round the ring saw it, but not Ronnie. He almost somersaulted backwards on to the canvas. It seemed all over, but Ronnie rolled over and crawled to his knees, then slowly to his feet. He didn't know where he was, but he survived the round. He was still in another world when he came out for the second and he took a hammering. But when the bell went for the third, his head suddenly cleared and he tore into his opponent, knocking him out after a series of crushing blows to the head.

In the dressing room afterwards, I said, 'That was very clever.'

Ronnie barely looked at me. 'What did you want me to do?'

'I told you to keep your chin down otherwise you'd get knocked over.'

Ronnie looked pained. 'Oh, stop nagging. I won, didn't I?'

Another time, at a dinner-jacket affair at the Sporting Club in London's West End, I took a look at Ronnie's opponent – a tough-looking gypsy type. I knew what to expect and I said to Ronnie, 'He'll be a strong two-handed puncher and he'll come at you from the first bell trying to put you away. So take it easy. Keep out of trouble for a bit.'

But, as usual, Ronnie wasn't too interested in what I had to say. In sport, it's good to have some nerves, it gets you keyed up, helps you perform well. But Ronnie didn't have any nerves. He didn't care.

When the bell sounded the gypsy almost ran from his corner and then started swinging at Ronnie with both hands. Ronnie looked totally shocked. He was battered about the head and forced back against the ropes taking massive lefts and rights to the head.

25

The gypsy's brothers, sitting near me, grinned. 'That's it. It's all over,' they said triumphantly.

Suddenly Ronnie found his breath. He started ducking out of the way of the gypsy's punches, then got in a few of his own. The gypsy's onslaught stopped. It was all Ronnie needed; he was in, smashing rights and lefts into the face and body as though he was possessed. It was quite devastating.

I knew the signs, and turned to the brothers. 'Yeah. You're right. It *is* all over.'

Less than a minute later the gyspy was being counted out.

I think Ronnie was secretly annoyed with himself for being caught cold because in the communal dressing room afterwards, he acted out of character. He overheard the gypsy moaning to his brothers about being caught unawares. It would never happen again, he said.

Before I could stop him, Ronnie had walked over to them. 'Stop making excuses,' he told the gypsy quietly. 'If you want, I'll do it again. I'll catch you unawares again.'

I stepped in and took Ronnie away. But that was him all over: he always believed that what was done was done and there was no point whingeing or trying to change it. Reggie would always be prepared to discuss matters, but Ronnie was withdrawn and would say, 'I don't want to talk about it.' And he was always right: there would be no argument, no discussion, no possible compromise.

Once, as boys, the twins were due to box at Leyton Baths, and Ronnie did not turn up. Reggie and I waited for him at home, but in the end had to leave without him. We were worried about his safety, naturally, and about the inquiry that would be launched by the boxing board: it was bad news not to turn up for a bout.

A few minutes after we got back home, Ronnie walked in with a school pal, Pat Butler.

'Where the hell were you?' I wanted to know.

'I had to go somewhere with Pat,' was all Ronnie replied.

'You know you could lose your licence.' I was livid.

' I don't care,' Ronnie said. 'Pat was in trouble with some people.'

'You're out of order, Ronnie. You should never not turn up for a fight.'

But Ronnie just shrugged. 'I don't care about not turning up. This was more important to me.'

Then Reggie chimed in. 'You could have helped Pat out tomorrow.'

'No,' Ronnie said, quietly but forcibly. 'It had to be done tonight.'

Reggie and I continued to argue with him, but Ronnie just said, 'Anyway I had to do it and it's done now. I'm not apologizing.'

We pointed out that Mum had stayed at home because she was worried about him. Ronnie was sorry he'd caused her to miss the fight, but otherwise he couldn't care less.

The twins seemed unaffected by their local Press coverage and the local fame that went with it. They still went to school regularly, didn't throw their weight around and were never loud-mouthed, like some kids in the neighbourhood. If anything, they were quiet and modest and always respectful. Someone who saw this side of their character was the Reverend Hetherington, vicar of St James the Great, in Bethnal Green Road. The church youth club, which the twins belonged to, ran jumble sales and other fund-raising functions, and they were always keen to help set up stalls and so on. The twins admired the vicar and went out of their way to oblige him whenever he wanted a favour. He liked them too, and

27

always spoke well of them. That friendship was to last a lifetime.

One night, the vicar was standing in the doorway of the vestry when the twins walked up.

'Can we do anything for you, Father?' Ronnie asked.

Mr Hetherington was a heavy smoker and had a cigarette going at the time. He drew on it. 'No, I don't think so, Ronald.' he said. 'But it's very kind of you to ask. Thank you.'

He asked them one or two questions about what they were doing with themselves and was generally as pleasant and friendly as usual. Then he said good-night and went into his vestry.

Half an hour later he felt in his cassock for his cigarettes and was amazed to find an extra packet. The twins had bought the cigarettes for him. But they knew he would not have accepted them had they offered. So they slipped the packet into one of his pockets without him knowing.

Later, I learned that Mr Hetherington said no when the twins asked if he wanted anything because he always wondered: 'What on earth are they going to do to get it!'

That immediate post-war period in the East End was a happy time. Life was getting back to normal after the horrors of the Blitz, and the family atmosphere Mum created at Vallance Road was warm and cosy and very secure.

As boys, the twins were very disciplined about their boxing. They went to bed early, ate well and regularly, and were almost fanatical about their fitness; they were always pounding the streets early in the morning.

Just after their fourteenth birthdays, however, the twins started to change. For the worse. Suddenly they started staying out late and neglecting their morning roadwork. They became very secretive about where they were going, what they were doing, who they were seeing. Mum was very concerned but she bit her tongue. She put it down to their age: they were probably going through that 'growing up' stage and she didn't want to appear a moaner. But then I discovered the twins were calling in at Aunt Rose's house late at night to clean themselves up before coming home.

The reason for their secrecy was suddenly very clear. They had been fighting in the street and knew that Mum would give them hell if she found out.

The East End had been relatively free of violence during the war and the couple of years after it. But now that the wartime controls were being relaxed, teenagers roamed the streets looking for excitement. It was, perhaps, inevitable that the twins, tough, utterly fearless and locally famous, would be involved, and with their flair for leadership it was hardly surprising that they were out in front when the battles began.

An incident that stands out involved a Jewish shopowner, aged about seventy who made a point of coming round to our house to say how wonderful the twins were. Apparently they were walking home one night when they saw some boys smash the old man's shop window and help themselves to some of his goods. As they ran off, the twins chased them – not to have them arrested, but to give them a good hiding and to get back what they had stolen. They didn't catch them, but the thieves never came back. The shopowner was very grateful to the twins, but it was nothing to them; they were always eager to help someone in trouble. Once Ronnie pawned a gold ring for a couple of quid to help a kid out. Another time he came home with no shoes. When Mum asked where they were, he said, 'I've just given them to a poor kid who didn't have any.'

They could not stand bullies, especially if our family was involved. When they were fifteen they heard that the old man had been slagged off by a crowd of young blokes in a pub. The old man and some friends were having a singsong when the crowd started taking the mickey out of them.

'Leave us alone,' the old man said. 'We're enjoying ourselves.'

'Who are you, you old bastard?' one of the youths replied, and he went to give him a smack.

One of the old man's friends warned, 'I wouldn't do that if I were you,' and the trouble was stopped.

But a few of the bullying crowd said, 'We're not finished here.'

The next day the old man told Ronnie and Reggie what had happened. 'Who were they?' the twins wanted to know. The old man thought they worked for a chap called Jack Barclay, who owned a big East End store. The twins were round there like a shot.

'Hello, Mr Barclay,' Ronnie said respectfully. He asked for two people by name.

'They're out the back,' replied Mr Barclay.

'Thank you,' said Ronnie. And he walked straight through with Reggie and confronted the two bullies.

'You had a go at our old man last night. And we don't like it.'

With that, Ronnie floored one of the guys and Reggie did the other. Then they went out, saying goodbye to Mr Barclay on the way.

Several times in that long hot summer of 1948, I talked to the twins. I tried to tell them what fools they were; that the only place they should be fighting was in the ring, where they could made a *good* name for themselves. I should have saved my breath. My twin brothers were not interested in what I had to say or what I felt. They were not fifteen yet, but almost overnight they had become men and nobody, not even their elder brother, was going to tell them what to do.

Adolescence, tragically, had passed the Kray twins by.

Chapter Three

My own life as I entered my twenties was going along nicely. I was earning a few quid with the old man. My boxing was fine; I was winning most of my fights and thinking seriously of turning pro.

And then I fell in love.

I was dedicated to fighting. I trained hard and nearly always went to bed early. But every sportsman needs a break some time, a chance to unwind, and one of the favourite places to do that in the East End was the Bow Civic dance hall. It was there that I met a stunning blonde who lived in nearby Poplar, the youngest of four sisters and a very talented dressmaker. She was two years younger than me and we hit it off immediately. We soon started going out seriously together.

Her name was Dorothy Moore and we felt we were destined to get married.

Mum and the old man approved of Dolly, and wedding bells rang out for us on Christmas Day 1948. Mum solved our housing problem by dismantling the gym in Vallance Road and redecorating and furnishing the room for us. We spent our honeymoon there. A week later I was in the ring at Leyton Baths, cruising to a points win in my first professional fight.

After that, I was much in demand and picked up between five and ten quid a fight. I trained hard and took everything that came my way, hoping to catch the eye of a leading promoter. The twins came to watch me fight at Hoxton, Stepney, West Ham and the famous Mile End arena, eager to pick up tips that might help them in the ring. I gained a reputation as a useful and reliable fighter, and although I didn't have that extra touch of class that makes a champion, I was proud of my skills and my considerable local fame.

Certain necessities were still rationed, but life had more or less got back to normal after the horrors of war. We ate and slept well, and the family atmosphere Mum created for us all at Vallance Road was warm and cosy and very happy.

It seemed too good to last. And it was.

One evening in March, the old man and I came home after working in Bristol and found Mum dreadfully upset. There had been a nasty fight outside a dance hall in Mare Street, Hackney, and a boy had been badly beaten with a length of bicycle chain. The twins had been arrested. Mum couldn't believe it; neither could the old man and I, because the twins had never once needed to use anything other than their fists to settle an argument.

The case went to the Old Bailey. The twins were innocent of the offences with which they were charged and they were rightly acquitted. But they had come face to face with that uniformed authority which they neither respected nor trusted. Just seven months later there was to be a more far-reaching and damaging confrontation.

It was a Saturday evening in October. There had been a fight near a youth club in Mansford Street, off Old Bethnal Green Road, and Police Constable Donald Baynton wanted to know about it. He went up to a group of youths on a corner outside a restaurant. Picking one out, he asked if he had been involved in the fight. The boy shook his head. 'Nothing to do with me.'

PC Baynton went up to the boy and pushed him in the stomach. The boy told him to leave him alone; he said again the fight had had nothing to do with him. The officer poked him in the stomach again.

It was a mistake. The boy was Ronnie. He didn't like the PC's manner one bit.

And he lashed out with a right hook to the jaw.

It wasn't a hard blow; PC Baynton didn't even go down. Ronnie ran off, but not very fast, and Baynton caught him. There was a brief struggle and Ronnie went quietly to Bethnal Green police station.

What happened inside that station during the next few minutes almost certainly changed Ronnie's life for ever.

Reggie heard about the incident from one of Ronnie's friends. Immediately, he went to the police station and waited outside. After a while, PC Baynton came out. Spotting Reggie, he grinned mockingly. 'Oh, the other one now,' he said. 'I've just put your brother in there and given him a good hiding. He ain't so clever now.'

Reggie sneered. 'You won't give me one,' he said. Then he darted into a side street, but not too quickly.

Thinking Reggie was running away, Baynton chased after him. It was his second mistake of the evening. When he turned the corner, Reggie was waiting, and he slammed into the surprised officer's face with a few right- and left-handers then walked away.

I was at home with Mum when someone knocked at the door and told us what had happened. When I got to the police station I couldn't believe it. Ronnie was in a terrible state: blood all over him, his shirt ripped to pieces.

'What the hell happened?' I asked.

Ronnie was still defiant. His eyes hardened. 'They got flash. A load of them came in the cell and gave me a hiding.' He glanced over to some of them watching. 'They all think they're big men. If they want a row it's ten-handed.'

I turned round on them angrily. 'Aren't you lot clever?'

33

I said sarcastically. 'Not one of you is man enough to fight him on your own.'

'Look, Charlie,' one of them said in a friendly tone. 'We don't want any trouble – any problems.'

'No problems!' I yelled. 'I'm going to cause you plenty of problems. This is diabolical, what's happened here. You're not getting away with beating up a sixteen-year-old kid!'

I started ranting and accused them again of being cowards. They threatened to arrest me and suggested I left. Finally I agreed but I warned them I was taking Ronnie to a doctor.

Later that evening it was bedlam at Vallance Road. Mum was crying her eyes out at the sight of Ronnie's smashed face; Ronnie was trying to console her, saying he was all right and he hadn't hurt the policeman anyway; the old man and I were wondering if we could take legal action. Then there was a knock at the front door. It was an inspector the old man knew from the local nick. PC Baynton was with him, looking the worse for wear. The Inspector wanted to speak to Reggie.

When I said he wasn't in, the Inspector motioned towards Baynton. 'Look what he's done to him,' he said.

'Oh, yeah,' I replied scornfully. 'Come in and have a look at what your officers have done to Ronnie.'

'I don't know anything about that,' the Inspector said.

I made them come in and see Ronnie anyway. 'You're dead worried because one of your men copped a right-hander,' I said. 'Ronnie got more than that – from half a dozen of them.'

The Inspector didn't want to know. All he wanted was to arrest Reggie and charge him with assault. A few minutes later Reggie walked in. After a brief chat I advised him it was best for everyone if he gave himself up, and he did. But I warned the Inspector that if Reggie was so much as touched, I'd blow the whole thing wide open to the papers.

A day or so later, the old man was told the police didn't want to make a song and dance about it unless they were forced to. The twins had to be charged because they had unquestionably assaulted a policeman, but they would be treated leniently – probably just put on probation – if I kept quiet about Ronnie's beating. If I didn't, the police would make it unpleasant for the whole family – starting with nicking the old man for dodging the call-up. I decided to swallow it.

A few days after their seventeenth birthday the twins appeared at Old Street in North London, accused of assault. For some reason, the magistrate, Mr Harold Sturge, praised PC Baynton's courage in a 'cowardly attack'. No mention, however, was made of the cowardly attack behind closed doors at Bethnal Green police station.

Not long afterwards Baynton was moved to a different area. But the PC had fuelled the twins' resentment and distrust of uniformed authority and the legacy of his arrogance that autumn evening was to last a lifetime.

The Baynton episode did nothing to destroy the myth that was growing up around the twins. They were tough and fearless and, in the tradition of the Wild West where the 'fastest guns' were always the target of other sharpshooters, they became marked young men in the East End. Hard nuts from neighbouring districts came looking for them in search of fame and glory as The Kids Who Toppled The Krays. Like the police, they came mob-handed. But they never came back.

One evening Reggie walked into the house at just after ten at night. I told him Ronnie had left a message saying he was in the Coach and Horses with his friend, Pat Butler. It was nearly closing time and I said it was a bit late to go, but Reggie had a strange feeling he ought to. He left quickly. What happened when he got there became the talk of the East End for months.

Ronnie was in the saloon bar with Pat. As Reggie walked in, Ronnie said, 'Just in time.' He nodded to nine youths at the other end of the bar. 'That little firm are looking for us.' ·

A few minutes later, the twins told Pat to make sure he stayed out of the way, then dashed out of the door, as though they were scared. But it was only a ploy to reduce the odds a little. As four of the rival gang followed them into the street, the twins doubled back into the saloon, through the public bar, taking the remaining five by surprise.

It was an almighty battle. Fists flew, chairs were thrown, tables overturned. Although the twins were out-numbered by more than two to one, they floored the whole lot. And when the other four ran back in, they knocked them out too. Amazingly, the twins came out of that scrap virtually unscathed. But one of the kids, Bill Donovan, who Ronnie had hit with a chair, was taken to hospital with a badly damaged eye.

The twins were very concerned about Bill and asked me to ring the hospital. I pretended to be a relation and asked how he was. A nurse said he was stable, but nobody knew if the eye was going to be permanently damaged. It was a worrying few days. The twins kept telling me to ring and eventually, to the twins' relief, we learned Donovan was going to be all right.

Pat Butler told me later that he was in the street after the fight had ended and an old man had asked him who the twins were. He'd never seen anything like it; it was like a scene from a Western.

One night a few weeks later the twins were spotted going into a café in Commercial Road. When they came out, they found themselves facing ten members of the so-called Watney Street Gang who, it seemed, were intent on teaching them to stay in Bethnal Green. The twins did not want to risk waiting for the usual preliminaries to a punch-up; they waded into the mob, laying six of them out on the pavement. The rest, not fancying the new odds, ran off.

Incidents like this built up the legend that the twins were tough guys who went around the East End looking for people to punch. That is far-fetched and unfair. What *is* true is that they were tasting power for the first time. They had been accustomed to victory in the ring against one opponent but now they knew they were hard and tough and skilful enough to take on, and beat, eight or nine between them.

And they enjoyed the feeling.

The Albert Hall was packed that night, 11 December 1951. Tommy McGovern, one of my contemporaries at the Robert Browning Institute, was defending his British light-heavyweight championship. And five of the other seven bouts involved Bethnal Green fighters – including the three Kray brothers. It was the first time we had appeared on the same bill together, and it was to be the last.

In those days, a boxer had really arrived when he appeared at the Albert Hall or Harringay Arena; it had taken me eighteen victories in twenty contests. But the twins, who had turned pro in July, had made it there after just six fights – and six wins. That's still a British boxing record.

My appearance almost never happened. I had decided to quit boxing and hadn't been in the ring for several months. But I wanted an extra bit of money for Christmas and agreed to take on an unbeaten Aldgate welterweight called Lew Lazar for twenty-five quid.

We were the first three fights on. First, Ronnie lost to a clever boxer from King's Cross named Bill Sliney, whom Reggie had outpointed two months before. Sliney was not too keen to continue after a first-round mauling by Ronnie, but he was persuaded to, and won a points verdict. Reggie's cool, scientific style earned him an easy points win over Bob Manito, of Clapham, and then it was my turn.

Unfortunately, it was a night when the deafening cheers of the Bethnal Green faithful could not help me. I'd been out of action too long and my timing was haywire. My pride got me to my feet after two counts of nine in the first two rounds, but a left hook in the guts finished me in the third.

I spent some of the twenty-five quid on a white fur coat for my baby son, Gary, who had been born two days after the twins turned pro. But it was my last boxing pay-day. I never put the gloves on in public again. Neither did the twins. For the next two years they were to pit their strength against a very different opponent.

The Army.

The twins filled in their time between call-up and reporting by joining the old man and me on the knocker. But they didn't show much enthusiasm, and it was a relief to them when they were ordered to report at the Tower of London for service with the Royal Fusiliers. They left Vallance Road early one March morning in 1952.

And were back in time for tea.

Mum asked what on earth had happened, but the twins were in a foul temper and refused to tell her. They went out and didn't come back until the early hours when we'd all gone to bed. Later that morning, they were arrested for deserting.

They had, it transpired, reacted badly to uniformed authority once again. An NCO had shouted some orders to them. The twins didn't like his attitude, his lack of respect, and one of them had thumped him. Then they had walked out, deciding Army life wasn't for them.

And after an uncomfortable week's punishment in the guardroom, they walked out again.

To me, it all seemed a terrible waste. Just four months before, they had been promising young boxers with just one minor blot on their record, for which they had been treated leniently. Now they were wanted men facing serious disciplinary action and, almost certainly, jail. I went to see them in hiding in various parts of London, and tried to persuade them to give themselves up. I told them the Forces favoured sportsmen; they could do well with their boxing talent. But it was a waste of breath, as usual. The twins were not going to serve in the Army and that was that.

They stayed on the run until early November, two weeks after their nineteenth birthday. Then one cold, snowy night Reggie suddenly turned up at Vallance Road. Mum was desperately worried for him but Reggie assured her he was all right. He stayed with her for about an hour then left. As he walked into the street, a voice called out, 'Hello, Reg. I'm going to take you in.' It was PC John Fisher, who knew the twins by sight.

Reggie asked him calmly to do him a favour and go away; he didn't want a row. But PC Fisher said he couldn't do that and lunged forward to grab him. Reggie ducked and threw a right hand. PC Fisher fell to the ground and Reggie hurried away in the snow.

It was only a matter of time. The police knew both

39

twins were in the area and they were picked up a few hours later.

At Thames Street Court that morning the magistrate, Colonel W. E. Batt, jailed them for a month. It was the first time they had seen the inside of a prison as convicted persons.

After their sentence, a military escort took the twins to Wemyss Barracks at Canterbury, Kent, where they were court-martialled for desertion. They escaped yet again, but it was a short-lived freedom and on 12 May 1953 the twins found themselves serving nine months' detention in the notorious military prison of Shepton Mallet in Somerset.

It was to be a tough nine months . . . for the Army! The prison staff at Shepton Mallet had never seen anyone like the twins before, and several sergeants were replaced because they couldn't handle them. The twins were so uncontrollable that the Commanding Officer sought my help. He wondered why it was impossible to get through to the twins with words, why they resolved everything with violence. I tried to explain that life was like that in the East End; if anyone tried to threaten you, you hit them first. It was a world which that polite, charming CO would never understand, and he asked me to have a quiet word with the twins. I agreed to try.

The twins were unimpressed that I'd been having a cosy chat over a cup of tea with the CO; all the guards understood was a punch in the face, they said, and that was what they'd get. Nothing I tried to say cut any ice with them. They simply would not tolerate being ordered around. Tell them to do something and they'd rebel. Ask them, in a civil tone, and they would be fine. Ronnie, particularly, would rebel against a strong person, unless he had reason to respect him. There was one sergeant there they *did* like: he was firm but courteous, and they did what he told them.

The twins didn't always use violence to make their point. One day a military policeman who had been giving Ronnie a hard time was standing outside the cobbler's shop where Ronnie was working. Suddenly Ronnie rushed out, blood all over his face, screaming, 'That's it! I've done it now! It's all over! Better get in there!'

The guard, convinced there had been a murder, dashed off to get reinforcements, but by the time they arrived everything was calm. Ronnie, who had smeared the blood over his face after cutting his hand slightly while working, was back at his bench.

'What the hell happened here?' demanded a senior officer.

Ronnie looked at him blankly. 'Nothing,' he replied. Then he looked at the embarrassed MP. 'He must be going round the bend. Been working too hard or something.'

It is a pity that the NCO at the Tower of London rubbed the twins up the wrong way that March morning in 1952, because I'm sure they could have made something of themselves in the Army. They were fit and strong, and they would have loved the physical side; I'm sure they would have become physical training instructors in no time. They both had a lot of guts, too: once, on an assault course, Ronnie jumped from something and landed awkwardly, crashing his knee sickeningly into his chin. But he forced himself to carry on; he had unbelievable determination and hated quitting anything. They both had a gift for leadership, too, and had it been wartime I feel it would have been a very different story. They were the type who could so easily have distinguished themselves with courage in the face of extreme danger.

As it was, the twins spent what should have been the rest of their National Service giving the Shepton Mallet staff a very hard time. And when they were thrown out on to Civvy Street towards the end of 1953 each of their records bore that ugly scar: Dishonorable Discharge.

What, I wondered, were they going to do with the rest of their lives?

Chapter Four

What they could have done was box for a living. They were both above average, particularly Reggie, and I'm sure they could have earned a few bob. I'd seen what boxing in the Forces had done for me and I'd urged them to give it a go in the Army. But, as usual, the twins felt they knew best. When they found themselves back in civvy street, Ronnie had lost interest in fighting and Reggie used the excuse that he would not get a licence because of his Army record. He did train with me, though, and the fitter he became, the more he felt he would like to box professionally.

Finally he did apply for his licence. However, the Christmas incident with PC Fisher was on his record and would have gone against him but for a lovely gesture by the policeman. He wrote to the boxing board explaining that Reggie's punch that night was thrown under provocation. 'Reggie told me to walk away, but I didn't accept his advice,' PC Fisher wrote. 'I tried to grab him, thereby provoking him to hit me to evade arrest.'

That letter swayed the decision in Reggie's favour and he was granted his licence. But within a few months he had lost all interest in the sport: he felt that all the managers and agents were too ruthless and only wanted to know those fighters who were going to become champions. The irony was that Reggie was good enough to become a champion; I didn't doubt that for one moment. But he didn't like the atmosphere and that was the end of that. Reggie never went in the ring again, although I believe he knew in his heart that he was good enough.

It quickly became clear that the twins were not cut out for a life on the knocker. I lent them some money and they did spend several weeks trying to generate some business, but they were always looking for something else. It came in the form of a filthy, neglected billiard hall in what had once been a small cinema in Eric Street, off the Mile End Road. The takings were low, mainly because the manager preferred playing snooker himself rather than encouraging business. But the twins saw the potential and put a proposition to the owner: they would take over the place, smarten it up and make it pay; in return, they would give him a weekly cut of the takings. Since the owner was receiving next to nothing, he accepted the deal. The manager was fired, the former 'flea pit' spruced up and, at just twenty-one, the twins were in the entertainment business.

They had the Midas touch. Word spread that the twins had taken over the billiard hall and business boomed. One aspect, however, I found disturbing: the clientele. No one expects an East End billiard hall to look like a church fête in Cheltenham, but I was shocked at the number of young tearaways and villains who gathered there, simply idling their time away. Some, who had been with the twins in Shepton Mallet glasshouse, should have been given a cool reception. But that wasn't in the twins' nature: it is a family characteristic that we accept people for what they are, not what they have done. Others who came to regard the billiard hall as a regular meeting place were hard people, who were not fussy how they earned a few bob.

I had no idea Ronnie was homosexual until he told me himself a few months after the billiard hall opened. As well as all the tough nuts, a lot of younger, very good-looking guys used to congregate there and I noticed they always stopped laughing and joking whenever I walked in.

After a while I got a bit paranoid. 'Why have you suddenly gone quiet?' I'd ask.

Someone would snigger. And I'd say, 'I don't find it funny.'

They would say they meant nothing by it. But it would happen again and I'd get really annoyed.

Finally, Ronnie said to me one day, 'You don't know, do you?'

'Don't know what?'

'That I'm AC/DC,' Ronnie said.

'Leave me alone,' I scoffed.

'It's true. That's what I am, whether you like it or not.'

I didn't know what to say. I just stared at him, shocked. I knew he had not had many relationships with women, but I certainly hadn't given a thought to him being the other way.

'That's what we'd be talking about when you walked in,' Ronnie said. 'They all knew and would be laughing about it. Then I'd say, "Sssh, here's Charlie." And they'd all shut up.'

All I could think to say was: 'I can't believe it.'

'Well, it's true,' Ronnie said. 'That's how I am and you're not going to change it.' He went on to say he'd always been that way and could not care less who knew. He could not understand why so many people took a pop at homosexuals. 'They can't help what they are,' he would say.

In the main, though, the billiard hall was a place for hard, tough men. One such man was Bobby Ramsey, and he, more than anyone at that time, was to influence the course the twins' lives would take.

Ramsey was an ex-boxer who could have made a good living from the sport. But he fell into bad company and had settled for being 'minder' for the notorious Jack 'Spot' Comer, one of London's underworld kings of the fifties. Ramsey, several years older than the twins, had been around and the twins admired him; they listened in some sort of awe as he described the high life the likes of Comer enjoyed through controlling clubs and spielers.

I didn't like Ramsey. I had a feeling he would cause the twins problems and I told him, 'If you've got trouble, don't take the twins with you.' He promised he wouldn't. I warned the twins about him, too, but they scoffed. They were quite capable of handling Ramsey, and half a dozen like him, they said. It hit home to me then that they were probably right. They were not my little kid brothers any more: they were men in a man's world, and formidable men at that. They were identical twins, with identical thoughts and opinions – a language of their own. They had proved their strength, power and tenacity, both in the ring and against heavy odds outside it. They had taken on the police and the Army and had not been intimidated. They had survived a short spell in prison and a longer spell on the run. And now, at just twenty-one, they were running their own business – not an empire by any means, but it was their own and it was profitable. They ate, drank, and dressed well. And there always seemed to be enough money around to give to others who were not so well off. The East End may have been a small pool, but the twins were very big fish in it. Perhaps they were right. Perhaps they *could* handle the problems I feared Ramsey might create.

Over the next eighteen months the Regal billiard hall became more and more popular. The twins ensured there were no fights or disorders of any kind that might bother the police, and the business still made money. Inevitably, though, it became a meeting place for thieves where robberies were planned. The twins were never involved, I know; but if any of the pals they helped out had a good tickle, I'm sure the twins made sure their debts were repaid with interest.

All was going well. The twins – particularly Reggie – were becoming more ambitious and thinking of opening a more respectable club where decent East End families could go.

And then Bobby Ramsey turned up. He hadn't been at the billiard hall for several weeks and when he arrived one hot August night in 1956, I learned why: he had been hit on the head with an iron bar during a fight with a gang from the Watney Street area, the other side of Commercial Road. Now that he had recovered, he wanted revenge. He'd come into the billiard hall with a pal, Billie Jones, and asked Ronnie to go with them to a local pub called the Britannia. A villain called Charlie Martin, who had wielded the iron bar, was drinking there with Jimmy Fullerton, a local tearaway who'd helped in the attack. Ramsey was in a dangerous mood: he said he had several weapons in his car, including a bayonet. He asked Ronnie to go with him. Before they left, Ronnie went behind the bar. He opened a drawer and took out a loaded revolver.

Martin and Fullerton were not at the Britannia, but Martin's younger brother, Terry, was. On the principle that one of the Watney Street mob was better than none, he was dragged outside. Ramsey, his bayonet tucked in his trousers, laid into him, then pulled out the bayonet and stuck it up the young man's backside.

At that time, East End gang feuds were commonplace. Normally, a victim was carted off to hospital, mouths were kept shut and the police never got involved. But that night Ramsey was a reckless fool: as he drove away from the Britannia, he got stopped for speeding. The officers in the patrol car couldn't believe their luck when they found a blood-stained bayonet, a crowbar and an axe in the car. Ramsey, Jones and Ronnie were arrested.

At the station, the gun was found in Ronnie's pocket. It had not been fired, but that made little difference.

While the three of them were being questioned, a report came in that a man had been taken to the London Hospital with serious stab wounds. The police put two and two together and spoke to Terry Martin, who confirmed he had been attacked. The case against Ramsey, Jones and Ronnie was cast-iron and on 5 November 1956 they appeared at the Old Bailey charged with causing grievous bodily harm. Reggie, too, was charged, even though he wasn't aware of the attack until afterwards.

Ramsey was jailed for seven years; Jones and Ronnie got three each.

Reggie, thankfully, was justly acquitted. But the immediate future would be difficult for him, too. As identical twins, he and Ronnie had lived virtually in each other's pockets all their lives. Now, for the first time, they were going to have to exist separately.

Dolly and I were still living at Vallance Road but were desperate to find a place of our own. Mum was kind and understanding, as usual, and treated Dolly like a daughter, and the old man, bless him, was a diamond. But a house – no matter how warm and friendly – is not the same unless it's your own, and I was always on the lookout for a place where Dolly and I could live a proper and private family life.

In those early days Dolly was a good wife. She didn't make friends easily and was extremely possessive and money-mad; but she seemed to care for me and Gary and was very neat and clean about the house. She was a highly strung woman with a vivid imagination, though, and when

Gary needed surgery to correct a squint, she convinced herself he would be blind for the rest of his life.

I'd had a couple of insights into her strange behaviour when we were courting. Often Dolly would stay overnight at Vallance Road, sleeping with Mum upstairs while I shared the twins' room downstairs. Once, at about three in the morning, there was an almighty crash and I found Dolly staggering around in the hall, covered in blood. She'd had a nightmare and thrown herself through a closed window on to the scullery roof. Amazingly, she escaped with just a badly cut face.

The other occasion was when I was boxing in a competition in Watford. Dolly was at the ringside, having seen me qualify for the semi-final. But when she saw the man I was to meet knock out his opponent in the first round, she fled. She came back after I'd won the competition, but I don't know to this day whether it was the prospect of seeing me hammered that made her run – or the thought that I wouldn't win the £15 prize money.

Life on the knocker did have its moments, and I'd get a terrific buzz coming home with a load of gear that would fetch ten times as much as I'd paid, but I was eager to better our standard of living. The chance came when Reggie and I became closer in Ronnie's absence.

Reggie was a real go-getter and when he came across a dilapidated old house near Poplar Town Hall, only two hundred yards from Bow police station, he saw the potential immediately. He asked me to help him renovate it and, with the help of a few mates, we transformed that house into a sparkling club with a stage and dancing area – the East End had never seen anything like it before. We called it The Double R, after the twins.

The only clubs around at that time were 'dives': dark and dingy 'Men only' drinking places where pints were pulled but punches were not. We wanted The Double R to be different. We didn't want the billiard-hall clientele – layabouts and villains who liked a bit of trouble. We wanted the club to have a family atmosphere, a club where respectable working men could enjoy a quiet drink and listen to a band with their wives and families.

It took us six months to make our point.

The local tearaways had never seen anything like The Double R and assumed it was a 'dive' like all the other places in the area. And they treated it as such.

Few unwanted visitors got by our twenty-two-stone doorman, 'Big' Pat Connolly, but one quiet afternoon when security was relaxed three burly coalmen barged in. They were covered in coal dust and leaned against the newly decorated wall, demanding drinks. Reggie quietly asked them to leave. They started to argue and one of them aimed a punch at Reggie. I was serving behind the bar and raced round to give Reggie a hand. It wasn't necessary. By the time I arrived all three were laid out.

Reggie was extremely swift to nip problems in the bud. He hit first and did not bother to ask questions afterwards. One night an over-enthusiastic customer made the mistake of trying to take the microphone from a woman singing on stage. Reggie took the mike away and handed it back to her. The customer's second mistake was trying drunkenly to pull our mum up from her table to dance when she was happy minding her own business. Reggie felled him with a right hook then ordered him to be carried out. Two days later the customer came back and, rather sheepishly, apologized.

I'd always settled disputes with words, not fists. And up to the day we opened The Double R, I'd never had a fight outside the ring. I had had arguments with the twins over this when they resorted to violence. I told them they should not get involved in fights, but they would sneer and say I had no idea what was going on, what it was like when someone was spoiling your business.

I found myself taking a different view when the trouble-makers started getting busy at The Double R. After all the hard work that had gone into transforming that Bow Road house I was damned if I was going to stand by and watch some mindless Jack the Lads ruin the venture before it had properly started. So: when there was no other way out I met violence with violence. I spoke to the idiots in the language they understood and, since I was fit and technically well equipped, I was able to handle myself more than adequately.

Reggie was amused and quietly pleased by my attitude. The afternoons were worst; if there was going to be trouble, that was the time. I had asked Dolly to stay away during the day but one afternoon she came in for something. Three blokes were drinking at the bar and one said, 'Hello, darling.' I let that pass because I was all for being friendly, but then they all started making stupid, unsubtle remarks, generally being lairy and showing a lack of respect to a woman. I was serving behind the bar and politely asked them to be quiet because Dolly was my wife.

Unfortunately, they took no notice and finally I went round the other side of the bar to show them the door. One of them threw a punch and before I knew it I was having a row with all three.

Bill Donovan, who had been badly hurt in the Coach and Horses battle several years before, was on the door, and helped me out. We finally sent the troublemakers on their way with a message not to come back.

When Reggie heard about it he said, 'Now you know. Sometimes you've got to fight.'

I could not argue. But all the aggro got on my nerves and made me sick. I found it hard to understand the

51

mentality of people who took a delight in smashing up something that was nice.

We turned the room above the club into a gymnasium and, although I left it very late to ask him, Britain's favourite boxing champ, Henry Cooper, came along with his manager, Jim Wicks, to open it. This helped publicize The Double R and more and more people came along to see what it was like. The message finally got home to the sort that took pleasure in trouble, and gradually the club became the sort of establishment we had wanted in the beginning. The twins attracted all sorts – good, bad and indifferent – but everyone knew the rules and respected them. Some hard gangland men from South London crossed the water to drink there. They may have been enemies with some of the East End clientele but after those first six months there was hardly any hint of bother. The Double R, it seemed, was welcome neutral ground, a 'Little Switzerland' in the middle of Mile End.

Reggie, who had a natural flair for mixing with all types, was the perfect host, and I ran the bar with Barry Clare, an engaging homosexual, who also doubled up as compere, calling up amateur talent from the customers.

One night a lady asked Barry if she could sing a number. It was a beautiful blues song and she was so good I asked her if she would come along and sing a couple of times a week. She was thrilled and said, 'I'd be delighted.'

'How much do you want?' I asked.

The lady laughed. 'I don't want any money for singing.'

But I insisted and she finally gave in to shut me up. I forget how much we agreed; it was probably a fiver.

After her first performance I went up to her and tried to give her the money. She refused, but I forced her to take it: she had been excellent value and had earned it.

She immediately went to the bar and put the money on the counter.

'What are you doing?' I said.

'You've paid me, Charlie,' she replied. 'I can do what I like with my own money. And what I'd like to do is buy everyone a drink.'

And she did. Not just then, but every time she came in. She was a lovely woman who just loved to sing, and her name was Queenie Watts.

For the rich and famous, the West End had always been the place for a night out. But in the middle fifties the other side of the river became fashionable, and wealthy, titled gentlemen and showbusiness stars – including Danny La Rue and Joan Collins's sister Jackie – started coming to The Double R.

For me, the work was tiring. But it was our own business and the financial rewards were worthwhile. Most of the time, too, I was meeting very nice, genuine people. It certainly beat life on the knocker.

With business booming, Reggie and I decided to expand into gambling. At that time it was illegal: bookmakers were not Turf Accountants with shops in the High Street; they operated on street corners and anyone who wanted to put a couple of bob on a horse risked being nicked. Card games, too, were against the law. Anybody who wanted to play for money had to go to a spieler – a club, normally in a basement, where chemin de fer and poker were played away from the prying eyes of the police.

Reggie and I saw the financial possibilities in spielers and we acquired one across the road from The Double R. Within a couple of months, we opened two more. Money, suddenly, was coming out of our ears.

To make life even sweeter, a member of The Double R tipped me off about an empty flat in Narrow Street,

Wapping. It was a two-bedroomed flat on the second floor of a shabby block called Brightlingsea Buildings, built for dockers and their families nearly a hundred years before. A palace it wasn't. But it *was* a place Dolly, Gary and I could call ours at last and I snapped it up the same day. I had the money to move to a posher pad away from the manor, but the thought didn't occur to me. The East End was in my blood, and anyway, that was where we were making a very good living.

Dolly adored the new lifestyle. She had always dreamed of being rich, and now that there was a few bob around, she made the most of it with lots of new clothes and regular hair-dos. We went to West End clubs with upper-crust patrons of The Double R who accepted us as friends, cockney accents and all, or we enjoyed ourselves with old friends in the East End. Wherever we went, Dolly always looked lovely and attracted a lot of attention. I was proud of her.

One bloke at The Double R seemed to be taking more than a passing interest in Dolly but I felt secure in our marriage and didn't think much of it. She was a stunning looker and it was hardly surprising that other men found her attractive. My life was full to the brim with money and excitement and plans for the future, and I didn't give George Ince another thought.

In Wandsworth Prison Ronnie was delighted that business was going well on the outside; he knew he would have a share in it when he was released, and because he'd earned full remission through good behaviour in his first year it seemed he would be home in time for Christmas 1958.

In one day, however, the whole situation changed. From being more or less a model prisoner without one black mark on his record, Ronnie found himself in a tiny, concrete cell in a strait-jacket. Dreams of freedom vanished. The nightmare from which Ronnie never escaped had begun.

During the year he'd been in jail, Ronnie had been a loner. He had had his place in the prison hierarchy and made sure everyone understood it, but he had made it plain that he wouldn't cause trouble if he wasn't bothered. Ronnie has an overpowering manner, bordering on hypnotic, and often sounds as though he's demanding when in fact he's merely asking. Whether this led to the problems in Wandsworth I don't know, but a prison officer reacted badly to something he said and Ronnie snapped. The officer went down but within seconds other officers were on Ronnie who, strong as a bull, chinned a couple and they went over. An almighty fight broke out with fists flying, boots kicking. More officers, some armed with truncheons, joined in. Ronnie laid into them until they grabbed his arms and pushed them behind his back. Then they forced Ronnie's head down and rushed him along the cell corridor into a post. Someone came running with a strait-jacket. Somehow they got Ronnie into it. Then they dragged him along to a concrete cell they call the 'chokey' block. They held him down while an officer injected him with a drug, then slammed the door. Ronnie was left in that cell for a week.

Then they transferred him to the psychiatric wing at Winchester Prison in Hampshire.

And a doctor certified him insane.

The family all reacted differently. I was very worried and disturbed because I realized the implications: Ronnie could be kept in jail indefinitely. Mum couldn't believe it, but she tried to keep cool about it and was as optimistic as usual, saying everything would be bound to sort itself out in the end. The old man *wouldn't* believe it. Ronnie was being clever, he said; he was getting the authorities at it, working his ticket. No way was Ronnie mad.

55

And Reggie? Reggie was beside himself with fury and worry. If his identical twin, the man who shared his innermost thoughts, had been officially declared a nutcase, what on earth did that make him?

The news from Winchester that spring of 1958 shattered us all and for weeks we tried to change the prison rules that did not allow us to have a second opinion. Meanwhile, Ronnie was given massive doses of a tranquillizing drug called Stemetil. We were told this was to stabilize him and curb his violent tendencies. But it dulled his mind and affected his memory, and we were powerless to do anything about it. We watched him deteriorate before us to a point where sometimes he didn't even recognize us.

Out of my mind with worry, I decided to find out just what Stemetil was. When I did, I was horrified. A Harley Street specialist confirmed that Ronnie was being treated for schizophrenia with a drug normally used for treating vertigo and vomiting! To make matters even worse he said, 'The precise mechanisms of the action of this drug are not yet fully understood.'·

It was too much to take. Reggie and I decided that Ronnie was coming out of Winchester even if we had to blow a hole in the prison wall to get him. Happily, this wasn't necessary. A week or so later, in May 1958, Ronnie was transferred to a mental hospital just fourteen miles from London. It was Long Grove near Epsom, Surrey. And springing him from there was going to be a doddle.

The Strange Case of the Vanished Twin hit the headlines later the same month. Millions probably thought it was just another piece of Kray skulduggery, another cheeky swipe at authority, but we removed Ronnie from that hospital because we were far from convinced of his unbalanced mind. Also, we were very concerned at the bad effect the drugs were having on him.

One thing the drugs hadn't done was change Ronnie's appearance; he still looked like Reggie. When Reggie put on a blue suit, white shirt and blue tie, similar to those Ronnie wore in hospital, only those who knew them well could spot the difference. When Reggie had his hair cut as short as Ronnie's and put on a pair of glasses, even I had trouble telling them apart.

The switch was a simple operation. Leaving some friends in a couple of cars outside the hospital grounds, Reggie went in to see Ronnie as though it was just another routine visit. They sat chatting at a table in the small visiting hall and waited until a patrolling male nurse's back was turned. Ronnie whipped off his glasses; Reggie slipped his on. Then they quickly but discreetly changed places.

When they were sure no one had noticed the change-over, Ronnie got up and sauntered over to a door which visitors were allowed to go through to fetch tea and biscuits. The nurse, assuming he was Reggie, opened the door and Ronnie walked out. But he didn't go for tea; he walked straight out of the hospital into the grounds. One of the hospital staff came towards him on a bike and Ronnie tensed. But the man merely nodded a greeting and rode past. Ronnie walked on and on until he reached the gate, and then he spotted the cars Reggie had told him about and he was gone.

Reggie waited for about half an hour, then he went up to the nurse on the door and said, 'Excuse me, Ron's been a long time getting the tea. I didn't think they were allowed to get the tea.'

The nurse looked puzzled. '*You're* Ronnie,' he said.

Reggie shook his head. 'I'm Reggie. Ronnie went to get the tea. I'm getting worried.'

The nurse stared at Reggie closely. He must have believed him, because he ran off, a worried look on his face. Then all hell broke loose. An alarm bell went off. Hospital staff started running around. And then the police arrived.

Someone said to Reggie, 'This is all down to you.'

But Reggie pleaded innocence. 'I just came to see him. He went to get the tea, then everyone got excited.'

To confirm Reggie's story, the police took his finger-prints and checked them with the Criminal Records Office at Scotland Yard.

'You *are* Reg Kray,' someone commented.

'That's what I've been trying to tell you for the last hour,' said Reg. Then he added, straight-faced, 'I'm worried. What's happened to him?'

'Do us a favour,' one copper said impatiently. 'You know what's happened.'

But Reggie kept saying he didn't. And they kept him there for a couple of hours before letting him go.

By then, Ronnie was in a beautiful, expensive flat in St John's Wood. Not for long, though. When he arrived, he took one look round and said, 'I don't like this. You can get me out of here.' And we did – the next morning. Ronnie was like that. It wouldn't have occurred to him that we'd gone to a lot of trouble and expense to get him a 'safe' house. He just didn't like the place and that was that.

That day, the Superintendent of Long Grove got in touch with us and asked us to see him at the hospital. He said we'd made a serious mistake: Ronnie wasn't well and should have stayed there for treatment. We played dumb, but the Superintendent laughed. He said he admired how it had been done: there had been no trouble, no one had been hurt. But, nevertheless, we had made a mistake. And he warned us that we would find out he was right.

For the next few months Reggie and I had our work cut out running our businesses while keeping Ronnie ahead of the law. The escape was big news and stories of his whereabouts flooded the East End: he was reliably reported to be in the Bahamas, New York, Malta, the Cote d'Azur, Southern Spain and goodness knows where else. In fact, he never strayed further north than Finchley or further west than Fulham. He took a few chances to visit Mum in Vallance Road, and the first visit proved very traumatic for him. While he was there, he wanted to see Aunt Rose. But she had died while he was in Winchester and Mum had decided not to tell him until he was better. When she did break the news, Ronnie got up and went into the yard. He stood there, looking up at the railway arch. The death of his Aunt Rose was the biggest blow of his life then. He stood out there, looking up, trying to take it in.

Ronnie didn't want to be on the trot for the rest of his life. But he didn't want to go back to a mental hospital either. While he had been in Wandsworth, he had heard about people who had been in and out of mental institutions for years and was terrified of ending up like them. One had actually been certified insane and was being detained without a firm date for release. Ronnie dreaded the same thing happening to him.

To solve the problem, we had to prove that Ronnie was, in fact, sane. So we booked an appointment with a Harley Street psychiatrist under an assumed name and asked him to give an opinion on Ronnie's mental state. Ronnie made it sound plausible with a cock-and-bull story about getting married and being worried about insanity way back in the family. The psychiatrist was highly amused and, after asking a few questions, sent Ronnie on his way with a document stating that he was, indeed, in possession of all his marbles.

The effect on Ronnie was startling, and very worrying.

Relieved that the dark shadow of madness was lifted, he started taking even more risks. He would have a few drinks here, a few drinks there, and once he strolled all the way along Bethnal Green Road, cheerfully returning the greetings of people who thought he was Reggie.

But after five months the strain of being on the trot began to take its toll. He'd put on a lot of weight through heavy drinking, his face was drawn and haggard, and he'd become morose and anti-social, preferring to stay in and read or sleep. None of us knew what to do for the best. I was told Ronnie was suffering from the after-effects of the drugs pumped into him. He needed medical treatment very quickly, but to get it would mean revealing his identity and recent history.

In the end, the problem was solved for us. Ronnie took one risk too many and was recaptured. He suspected police would be waiting for him to turn up at Vallance Road to celebrate his twenty-fifth birthday, so he waited until the day after and arrived after dark. But the police were still waiting and let themselves in quietly at three in the morning as one of the party guests left.

A few days before, Ronnie had been acting very strangely; sometimes he didn't even recognize Reggie or myself. But when those two uniformed policemen and two male nurses walked into the house that night Ronnie was perfectly normal. He said he knew they had to take him back, and went to get his coat. I think he was relieved it was all over.

The police said they would take Ronnie to Long Grove for a formal discharge, then return him to Wandsworth where he would finish his sentence. But first he would stay overnight in Bethnal Green nick. Alarm bells rang loudly in my mind and Reggie's: we had not forgotten the PC Baynton affair. And although it was now nearly four in the morning, we rang our solicitor, a doctor and a national newspaper reporter.

Two hours later, Reggie and I walked into the police station with the lawyer and the doctor. We were not welcome. A high-ranking officer refused to let us see Ronnie and, in spite of the lawyer's protests, ordered us out of the building.

If someone had talked to us civilly, assuring us that Ronnie was all right and would get the proper treatment, I'm sure that would have been the end of it. But when Ronnie eventually came out, the police laid on a security pantomime that got everyone's back up. He was in a taxi – with a police escort – and they roared past us as though Scotland Yard was on fire. Angry now, as well as concerned, Reggie and I gave chase in our car, with the doctor and lawyer behind in theirs and the reporter behind them. It was like something out of those pre-war Keystone Kops silent movies. And it got even crazier near the Oval cricket ground in Kennington, South London, when a second police car, probably called on the radio, cut in front of Reggie, forcing him to swerve on to the pavement. It was all so stupid and irresponsible.

The security farce continued even when we reached Long Grove. The police escort let the taxi into the hospital grounds, then parked across the drive, blocking the entrance. We simply got out and walked. But then the second police car was allowed through and it crawled behind us as we walked to Reception. What on earth did they think we were going to do? Hurl hand grenades and rush Ronnie to freedom under cover of machine-gun fire?

At Reception, we asked to see Ronnie. The request was turned down. Instead we were shown into the Superintendent's office. He was as charming as before, but repeated that we'd done Ronnie no favours by helping him escape: he was very sick. We agreed, but argued very strongly that he wasn't insane. The Superintendent listened politely, promised to consider Ronnie's case carefully, then arranged for us to see him there and then.

That Superintendent didn't have long to consider the case. Within a couple of days Ronnie was taken back to Wandsworth. He was *not* re-certified, but he was put on tranquillizers. He hated this, but he finished his sentence without further trouble and walked out a free man about seven months later, in May 1959.

The release date surprised us. Ronnie, sentenced to three years, had belted a prison officer, caused a certain amount of damage to others, then escaped from captivity for five months. Yet he still earned full remission and served just two years.

Did someone blunder, I wonder? Was Ronnie diagnosed wrongly? Did a doctor or psychiatrist prescribe the wrong treatment? Was Ronnie allowed out earlier than he should have been just to keep him happy?

And to keep us quiet?

Chapter Five

The weight Ronnie had put on before he went back to prison had dropped by the time he came out. He looked awful: he was very pale and drawn, and his eyes had no life in them. He would spend much of the time staring into space, unaware of what was happening around him. He recognized Mum and the old man, and he trusted them, but he looked blankly at Reggie and me, refusing to believe we were his brothers.

We'd laid on this big party at The Double R. Dozens of old friends were looking forward to seeing Ronnie again. But he refused to go and I had to apologize to everyone and make up an excuse. All Ronnie wanted to do was sit in the kitchen at Vallance Road and drink tea and smoke. Reggie would sit with him for hours and then ring me to say he couldn't handle it any more. Then I'd go and sit with him. Poor Mum! She didn't know what to make of it all. She didn't understand when Ronnie would suddenly look at me strangely and say, 'You're not Charlie. Why do you keep coming here?' It got worse and worse and he got more and more suspicious, even of Reggie.

And then, inevitably, Ronnie exploded.

We had taken him to a pub to try and cheer him up. Throughout the evening he was very strange, talking funny and making no sense at all. And if he caught Reggie or me looking at him, he'd snap, 'Who you looking at?'

Mum or the old man would say gently, 'Ronnie, that's Charlie, your brother.'

'Yeah,' Ronnie would scoff. 'That's what he tells you.'

It was frightening for all of us.

At about ten o'clock, Ronnie slammed his glass on the table and dashed out of the pub. We all looked at each other, not knowing what to do. Then Reggie and I jumped up and ran after him. We found him trying to smash a shop window with his hands.

'What the hell are you doing?' we yelled.

But all Ronnie said was, 'Go away. I don't know you.'

Luckily for us, a chap we knew – Curly King – pulled up in a car. He seemed to sense a problem. He said hello to Ronnie. Ronnie recognized him and stopped bashing the window.

'Come on, Ron, take me down the billiard hall,' Curly said.

It saved the situation. Ronnie liked the idea and I went back into the pub for Mum and the old man and we all went to the billiard hall. What happened there was one of the most terrifying experiences of my life.

While the rest of us chatted amiably, Ronnie was restless, prowling up and down all the time like a caged tiger. We all tried to calm him down but it was no good: Ronnie was in a world of his own and no one, it seemed, could get in. None of us could relax. Everyone kept looking at me to do something. But every time I tried to talk to him, he kept telling me he didn't know who I was. He just kept prowling up and down . . . up and down . . . up and down . . .

It seemed to go on for ages. And then suddenly Ronnie stopped. He looked all around him, a strange look on his face, staring at us all as if trying to remember us or recognize somebody. Then he turned and walked quickly to the middle of the room where he stood deep in thought, as though he had some major decision to make and he didn't know what to do. His whole body suddenly stiffened as if someone had given him an electric shock. We all stared at him, transfixed. We'd never seen anything like it in our lives and we didn't know what to do. Gradually, Ronnie's stiff, straight body lost its tenseness. The electric shock had been switched off. Slowly, he sank to his knees as if he was praying. He stayed like that for several seconds.

We were all staring. Then I heard someone shouting, 'Charlie, for God's sake, do something!' I don't know who it was but it snapped me out of my shock. I ran over to Ronnie and put my arm round his shoulder, but he shrugged it off and pushed me away. 'Go away!' he shouted. 'Go away from me, I don't know you.'

He stayed like that for a few more seconds, then slowly got to his feet. I told Reggie we had to get him to hospital and he shouted to someone to call an ambulance. When it arrived, Ronnie refused to get in. Then the police came and we all coaxed Ronnie gently, telling him it was for the best, that he was unwell and we needed to make him better. Finally he agreed to get in.

They put Ronnie in a bed with curtains round it and then, at about midnight, a doctor told us there was nothing wrong with him.

We were shell-shocked. I told the doctor what had happened in the billiard hall.

'We're not trying to get him certified, you know,' I said. 'We think the world of him. We brought him here because there's something badly wrong.'

The doctor wouldn't have it.

'He must be developing a cunning mind,' I said. 'Because you're a doctor, he's behaving differently.'

The doctor wasn't impressed. But the situation was too critical for us to be fobbed off and I persisted. 'Ronnie doesn't even believe we're his brothers. Just stand outside that curtain and listen.'

Somewhat reluctantly, the doctor agreed. Reggie and I went in. 'How are you, Ron?' I asked.

Ronnie reacted as we expected. 'What are you two doing here?' he said. 'Get out!'

We pointed to small scars on our faces as proof of our identities but Ronnie said, 'You've had them put on. How clever. Go on, get out – you imposters!'

Ronnie's behaviour didn't please us, but it did convince the listening doctor and he apologized for doubting us. He arranged for Ronnie to be admitted to St Clement's Hospital in Mile End immediately.

For the next two weeks Ronnie was given tests and more drugs to stabilize him. The family visited him every day. He always knew Mum and half-knew the old man, but for the first week neither Reg nor I had a chance: we were still imposters. And then one day I walked in and I could tell straight away that he was all right again.

For the first time Ronnie talked about what he had been going through. It was weird: some of the time he realized the stupid things he was doing but he couldn't stop himself; most of the time he knew I was Charlie but couldn't help denying it.

The doctors told me that the terrifying experience in the billiard hall was a seizure and Ronnie could have gone one way or the other. If he had gone the wrong way he would never have come out of it; he would have gone mad. But he fought it and because his will-power was so strong he came through it.

The price he had to pay was immense. Drugs would be part of his life for ever: four different tablets a day, an injection once a month. Ronnie accepted it without complaint; he realized how unwell he was and he knew that the drugs kept away the paranoia and the eventual distrust that led to extreme violence.

The Ronnie Kray who came back into the world to join

us in the enterprises we had built in his absence not only looked different from the one who had picked up that gun two years before. His movements were more ponderous, his speech slower, his mind numbed. He wasn't the Ronnie we had known.

Things changed when Ronnie got involved in The Double R. He had always been the dominant twin and immediately took over. While he was away, Reggie had more or less had a free hand and made his own decisions, but now Ronnie insisted that everything had to be discussed. And even then he would always have to be right. They would argue, as they had always done, but if it came to the crunch, Ronnie would keep on and on until he got his own way. This had a bad effect on all our finances because it was Reggie who had the better business brain. Ronnie, as generous and kind-hearted as ever, preferred to give money away.

In those late fifties, lots of people were coming out of prison and word soon got around that Ronnie Kray was a soft touch. People I'd never seen before would come into the club and Ronnie would give them fifty quid out of the till. The next day it would be someone else. It never seemed to stop.

Reggie and I would get very uptight about it. We said we didn't mind helping people, but we had to draw the line somewhere. It didn't cut much ice with Ronnie.

'What do you want to do – show ourselves up?' he said. 'People come home expecting to be given something. Do you want us to get a bad name? Do you want people to think we're tight?'

Reggie said, 'We'd better slow down, that's all. We're overdoing it.'

Ronnie wouldn't have it. 'You may think we are, but I

don't. It's not going to change. That's how it's going to be.'

It was frustrating not being able to reason with Ronnie. I'm sure he thought there was a bottomless well of money he could dip into when he liked. And when there wasn't any there, he'd moan about it.

One day he came in for some for himself. The till was empty. 'Where's the money?' he said, all surprised.

'You've given it all away,' I told him.

'We have to do something,' he said impatiently. 'We've got to earn some money.'

'How can we?' I asked, pleased to make the point. 'You give it away as fast as we can earn it.'

But it didn't make the slightest difference. In those days, when the average weekly wage was less than £10, our combined enterprises were bringing in around £200 a week. Ronnie continued to give away twenty, thirty and fifty pounds if he felt people needed it. Children, old people, families who were skint – Ronnie would help them all. But as usual he did it all quietly, without fuss; he didn't want people to know. One day, however, his generosity was made public, much to Ronnie's embarrassment.

Every Wednesday a show was put on for old people at Oxford House in Hackney. Ronnie took great delight in arranging for boxes of apples and pears to be sent over to them. This went on for several months, then one night Ronnie delivered the boxes himself. The owner of the little theatre called out, 'I'm on the stage.' As Ronnie walked out, the man quickly pulled back the curtains, revealing scores of old ladies and gentlemen waiting for the show to start.

He pointed to Ronnie and said, 'I thought you'd like to know that this is the gentleman who sends the fruit.'

Then, to Ronnie's horror, he said, 'Let's have three cheers for Ron!'

Ronnie blushed. He couldn't wait to get off that stage.

If we had to pay a bill for, say, a hundred pounds, Reggie or I would put the money away. But if someone came in and Ronnie felt they needed the money, he'd give it to them without thinking about it. Then later, he'd start worrying about how the bill was going to be paid. If several people wanted help, Ronnie would go out of his way to help them all. Reggie was generous, too, but he was sensible; he wouldn't leave us with no money for the bills. Money meant everything to Ronnie – but it also meant nothing. If he had a million pounds, he wouldn't be happy until he'd given it all away.

His charity didn't stop at cash handouts either. If a kid came into the billiard hall looking for a job, Ronnie would take him on, helping our old man behind the bar or cleaning the tables. We had all the staff we required but Ronnie found it hard not to help someone if he felt they needed it.

With him around, business was like a benevolent fund or welfare office and one day I told Ronnie he'd missed his vocation in life: he'd have made a fantastic welfare officer. In one respect it was true: he was capable of so much patience with people. One of our customers had a sister who was very ill in a mental hospital, and Ronnie visited her a few times. He just sat talking and listening, trying to help her.

Another customer had a sister who had become a drug addict and changed from a lovely girl into an old hag. Ronnie paid doctors a lot of money to try to help her, then bought her a hairdressing salon to give her an interest. Sadly, the girl was hooked for life and became a registered addict. But she appreciated Ronnie's help and wrote to a newspaper explaining what he'd done. When

Ronnie learned that a certain bloke had ruined her life by forcing her to have drugs at a party, he smashed in the door of his home and gave him a hiding.

Ronnie had this thing about the underdog – anyone underprivileged, weak or in trouble. He loathed bullies and flamboyant, overpowering people who thought they were God's gift; and he couldn't stand blokes who took liberties, either. Once, I was with him in a crowded pub when a cocky Irishman came in and ordered drinks all round. When he was asked for the money, he said he would pay the next day because he had none on him. Ronnie was fuming and laid the big Irishman out with a right to the jaw. I picked the guy up and took him outside. When I got back, Ronnie was still seething. 'What a liberty!' he said. 'Walking in like that, then saying he'll pay when he feels like it!'

The irony is that if that arrogant Irishman had gone up to Ronnie and asked to borrow some money to buy a round, Ronnie would no doubt have given him some.

Most of us in a situation like that would have felt like saying something to put the man in his place. But Ronnie had an abnormally quick temper. If someone did something he didn't like, he would see red and lash out.

One night there were about twenty of us having a quiet drink in a pub when two guys came in and started staring at us. I asked the group if anyone knew who they were. No one did. I said that when I bought the next round I'd go over and see if they said anything. A little while later I strolled over, unaware that Ronnie had followed me. I was ordering the drinks, waiting for the two blokes to say something, when there was a scuffle and they both ended up spark out on the floor.

The guv'nor looked at me, stunned. 'I don't know if I saw that, or I didn't.'

Ronnie got the two guys to their feet and took them

outside. When he came back, he said to the guv'nor, 'I didn't want you to have any bother in your pub.'

I told Ronnie I had gone over to see what was happening, but he said he knew what they were up to, and didn't want any part of it.

Strangers who took liberties were always in danger with Ronnie. People he knew were not. He'd bawl and shout at them perhaps, but knock them up in the air? Never.

For the next six months, money continued to flow in, despite Ronnie's philanthropy, and we lived well. We didn't have a lot of staff as such, but we did gather around us a number of loyal and trusted allies who looked after us and who, in turn, expected to be looked after.

There was 'Big' Pat Connolly, a huge, happy man, who was doorman at The Double R; Alf 'Limehouse' Willey, who had a brain like a computer when it came to calculating gambling odds; Tommy Brown, a quiet, withdrawn, but immensely strong young man, nicknamed The Bear of Tottenham; Billy Donovan, one of the hardest men I'd ever met; and two lifelong close friends of the twins, Ian Barrie and George Osborne. We had premises, clients and large sums of cash to protect, and these men helped us protect them. In the East End in those days there were 'firms' and 'mobs'. The mobs consisted of villains and thieves, who specialized in robbery with violence. A firm was a group of people who ran an enterprise which dealt in cash – readies – didn't keep books or records and handled their own social security. We were not the only firm operating in Bethnal Green but we were the best organized and most successful – and, because of that, the best known.

Just as the twins had said they would not tolerate trouble in their clubs, they also made it plain they did not approve of rival spielers opening in their manor. If anyone did open one, the twins went along, said they felt it was a liberty, and asked for a percentage of the takings. It was not so much the money they wanted – they had enough interests of their own – it was the principle. They hated the idea of someone taking a liberty. Such was their reputation that they always got a share. But it wasn't always like that. Because there was rarely any trouble in Kray premises, spieler owners came to the twins asking them to be involved. It was a sensible, practical arrangement and, in most cases, they accepted the offers. But not always. Danny Green, who owned The Grange in Stoke Newington, for example, came to us, saying he was having a lot of bother with local tearaways. With tears in his eyes he begged the twins to give him protection in return for a share in his business. The twins were sorry about Danny's problems but declined his offer. Stoke Newington was outside our manor and we had enough on our own plates.

I understood the principle of discouraging a rival operation starting up in the same area, but I did not approve of the twins leaning on people. If I was around and saw or heard anything I did not like, I would say something about it and we'd have an argument. But the twins rarely listened to what I had to say, so it was really a waste of time saying anything. Ironically, they would ask my advice on many things. They would listen for five minutes, then start arguing with me. Finally I would blow up and say, 'Why ask my bloody advice when you never agree with me?' In the end, I started looking around for other interests, because they got on my nerves.

I could not be with the twins twenty-four hours a day, so I don't know everything that went on. But they only ever approached spielers for money, not shops or pubs.

People on our payroll were well paid and well looked after if they were totally loyal and honest; if there was one thing none of us – particularly Ronnie – could bear, it was dishonesty. One of our most trusted and valuable employees was Barry Clare. We were all devastated to learn that he'd gone home one night and stuck his head in the gas oven. Determined to find out why, we put the word out and soon discovered that Barry was being blackmailed.

I discovered the blackmailer by chance because, from a distance I resembled Barry and was mistaken for him in the doorway of the club. A car pulled up and a bloke in the passenger seat called out, 'Hello, Barry, got it for me?'

I sensed immediately it was the blackmailer. But I resisted the temptation to grab him by the throat. Instead, I said, 'Sorry, mate, I'm not Barry. He's round the billiard hall.'

I knew Reggie was at the hall. And as the car pulled away, I rang and told him what had happened. When the guy arrived for his 'pick-up' Reggie was waiting. The man was given such a hiding it's unlikely he ever put the squeeze on anyone again.

Reggie, like Ronnie, never forgot a favour. And someone who had been very helpful while Ronnie was staying in Finchley when he was on the trot from Long Grove, was a car dealer and gambler called Danny Shay. One day, towards the end of 1959, he came to the billiard hall and asked Reggie to help him collect a hundred-pound gambling debt. The man who owed it, he said, was a Pole called Podro, who owned a small shop in Finchley Road. He was a notorious welsher, it seemed.

The task didn't seem too difficult and Reggie said he was happy to try to persuade Mr Podro to pay up. As an afterthought, he asked George Osborne if he'd mind driving them to Podro's shop. Georgie didn't mind, and off they went.

What the three of them didn't know was that Podro, who obviously expected a visit, had told the police. Three of them were hiding in the back of the shop listening to Reggie's own brand of persuasion, and when Reggie finally hung a right-hander on Mr Podro's chin they ran out and nicked him, Shay and Georgie.

The next day the newspaper headlines screamed: 'Chicago-style gangsters' methods!' And later, at the Old Bailey, Shay got three years and Reggie and Georgie eighteen months each for demanding money with menaces.

It was all so stupid. Reggie didn't need money, he was doing someone a favour. And poor Georgie Osborne had just gone for the ride.

'Demanding money with menaces.' It was a phrase that would plague the twins for ever.

Just before Reggie was jailed, a Leyton car dealer named Johnny Hutton introduced him to Leslie Payne, a big man with a quiet chuckling laugh and great charm. Payne, a year older than me, was talented and knowledgeable and could have made a lot of money honestly, but for some reason he seemed to prefer bending the law. He and a financial wizard named Freddie Gore were operating a second-hand car racket in the East End – at the expense of the finance companies – and after Reggie went away they often turned up with ideas and propositions for us to consider. Although we did a couple of deals with them through a second-hand car business of our own, other projects rarely got beyond the discussion stage.

But then they suggested something that was right up our street.

There was a lot of talk in the early part of 1960 about the Government legalizing gambling, and Payne had been tipped off that a first-class West End club was coming on the market. We had a great opportunity to get in on the ground floor of what promised to be a bonanza.

A meeting to sort out the details of the takeover was held in a flat over the Scotch House, in Knightsbridge: it was the home of Commander Drummond, a retired naval officer with blue eyes and a small moustache. Apart from him, Ronnie and myself, there were four others present: Payne, who just sat and smiled, Gore, who scribbled figures on a piece of paper, and the major shareholders in the club, two gentlemen called Faye and Burns. Why the commander was involved I didn't know, but he did most of the talking. After a pleasant enough chat, a price was agreed, a deal struck and Ronnie and I went home to celebrate. The Kray brothers from the backstreets of Bethnal Green now had a club in Wilton Street, Belgravia, one of the wealthiest parts of London.

It was called Esmeralda's Barn. And it turned out to be a gold mine which was to open up a new life for the three of us, our mother and the old man.

The twins particularly were well suited to the West End club circuit and popular among the expensively dressed pleasure-seekers who frequented it. They loved mixing with the aristocracy, showbusiness stars and millionaire businessmen; they rarely missed out on having their photographs taken at social and theatrical gatherings. In their identical, well-cut, midnight-blue dinner jackets, they certainly looked the part. And their behaviour was always respectful and proper.

Although I was on the spot when it mattered, I preferred to keep in the background. Most of my work was done behind the scenes, keeping a close eye on day-to-day events in a business empire that was rapidly expanding. I had been granted a licence to operate a theatrical agency, which meant I booked all cabaret acts for our own clubs, and others, instead of going through other agencies.

It also meant I could spend more time at home, which was important since Dolly had made it clear that she was being neglected and was bored and frustrated at spending so much time on her own. Something happened, however, that made me wonder whether Dolly had, in fact, been neglected or bored in my long absences.

There was a big group of us in a pub called The Green Dragon. I was standing at the bar talking to a couple of friends and Dolly was sitting at a table talking to George Ince. Dolly's two brothers and the twins were also there.

Suddenly Reggie came over to me, looking tense. He told me to get Ince out of the place or there would be trouble. I was confused but I knew the look in Reggie's eyes; it wasn't time to argue.

I went over to the table and took Ince out of Dolly's earshot. I told him I didn't know what it was about, but he should make himself scarce. He did – quickly. Then I rejoined the twins, who proceeded to tell what everybody, it seemed, knew except me.

George Ince and Dolly had been having an affair for some time.

Boiling with rage, I dashed into the street looking for Ince. It was probably just as well for both of us that he was nowhere to be seen. I went back and confronted Dolly, and we agreed to discuss it when I was calmer and more rational. When we did, she denied the affair. But I was not convinced. I had to make a decision: let sleeping dogs lie, or walk out and let her get on with it. In the end I decided to stay, because Gary was at an impressionable age and I couldn't bear him to suffer the trauma of his parents splitting up.

But something in me died that night in The Green Dragon. And when just a few months later I was attracted to a young lady, I threw myself into a full-blooded affair, which, ironically, nearly destroyed the family unit I so wanted to save.

The young woman was beautiful, bubbly and also blonde. Her name was Barbara Windsor and she was an actress.

Our relationship started when she was appearing in the hit show *Fings Ain't Wot They Used To be* in the West End. An actor friend of mine, George Sewell, was in the show too, and arranged front-row seats for myself and Dolly's brother Ray.

I had met Barbara only once before, with other people, but as the cast took their bows at the end of the performance she kept motioning to me to go backstage for a drink. The audience must have wondered who I was! Ray and I enjoyed a drink with the whole cast, then I asked Barbara to come to a club with me on her own. She agreed, and afterwards I took her home to Harringay, where she lived with her parents. Apart from being a beautiful young woman, with a sexy, shapely body, Barbara was a joy to be with – everything, in fact, that Dolly was not. We agreed to see each other the next night and, making my way home to Wapping, savouring the sweetness of her good-night kiss, I could hardly wait.

Being unfaithful to Dolly did not bother me unduly and I met Barbara as often as I could. I saw several sides of her, but one that surprised me was her kindness and generosity. As we all know, showbusiness people are not known for putting their hands in their pockets, but Barbara found it hard to say no if someone said they were in trouble. She was becoming quite a big name then and people – mostly men – were always tapping her for a few quid. I told her she was too kind for her own good and people were taking advantage. Unless she toughened up, I said, she would never have any money for herself when she needed it. But Barbara said she could not help herself, and in a way I loved her all the more for that.

She worked hard and played hard, and was always lively and happy. Most of the time we were together there was a lot of laughter – something there wasn't at my home.

Once, early in our relationship, Barbara and I were having a drink in a Wardour Street club with some of the cast of *Fings* when a row broke out and someone went tumbling down the stairs. Barbara and the others, worried about their reputations, wanted to get out quickly, but one of the guys in the fight warned everyone to stay where they were: nobody, he said, was leaving the club that night; anyone who tried to would be in trouble. That suited us all fine: we ordered more drinks and carried on enjoying ourselves.

After an hour or so, however, the cast started getting worried, so I decided to take matters into my own hands. I went to the top of the stairs and shouted out that whoever was barricading us in had better get out of the way because we were all coming down. With a friend called Harry, I bounded down the stairs and charged down the door leading to the reception foyer. It opened very easily . . . because it wasn't locked! No one was there. Our captors had probably left hours before. We never did find out what the row was about, but Barbara found it very amusing that we'd waited all that time and I'd charged down that door for nothing.

In her early twenties, Barbara had one of those eye-catching figures that was quite dangerous: how many young men, I wonder, walked into lamp-posts or trees because their heads had been turned by that pert little bottom, tiny waist and big boobs? Even today, Barbara and I still laugh at the time a railway porter at Eastbourne thought he was seeing things when the famous Windsor bustline turned up at his station at the unlikely hour of six in the morning. Barbara and I had been in the Astor Club. Remembering that I had an appointment in Eastbourne later that day, I asked Barbara if she fancied riding down there with me. She phoned her mum to tell her where she was going and we got a train. At the other end, Barbara was clip-clopping along the platform in monstrously high-heeled boots, short skirt and clinging white jumper when the porter, eyes out on stalks, mouth open, stumbled over his trolley. Barbara, used to such attention, just giggled. ''Ere Charlie, look, that bloke's fallen off his barrer!'

The laughing could not last, of course. All the time I was married, I could not devote as much time to Barbara as I wanted. And although she never put any pressure on me, I knew I had to decide whether to leave home for her. If it had been a straight choice between Dolly and Barbara I would have walked out of my Wapping flat without a second thought, but Gary was still my main consideration. I would not do anything to hurt him.

It was a hard decision to make because I loved Barbara and really cared for her. I agonized over it for months, but in the end I said we had to finish because I couldn't bear to put Gary through all the upset of a divorce. I told Barbara she needed a fella who could take care of her, and I was so happy when she told me some time later that she had met someone she loved and was getting married. His name, she said, was Ronnie Knight, and she was sure she was making the right decision.

Chapter Six

Mum, as always, was the centre of our lives. And when Esmeralda's Barn started lining our pockets, the twins and I were keen to give her everything she had ever wanted. She wanted very little, however; she certainly didn't want to leave Vallance Road for a bigger house in a posher street. But she and the old man did not say no to holidays. They had never been further than Southend in Essex, and now there was some money around they seized the chance to be more adventurous. Mum had had nothing for herself all her life and I was thrilled to be able to give her a taste of the 'jet-set' life. We went to Tangier, Italy, the South of France, and even lashed out on a wonderfully expensive cruise. It was lovely to see someone who had been nowhere suddenly going everywhere, and enjoying every sun-soaked minute.

Exotic places abroad were all very well for a couple of times a year. But we wanted to enjoy Steeple Bay, a nice little spot I had discovered near Burnham-on-Crouch, Essex, so I bought a caravan and a little motor cruiser and I'd pop down there with Mum and the old man every weekend. They were blissfully happy times. The twins were very funny about me going away at weekends. They would say: 'Going away *again*! Leaving us to do all the work!' We'd argue every weekend. They would call me a playboy and it really got on my nerves. Then they would suddenly turn up in Steeple Bay with their mates. They always had loads of people with them; they attracted people all the time.

Mum lapped up the good life at home, too. Two good

friends of ours, Alex Steene and his wife, Anna, made a point of taking Mum to the Royal Command Performance at the London Palladium every year, followed by a slap-up meal in a top restaurant. Mum always looked forward to that.

It was all a dramatic change from the modest lifestyle Mum had previously enjoyed. But the money that was suddenly available did not change her one bit: although she now mixed with dukes and duchesses, lords and ladies, she was always herself. She wasn't one for intellectual conversation, but what she had to say was said with a simple honesty that endeared her to everyone she met. The twins and I were proud of her.

Ronnie and Reggie never put on airs and graces either. Far from being ashamed of where they came from they were proud, and took a delight in taking friends and business acquaintances home to meet Mum over a cup of tea in the upstairs sitting room.

I was sitting in that room talking to Ronnie one day when the phone rang: it was Lord Effingham, whom we paid to sit on the board of The Barn for prestige. When Ronnie put the phone down he said the friendly peer had told him he needed two hundred pounds immediately; if he couldn't get it, he was going to kill himself. When Ronnie told me he was arranging for someone to deliver the money within an hour I went spare. I said it was an obvious ploy to get money, and Ronnie was mad if he fell for it. But he would have none of it; he said he wouldn't be able to live with himself if something happened to Effingham. I suppose I should not have been surprised. Nothing had changed; Ronnie had been a soft touch when he didn't have much money and now that he had it coming out of his ears he was even more charitable. I'm sure that the word went round London that if you were plausible you could get anything out of Ronnie Kray.

Lucien Freud, a heavy gambler, owed the club £1,400 and I told Ronnie that someone should speak to him about it. A few days later he came up to me and said triumphantly, 'It's all sorted out.'

Relieved, I asked, 'He's going to pay up?'

'No,' Ronnie replied. 'I told him to forget it.'

'What?'

'I said we wanted to see him back in the club,' said Ronnie casually. 'It's better for us to have his custom.'

I tried telling him he had made a bad mistake but Ronnie just said, 'Don't go on about it. I've done it now.'

My dismay at his misguided generosity deepened a few days later when I learned that Freud had offered a very valuable painting as collateral for his debt and Ronnie had turned it down.

One of our customers was Pauline Wallace, a lovely, well-dressed, well-spoken Irish lady. What she didn't know about gambling was not worth knowing, so when she hit hard times we gave her a job supervising the croupiers. A month or so later she told Ronnie she was being evicted from her Knightsbridge flat unless she paid £800 rent arrears. Quick as you like, Ronnie took the cash from the club coffers and gave it to her. When I had a go at him he said, 'It's all right. I can use the flat whenever I like.'

When Pauline got on her feet she never forgot what we had done for her. She would visit Mum in Vallance Road, always with some beautiful flowers. Then one day she told the twins she wanted to give them some money every week to repay them for helping her when she needed it most. The twins refused, so Pauline said she would give it to Mum. They told her it was not necessary, but she insisted. Every week Billy Exley went to Knightsbridge and collected some cash. It was something Pauline wanted to do; she was that kind of woman.

A couple of years later she married a multi-millionaire in Texas and the last I heard of her she was running all the greyhound racing in Miami.

Ronnie did not spend all his time playing the nice guy, however. If someone stepped out of line he'd be swift to crack down on them. Lord Effingham was given a fee, plus all he wanted to eat and drink, but that was not enough for him. One of our senior employees complained that the noble lord was interfering in the running of the club, so Ronnie asked to see him.

'Yes, Ronald?' Effingham said.

'Mowbray,' Ronnie said quietly, using the peer's Christian name. 'You're getting above yourself. You're getting paid for nothing, so you can shut your mouth or leave.'

Effingham knew what side his bread was buttered. 'You're so right, Ronald,' he said. 'I do apologize.'

The people who flocked to The Barn in 1960 seemingly had money to burn; it would shake me when I watched thousands of pounds being risked on the turn of a card at the chemin de fer tables.

Neither the twins nor I were gamblers, but I do remember one night I tried my hand at chemmy and won £350. Well pleased, I told Reggie, who immediately thought he'd have a go. I saw him about two hours later and he was falling about laughing.

'How much did you win?' I asked.

'Nothing,' said Reggie, highly amused. 'I did £750 in an hour.'

Reggie was not as careless with money as Ronnie, but when he had it he was not afraid to spend it.

It was during the early days of The Barn that Reggie developed an outside interest that in time was to change his personality and, eventually, his life.

She was a sixteen-year-old girl and her name was Frances Shea. Like us, she was from the East End and

83

Reggie had watched her grow from a child to a beautiful young woman. When he fell in love with her it was with the same intensity, commitment and passion he showed in everything he did. Although eleven years younger, she was everything he wanted in a woman; it was as if even then he knew that this was the girl he wanted to marry, and he courted her in the old-fashioned sense, with roses and chocolates, the deepest respect and impeccable manners. Reggie put Frances Shea on a pedestal that would eventually destroy him.

Early in 1961 we got our first warning that the police were not impressed with the Kray success story and that someone somewhere had decided a couple of East End tearaways and their elder brother had no right making a few bob and mixing with wealthy folk far above their station.

Ronnie and I were at Vallance Road when Big Pat Connolly's wife phoned from a call box saying Pat had been taken to hospital. A friend of ours, Jimmy Kensit, ran us to the Connolly home to see if there was anything we could do. When we arrived, we discovered Pat had suspected polio: since we had all been in recent contact with him my first thought was to tell Dolly and Gary to go to the hospital for an anti-polio injection. I made a call from a kiosk in Queensbridge Road, then we all headed back to Mum's house where we could phone everyone who had been in contact with Pat.

We did not get there until several hours later – after a spell in Dalston police station.

Jimmy Kensit had decided to call in for something at his flat in Pritchards Road, in Haggerston. Ronnie and I were sitting in Jimmy's banger when a squad car roared up. We thought there must have been some big robbery – a murder perhaps – but in fact we were the lucky ones to be under investigation. A detective constable called Bartlett started asking Ronnie and me who we were, where we were going, etc, while two uniformed constables inspected Jimmy's car.

Fortunately, just as Bartlett was preparing to take us to Dalston nick for further questioning, a friend of ours named Billy Gripp walked by. Billy, who trained for judo at the gym above The Double R, was a respected citizen of Bethnal Green and I admitted to him I was worried about a frame-up: would he mind searching Ronnie, Jimmy and myself, and the car, to satisfy the police and a gathering crowd that we didn't have anything we should not have? Bartlett objected, but Billy went ahead anyway. Then we were taken to the police station. While Bartlett strutted around, warning us that we'd be inside soon, our homes were searched – without warrants – and later we were charged with . . . loitering with intent to commit a felony!

Poor Pat Connolly had to take a back seat for a while, as did all the people we were keen to warn to have anti-polio jabs.

The case actually went to court but, happily, did not last too long. Bartlett told the Marylebone magistrate under oath that Ronnie and I had been seen in Queensbridge Road trying the door handles of parked cars, and that we fled after Kensit hooted his horn to warn us we were being watched.

Jimmy's car horn was found to be out of action, and we proved we were somewhere else at the time of the alleged offences. But we were far from happy walking out of Marylebone Court that day. It was obvious we were marked men.

Bartlett – a pervert later convicted of molesting young girls – was merely a pawn in a game controlled by far more senior and influential officers.

A few days later I arrived at Vallance Road to find Mum comforting Frances, who was crying: some policeman had turned up and arrested Reggie for breaking and entering an East End house. Seething, I raced round to Bethnal Green nick and told them I knew it was a 'get up'; that they were framing Reggie for something he didn't do.

The police said they had a witness – a Jewish woman in her seventies called Lilia Hertzberg who claimed to have seen Reggie and another man running out of her husband's Stepney home with jewellery and cash valued at £500.

The case was a laugh throughout the East End, for most people knew that Reggie would rather give an old couple £500 than steal it from them. But Reggie was still sent for trial at Inner London Sessions. We were not sure if there had actually been a robbery or if Mrs Hertzberg was being paid by the police to invent one. But we knew she had not seen Reggie so we offered her £500 to encourage her to tell the truth in court. Since she and her husband were due to leave to begin a new life in Australia shortly, they both jumped at the idea.

It was decided that on the day of the hearing someone would go to the old man's house with the £500. As soon as Reggie was released, the husband would receive a phone call from the court and the money would be handed over.

That's exactly what happened – except that the old man never got the £500. When the phone call came through and he asked for it, our friend said, 'You've got to be joking. You're lucky you're not younger – I'd knock you up in the air for what you've tried to do.'

Since we had discovered he was a paid police informer, none of us had any qualms about not giving him the £500.

As for Reggie, he was awarded costs against the police

– satisfying in a way, but hardly compensation for the seven weeks he had been held in custody.

Later, Reggie admitted to me that he'd panicked when the police arrived at Vallance Road. I was amazed because Reggie had never been intimidated by the law. But it was all to do with Frances. Reggie knew the robbery allegation was a joke and he felt they might go the whole hog and claim the woman had been assaulted. The thought of Frances thinking for a second that he had touched another woman sent him into a cold sweat; and when the police said it was only robbery he was relieved, and went quickly and quietly – even though he hadn't been anywhere near the scene of the alleged crime.

The warnings were there for the future: the police had played two tough games against the Krays and lost badly each time. But there was bound to be another time. We had bought cars, clothes, jewellery, exotic holidays, and other luxuries that make life sweeter. But we had not bought any policemen.

When the police moved in and closed The Double R, the twins got the hump. Why did the Old Bill have it in for them? they wanted to know. One minute they were millionaires, demanding with menaces all over London, the next they – and I – were supposed to be pilfering from cars. Now a harmless club was shut down. It did not make sense.

Around this time Billy Hill gave the twins some advice, which he urged them to take and never forget. Over drinks at his sumptuous flat in Moscow Road, Bayswater, the notorious gangland figure of the fifties told Ronnie and Reggie that they were fortunate in having a brother who was straight, who had no criminal convictions and was not involved in villainy of any kind. It was vital to

87

keep it that way, he said, because I would always be an ally; an important weapon they could use to set legal machinery in motion if things went badly with the law. 'Never involve Charlie in anything crooked,' he said.

And he begged them to remember that advice.

Billy's remarks gave the twins an idea. Since I was trusted one hundred per cent by the Old Bill, could I not have a word with someone to find out just why they appeared to be marked men. I said I'd speak to someone in the know, which is how I came to be talking to two plain-clothes coppers in an out-of-the-way pub in Walworth, South London.

The men arrived with a load of papers. And what they contained blew my mind. To me, the twins were just two ordinary cockneys from the back streets of Bethnal Green: tough, certainly, but likeable and respectful unless their feathers were ruffled by idiots. But to Scotland Yard, it seemed, the twins were a highly important duo, worth watching closely. I was shown telexes to Scotland Yard from forces in other countries, giving details of where the twins had gone and who they had met. There was a lot of stuff on Tangier and Ronnie's meetings with Billy Hill, who had a house there.

I told the two coppers that I couldn't dispute that the twins had had a few rows. But they were not robbing people; they were just club owners who wanted to make a few bob. Why, I asked, was the Yard going to such lengths to find out what they were up to?

The coppers told me that, quite simply, the twins had become too powerful. They may have started out as two ambitious, but insignificant, East Enders of modest intelligence, but now they were powerful; too powerful. They had money, and friends in high places with a lot of influence. The mixture was too dangerous.

I said I couldn't understand it. How could the twins be

a danger? All they wanted to do was to run a few clubs, have no money worries and be able to count the rich and famous – particularly sporting and showbusiness celebrities – among their friends.

Top political figures, it seemed, believed the twins could get 1,000 men behind them from all over the country, with a few phone calls.

The twins knew a lot of people, I agreed. But if they could get 1,000 people, what would they want them for? What would they all do?

The coppers didn't have an answer to that. They just said that the people who ran the country considered them too powerful and were thinking of ways to control them. But I could be sure of one thing, they told me, and the twins ought to be aware of it: they would not be allowed, under any circumstances, to become more powerful.

I paid the coppers the agreed £100 for their information and went home, my head swimming with the implications of what I had been told.

Surprisingly, the twins were not at all bothered. Ronnie, particularly, thought it a big joke.

'What do they think we're going to do?' he quipped. 'Take over the bleeding country?'

Chapter Seven

With Esmeralda's – and other projects dreamed up by Leslie Payne – bringing in hundreds every week, it wasn't long before we decided to open another club in the East End to replace the much-missed Double R. We called it The Kentucky and it was packed every night after it opened early in 1962.

I must admit the way the twins chucked money around worried me and, since the Betting and Gaming Act had made gambling legal, I suggested investing some of our profits in betting shops, which were springing up all over the country. But Ronnie and Reggie did not fancy the idea.

What we did agree on, however, was using some of our money and growing business and showbusiness contacts for charity work. The three of us had always been eager to help old people and children and now we took huge pleasure in organizing fund-raising activities for Mile End Hospital, the Queen Elizabeth Hospital for children, the Repton Boys' Club and various other organizations.

One of Reggie's promotions at the York Hall in Bethnal Green was unique. He matched Bobby Ramsey – who had been responsible for the ill-fated bayonet attack in 1956 – as a properly gloved boxer against a judo and karate expert called Ray Levacq. Although the 'anything-goes' bout lasted only a few minutes – Ramsey winning by a second-round knockout – the star-studded audience loved it, and local charities benefited by several hundred pounds.

The Kentucky had a colourful, if short, life. A number

of international stars – including Billy 'That Ol' Black Magic' Daniels – came there for a few drinks after their shows and the club even provided the setting for a film, *Sparrows Can't Sing*. The mayor of Bethnal Green, Mr Hare, asked if we could help him by selling tickets for the charity première at the Empire Cinema opposite The Kentucky. We bought £500 worth – and sold the lot. Later, people would say this was 'demanding', but it wasn't. East Enders were keen to support charities, always had been. And anyway, people liked a good night out. After the première we threw a party for the whole cast that was talked about for months. Throughout 1962 and early 1963 the East End in general, and The Kentucky in particular, was the place to be.

You could never be quite sure what was going to happen. One night, for instance, a midget singer called Little Hank took the stage for a cabaret spot when Ronnie suddenly emerged from the wings, holding a donkey on a leash. Little Hank – no doubt as surprised as the rest of us – gravely climbed on it and sang his opening number as Ronnie stood alongside with a straight face. After Hank's performance, Ronnie led the donkey down to the bar and it waited next to him patiently while he had a few drinks. Later he gave the donkey to a club member for one of his children.

At around three in the morning, Ronnie was woken up by a knock at the door in Vallance Road. The recipient of Ronnie's thoughtful gift was extremely grateful, but wanted to know what to do to stop the blessed animal's deafening hee-haws, which were keeping everyone awake.

'Put its bloody head in a sack,' Ronnie offered, and went back to bed.

Charitable Ronnie even gave some local buskers a chance to take the Kentucky stage. We were walking along Bethnal Green Road one day when Ronnie pointed at four or five blokes playing trumpets and various other instruments on the pavement.

'They're terrific,' said Ronnie. 'I always give 'em a few quid.'

I nodded. A few quid probably meant ten.

'Oh, by the way,' he added, 'I've told a couple of them to come to the club tonight and play us a tune. I said we'd give 'em a few quid.'

'Do me a favour, Ron,' I said. 'They're amateurs.'

'They're very good, let me tell you,' Ronnie said indignantly.

'You can't have them in the club,' I told him.

But, of course, he did. They played a tune and Ronnie paid them. That's how he was.

Both the twins had a lot of will-power, but Ronnie's was phenomenal. He had a sort of obsession about it: if you really wanted to do something, he'd say, nothing should be able to stop you.

One night in The Kentucky, Ronnie was at the bar, having a heated discussion about will-power with a much younger guy.

'I'll prove you can do anything you want,' Ronnie was saying. And he took a knife out of his pocket and plunged it into his left hand. Blood spurted everywhere. Reggie and I looked at each other, not believing what we had seen. We ran behind the bar and got a towel and wrapped it round Ronnie's hand, which seemed nearly cut in half.

'What were you doing?' Reggie yelled. 'Are you mad?'

Ronnie just said he was trying to prove a point.

'Fantastic!' I said. 'You're so bright.'

We took him to The London Hospital at Whitechapel and a doctor told him he had come within a fraction of an inch of losing the use of the hand.

Ronnie said he had put his hand through a window, but

the doctor did not believe him. When we got home, Mum broke her heart. She kept asking Ronnie why he had done it, but all he would say was, 'To prove a point.'

When I told him I thought he was barmy trying to prove a point to some idiot, Ronnie said, 'Shut your mouth. It's done now. It's finished.'

You could never tell Ronnie anything.

Both he and Reggie could not bear anyone who took liberties, particularly where women were involved. One afternoon, some girls from a dress-making factory hired The Kentucky for a firm's party. The twins and I greeted them, then left them to enjoy themselves. Later we learned that two brothers named Jordan had gone to the club and made themselves busy with the girls, grabbing them and generally trying it on. The bloke in charge of the club had not tried to stop the brothers because he feared they would smash the place up.

We hit the roof. I was happy to find the brothers and warn them verbally but the twins didn't think that was enough. The next morning Ronnie got up at five o'clock to go to Smithfield market where one of the brothers worked; he told Reggie and me to go to a local glass factory to find the other one.

When we got there, Reggie told me to leave everything to him because two on to one wasn't fair. One massive punch to the jaw did it: Jack the Lad Jordan didn't know what hit him. But, as usual, Ronnie was not able to throw just one and walk away. Apparently, he charged around Smithfield and when he found his Jordan, knocked him all over the place, leaving him in a right mess. The brothers never came into The Kentucky again.

Sadly, it was only a few months later that no one came to the club at all. Mysteriously, our request to have our licence renewed was turned down by the local justices. The club had been run properly, with no complaints from anyone, and applications for extensions had always been granted. But our renewal application was thrown out anyway. The local justices were not obliged to say why, and they didn't.

It did not need an Einstein to work out the reason. Because we refused to give the police back-handers to leave us alone we were still marked men. The daft charges of fiddling with car doors and robbing defenceless old-age pensioners had blown up in the police faces, so other tactics had to be used. They had easily closed The Double R without good reason, and they did the same with The Kentucky.

The closure had a bad effect on all of us, but particularly Ronnie. He hated the police aggravation and the violence. He would often say to Mum, 'I'm going to move. I can't stand it any more.' He wanted to get away from an area that bred violence and people who revelled in it. Ronnie, of course, was violent himself. But afterwards he would hate what he had done. I remember once he got extremely depressed and said, 'That's it. I've had enough.'

Leslie Payne had come running to the twins asking for help because Bobby Ramsey had taken a pop at him. Ronnie and Reggie were going to see Ramsey at a garage in Stratford and they asked me to go with them; why, I can't remember.

Ramsey came out into the courtyard. Ronnie told him not to take liberties with Payne, then laid him out with a right to the jaw. As Ramsey went to get up, Ronnie picked up a shovel and raised it menacingly. Reggie and I were convinced he was going to kill Ramsey before our eyes, but he calmed down and later went into the office to apologize. But he told Ramsey he had been wrong to hit Payne.

In the car going home, Ronnie was extremely

depressed. 'I'm sick of all this,' he said. 'I had to go and hit Ramsey on the chin because of Payne. I'm sick of the whole life. I want to get out. I've had enough.'

When he got like this he would go to Turkey or some other sunny place to get away from it all. But he badly wanted to move away for good.

Eventually he was to buy a place in that part of England he had loved so much as a war-time child. But by then it was too late.

We were sorry to see The Kentucky go: it was well liked and well used by respectable local people, and enhanced the area. But if the police thought the closure would put the Kray brothers out of business they couldn't have been more wrong. Esmeralda's Barn, which now had a basement disco, had enabled us to buy into other, smaller West End clubs. The twins also bought a small hotel, The Glenrae, in Seven Sisters Road, North London. And Leslie Payne, who was buying a controlling interest in The Cambridge Rooms on the Kingston bypass, was about to launch a legitimate company, The Carston Group, with a posh Mayfair office.

The police may have hit our East End connection. But up West, the money was rolling in.

To three East End blokes in the nightclub business, Leslie Payne's scheme sounded senseless. He had returned from the Eastern Nigeria city of Enugu and partly committed us to building a new township in the bush. It was a project more suited to merchant bank investment, but the more Payne explained the financial possibilities the more excited we all got. Ronnie and Reggie flew to Enugu with Payne and Gore to see the development site and when they returned plans were made to approach wealthy and influential people for investment. One of these gentlemen was Lord Boothby; another was Hew McCowan, son of a rich Scottish baronet and landowner.

What we did not know at the time was that Ernest Shinwell, son of the late, much-respected Labour MP, had hawked the proposition round for a long time without finding any takers. He must have gone to Payne as a last resort. Blissfully unaware of this, we happily poured money from our various London enterprises into the Great African Safari – GAS for short – confident that Payne knew what he was doing. As 1964 wore on, however, we became worried: not only was more and more money being swallowed up by GAS, we also got word that the police were taking an even closer interest in our activities. So it was with some relief that we greeted Payne's assurances in October that it was pay-off time and we would soon all be rolling in money again. Four of us – Payne, Gore, a well-connected Canadian called Gordon Anderson and myself – flew to Enugu full of hope.

It took me just three days to sense that all was not well.

Payne, as usual, strutted around like a Great White Chief – the faithful Gore forever in his wake – but I could not fail to notice he was always avoiding a native building contractor who, I knew, had paid us a £5,000 introductory fee months before. The man wanted to get on with the building work and was always in the foyer of the Presidential Hotel looking for Payne who, in turn, was forever dodging him. I talked to Payne about it but he told me not to worry.

Payne gave the impression he knew what he was doing. But he didn't. That contractor got fed up and opted out of the scheme. He managed to track Payne down and demanded his £5,000 back. After a blazing row in which Payne said he didn't have the money, the man went to the

96

police. Payne and Gore were arrested and thrown into jail.

Overnight the warm, friendly atmosphere became cold and frosty: no more smiles, polite bows and handshakes from Government officials; no more smart cars with motorcycle escorts at our disposal.

Payne was still playing the Great White Chief in his prison cell, vehemently insisting that he and Gore would join us at the airport as soon as he'd put the local police chief in his place. When they didn't show up, I told Anderson to go on to Lagos while I dealt with the matter. The only way to sort it out was to pay back the £5,000, so I rang the twins and told them to wire the money at once. I sat by the phone for the next twenty-four hours until I had absolute confirmation that the cash was on its way. Then a solicitor I'd met on previous visits found a judge who would sign the necessary bail forms if I arranged for £5,000 to be paid.

The journey to that judge was a nightmare. The solicitor and another black guy drove me off into the jungle, along a narrow road that looked as if it didn't lead anywhere. The solicitor assured me we were going to the judge's house but the way Payne had behaved made me fear for my life. As we drove deeper into the jungle I had visions of being bumped off and dumped – just another mysterious disappearance. But after the longest fifteen minutes of my life, the jungle opened up and there was the judge's bungalow, set in beautiful gardens. I showed the relevant documents, signed some forms, tingling with relief, then went back to get Payne and Gore out of the nick.

They were filthy, thirsty, hungry and exhausted. Gore was demoralized; Payne on the brink of a breakdown. I didn't give either of them any time to say much: I spelled out the seriousness of our predicament and told them we

97

were leaving – right then. It was not until the plane had left the runway at Lagos Airport that I was able to relax for the first time in three days.

The GAS had blown up in our faces and, once back in England, the twins and I gave Leslie Payne the elbow.

Towards the end of the Nigerian affair, the Boothby Photograph 'Scandal' hit the headlines. What a storm in a teacup that was! The whole nation, it seemed, was led to believe that Ronnie and the charming, multi-talented peer were having a homosexual affair. But nothing was further from the truth.

Ronnie went to Lord Boothby's home in Eaton Square just twice – on business. Boothby seemed keen to invest some money in the Nigerian project, but ultimately wrote to Ronnie saying he did not have the time to devote to it. That's where the matter should have ended. But Ronnie's passion for having his photograph taken with famous people set off a dramatic chain of events that ended with Boothby being paid £40,000 libel damages by the *Sunday Mirror*.

The photograph in question – one of twenty or so taken during Ronnie's second visit to Boothby's flat – was an innocuous one, showing the two men sitting side by side on a settee. They were both dressed in suits and, since they had been discussing a multi-million pound business proposition, they looked fairly serious. Keen to make a few bob, the photographer showed a print to the *Sunday Mirror* and on 12 July the paper ran a sensational front-page story – under the headline PEER AND A GANG-STER: YARD PROBE – alleging 'a homosexual relationship between a prominent peer and a leading thug in the London underworld'.

The story did not name Boothby or Ronnie, but claimed that a peer and a thug had attended Mayfair parties, that the peer and prominent public men had indulged in questionable activities during weekends in Brighton, that the peer was involved in relationships with clergymen, and that people who could give evidence on these matters had been threatened.

Not surprisingly, the *Sunday Mirror* story – based on little fact – blew up into a major scandal. The questions on the lips of the nation, it seemed, were: Who is the peer? And who is the gangster?

Well, the satirical magazine *Private Eye* did its best to put people out of their misery by naming Ronnie as the thug. And then Boothby himself brought the whole thing into the open in a frank letter to *The Times*, in which he referred to the *Sunday Mirror* story as 'a tissue of atrocious lies'.

On 4 August, both Ronnie and Boothby agreed for The Photograph to appear in the *Daily Express*, and the next day the International Publishing Corporation, which owned the *Sunday Mirror*, paid Boothby £40,000 compensation for the paper's unfounded and libellous story. IPC chairman, Cecil King, also made an unqualified apology. Ronnie was given no cash compensation but on 19 and 20 September the *Daily Mirror* and *Sunday Mirror* did allow four column inches to apologize to him.

To celebrate the end of the affair, Ronnie threw a party at a Bethnal Green pub. Boothby didn't come; nor did Reginald Payne, who was fired as editor of the *Sunday Mirror* on 14 August. But many celebrities *were* there. And among those who showed no fear at being photographed with the so-called thug, Ronnie Kray, was someone who was to become a dear, dear friend: Judy Garland, the Hollywood moviestar.

The spider spinning a web to trap the twins made his first move in January 1965. Detective Inspector Leonard Read

– known as 'Nipper' in criminal circles – walked into the basement bar of the Glenrae Hotel and charged Ronnie and Reggie with demanding money with menaces from a Soho club owner. They were said to have threatened Hew Cargill McCowan with violence unless he gave them a percentage of the takings of the Hideaway Club in Gerrard Street. When McCowan refused the twins' offer, the prosecution alleged, a drunken writer called Teddy Smith smashed some bottles and glasses at the club, causing twenty pounds' worth of damage.

The evidence was wafer-thin and, thankfully, Ronnie and Reggie were acquitted. But they were subjected to two Old Bailey trials and three months on remand in Brixton before being cleared. Police objected to bail four times because they feared Ronnie and Reggie would not turn up to stand trial. But the twins offered to give up their passports, report to the police twice a day and undertake not to interfere with witnesses – all this in addition to sureties of a staggering £18,000. The court's refusal to allow bail caused widespread controversy and Lord Boothby was so incensed he asked the Government in the House of Lords whether 'it is their intention to imprison the Kray brothers indefinitely without trial'.

The trial took place at the Old Bailey in March 1965, but after a nine-day hearing the jury failed to agree. The retrial started on 30 March, and I was spending money and time trying to find witnesses who could help the twins. I went to the solicitors' at 9 A.M. every morning to tell them what I was doing. I had a private detective running around all over the place. And I had a tape on my phone, to cover every call.

The police had the hump with me for trying to help the twins and tried to fit me up one night.

I arrived home and Dolly told me a man had just phoned from Finchley saying he had some information that would interest me; he was going to ring back. About fifteen minutes later, the phone went. The guy was at Aldgate; could I meet him there? And would I be in my white Mini? I smelled a rat. How did he know what car I drove? And if he had rung from Finchley the first time, how had he got to Aldgate in fifteen minutes? I pulled him on this and he gave me some story, but I wasn't fooled. I told him I knew he was a copper and if he thought he was going to fit me up he had another thought coming. Both conversations had been taped, I said, then I put the phone down. I did not keep the appointment. And I never heard from the guy again.

I was spending so much time on the case – chasing witnesses, helping the private detective or attending court – that I had no time for my work as a theatrical agent. No work meant no bookings. And no bookings meant no money. But money was what was needed if the twins were to get off; for lawyers want paying, no matter which way the verdict goes.

I had been dipping into my savings and was absolutely boracic when I got a call from the solicitor representing the twins. The legal costs had been paid up front, but they had run out, the solicitor said. He wanted £1,500 for the next day's hearing, or he and the barrister were pulling out of the case.

I was owed money that would have more than covered the required amount, but I would not get it until the end of the week. I needed the £1,500 urgently and racked my brains for someone who had that sort of money at the drop of a hat.

I could think of only one person: Lord Boothby.

I rang his Eaton Square house and Boothby's charming butler arranged for me to see the noble lord that afternoon. Boothby was very pleasant: he offered me a drink and allowed me to say my piece. I explained why I needed the money so quickly and stressed that I wasn't broke, just in a tight financial corner.

I honestly felt Boothby would agree to a loan: he'd just been awarded £40,000, and he knew the 'menaces' charge against the twins was nonsense. So I was shell-shocked when he said, 'I'm sorry, my dear boy. The forty thousand's all gone. I owed so much.'

I was choked. I didn't know what to say; there wasn't anything I could say. I'd blown out. I needed to get out of there quickly and try someone else, or else the twins would find themselves with no legal brief the next day – which would almost certainly mean a verdict of guilty and a prison sentence.

I left Eaton Square a very worried man, and not a little disappointed in Lord Boothby who, I'm sure, could have found £1,500 if he had really wanted to.

Of course, I got the money in the end; you always find a way when it's critical, don't you? And then I got on with the business of tracking down witnesses willing to tell the truth and get the case against the twins kicked out once and for all.

They *did* get off. But, sadly, I wasn't there to hear the Not Guilty verdicts.

On the sixth day of the retrial I went to see a possible witness instead of going to the solicitor's office first. When I finally turned up an hour or so later to tell them I'd found someone willing to give evidence, one of the clerks said, 'That was good, wasn't it, Charlie?' I didn't know what he meant. A minute later, in an upstairs office, a solicitor said, 'Congratulations.'

'What for?' I asked.

'Your case,' he said. 'It was thrown out this morning. Your brothers have been cleared.'

I was pleased, of course. But also cheesed off. It was the first day of the case I hadn't been in court, and I'd missed the best moment. By the time I got home to Vallance Road, the Fleet Street hounds were outside the house and the twins were having cups of tea – free men for the first time since their arrest three months to the day before.

That homecoming made even bigger headlines than the trial itself and when all the reporters and photographers and well-wishers had left Vallance Road, I took the twins in the front room and gave them some strong advice that, had they heeded it, could have changed the tragic course their lives were to take. They had proved their point, I said. Once again, the police had tried to put them away on trumped-up charges – and failed. But Nipper Read and his men would not give up; if anything, they would take the latest setback to heart and try even harder next time. Whatever the twins had in mind, I said, they should stop and think and be very careful. If they stopped now we could go on for ever and be looked on as respectable businessmen; we could have everything we ever wanted, with no villainy, no worries, no police harassment. Having won a few battles, we could go on and win the war.

Ronnie and Reggie nodded. What I said was right, they agreed. They had indeed proved their point to the police. It was time to quieten down and become respectable businessmen. Reggie even admitted that he and Frances were getting married.

But already it was too late. Reggie's marriage was tragically doomed. And in Westminster's corridors of power, one of the top men in the country was preparing a Top Secret document that was to lure the twins into the spider's web and trap them for ever.

Chapter Eight

Reggie could have married Judy Garland. She truly loved him, fawned all over him and was always trying to persuade him to stay at her house in Hawaii. But Reggie only had eyes for Frances Shea. She was all he had ever wanted in his life and could ever hope to want: the beginning and the end of everything. Reggie was very old-fashioned in his attitude to women and he courted Frances in an old-fashioned way. He took her to the top clubs and restaurants, always making sure she had the best of everything, but he liked the less flamboyant touches, too. If they were walking down a street together, Reggie would think nothing of stopping at a florist's to buy her a bunch of roses. It was a beautiful love affair, and the flower of their love grew and grew until it blossomed into marriage on 19 April 1965.

The wedding took place at St James the Great in Bethnal Green Road, and photographs of the happy event were taken – as a wedding present – by David Bailey, himself an Eastender, and the most famous photographer on the scene at the time. Hundreds of Cockneys turned out that sunny spring afternoon to wish the newlyweds good luck. But good luck, it seemed, was a luxury Reggie and Frances did not need. Fate had dealt them a kind hand. Although Reggie was eleven years older than his bride they were well-matched, joyously in love, and looking forward to spending their lives together. Reggie was already confiding his excitement at the prospect of becoming a father.

On the business side, too, he and Ronnie had fallen on

their feet after the nightmare of the two Old Bailey trials. Gilbert France, who had rented the Hideaway club to McCowan, had told the jury the twins did not need to demand from anyone; because they were so successful with clubs he would have been happy to give them a share. And when the twins were acquitted this is precisely what he did.

While solicitors prepared the paperwork for the partnership, Reggie and Frances flew off to the Greek sunshine. Their new-found good fortune quickly brought them into contact with high-ranking officers from the *Saratoga*, the renowned US aircraft carrier, who took a liking to the honeymooners and invited them on board. For two impressionable Cockneys it was a rare honour, and for years afterwards Reggie treasured a specially engraved lighter, given to them as a memento of their visit.

Back in London, it was decided to give the Hideaway a new name – El Morocco. When a star-studded party was arranged to mark its opening on 29 April Reggie and Frances cut short their honeymoon to be there, with a host of current celebrities – and 'Nipper' Read who, for some reason, popped in for a glass of champagne. One of the celebrities was Edmund Purdom, a very well-known film star who was living in Italy. Like most of the celebrities we encountered, Edmund took to the twins, particularly Ronnie, and he would always make sure he spent some time at El Morocco when he was in London.

One night Edmund came up to Ronnie and said he desperately needed to borrow two hundred pounds. Ronnie agreed to lend it to him, but said he would have to go to Vallance Road in the morning to collect it. Ronnie always preferred the house as a meeting place, feeling that if it was not grand enough for anyone they probably were not worth knowing anyway. It was perfectly acceptable to Edmund and he arrived on time the next morning, much to Mum's delight.

Always ready for a giggle, she asked me not to mention Edmund's presence to a neighbour, Rosie Looker, who came in every morning to help Mum around the house. When Rosie arrived she went into the kitchen at the back of the house while the twins and I talked to Edmund in the front room. After a while I went out there and asked Rosie if she would take some tea in to the twins and their guest. I stayed in the kitchen with Mum, waiting for Rosie's reaction. She did not disappoint us: she came running out, her face flushed with embarrassment, saying, 'Oh, Charlie, you should have told me. I'd have put something different on.' Mum and I laughed. It was the equivalent of coming face to face with Paul Newman today.

On 19 June that year Dolly had a baby. It was a posh affair in the exclusive London Clinic and the baby girl was wheeled into her ward in a cot fringed with lace. She was blonde and beautiful, and as I held her in my arms I knew what love was. She had marvellous laughing eyes and we called her Nancy, after the famous Sinatra song.

Ronnie, thankfully, was anxious for violence to play no part in the new operation. One night, for instance, he took care of two massively built bodybuilders – one black, the other white – with little more than a tug of the sleeve. I wasn't in the club at the time, but I gather the two blokes started shouting and swearing and generally making a nuisance of themselves shortly after coming into the club late one night. Ronnie, who was sitting at a nearby table quietly talking with a friend, did not like their behaviour at all. After tolerating it for a few minutes he got up and walked over to the musclemen who were standing at the bar.

'Excuse me,' he said softly and pleasantly. 'Could you be quiet, please? There are ladies present. They don't like your language. Nor do I.'

Ronnie never gave anyone the chance to argue with him. He always said what he had to say and that was it. So, having said his piece, he turned and walked back to his table. His request did not cut any ice with the two unwanted customers: no sooner had Ronnie sat down than they started mouthing off again. Ronnie's face, I was told later, was a picture: it tensed in irritation then, as the swearing got louder, it tightened and went white with anger. I had seen that look many times and, to strangers, it must have been quite frightening. Finally, unable to stand it any longer, Ronnie got up again and walked over to the two hulking giants. Grabbing each by the arm, he said quietly but convincingly, 'You're leaving.' And he started walking them to the door. As he bundled them into the street he said, 'Don't come back. You're not welcome here.' Then he returned to his seat and calmly carried on talking to his friend as though nothing had happened.

For Ronnie to restrain himself when so angry was remarkable. I would not have been surprised to have been told he'd laid them both out at the bar. I was pleased when I heard the story. Maybe for once he was heeding my advice.

From the early days of their club life the twins had always liked to rub shoulders with famous people and now, in 1965, they were given an opportunity to meet more big American stars, not only from the showbusiness world, but boxing, too. The chance came when they were introduced to a genial, nineteen-stone former American football star named Eddie Pucci, while he was in England as bodyguard to Frank Sinatra's son.

Eddie, who had been connected with Sinatra for five years, was getting involved in arranging for American showbusiness stars to perform in England. As the twins knew the club scene backwards, he asked them if they would entertain the stars and generally make them feel at home. It was through Eddie we met the actor, George Raft, singers Tony Bennett and Billy Daniels, and goodness knows how many other celebrities who were household names in Britain then. The twins persuaded several to come to meet Mum at Vallance Road but none made more impact than the unforgettable Judy Garland. She was very warm and friendly and Mum adored making her feel at home. Once, we amazed the regulars at the Crown pub – just around the corner from the house – by taking Judy to a party there. The pub was packed and people were standing on chairs trying to get a glimpse of her. We were besieged by people wanting us to ask her to sing, but we told them we had brought her as a friend, not as a star. We said Judy just wanted to relax and be herself and, thankfully, everyone understood and respected her wishes. All our relatives and friends were there, and for several hours Judy sat in an armchair, drinking and chatting away about life in general and the East End in particular. We had records on all the time and some of them were Judy's but no one asked her to sing. When we left she said it was one of the most pleasant nights she had spent anywhere because she had been allowed to be herself. I like to think she meant it.

Life in 1965 seemed to be one long, glittering merry-go-round of star-studded events and Reggie delighted in taking Frances to all of them. He had put her on a pedestal high, high above any other female, and he seemed to live in constant fear of looking less than perfect in her eyes. When she was with him he seemed to be on a knife-edge, always worried about whether she was all right. Once we all went backstage at the London Palladium to see Judy Garland after one of her performances. The dressing-room door suddenly opened and Judy rushed out and threw open her arms to give Reggie a hug. But Reggie backed away nervously, and Judy almost fell over. Frances was not in the least concerned or worried by Judy Garland, but Reggie was terrified to get in a clinch with her in case Frances thought something was going on. That's how he was all the time. He even took her to the opera and was invited backstage to meet the fabulous Australian singer Joan Sutherland. Nothing seemed out of reach. Mum, for instance, always dreamt of meeting the French film heart-throb Charles Boyer and, of course, the twins set it up. As they prepared to escort her to the rendezvous, Ronnie kept winding up the old man that he was about to lose her to the most romantic, charming celebrity of the day. The next day I asked Mum how it had gone and she just said, 'Amazing.' It was a dream come true, and the twins were delighted to have made it possible.

Not all their thoughtfulness had such pleasing results, however. The time they extended a helping hand to American boxing hero Joe Louis, for example, rebounded on them nastily and showed how much they were marked men. Eddie Pucci told us that the former world heavyweight champion was coming to England and, as he was down on his luck, could do with some work. Joe was no song-and-dance man like Sugar Ray Robinson, but he was a gilt-edged celebrity who was still a big-name attraction and the twins – particularly Ronnie – wanted to help him. They knew some club and restaurant owners in Newcastle who would pay Louis to promote their premises and so they took the train up there, planning to spend some days trying to earn the genial giant a few bob. They had not been in the city two days when a posse of police pounced on them in their hotel room. Ronnie told them why they were there but an inspector would have none of it: the twins were the 'London mob' and were now trying to take over Newcastle; he wasn't going to stand for it and he wanted them on the next train back to London. It was like something out of a western, with the sheriff giving the bad boys an ultimatum to get out of town. Ronnie said if the stories about them taking over London were true, why did they need to bother with a smaller city nearly four hundred miles away? But that argument didn't impress the inspector. Frustrated by it all, the twins called Louis in his room and told him what was happening. Dear old Joe was bewildered. He told the police the truth, that the twins were friends trying to help him, but the inspector didn't want to know. He handled the Brown Bomber very carefully but told him he was just an excuse; he'd heard all about the Kray twins and they were not going to bring trouble to Newcastle like they had to London. There was a train to London very soon – and the twins would have a police escort to see they caught it.

In the end, the twins had no choice.

They asked Louis to stay on with some friends, then phoned me with the full story. Convinced the police would try to frame them in some way, they asked me to arrange for our solicitor, Ralph Haeems, to be waiting for them.

When the train arrived at Euston, I was surprised to see Reggie in shirtsleeves. He told me he had held his jacket the whole journey because some Newcastle police had travelled with them and he wasn't risking anything being planted.

When Louis returned to London he apologized to the twins for inadvertently getting them into trouble, but they told him not to worry about it. Many of the worthwhile things they did were misconstrued, they said, and they had grown used to it. Later, Eddie Pucci told us that the much-loved American hero really appreciated what the twins had done for him. But they thought nothing of it; Joe Louis had the same courage and dignity when his luck was low as he had when he was riding high as one of the greatest boxing champions ever. Ronnie and Reggie considered it an honour and privilege to help him in some small way.

Around that time, Reggie did a favour for another world boxing champion. But this time it did not go down well at all.

Sonny Liston, who held the heavyweight crown from 1963 until he was beaten by the then Cassius Clay in 1966, visited the twins at the Cambridge Rooms one night. After a pleasant evening drinking and chatting to various friends and acquaintances, he accepted Reggie's offer to drive him back to the May Fair Hotel in Stratton Street. As they pulled away, Reggie drove the wrong side of some bollards in the road. I thought, 'Good luck, Sonny, you're going to enjoy that drive.'

A friend of ours, John Davis, who was in the front passenger seat, told me it was a wild ride, even by Reggie's hair-raising standards: they went through red lights, screeched round corners, narrowly missed other cars and clipped a couple of kerbs before shuddering to a halt outside the May Fair.

Jauntily, Reggie climbed out and opened a back door for Sonny and his manager, then he pumped Sonny's hand cheerily and said, 'I'll see you tomorrow, Sonny.'

The world champion returned the handshake but then looked seriously into Reggie's face. 'Reggie, I'm going to tell you something,' he said. 'There's no man in this world I'm afraid of . . .'

111

Reggie nodded knowingly: it was the sort of comment you'd expect from a huge, hulking bear of a man who was heavyweight champion of the world.

'. . . except one,' Sonny added.

Reggie frowned, mystified.

'Who's that?' he asked.

'You,' said Sonny. 'I've never been so terrified in my life. You'll never drive me again. Ever.'

Reggie laughed. And no doubt zoomed off through the Mayfair traffic in precisely the same reckless manner. He simply didn't appreciate what it was like for his passengers. His adrenaline was always running fast; he was always in a hurry. In his life, as in his boxing, he was always lightning quick, but his brain was one step ahead. Behind the wheel of a car, though, he was a menace. A lot of it was to do with his short-sightedness.

One night, driving me from his house in Casenove Road, he suddenly said, 'Is that a bus coming up here?'

'You *are* joking!' I said, staring at the huge red monster bearing down on us.

'Well, I haven't got my glasses,' Reggie said, matter-of-factly.

'For Christ's sake, stop then, and let me out!' I roared.

Once I went with him to collect a new Humber from Commercial Road. Driving back along Cambridge Heath Road we approached a badly parked lorry on our side of the road. A bus coming towards us was already alongside the lorry and the space was obviously too small for Reggie to get through. Anybody in their right mind would have stopped but Reggie steamed on through, and duly scraped the side of the car from front wing to the back.

'That's clever,' I said. 'You've ripped a car you've only just bought.'

Reggie shrugged. 'That's all right. I can soon get it done.'

112

A Buick also had an eventful life in Reggie's hands. One night he was driving a load of his mates along Commercial Road when they came to some road works. The area was roped off, with lanterns warning drivers, and Reggie's passengers thought he was larking about as he headed straight towards it; they were convinced he was going to swerve at the last minute. But Reggie drove straight on . . . and the big American car disappeared down a hole. Reggie was lucky the hole wasn't that deep, otherwise some of those passengers – and maybe himself – could have been killed. As it was, they all climbed out unhurt. Reggie merely looked down at the wrecked car and said, 'We'll have to walk home.'

The next day a police inspector called at Vallance Road, asking for Reggie.

'Do you own a Buick, registration number . . .?'

'Yes,' said Reggie.

'Well, I don't know how it got down a hole in Commercial Road but you'd better get a breakdown truck to pull it out.'

Reggie just said, 'Oh.'

He never cared about cars – or any material thing, come to that.

The Cambridge Rooms should have been a profitable venture but Ronnie's generous nature sent it into bankruptcy. He paid the staff too much and gave free drinks to too many people. He even took £1,000 out of the till to buy a racehorse – then gave it away!

The horse, called Solway Cross, never won anything, and a leg injury finally ended an undistinguished racing career. We were wondering what to do with it when Ronnie had a brilliant idea: we would raffle it at a big party we planned to throw at the Cambridge Rooms in aid of an East End charity, the Peter Pan Society for

Handicapped Children. The party was held towards the end of the summer of 1963 and we had a big turnout of East End bookmakers and publicans, showbusiness celebrities including our old mates Barbara Windsor, George Sewell, Victor Spinetti and Ronald Fraser, and boxing stars Ted 'Kid' Lewis, Terry Downes and Terry Spinks. There were a few titled gents too, including Lord Effingham and Vice-Admiral Sir Charles Evans. Guest of honour was Sonny Liston.

The main event of the day was the raffling of Solway Cross at £1 a ticket – the entrance fee – and it was won by a Stepney publican, who said she had not time to enjoy the horse and put it up for an impromptu auction.

Lord Effingham mounted an improvised rostrum and within a couple of minutes Solway Cross had a new owner – Ronnie Fraser. The genial actor had had a couple too many and had got landed with the horse for £200. He couldn't believe it; he'd only joined in the bidding for a giggle. He turned to me and grumbled, 'Apart from getting ratted, I'm going home with a filly I hardly know.'

Fraser may not have been too pleased with that lovely summer afternoon party. But the Peter Pan Society was delighted. Their representatives went away with £1,200 all collected on the day.

Alan Bruce Cooper's name spelt ABC. But he was a trifle more difficult to read than the alphabet. He came on the scene around the time the El Morocco opened and we did not know what to make of him. He was rumoured to be one of the organizers of an international arms smuggling ring, supplying the IRA, Palestinian terrorists and groups of mercenaries. It was also suggested that he had a finger in gold and narcotics smuggling. At one time the twins and I even thought he was part of the Mafia.

Three years later – as the spider's web was closing

around the twins – we discovered that the little man with the moustache and a stutter who lived in great style in Kensington and drove a Rolls Royce was indeed in a sinister line of business.

From the moment they met him the twins were impressed with Cooper: he talked in telephone numbers and had an air of mystery that fascinated them. It was clear he was trying to involve them in some form of international intrigue, but the twins did not seem to mind. When he suggested a trip to New York, Ronnie jumped at it. People with criminal records are not allowed to have a visa for entry into the US but Cooper, who travelled on an American passport, got round this by taking Ronnie to Paris and obtaining a visa from the US Embassy there. Ronnie thought it was great fun, not only because he spent a lively week in New York but also because it was a victory against the Old Bill at home, who seemed to be going round the bend wondering where he was.

Cooper, who was about thirty-five, captured Ronnie's imagination with stories of how he was responsible for several assassinations in which he used highly sophisticated lethal devices, including a hunting crossbow and a briefcase containing a hypodermic syringe full of deadly poison. He was a nondescript character, who could easily have passed for an insurance salesman. But behind that bland exterior there must have been a clever man, for I checked him out and found no trace of a criminal record, either in Britain or the US. He thrived on mystery. One day he would be in his office in Mayfair then he would be off to the States, saying he had to visit a daughter who had meningitis. When he returned, there would immediately be phone calls from Madrid or Paris or Geneva or Brussels; it was difficult keeping track of him. One day he walked into the Carpenter's Arms with a mild-mannered gentleman with glasses who looked like a school-teacher.

In a dramatic whispered aside, Cooper informed me he was a hit man for the Mafia.

A friend of ours, Tommy Cowley, said early on that Cooper was a police spy. I laughed it off. He was a harmless Walter Mitty no one should take seriously, I said.

Chapter Nine

The three bullets that shattered my dreams of a quiet, peaceful and successful future were fired in the saloon bar of The Blind Beggar pub in Whitechapel Road, around 8.30 P.M. on 9 March 1966. The first was fired by Ronnie into the head of a man sitting at the bar. The next two were fired into the ceiling by a member of the twins' Firm, Ian Barrie.

The victim was George Cornell, a member of a gang operating in South London. He was known to the twins as flash and loud-mouthed and was supposedly going around town boasting that he was 'going to put that fat poof Kray away'.

On that Wednesday evening, Ronnie and the Firm were drinking in a pub we called The Widow's. Suddenly Ronnie got up and said to Barrie and Scotch Jack Dickson: 'Let's go for a drive.' He often suggested this if the mood took him and the other two thought nothing of it. They followed Ronnie out of the pub.

Cornell often spent some weekdays in the East End; that night, Ronnie wanted to have a look in a few pubs to see if he was, in fact, around. There's not much doubt Ronnie hoped he was. For he didn't like what Cornell was saying, and was determined that if anyone was going to be 'put away' it would be the South Londoner, not him.

After the fatal shots, Dickson drove back to The Widow's. Ronnie told Reggie and their close friends, 'I've done Cornell.' He suggested they went to a pub away from the scene of the crime and within minutes they were on their way to Walthamstow.

Earlier that day I'd seen Reggie at Vallance Road and he'd asked if I was going drinking that night. 'We'll be in The Widow's,' he said.

'I may see you later,' I replied. I never committed myself. If I fancied a drink with the boys I would go; if I didn't, I wouldn't. I liked to be able to please myself.

That night I did fancy a drink. But when I got to the pub it was half empty. 'Where did they all go?' I asked Madge, the missus.

She shook her head. 'They had to see someone. Don't know where.'

I walked round to Vallance Road and asked Mum but she did not know where the twins were either. I nipped back to The Widow's in case I'd missed them and no sooner had I walked in than the phone rang. Madge looked at me. 'It's Reggie. For you.'

I took the phone. Reggie quickly gave me the name of a pub in Walthamstow. 'If I was you I'd pop over here and see us.'

When I got there Reggie motioned towards Ronnie and said, 'He's just done Cornell.'

I looked at Ronnie. 'I shot him,' he said.

He spoke so matter-of-factly, I couldn't take it in at first. Then I started asking questions: Where? How? Was it bad? Was he dead?

Ronnie told me what had happened. But he didn't know if the shots were fatal. Just then the news came on the pub radio. Everyone was listening to it: 'A man gunned down in a Stepney pub earlier tonight has died in hospital.'

I looked at the faces of all Ronnie's friends then told Ronnie, 'You're in trouble. Everybody knows.'

But he just said, 'I don't care.'

After a couple of drinks I decided to make a move.

'Better not go home,' Ronnie said.

'Why not?'

'The law will be about.'

'Why should I worry about that?' I asked. 'It's nothing to do with me.'

'You know what they're like. They'll try and involve you.'

'I'll take my chances,' I said.

'Well, we're not going to be around for a few days.'

And they weren't. As the law buzzed around the East End looking for witnesses to the killing, the twins stayed in Walthamstow, out of sight in a friend's flat. About a week later they surfaced and carried on as if nothing had happened. The heat was off. No one was coming forward to say who had shot Cornell. Ronnie, it seemed, was getting away with murder.

If the police were not sure who had killed Cornell there was one person who was in little doubt – the dead man's widow. She came round to Vallance Road and threw a brick through Mum's front window; fortunately she and the old man were out at the time. Cornell's widow stayed outside the house, yelling insults and accusations until Aunt May told her that, no matter what the woman thought the twins had done, it was nothing to do with the parents. Finally, Mrs Cornell left. I can understand her wanting to vent her anger and hate, but her reaction did nobody any good.

The Cornell murder shook me, naturally, but I should not have been too surprised. The twins and I had had our rows about guns. I tried to make Ronnie see that it was daft to walk around London armed to the teeth like some commando but he would reply, 'If they're tooled up, so will I be. They won't have me over.'

'Hold up,' I'd say. 'Think about what is going to happen.'

But of course he wouldn't. 'I'd rather accept the consequences than have my head blown off,' he'd say.

The twins were very disappointed in me for not sharing their views about weapons, and I did not endear myself to them when I put my foot down over a row between two of their Firm – Connie Whitehead and Scotch Jack Dickson. Ronnie had already told them to cool it but Connie and Jack took no notice. Then one night when I went to one of our clubs, The Starlight in Oxford Street, the doorman, Tommy Flanagan, said, 'I'm glad you've come, Charlie. Jack's inside, waiting for Connie. With a gun. He's going to do him.'

'It's not going to happen,' I assured him.

Relieved, Tommy said, 'Tell him, Charlie.'

When I walked through into the club Ronnie came up, wanting to know why I was there. I told him I'd popped in for a drink, then asked what was going on between Connie and Jack.

Ronnie said, 'I could have guessed you'd interfere.'

I went up to Jack and asked him if he had a gun. He admitted he had. 'So you're going to shoot Whitehead.' I said. 'You were pals a little while ago. Now you've had a row, you want to shoot him.' I turned to Ronnie. 'Are you just going to stand there?'

'Let 'em get on with it,' Ronnie said. 'If he wants to shoot him, let him. It's nothing to do with me.'

'You can't just stand by and watch,' I told him.

But Ronnie said, 'Don't interfere. Get on with your own business. I couldn't care less.'

I turned to Jack again. 'The only reason you have a gun and you're standing there like a big guy is because Ronnie is standing with you. You wouldn't have the bottle on your own.'

120

Jack said nothing. Ronnie drew on a cigarette, watching me. We stood there in silence.

'Well, it's not happening,' I said finally. 'I promise you that.'

'What do you mean?' Ronnie asked.

'If Connie comes down here, I'm taking him away. I won't let it happen.'

Ronnie launched a tirade of abuse at me, but I ignored him and I looked at Jack. 'Give me the gun,' I said.

He didn't want to, but after a few minutes he handed it over.

'Happy now?' asked Ronnie.

I continued to ignore him and went upstairs with the gun and told Tommy to dump it.

'Thank God for that,' Tommy said. He was pleased I'd intervened. No one else would have stood a chance of overruling Ronnie.

But Ronnie thought I was an idiot.

For the next five months the East End was alive with rumours: everyone, it seemed, knew who had shot Cornell. People would come up to me and try to pump me, hoping I would confirm what everyone suspected. 'I hear old Ron had Cornell over, then,' they'd say. 'Is that right?'

'News to me,' I'd reply. 'Better ask Ron.'

I was up to my eyes running my theatrical agency, a coat factory and distributing potatoes, and did not see a lot of the twins. When I did see them, neither mentioned the murder. They did not seem the least concerned; it was as if it had never happened. But throughout that spring and summer I was on edge all the time, expecting something to happen – waiting for it, almost.

In August, it did. Detective Chief Superintendent Tommy Butler swooped on a number of East End houses

– including the twins' in Vallance Road – and took in several men he felt might be able to help with his inquiries into the Blind Beggar mystery. Ronnie and Reggie appeared in identity parades at Leyton police station; neither was picked out, but it was clear that if they felt the heat had gone out of the police investigation they were wrong.

I came up with a suggestion that the twins should leave the country for a while, and for once they took the advice. I insisted that only two people, apart from the three of us, should know where they were going – Mum and the old man. The twins loved that idea, too, and a few days later took a private plane from Lydd in Kent to France, where they picked up a scheduled jet to Tangier. To keep the secrecy watertight, I told them never to phone the house but to dial the number of a public call box in Bethnal Green Road. They agreed to phone every Tuesday and Thursday at 8 P.M.; if the phone was engaged they would keep ringing until I picked it up. For the next month I felt like a spy, slipping out quietly just before eight and waiting for the phone to ring, and of course the twins loved the intrigue.

The effect on the East End was startling: the twins' friends were very curious, but not as much as the police were. Soon, rumours started flying around, including one that the twins had been murdered. When I told them, they roared. It wasn't easy keeping the secret for four weeks but somehow we managed it. And it was worth it. It gave the police something to think about and, as far as the twins' so-called friends were concerned, the rumours proved something I'd always suspected: that they couldn't stop bragging that they knew everything about the twins when, in fact, they knew absolutely nothing.

When the twins were due to return, I decided to see how fast the truth travelled by telling just one person where they'd really been. It was all over the East End in minutes.

When they finally arrived home, tanned and rested, Ronnie and Reggie took a great delight in the fuss their sudden absence had caused. A lot of people were glad to see them back, but in Tangier many – chiefly hotel waiters and taxi drivers – had been sorry to see them go.

Ronald Kray was the biggest tipper the city had ever seen.

With the law still buzzing on the Cornell mystery, Ronnie and some pals started spending their evenings at the Baker's Arms, a quiet pub a couple of miles away in Northiam Street, Hackney. One summer night Detective Sergeant Leonard Townsend from Hackney police station walked into the saloon bar with a colleague called Barker. Ronnie and most of his friends walked out.

Townsend looked at one who stayed behind. 'They have got to drink somewhere,' he said. 'And they might as well use this pub. If you see the Kray twins tell them if they want to play ball with us, we'll play ball with them.'

When Ronnie heard this he went spare, but he agreed to meet Townsend in the pub the following night.

They went into a private room at the back of the pub and Townsend quickly came to the point. 'I know you like it here because it's nice and quiet. But if you want to be left alone it's going to cost you a little bit of rent. There are two of us in it – a pony a week each.'

Inwardly Ronnie was boiling. Fifty quid a week to be allowed to drink in a pub! He felt like laying Townsend out on the spot, but he controlled himself – he had had an idea. He asked for a day to talk it over with Reggie and agreed to meet Townsend in the pub again the next night.

When Townsend left, Ronnie told the licensee, Eric Marshall, who exploded. 'I'm going to Scotland Yard,' he said. 'I'm a straight man. You've done nothing. You and your mates spend your money here. You're always treating the old people. The police are driving you away. I'm not having it.'

Ronnie quietened him down. They needed proof, he said, and he knew how to get it. He would meet the greedy copper the next night, as arranged, but this time the conversation would be taped.

When Ronnie asked my opinion of the plan I said it sounded a good idea because it would put a stop to the police corruption we knew had been going on for years. It would do the public good to learn that while the Kray twins had been accused of demanding money from people, the police had been demanding it off them. But I knew Ronnie well and suspected he wouldn't follow it through all the way. 'You'll get them nicked all right,' I told him. 'But when it comes to court, you won't give evidence.'

'Oh, yes I will,' Ronnie said. 'They asked for this trouble. And I'm going to give it to them.'

I shook my head. 'Don't bother wasting your time. You should go through with it, but you won't.'

I suppose Ronnie really believed he would. But I knew him better than he knew himself.

Before the meeting Ronnie contacted a private detective friend who set up two tape recorders in the room – one in an empty tin, the other strapped to Ronnie's chest under his shirt. The trap worked like a dream: Ronnie got Townsend to spill out all the incriminating evidence of corruption, then he took the recording to a solicitor who went to Scotland Yard.

Four days later Eric Marshall kept a rendezvous with Townsend carrying ten £5 notes, the numbers of which had been listed by a Scotland Yard Detective Chief Inspector. Townsend got into Mr Marshall's car at the

Triangle, Mare Street, Hackney, and a microphone hidden under the front seat recorded the conversation as the money was handed over. The hard part of the plan was over: the greedy cop had taken the bribe. But sadly, the watching police made a mess of the next part of the plan. Over-zealous C11 men blew their cover too soon and Townsend made a run for it, throwing the incriminating packet into the road. He was caught after a mild chase, but not with the evidence on him. As it turned out, it didn't matter; the tape recordings were enough to convince the police Townsend was guilty of corruption and he was duly charged.

All that was needed now was for Ronnie to make a statement and go to court and Townsend would be kicked out of the force, possibly jailed.

Surprise! Surprise! Ronnie said he couldn't, and wouldn't do it.

I tried to reason with him. I told him he had gone through all the aggravation so far and it would be easy to follow it through. When Ronnie still refused I said he owed it to other victims of police corruption to try to end it once and for all. No joy there, either. Finally, I told him straight out that he would be totally in the wrong if he turned his back on the case: not only would a bent copper go free on his money-grabbing way but Ronnie would have wasted everyone's time: his own, Eric Marshall's and God knows how many police.

I may as well have been talking to a brick wall. Ronnie said he would never go into a witness box to put somebody away, no matter who they were. Yes, Townsend was a bad copper, but giving evidence against him would make them as bad as each other, Ronnie argued. It was a strange, maddening philosophy and I tried my damnedest to change Ronnie's mind. I should have saved my breath, for when a summons arrived in December ordering

Ronnie to attend Old Street Court in North London as a witness, he promptly went into hiding. The case opened, but without Ronnie there it could not get very far and, not surprisingly, Townsend was remanded on bail.

We found Ronnie a flat in Kensington, near Olympia. He took a few chances to come to Vallance Road to see Mum, but generally he stayed in that flat. The police did not make a huge effort to find him and whenever I got the chance I told them they didn't want to. The absence of a key witness was a good excuse for their man to get off, wasn't it? With the case unlikely to be heard for a few months, Ronnie prepared himself, somewhat reluctantly, for a Christmas away from the family.

The case against Townsend started at the Old Bailey in April 1967. He was accused of trying to obtain £50 from Ronnie as an inducement to show favour and of corruptly accepting £50 through Eric Marshall for showing favour to Ronnie.

The jury was out nearly eight hours, but could not agree and a new trial began two months later. The tape recordings were present, but Ronnie wasn't; he was still holed up in Kensington. It didn't matter. Again, the jury could not agree and Mr Justice Waller ordered the detective to be found not guilty and discharged. Townsend was dumbfounded – he knew how lucky he was – but one person who probably was not surprised by the verdict was the prosecution's own counsel, a barrister named John Mathew. As prosecuting counsel his job was to prove Townsend guilty. For some inexplicable reason, however, he gave the jury the impression the twins were on trial. In his opening speech, he said: 'It may well be that some of you have heard of two persons known as the Kray brothers, Ronald and Reginald Kray. They are notorious characters. They are persons of the worst possible character. They have convictions between them for violence, blackmail and bribery. Their activities were always of interest to the police.'

Mr Mathew, one might be interested to learn, was prosecution counsel when the twins were cleared of demanding money from Hew McCowan two years before!

The day after Townsend walked free Ronnie came out of hiding, pale and wan from his self-imposed imprisonment. As we were leaving an outfitter's in Bethnal Green Road next to the police station two policemen saw us. 'All right, Ron?' one of them called out casually, as though Ronnie was a dear friend he saw every day.

'I'm all right now,' Ronnie replied. 'Do you want me?'

The policeman said, 'No. We heard you were in Tangier. You don't look very tanned.'

'No,' Ronnie said. 'I've been here all the time.'

The policemen laughed and walked on. We got in the car and drove to Vallance Road.

That ended one dramatic episode in Ronnie's life. But another was already hitting the headlines and it was to end at the Old Bailey with Ronnie facing a charge of murder. It was The Strange Case of Frank Mitchell, a giant whose brutality had earned him the nickname 'Mad Axeman'.

Mitchell stood over six feet, had enormous muscles and was immensely strong. Yet he was shy and inarticulate, with the mentality of a child. He had had a sketchy education at a school for the sub-normal and turned to crime early in life, quickly progressing from remand homes to Borstal, then to prison. He was four years older than the twins and had spent most of his life in one institution or another.

Reggie met him in Wandsworth Jail in 1960 while serving eighteen months for demanding money from Podro the Pole. Almost from the moment they came into

127

contact Reggie felt compassion for the gentle giant. Mitchell was constantly being beaten up by sadistic prison officers, but he never complained and always came back for more, fighting his persecutors with the power and strength of a bull. At the same time, though, he responded readily to a kind word or gentle gesture, and when Reggie went out of his way to make his life more tolerable, Mitchell developed a bizarre sort of hero-worship for him.

He demonstrated this in a spectacular way that endeared him to Reggie and, with tragic irony, prompted a chain of events that would lead to him being murdered in the most violent way.

Reggie had just three weeks of his sentence to go when some officers started winding him up, tried to light his notoriously short fuse. It was not difficult. From the moment he had gone into prison he seemed to be the target for officers' bullying and he had never taken it lying down; this occasion was no exception. He was just about to retaliate when Mitchell roared from his cell, 'Leave the bastards to me, Reg. You've only got three weeks. They're only trying to keep you in here.'

For some reason it did the trick and made Reggie see the sense in swallowing it. He didn't lose any remission and left the jail three weeks later. But he never forgot Big Frank and ensured, through various means, that he never went short of comforts. Some time later, Reggie got a chance to prove his friendship in a more profound way. Mitchell was accused of stabbing another prisoner with a knife, and Reggie arranged for him to be defended at Marylebone Magistrates' Court by a brilliant young barrister named Nemone Lethbridge.

Thanks to her superb defence Mitchell was acquitted on a charge of causing grievous bodily harm. He returned to Wandsworth, but was later transferred to Her

Majesty's Prison, Princeton, Devon, a massive, dark, forbidding Dickensian building more commonly known as Dartmoor. And although he often worked outside the prison he wanted nothing more than to be free permanently. Reggie had been doing his best to get his case investigated by persuading influential friends to write to the Home Office. But no hope was on the horizon.

Then, one wintry afternoon – while Ronnie was playing Puccini in his Kensington hideaway – Scotch Jack Dickson went to Reggie with a story that Mitchell was threatening to kill one of the prison officers to draw attention to his case. Reggie thought about it carefully, then made one of his swift decisions. He gave Dickson a couple of hundred quid and told him to get Mitchell out of jail for Christmas.

Dickson enlisted the help of a couple of mates – Albert Donaghue and a former boxer named Bill Exley – and planned the escape. It was surprisingly easy: on the morning of 12 December the three of them turned up in a car at a pre-arranged spot and Mitchell, who had slipped away from a group building fences on a military range, was waiting for them. Later that day, radio and TV news reports informed the nation that helicopters and commandos were scouring the moors for 'Mad Axeman' Frank Mitchell. But by then the subject of their search was tucking into a fry-up at a council flat in Barking.

As Londoners packed the shops in the frenetic pre-Christmas shopping build-up, two of the most infamous men in Britain sat it out quietly in their comfortable 'prisons' on opposite sides of the city: Ronnie in upper-crust Kensington in West London, Mitchell on the outskirts of the more modest East End.

I was a virtual 'prisoner', too. I'd developed a throat infection, which confined me to bed at the time of Mitchell's escape and for some days afterwards. I could not get involved in the big man's problems, even if I'd wanted to. For no sooner had I recovered than I had to get busy, tending to Ronnie's needs. I felt like someone from MI5 again when I went over to Kensington to see him: just in case I was being followed, I jumped on and off buses, in and out of taxis and sometimes walked round in circles just to shrug off would-be pursuers. With Ronnie wanted by every policeman in London I couldn't be too careful. It was a bit of a drag sometimes, having to go through all that fuss, but I didn't mind. I couldn't expect Reggie to spend a lot of time with Ronnie: he was having great problems with his in-laws over Frances who, sadly, was suffering from depression.

I quickly discovered that Mitchell had had no intention of killing anyone: Dickson, Donaghue and Exley had dreamt it all up as some sort of exciting escapade. To them, minding a dangerous man on the run was a huge joke. But, tragically, the joke misfired. An attractive nightclub hostess, Lisa Prescott, was hired to satisfy Mitchell's sexual urges, but the poor man – unworldly and naïve as they come – mistook her professional competence for true affection and fell in love with her. Then he got hold of Exley's gun and suddenly what had been a manageable, if troublesome, situation was out of control. Something had to be done.

It was decided that Mitchell would be smuggled out of the country. More money was provided and Donaghue was told to take him to a remote part of Kent, on the first leg of his journey. On Friday night, 23 December, the two men left the Barking flat together. Frank Mitchell was never seen again.

As that 1967 spring turned into summer, tension in the East End mounted. The police were no nearer to bringing Cornell's killer to court and now they had another East

End mystery on their hands. However, a far more significant event had been taking place at the Old Bailey which was to have a serious knock-on effect for the twins, their Firm and me. A South London gang, led by one Charles Richardson, had received massive sentences in what had become known as The Torture Trial. The victory had given police chiefs at Scotland Yard a tremendous boost in their war against London's gangland. The spotlight, we quickly discovered, switched from south of the Thames to the East End, and the twins' manor in particular.

I didn't see a lot of the twins but whenever we did meet I got the feeling that they were under scrutiny – in their favourite pubs there always seemed to be somebody in a remote corner, watching points, taking notes.

Ronnie and Reggie had followed the sensational month-long Torture Trial and appreciated the dangers ahead. But they had such a total lack of fear that they took the increasing pressure lightly, particularly Ronnie. In the Grave Maurice pub in Whitechapel Road, for example, he would wave a mocking greeting to anyone he detected was a copper, and invite him over for a drink. Once he walked down Vallance Road to find detectives watching the house from a car. He apologized for keeping them waiting, then went in and told Mum to make some tea. He took it out to them in four of her best china cups and told the surprised policemen to make sure they returned them when they had finished.

Always the more dominant, more fearless, more reckless twin, Ronnie was convinced that he was above the law and that the Cornell business proved it. It was over a year since the killing. If the Old Bill were going to nick him, he said, they would have done it by now. The fact that nothing had happened proved they couldn't touch him.

I told him to cool it and warned that both he and

131

Reggie were heading for serious trouble. But as usual Ronnie didn't listen. With this air of invincibility he started embarking on wild, extravagant plans to make vast fortunes with Alan Bruce Cooper, the moustachioed, stuttering American who was now permanently on the scene. I didn't trust the man; he reminded me too much of Leslie Payne, whose elaborate plans also came to nothing. I was to discover that my intuition was right.

In the spring of that eventful 1967 I went to Spain with Dolly and my daughter Nancy on an all-expenses-paid trip organized by an American friend, Joe Kaufman, who had gambling connections and an antique shop in New York. Shortly after our arrival at the Avienda Palace Hotel in Barcelona, Joe, a keen amateur photographer, told me he'd been taking some long-range pictures from his balcony and seen someone else's telephoto lens focused on him. At the time I was amused: I told Joe he probably wasn't the only photographer in Barcelona. However, the incident was to have sinister implications.

We all went on to the resort of Sitges, further along the Costa Brava, and who should turn up but A. B. Cooper and his wife. He claimed he was in Spain on business and had decided to drop in and say hello. I presumed that Joe had told him and thought no more about it. But we discovered later that Cooper was, in fact, an informer for the CIA or FBI and had provided the police with a comprehensive diary of the twins' movements over the previous couple of years. We tumbled him when he tried to trap the twins into parting with some incriminating evidence in a room bugged by police. Cooper's plan, almost infantile in its conception and execution, began with a spate of phone calls and telegrams to the twins, and culminated with a frantic phone call from a Harley Street nursing home. He was, he claimed, suffering from a duodenal ulcer and wanted the twins to visit him.

Precisely why was not clear. The twins were convinced it was a set-up and sent Tommy Cowley instead.

Tommy told me later that he smelled a rat the moment he walked in; Cooper simply did not look like a man with an ulcer. Then, shortly after they began talking, a nurse burst in, the Old Bill written all over her. She handed Cooper a menu and asked him what he wanted for dinner, which Tommy took to be a cue for Cooper to turn up the volume on the mike, probably hidden under the bedclothes.

As soon as the nurse left the room Cooper started talking about the gelignite Paul Elvey had gone to Scotland to get. Tommy looked suitably puzzled and asked why Elvey had gone there to get gelignite.

'To blow something up, of course,' said Cooper.

Tommy roared with laughter. 'You delirious or something?' he said. 'We're supposed to be the guv'nors in London. If you want any gelignite, I can get you some today.'

It was all too ridiculous for words, and shortly afterwards Tommy made his excuses and left, without giving the listening law one shred of information that could have landed the twins in trouble. That was the last they saw of A. B. Cooper – until he turned up at the Old Bailey to testify against them.

A friend of the twins', Harry Hopwood, called at my flat wanting £2,000. The twins had decided to buy a pub and needed the money. I wasn't very happy about the hurry-up approach and sent Harry back with a message that I'd see them tomorrow. In those days it was easy to buy a pub and within a matter of weeks The Carpenter's Arms in Cambridge Heath Road was ours. We suggested Harry's sister and her husband ran it for us, in return for a weekly wage plus a flat above. The couple had no home of their

133

own at the time and were delighted with the deal. A 'godsend' was the word used.

The pub was to become a regular meeting and drinking place for the twins and their Firm. But for a while a different type of customer made a name for himself. He was a tramp who Ronnie befriended after seeing him looking for dog-ends at the front of the house in Vallance Road.

Most of our family smoked, and the old man used to collect all the dog-ends and put them on the pavement, much to the delight of the local tramps who thought all their birthdays had come at once. The hoard was like gold dust, especially Ronnie's throwaways; he used to take only one or two puffs, leaving virtually a full cigarette. Ronnie, who had no idea the old man looked after the local tramps in this way, came out one morning and was horrified to see a shabby bloke with a beard and unkempt hair rummaging around the dog-ends.

'Throw them away,' Ronnie said. He took a packet of cigarettes from a pocket. 'Have some of these.'

The tramp, a shortish, stocky guy in his mid-forties, could not believe his luck. Later, Ronnie mentioned the incident at home.

'I've always left the dog-ends out there,' the old man said.

Ronnie shook his head. 'You can't expect people to smoke dog-ends, Dad,' he said, horrified.

After that, Ronnie used to wait until the tramp came along then go out and give him some fags. Over the next few days he got to know him quite well and took him to the public baths in Cheshire Street for a clean-up and shave. The next thing we knew, he had bought his new-found, fresh-smelling friend a new suit, shirt and tie and wheeled him into The Carpenter's Arms. 'Let's give him a few quid,' he said to Reggie and me. 'And if he wants a drink, don't charge him.'

The mounting police interest did not bother Ronnie. And Reggie had a far, far bigger problem on his mind early that summer – Frances. She was becoming more and more depressed and seemed on the verge of a nervous break-down. She had always been a highly strung woman; Reggie did not know it when he met her but she had had a couple of minor breakdowns in her teens. In the early days the Shea family had accepted Reggie but gradually as he became more and more successful and Frances was taken to West End shows and one champagne party after another, they grew to resent the relationship. In a strange way, they seemed jealous of their own daughter and this, I'm sure, played on her mind.

For several months, just before Christmas and after, she was very depressed. Reggie suggested it might do her good to stay with her parents for a while but Frances didn't seem too keen. A few days later, however, she suddenly disappeared. Reggie was out of his mind with worry. Nothing was heard of her for three or four days, then Reggie got word that she was in hospital. When he discovered that her family had known where she was he hit the roof, unable to understand why no one had bothered to tell him. He rang me at the time in a terrible state. 'How do you think this makes me feel,' he said, his voice shaking with emotion. 'A wife in hospital and the husband doesn't know!'

I couldn't say it to Reggie but I wasn't too surprised at the Shea family's behaviour. They had never treated Reggie with any respect. Whenever he called round at their house to pick her up – before they were married – the parents never invited him in. They would call down from an upstairs window, 'She'll be out in a minute.' And they would leave him to wait in his car. Sometimes he'd wait an hour. I told him I could not have stood for it, I would have driven off, but Reggie loved Frances enough to put up with anything.

Naturally, he went to see her in hospital and a day or two later she came home. But she did not look well: her eyes were lifeless, her face pale and drawn. All the vitality and effervescence she had displayed on her wedding day two years before had gone, leaving her looking much older than her twenty-three years.

Then she went to stay with her brother, and the next time Reggie saw her she was dead.

It was a Wednesday morning in June. I was at home when the phone rang, and the moment I heard Reggie's voice I knew something was wrong. He started breaking his heart. For some time I couldn't make out what he was saying but eventually he got out that Frances had taken an overdose. He had gone round to see her at her brother's house and when he hadn't got a reply he had located the brother and they'd found her in bed. Dead. I couldn't take it in. It didn't seem possible. Reggie was sobbing on the phone and I told him to go to Vallance Road; I'd see him there. I dropped what I was doing and raced round but Reggie was already there and had told Mum. She was as devastated as we were. Reggie just sat in a chair, staring ahead and repeating, 'If she'd been with me it wouldn't have happened . . . it wouldn't have happened . . .'

I told him it was an accident; Frances had surely not meant to kill herself. She was probably feeling neglected and took an overdose to try and get some attention. But Reggie did not even hear me. He just said, 'Why did she do it? Why?'

Reggie's heart was broken. He wanted to see Frances's body after the autopsy at Hackney mortuary, and he

Me, aged about six, with Mum

Inset The toddling twins: Ronnie, left, and Reggie, loving the limelight

Me at seventeen, shortly after I joined the Navy

Triumph in the ring – one of my eighteen
victories in twenty-one fights

The twins at school, aged eleven. Ron is on the right of the boy with the cup

Above Killer instinct: seconds after this picture was taken, Reggie knocked out his opponent at Lime Grove Baths, in West London

Right Three Krays on one bill. It was my last fight and I lost

ROYAL ALBERT HALL

Manager .... C. S. Taylor

AN INTERNATIONAL BOXING TOURNAMENT

—— TONIGHT'S CONTESTS ——

Fight No.

10 (3-min.) Rounds Lightweight Contest at 9st. 11 lbs.

1. **TOMMY McGOVERN** v. **ALLAN TANNER**
Lightweight Champion of Great Britain / BRITISH GUIANA

8 (3-min.) Rounds Light Heavyweight at 12st. 10lbs.

2. **Johnny McGOWAN** v. **Eric JENSEN**
WAKEFIELD / Light Heavyweight Champion of Denmark

8 (3-min.) Rounds Bantamweight Contest at 8st. 9lbs.

3. **Ron JOHNSON** v. **Jimmy CARDEW**
BETHNAL GREEN / HOLLOWAY

8 (3-min.) Rounds Welterweight Contest at 10st. 10lbs.

4. **Jackie BRADDOCK** v. **Chris. CHRISTENSEN**
MANCHESTER / Welterweight Champion of Denmark

8 (3 min.) Rounds Middleweight Contest at 11st. 9lbs.

5. **Jimmy DAVIS** v. **Jimmy JAMES**
BETHNAL GREEN / JAMAICA

6 (3-min.) Rounds Welterweight Contest at 10st. 9lbs.

6. **Lew LAZAR** v. **Charlie KRAY**
ALDGATE / BETHNAL GREEN

6 (3 min.) Rounds Lightweight Contest at 9st. 11 lbs.

7. **Reg KRAY** v. **Bobby MANITO**
BETHNAL GREEN / CLAPHAM

6 (3-min.) Rounds Lightweight Contest at 9st. 11 lbs.

8. **Ron KRAY** v. **Bill SLINEY**
BETHNAL GREEN / KING'S CROSS

OFFICIALS

Left Ron, left, and Reg with a couple of pals outside the billiard hall in Mile End Road

Below Family affair: me and my brothers with the old man, his brother, Billy, and our cousin, Ray, at one of the many Kentucky charity nights

Mum and the old man introduce former champion boxer Larry Gains to the horse actor Ronnie Fraser won in a raffle

Ron, left, and Reggie with two boxing champions – featherweight Terry Spinks and heavyweight Sonny Liston

Tough guys: from left, Eddie Pucci, once Frank Sinatra Junior's bodyguard, Ronnie, film star George Raft, Reggie, former world heavyweight boxing champion Rocky Marciano and me

Above So happy together: Reggie and Frances at Danny La Rue's club in Mayfair, shortly before their marriage

Left The playmate who brightened things up for me in Leicester

My first wife, Dolly, before the divorce

One of my favourite photos: my lovely son Gary with Nancy, the sister he missed so much

Above Reggie, left, and Ronnie
with gang boss Billy Hill at his villa
in Tangier

Right Ronnie in Nigeria, outside
the prison he was asked to visit

Below The picture that started
a political storm: Ronnie with
Lord Boothby at the peer's
Eaton Square home

asked me to go with him. There is a police station near the mortuary and while we were in a small room waiting to be called two policemen walked in. We couldn't believe it. Reggie started to choke with anger but I begged him to ignore them: they would probably have excused themselves by saying they were checking that Ronnie wasn't around. They just stood there, watching us. I felt like saying, 'Can't you find a better time?' but heeded my own advice to Reggie. Having a row in a place like that would have been dreadful; it would have made us lower than them.

Finally, we were called and went into another room where we could look through a window at the body. The two policemen moved so that they could half-see us in a mirror. Reggie and I stood looking at Frances and then Reggie started to cry, and I walked out of the room, leaving him to release the grief and heartbreak he'd been bottling up since that terrible Saturday morning. The policemen were watching him, and as I passed them I felt like lashing out. But I just sat down and ignored them and waited for Reggie, and when he came out, still choked, I just said, 'Come on, let's go home.' The policemen followed us out and were still watching us as we drove away.

It was then that I began to understand my brothers' rebellious attitude towards the police.

Mum, the old man and I tried to give Reggie support, but more than anything he needed the companionship of his twin, who could understand what he was going through without the need for words. However, the Townsend second trial had still to be heard and Ronnie was holed up in the flat in Kensington. He felt he would make things worse for everyone if he suddenly reappeared.

Reggie wanted Frances to be buried in her wedding dress but the family said no. They blamed him for her death, and their hatred was so deep that they tried to have her maiden name of Shea substituted for her married name on the coffin and memorial stone. But, of course, Reggie resisted that.

The funeral was held at the church where Frances and Reggie had been married just two years before and it caused a personal problem for Father Hetherington, who would conduct the burial service. He was a very Christian man and couldn't come to terms with his resentment towards the Shea family for the appalling manner in which they were treating Reggie: it hurt him to feel so badly towards them. Nevertheless, he refused to be hypocritical and insisted that Mr and Mrs Shea did not travel in the first car with Reggie. He also called me into the vestry and made it clear Ronnie must not turn up at the funeral. He urged me to make him promise not to come, even if he felt he had a duty to be present. Ronnie wanted to pay his last respects to his brother's wife but he thought too much of Father Hetherington and Reggie even to consider breaking his promise.

The police did not know this, of course, and on the day, police cars lined the route to the church and detectives mingled incongruously with mourners. The occasion was bad enough for all who had known and loved Frances. To have her death robbed of the dignity it deserved just made it worse.

Reggie did not speak to the Shea family after Frances was laid to rest. He didn't want to know them; they blamed him for their daughter's death and he blamed them; they said he had always been bad for her and he said they caused her mental problems by trying to pull her away from him. It was pure hatred on both sides.

For Dolly and me, our springtime trip to Spain had not changed anything: we continued to drift apart and by

138

August I was going through my own domestic crisis. I adored my kids, of course, and was enjoying watching them grow, but the marriage itself was virtually over. The rot had set in the night I learned about George Ince, and the relationship had never recovered. That summer I was ripe for another affair and, when the chance came I threw myself into it with all the boundless joy of a carefree teenager.

Her name was Diana Ward and she had been hired as a waitress for a casino-nightclub I was opening in Leicester with a partner, Trevor Raynor. The club was due to open officially in the autumn and one afternoon I went to Leicester with Tommy Cowley to see how it was progressing. Within a few minutes Tommy spotted Diana. He was knocked out by her beauty and eagerly pointed her out to me. My mind was more on business, and I told him to keep his eyes off the staff. Secretly, though, I admired Tommy's taste: Diana was stunning.

Over the next few weeks, I got chatting to her and learned that although she was married it was not a relationship made in heaven. I was not in a position to ask her out, though. In London I was up to my eyes with my other businesses and I was not able to pop up to Leicester as often as I would have liked.

However, I did have to see how the club was coming along, so I set aside Wednesday as my 'Leicester day'. Diana was on my mind a lot, and as I drove north a warm feeling of pleasure would flow through me at the prospect of seeing her.

What I did not know was that on the eleventh floor of Tintagel House, a towering office block on London's Embankment, behind a door marked 'Krayology', the spider's web was being spun carefully, hour after hour, day after day. A pile of damning documents was growing steadily – detailed reports and sworn statements on the movements and activities of the Brothers Kray by so-called friends and associates, eager to trade a lifetime of loyalty for the promise of freedom.

Suddenly that summer, betrayal was in the air.

Reggie could not cope with the loss of the beautiful woman he had idolized. For weeks after the funeral, he tried to drink himself into oblivion every night to ease the pain. Thanks to the Valium the doctor had prescribed him he found this relatively easy. Mum hated going to pubs every night, but she came with Reggie and me because we were so worried about him. He didn't seem to care about anything any more, he just drank and drank. And when he had drunk too much he would drink some more until the effects of too much gin and Valium would explode in his head making him incapable, and we would take him home and put him to bed.

Reggie had always taken immense pride in his appearance, but in his misery even this went out of the window. Once, someone saw him at five in the morning walking along Whitechapel High Street with no jacket and his shirtsleeves rolled up. Two policemen called out, 'What are you doing?' But Reggie just glared at them and walked on without saying a word. Evidently his look was enough for them to get the message. In the state he was in God knows what he would have done to them if they'd got busy.

Frances had been his life and now she had gone life would never be the same again. If she had not died so tragically young, if she had been around to give him love and a purpose for living, Reggie's entire existence would have taken a different direction. As it was, the whole appalling episode crucified him, and took away everything except an overwhelming desire to destroy himself.

The only reason he had for living, it seemed, was to

die, to join his beloved Frances. He pumped more gin, more Valium, into his body to take him away from the terrible reality of her death, and inevitably his personality began to change. I watched the transformation hopelessly with a kind of dread. Reggie was disintegrating before my eyes and there was nothing I nor anyone could do. He was on a wild, crazy rollercoaster that was hurling him round and round, faster and faster, and he didn't care where it took him or where he ended up. More gin. More Valium. As the heat of that summer of '67 cooled and autumn brought an early warning of winter's chill to the East End streets, the transformation was almost complete and Reggie's death-wish was about to shatter the barrier that separated him from Ronnie, and change all our lives for ever.

Chapter Ten

The early hours of Sunday 29 October 1967. The ringing of the phone shattered the silence of my bedroom. I reached out for the receiver and grunted, 'Hello.' It was Harry Hopwood.

'Something's happened,' he said. 'It's very urgent. You've got to come over.'

'What?' I asked sleepily. 'It's three in the morning.'

'Ronnie said you've got to come over. It's very urgent.' Harry sounded very worried.

'I'll get over as soon as I can,' I said. I put the phone down, wondering what could be so urgent that Ronnie would get Harry Hopwood to ring me in the middle of the night.

As I drove to Hopwood's house my mind ran riot with vivid imaginings. But nothing could have prepared me for the horrific revelation waiting for me at 14 Ravenscroft Street, Bethnal Green.

A distant cousin of ours, Ronnie Hart, opened the door. His face was pale, his expression worried.

'What's going on?' I demanded to know.

Hart motioned with his head to a back room. 'They're in there. You better ask them.'

I strode into the back room: Ronnie and Reggie were sitting in two armchairs.

I looked at Ronnie, then at Reggie. My heart raced with apprehension. 'What's going on that's so important at this time of the morning?'

'We've done McVitie,' Ronnie said in a matter-of-fact tone.

I knew Jack McVitie. He was a small-time villain, who

was always shouting his mouth off about what he'd done or was going to do. He was bothered by his baldness and always wore a hat to cover it. He was called Jack The Hat.

He was also a crank; everyone knew it. For weeks he'd been slagging off the twins saying what he was going to do to them. One day they collared him and warned him he was heading for a lot of trouble. Shortly afterwards he went into The Regency, high on drink or drugs, armed with a shotgun, and started shouting that he wasn't scared of anyone – the twins included. He was warned that he was going too far. But he said he didn't care.

I stared at Ronnie. 'What do you mean, you've done McVitie? How bad?'

'We've killed him,' was all Ronnie replied.

I couldn't believe what I'd heard, couldn't take it in. My heart raced faster; my head pounded. I could understand teaching McVitie a lesson. But, murder?

'You've done WHAT?'

'It's true,' Reggie said.

Between them, they told me the story: they'd all been to a party, Chris and Tony Lambrianou, their pals from Birmingham, Ray and Alan Mills, Ronnie Bender and Ronnie Hart. Someone told the twins McVitie had been shouting his mouth off in The Regency again and Ronnie arranged for him to be brought to the party in Stoke Newington. Things had got out of hand.

'That's lovely,' I said sarcastically. 'Well, that's it. You've gone over the top this time. End of story.'

Typically, Ronnie said, 'Well, it's done now. That's the end of it. He had it coming anyway.'

'He'd been mouthing himself off about what he was going to do,' Reggie chimed in.

Hopwood came in with some tea, and I drank some quickly to calm myself. I glared at the twins.

143

'Nice,' I said sarcastically. 'You have somebody over. Now you ring me up at three in the morning.'

'The Old Bill are going to be buzzing,' Ronnie said.

'So? What's that got to do with me? I wasn't involved. I wasn't there.'

They said nothing.

'What's happened to him?' I asked.

They shrugged. 'I don't know,' Ronnie said. 'Somewhere in South London, I think. The Lambrianous have taken him.'

I shook my head slowly from side to side. I didn't know what else to say to them; but I did know I wasn't involved and didn't want to be. I decided to stay out of it and let them sort it out themselves, so I left the house and went home. Dolly woke up as I went in. I made up some cock and bull story about the twins having a row and told her to go back to sleep. There wasn't much sleep for me. Since the Cornell killing, police pressure had been stepped up. With a second East End murder they would go potty. I'd been woken up from a dream and dragged into a nightmare from which there would be no escape from the ghost of Jack 'The Hat' McVitie.

As I lay there, it struck me that I didn't know how McVitie had met his death. I hadn't asked. And the twins hadn't told me. They never liked talking about their rows.

Later that morning Ronnie and Reggie changed their clothes and set off for Hadleigh, in Suffolk, where we had spent our evacuation. They took Ronnie Hart with them and left Ronnie Bender to clean up the flat in Evering Road, where McVitie had met his death.

The twins and Hart spent a week away, keeping on the move among the villages and hamlets of the pretty east coast country. They kept in touch with me by telephone and were relieved to hear that Jack The Hat's disappearance did not seem to have caused any undue police activity. When they returned they were buoyant and overjoyed, carefree almost. The only thing they could talk about was this fabulous Victorian house they had found in Bildeston, a few miles from Hadleigh. It was set in eight acres, with stables, a paddock and a stream running along one boundary. It was called The Brooks and it was on the market for £12,000. The twins snapped it up.

Mum and the old man, who had moved from Vallance Road to a tower block in Bunhill Road, not far from the Bank of England in the City, did not need much persuading to move to Bildeston and for the next few months The Brooks was the centre of the twins' lives.

They spent thousands doing it up and Ronnie took great delight in giving children from the village the run of the paddock, including a donkey which they could ride. Christmas was celebrated in style, with lashings of food and drink, and Mum and the old man were as happy as they had ever been, surrounded by family and friends in a house that surpassed their wildest dreams. The ugly face of villainy seemed a million miles away: a brief glimpse of a strange face in the village or a car cruising past the house were the only reminders that the police were still interested in us.

That period of the twins' lives was hardly idyllic, but the atmosphere was quiet and peaceful and they loved it. For two young men with a couple of corpses on their consciences they were remarkably relaxed. Far from worrying about being arrested, they started talking about retiring from the London scene and becoming country gentlemen.

It was the calm before the storm. For when the twins returned to London early in 1968, the East End was buzzing with rumours that the law had been busy and it wouldn't be long before the Kray Firm was nicked. Typically Ronnie and Reggie laughed in the face of the impending danger. They honestly believed that they were invincible and that no one would dare 'grass them up'. I advised them to go away for a few months, maybe longer, to take the heat out of the situation but they just said, 'Why should we run away? This is our home. No one can touch us.'

Every night they drank in the Carpenter's Arms with their Firm, oblivious, it seemed, to all that was happening around them. Night after night, drinking, drinking, drinking. It seemed to prove something to them: if you went drinking with them, you were a lovely bloke. I did not go drinking every night, with them or anybody. I knew what was looming and I didn't want to get involved. During the day, I kept myself busy with my coat factory and theatrical agency. At night, more often than not, I'd be at home with Dolly and the kids.

But one night I had to see the twins about something and went to the Carpenter's Arms.

All the Firm were there, as usual, sitting around like bit-part actors in a bad gangster movie. Ronnie started having a pop at me; mocking me for never drinking with them, for being hen-pecked, 'under the cosh'.

Then Reggie started putting in his twopenn'orth on the same theme and I lost my temper – 'went into one', as we say in the East End.

'See this lot here,' I said, my eyes sweeping the Firm sneeringly. 'They hang round you. They love whatever's going on. They love the violence. They love being bloody gangsters.'

'You're a nice bloke,' Ronnie said, taken aback. 'All these nice guys . . .'

'Nice guys!' I yelled, feeling all my anger at what was

going to happen to us welling up inside me. 'You know what's going to happen?'

I glared at Ronnie. 'You're going to get nicked.' I glared at Reggie. 'And you're going to get nicked. And I'm going to get nicked, too.'

I glared at the Firm. And they sat there, their mouths open, shocked at dear old Charlie, good old, quiet, straight Charlie, losing his rag.

'And I'll tell you something else,' I said, my voice rising. 'You see all these clever Jack the lads here? They're going to give evidence against you. And I'm going to have to stand there and take it all. For you.'

The twins stared at me disbelievingly. I don't think I'd ever shouted so loudly and been so angry in front of people before.

Finally Ronnie found some words, 'You're being disloyal, Charlie,' he said.

'No I'm not,' I said. 'I don't owe any of them any loyalty at all. They're your mates, not mine. But I can promise you this. You won't get any loyalty from them when the Old Bill gets lively. They'll grass you up as fast as you like.'

I didn't care that the Firm was there. Big Pat Connolly was all right except when he'd had a few and Bender was a bit of a laugh. But the rest I wouldn't give two bob for. I didn't give a monkey's what anyone thought. My views on them and what they would do to the twins was long overdue anyway.

Yuka Stuttgart was a ravishing blonde Swiss beauty who had earned the title Playboy Bunny of the Year in 1966 under her Playboy name, Surry Marsh. She looked me up in London at the suggestion of Joe Kaufman, and when the Leicester club opened she was the perfect partner for

147

me. She turned out to be something else, too – the unwitting catalyst that brought Diana and me together.

The club was bustling with activity that September night. Everyone was done up to the nines and no expense had been spared to give the club a champagne launch. I walked into the club proudly, the sumptuous Surry Marsh on my arm. Heads turned; knowing smiles were exchanged.

Later, Diana came up to our table to serve something. She motioned her head towards Surry, engaged in conversation with someone on the other side of the table. 'I must say you have beautiful friends,' Diana said quietly.

I grinned. 'Yes. She's very attractive.'

Diana's eyes twinkled. 'Well, you'll enjoy yourself there, even if the club's not up to much.'

I laughed. I admired her sauce. She always saw the positive side of situations.

And although it was a flippant remark, just a bit of harmless nightclub banter, there was something in Diana's warmth and friendliness that I found appealing and, in a way, exciting.

Surry and I spent the night together in Leicester and returned to London the next day. The following week I went back to the club, Di accepted my invitation to go for a drink and the affair began. After the dreariness and monotony of marriage to Dolly I found Diana's exuberance and love of life exhilarating and refreshing. She was so much fun she didn't have an enemy in the world, although she was having a very bad time with her husband who had beaten her up a few times; but she kept her unhappiness to herself.

Chemin-de-fer games were all the rage then and Trevor and I opened a new club in Coventry. I had to spend my Wednesdays there, but that didn't stop Diana and I seeing each other. She would ring the Leofric Hotel to find out if I'd checked in, then get a taxi from Leicester after work at the club.

Diana was such an attractive creature that she was never short of admirers. One of them was Con Cluskey, a member of the Bachelors singing group, which was appearing in Coventry at the time. Con was mad about Di; he would tell me so every time we had a drink. And he was always wanting Diana to dance with him. Happily for me, Di preferred my rough-edged Cockney and didn't fall for the Irish blarney. Those mid-week spells together were joyously happy for Diana and me – welcome breaks from our respective homes where we were less and less content. But as our feelings became deeper, the need to see more of each other grew. When, early in 1968, Diana said her marriage had got so bad she was going to leave home, I knew the time had come for me to make a similar decision.

It wasn't easy with the increasing activity around the twins. Diana was no fool, but she was blissfully innocent of any kind of villainy and I was worried she might hear bad things about the Krays and associate them with me. As tactfully as I could, I explained that the twins had been involved in the odd bit of trouble and had given the name a notoriety. I warned her that it was possible something might happen. Diana, bless her, told me not to worry: she knew me well enough to know I wasn't a villain and that was enough for her. She didn't care what people thought.

Relieved, I decided to tell Mum about the woman I wanted to share my life. But just before I was going round to see her, something happened which I had to put before everything else.

Reggie was having a drink in the Carpenter's Arms one night when two plain-clothes policemen walked in. Reggie told the barman to give them both drinks. They accepted, then asked to speak to Reggie privately. Reggie said, 'What about the toilet?' and they all went in there.

The two men said they were well aware what went on with fit-ups; sometimes they agreed with them, sometimes they did not. They had just come from a meeting where it had been decided to set somebody up. And this time they did not like it at all.

Because the person who was going to be fitted up was me. And everyone knew I was straight.

The plan, they told Reggie, was to plant drugs in my car, then stop me on some pretence. Reggie asked why they wanted to put me into the frame; the cops said the powers that be were upset at some of the things I'd done to get the twins out of trouble. They told Reggie to tell me to make sure my car was secure whenever I left it.

Before they left, Reggie offered them money for the tip-off but they refused, saying that if they took it he would think that was the only reason they had come, when in fact they had come because of the principle. It may be hard for Reggie to believe, they said, but it was true.

After the pub shut, Reggie rang me. He didn't want to talk about it on the phone but asked me to go round to his place very early the next morning.

When I heard what it was all about I went spare. I rang a friend on the *Sunday Pictorial*, Norman Lucas, and told him the whole story. I told other people, too, and I told them to tell their friends. And then, just in case that didn't make the Old Bill think again, I fitted my car with the most sensitive alarm system I could afford; it was so sensitive, the wind set it off one night!

I'm happy to say that, in the end, the fit-up never happened.

Thank God for coppers with principles.

* * *

Mum, as usual, did not criticize me when I finally told her about Diana. She listened intently as I explained that it was over with Dolly, that I'd met someone else who was everything Dolly wasn't, and then she said if that was what I really wanted, she would like to meet Diana. Whether she was tempted to tell me what she knew about Dolly and George Ince I don't know; she didn't say anything. I arranged to bring Diana to the flat the following Wednesday then I walked out along Bunhill Row in the late April sunshine feeling cheerful, and a little light-headed. Telling Mum had made a huge difference; had made it all right in a way. She was going to love Diana.

But Diana couldn't come to London the following week because one of her children fell ill. I was disappointed; I'd been looking forward to introducing the two women I loved deeply. But I wasn't too bothered. There was no rush. I would go to Leicester, as usual, next Wednesday, 8 May, and bring Diana back with me. Seven days wouldn't matter.

Sadly, it was to be nearly seven *years* before I saw Diana again.

They came for me that Wednesday at 6 A.M.

The doorbell rang and there was heavy knocking on the front door. Dolly sat up in bed. 'What's that, Charlie?'

I put on a dressing gown and shuffled sleepily downstairs. I opened the door to the full extent of the safety chain. I didn't get a chance to ask who it was or what they wanted because three plain-clothes detectives shoved against the door, breaking the chain.

'Hold up,' I said, suddenly wide awake. 'What's wrong?'

They all closed in on me so that I couldn't move.

'Let's go in here, shall we?' one of them said. They

151

ushered me into the lounge. One of them eased me into a chair; another took the phone off the hook.

My eyes went from one to the other searching for a clue to what it was all about. All I could think in my confusion was that they were not Metropolitan Police, and that they were probably armed.

By now Dolly had come down with Nancy, wondering what all the fuss was about. Then Gary appeared, looking bewildered. They all stood there, looking at me, hoping I'd tell them what was going on.

I looked at the senior officer and demanded to know what I was supposed to have done to warrant my front door being broken open at six in the morning.

He said I was being arrested on a charge of conspiracy to defraud. I stared at him in shock. I'd never defrauded anyone in my life, was all I said. They cautioned me that anything I said would be taken down and might be used in evidence against me. I decided to say nothing else. There was nothing *to* say: the allegation was utter nonsense.

They told me to get dressed as they were taking me to the nick. The three of them stood watching as I washed. I wanted to shave, but they told me not to bother. Then, after I'd dressed, Dolly made some tea and we all stood around drinking it and making polite conversation like strangers at a vicar's tea party. Finally one of the officers said we were leaving and produced a pair of handcuffs. He asked me to hold out my hands. Flabbergasted, I said, 'Are you joking?'

He ignored me and tried to put the handcuffs on me. But they were too small and he couldn't fasten them. I told him not to be daft; I didn't intend running away. But the officer wouldn't give up and kept pinching my flesh, trying to get the cuffs locked. The top man looked put out, but finally told his colleague not to bother.

I told Dolly and the kids not to worry: I would be back

as soon as I'd sorted it out at the police station. Then I was escorted to a police car, a copper on either side holding the sleeves of my jacket.

About an hour earlier, more than a dozen police had got out of the lift on the ninth floor of Braithwaite House, Bunhill Row. They padded stealthily to Number 12. One of them smashed the door with a sledgehammer then they rushed in, pistols at the ready. Some of the men darted into Ronnie's bedroom; the rest went into Reggie's.

Ronnie woke up with about ten guns pointed at his chest. He reacted with customary coolness. 'I'd be careful with those,' he told them. 'One of them might go off.'

They told him to get out of bed slowly and he said sarcastically, 'What do you think I do – sleep with a bloody machine gun?'

Reggie was in bed with a young woman and Ronnie in another bed, with a young boy. Both were naked, and the police ordered them to get out and stand there while the room was searched. Reggie asked if they could put some clothes on. He was told no. He was angry, not only at being arrested, but also because the girl was being degraded. He couldn't understand why they didn't just take him out of the room and leave her alone.

Suddenly the caretaker of the flats came up. He was shocked at the broken door and the mess inside. He made some protest and asked what was going on. A couple of the officers told him, 'Fuck off.'

About half an hour later Ronnie and Reggie were driven to West End Central police station.

As they left the flat in handcuffs, Ronnie looked at the once-beautiful Chinese carpet Mum adored. It was littered with dozens of cigarette butts stamped out by the dawn visitors.

* * *

153

Getting into the Rover I was not unduly bothered, because my conscience was clear: I was not guilty of fraud and that was that. When we got to Bow Street nick I'd call my solicitor and put things straight.

However, as the car pulled away from the house in Poplar I had a slight feeling of unease: police wanting to arrest someone on a charge of fraud did not force open doors early in the morning and treat the suspect as though he was going to shoot his way out of trouble.

And I knew I was right when the car roared past Bow Street nick and kept heading west. 'Where are we going?' I asked.

'You'll know soon enough,' one of the officers said brusquely.

As we sped through London's sleeping streets in silence, one thought kept coming back to me as my mind reeled with the possibilities of what lay ahead: whatever it was had better be sorted out quickly, because today was Wednesday and I was going to Leicester to see Diana.

I was thinking about her as the Rover swung into West End Central police station in Savile Row.

Inside it was bedlam. Dozens of police were racing around in organized confusion; giving or receiving orders, asking or answering questions, taking notes, speaking on the telephone. I had little time to take it in because I was hustled into a waiting room at the rear of the station, but I did get a fleeting glimpse of some familiar faces that confirmed what I'd begun to suspect: I had been dragged out of bed by something far more serious than an allegation of fraud.

Within minutes, a sergeant read out a charge and cautioned me. The charge had something to do with American bonds and was a load of nonsense. I asked for permission to ring a solicitor, but was refused. All my possessions had been taken from me at home, but I was searched again. Then I was put in a cell. It was now about 8 A.M.

Over the next few hours, there was a lot of rattling of keys, slamming of doors, and raising of angry voices as other cells filled up and people were questioned. Through the tiny bars of the cell's solid door, I saw a lot of faces I recognized: members of the twins' so-called Firm and other East End characters, including Limehouse Willey and Harry Hopwood. The procession seemed endless, and highly significant.

Two faces I didn't see were those of Ronnie and Reggie. When I finally did see them, it was nearly two days later – at 3 A.M.

I was taken from my cell into the charge room and there they were, looking as rough as me: dirty, scruffy, unshaven, and red-eyed through lack of sleep. Ronnie was in a shirt because the police had not allowed him to put on a coat. He asked if I was all right. I would be, I said, if someone would tell me what was going on.

Then all the rest were brought in and senior officers started taking particulars. Sitting at one desk, with inspector's pips, was someone I'd known for years, ever since he was a constable on the beat. He was a terrific rugby player and once, when we both found ourselves in the South of France, I played with him against the French Navy in a stadium at St Raphael. He was plain PC Vic Streeter then, but now he was Detective Inspector Streeter and he was sitting behind a desk taking down my details. We didn't mention the past.

I then had to stand before a young bloke at a typewriter, who asked daft questions such as: 'Do you have blond hair?' 'Have you got blue eyes?' I had not been through anything like that before and I didn't like it; besides, tension and lack of sleep had made me short-tempered. Finally I could stand the bloke's inane questions no longer and snapped, 'Do you need bloody glasses or what?' He shut up.

You could almost feel the tension in that small, crowded room. It needed something to break it and, of course, it was Ronnie who provided it.

Everyone's particulars had been noted and the law were wondering what to do with us, when Ronnie suddenly called out, 'Nipper!'

Detective Superintendent Read turned round. 'Yes, Ronnie?' he answered, respectfully.

'Any chance of a bit of bail?' said Ronnie, po-faced.

The whole room cracked up.

Read coughed quietly. 'Er, I don't think so, Ronnie,' he said, fighting to stop himself laughing.

'Just thought I'd ask,' Ronnie added with a grin.

Early on Friday morning things started to happen: it was orderly and purposeful, with no sign of Wednesday's confusion. I was taken from my cell, closely guarded by two coppers, and ushered into a Black Maria at the back of the nick. I had never seen inside one of those forbidding vehicles and I got a shock. A narrow passageway ran along the centre of what was a converted large van; on either side of the aisle were small cubicles – rather like tiny dog kennels – which allowed the prisoner to stand or sit but little else. Once inside the cubicle the prisoner was cut off from the outside world except for a restricted view from a small window.

When we were all inside, the Black Maria moved out of the yard and the sirens started. They howled deafeningly during the whole journey down Regent Street, around Piccadilly Circus to the Strand and up Bow Street to the magistrates' court, opposite Covent Garden Opera House. Through my tiny window I caught sight of startled pedestrians rushing to get out of the way of the high-speed van and its escort of motorbikes and cars.

It was an elaborate, costly pantomime.

At Bow Street, the twins and I and several others were charged with a number of offences from petty larceny to conspiracy, all of which were merely holding charges that were later dropped.

During the lunch break, we were all shepherded into a large room and left on our own. Something wasn't quite right; I sensed it and so did the twins. Then I realized that a door on the other side of the room led into a corridor which, in turn, led to the street.

'This is a get up,' I said. 'They've put us in here deliberately. They want us to make a run for it.'

I could picture the newspaper headlines: Dangerous Gang In Dash For Freedom. Everyone agreed with me and we just sat around in that room waiting for someone to come in.

When Read arrived Ronnie couldn't resist it. 'We're still here, Nipper,' he said. 'Sorry about all your little Firm waiting outside with their guns. You must think we're silly.'

For the twins, hearing they were being remanded in custody came as no surprise. To me, who had never been inside a jail, it was a great shock. But it was nothing to the humiliation I felt during my first few hours in Brixton Prison in South-West London. I was ordered to strip totally naked in front of two prison officers, then subjected to a most intimate search. I couldn't believe they seriously thought I'd had the foresight to insert money, tobacco or cigarette papers in my rectum, which, I learned, some forward-thinking prisoners do prior to being sentenced. I was told to take a bath. The water was tepid and just nine inches deep, but I attacked my body vigorously and thankfully. I hadn't seen soap or water for three days.

I was then allowed to put on my clothes and was shown into a room, where Ronnie and Reggie were sitting. They seemed in good spirits and Ronnie took great delight in telling us what he'd said to the armed copper who had disturbed his sleep three days before. I was not able to share their light-hearted approach to our predicament; I had businesses on the outside that would not run themselves. I had children who needed me. And what about Diana? But at least the twins and I were happy on one score: Mum and the old man were miles away from the aggravation, safely tucked up in that comfortable house amid the tranquillity of the Suffolk countryside.

We were not allowed to spend long together. We suspected the room was bugged so we kept our conversation to trivialities. Whoever was listening quickly got bored and we were taken to separate cells.

As the massive door clanged behind me, I looked at what was to be my home for the forseeable future: an expanse of painted brick wall around a rectangular area about 11ft by 6ft. To my right was a bed, a stout, tubular steel and wire contraption hinged to the wall. In the far corner an enamelled bowl and jug stood on a triangular table; underneath this was a Victorian-style bedpan. To my left there was a sturdy wooden table with a matching chair.

That was it.

I sat on the bed and thought, and my thoughts were about my kids, and Dolly and Diana, and Mum and the old man, and when I'd exhausted all my thoughts about them I thought about myself and then I started to think about freedom.

It was the first time it had been taken away from me and it was a bad, bad feeling.

*   *   *

I had always believed in justice. If you did wrong, then were caught and found guilty, you were punished. If you hadn't done anything wrong, you had nothing to worry about. I knew about police frame-ups, of course, but in those first few distressing days in custody I did not think for a second that anyone was out to get me, to stitch me up. Sitting in that cell, day after day, all I could think was that it was a mistake; a massive mistake that had put me temporarily behind bars but a mistake nonetheless. Someone, somewhere would realize that soon, and I would be released, with a suitable apology, to continue earning an honest living on the outside.

I saw the twins every day; we were allowed to take exercise in a small yard for half an hour each morning and we discussed the situation. They were still fairly relaxed and confident: they felt, as I did, that the charges made against them were nonsense and would be thrown out through lack of evidence. Although they had serious problems over the killings of Cornell and McVitie, both were convinced the police would not be able to prove they were responsible. I was not so sure but, from a personal point of view, I was not bothered. Even if someone did come forward to testify that Ronnie had shot Cornell, how could that affect me? I wasn't there. Even if the truth about McVitie came out, how could I be implicated? I'd got a phone call in the middle of the night after the event and knew it had happened; but I'd gone back to bed and left the twins and the others to get on with it. I told the twins this as we took our daily stroll, but they were uncompromising: they said I'd have to take my chance with them and seven of the Firm who were also on remand.

The days rolled into weeks as the machinery of the law moved ponderously along. The monotony of prison life was relieved by interviews with solicitors, noisy, high-speed journeys to Bow Street, and visits by Mum, the old man, Dolly and the children. I was tempted to write to Diana but always decided not to. We had a future together, I was sure of it; but that, like everything else in my life, had gone up in the air. How could I make long-term plans when I had no idea what was going to happen tomorrow? In that cell I thought about Diana a lot. I knew she would have read what had happened and secretly hoped she would get in touch one way or another. But I wouldn't, couldn't, blame her if she chose not to. Leicester was only 150 miles away, but the world in which she moved was a million light years from the one I was now in. How could Diana possibly begin to understand what was going on if I didn't myself? How could I possibly blame her if she had written me off as an exciting, but closed, chapter of her life.

Through the small, heavily barred window high above me, I stared at the blueness of the summer sky and found myself thinking yet again of the appalling injustice: innocent until proven guilty, cried the statute of our beloved, jealously guarded democracy. So why was I here? Why was I being treated like a criminal? Why was I incarcerated behind a massive steel and wood barricade as though already tried and convicted by the courts?

Slowly, my anger turned to bitterness and then, as I saw and heard what was happening around us, I started to worry.

With the twins and members of their Firm locked away on charges that could be thrown out later, Nipper Read got to work on the big stuff. He needed key witnesses – members of the trusted Firm – to betray the twins, to go over to the other side to help put them and others away on the more serious charges. He needed more statements, more damning documents and, with the twins removed, so was the desire to stay silent. With the fear of retribution gone, the men with a lot to say were free to say it, to do deals to save themselves. As London sweltered, first one then another Judas stepped forward to buy his freedom with a pocketful of lies. Now the spider's web was finally spun and out of the labyrinth of tiny, crowded dockland woodwork came the insects, creeping and crawling to the spider, and their names were Ronald Hart and Albert Donaghue and William Exley and Jack Dickson and Leslie Payne and A. B. Cooper and Billy Elvey.

Still the twins were optimistic. Still they had that air of invincibility, the confidence that when it came to it they wouldn't, couldn't be charged with murder. Even when we were put in a specially built two-floor cage, they didn't appreciate the significance of Donaghue, Hart and Dickson being excluded. Even when they heard that visiting friends were intercepted at the prison gates and warned not to have contact with us they didn't see the danger signals.

They were prepared for imprisonment on the lesser charges, though. At one of the early Bow Street hearings, Ronnie was so uninterested in the proceedings that he actually fell asleep during someone's testimony. When I heard the gentle rumble of his snoring I nudged him and told him to wake up. But Ronnie merely grunted, 'Leave me alone. I've got two clever brothers – you listen to it,' and went back to sleep. Suddenly the magistrate noticed and asked if Ronnie was all right. I said I thought so, and nudged Ronnie again. He opened his eyes and thanked the magistrate, saying he felt fine. But about ten minutes later he dozed off again. Later he said he knew they were going down so why should he listen to it all?

Then the twins were charged with murdering Frank Mitchell. The big man's body had never been found after

161

he vanished in December 1966, but Albert Donaghue had told the police the twins had arranged for him to be killed. The charge came as a shock, naturally, but the twins were still surprisingly nonchalant about their worsening predicament. They pleaded not guilty.

My barrister, Desmond Vowden, had given me real hope of getting bail at the next Bow Street hearing. Not one of the conspiracy or fraud charges against me had much substance, he said, and he was confident the magistrate would take a lenient view. My spirits soared; justice was smiling on me, as I always knew it would in the end. The prospect of freedom – albeit a conditional one – dominated my thoughts for the next few days.

At Bow Street, the twins and I were always kept in separate cells, but when we arrived for the next hearing they put us in one together. There, too, was another Mitchell: Charlie Mitchell. We'd known him for years. He was sitting at one end of the cell, away from the twins, and when I walked in he put a finger to his mouth and said, 'Don't speak too loudly. It's bugged.' Then he came up to me, saying to the twins, 'I'm going to say something to Charlie. He'll tell you later.' He whispered in my ear, 'You may hear something you think is terrible. But don't do anything about it because there may be a reason for it.' I didn't understand what he was talking about, but he said, 'Don't puzzle it out. Just remember, I told you.'

A few minutes later, the cell door opened. An inspector said, 'Charlie, we'd like to see you a minute.' I went outside into the corridor. The inspector was joined by another officer, who said, 'Charlie, we're charging you with the murder of Frank Mitchell.'

My mouth fell open. 'You're *what*?'

As we were speaking, Mr Vowden came along the corridor towards us. I told him what had happened. He was kind and sympathetic, saying he knew I'd had nothing to do with any murder, but there was nothing he could do until it came up in court. He did say he wished he could have taken a picture of me at that time because I would have been found not guilty by the look on my face.

I was gutted. For apart from the horror of facing a murder charge, my much cherished hope of bail was gone.

I went back into the cell and told the twins what had happened. They were stunned. Charlie Mitchell said it was diabolical; he was choked for me, he said. Fortunately, this trumped-up, stupid charge was thrown out at Bow Street for lack of evidence.

The cage made life bearable for us as the months rolled on: the beds were more comfortable and there was a TV room which we were allowed into, two or three at a time. But we were not allowed any contact with other prisoners. Nor were we allowed to go to church on Sundays. Security around us was elaborate and efficient, but we managed to find out a lot about what was going on. One new item that filtered through was that Nipper Read was visiting Brixton in various disguises for his growing Kray dossier.

The months rolled on and on and then, hard though it was for us to believe, it was Christmas. Mum and the old man, who had sold The Brooks and returned to London permanently, sent in as much food and drink as allowed, although money was beginning to be a bit short. It was my twentieth wedding anniversary but Brixton Prison is far from ideal as a venue for such a celebration. As the festivities passed and we moved on to yet another New Year, I thought of Diana. Had she, I wondered, followed through that decision to leave home? Whatever had happened, I hoped she was happy.

And then it was 7 January and the Old Bailey was set for the trial of the century. The cockney canaries had sung their hearts out to Nipper and his men. And when the twins and I, with seven members of their so-called Firm, emerged from the cells into the famous No. 1 Court that morning it was not to face the relatively innocuous charges of conspiracy to defraud but varying charges of murder and complicity in murder.

Ronnie was charged with murdering George Cornell, in The Blind Beggar, on 9 March 1966. Reggie was charged with killing Jack McVitie, in Blonde Carol's flat, in Stoke Newington, on 29 October 1967.

And I was accused of being an accessory to McVitie's murder. To be more precise, that I helped dispose of the body.

I was apprehensive, of course. Who wouldn't be? But I was relieved, too. Eight months in prison had knocked my self-confidence, left my nerves in tatters, and almost wrecked my spirit. Now, the nightmare was nearing its end. Twelve ordinary citizens, and a fair-minded judge, were going to see through all the lies and deceit and set me free, I was certain of that.

Justice, I'd always been told, must not just be done, but must be *seen* to be done. That cold winter's morning, I couldn't wait for the world to see it.

Chapter Eleven

People who have never been in trouble with the police will find it difficult, if not impossible, to understand why I didn't go into court and tell the truth about that terrible October night in 1967. That way, I could have thwarted every attempt by police and prosecution witnesses to convict me for something I did not do. But, quite simply, that was not the way we did things in the East End. Nobody – me included – thought for a moment that the twins would plead anything but not guilty to everything, which meant that I would have to deny all knowledge of Jack McVitie's murder and take my chances along with everyone else.

Lying, I appreciated, would make things difficult for me, because I *had* received a phone call in the middle of that Saturday night and *had* gone to Harry Hopwood's house, and both Hopwood and Ronnie Hart were going to say so. I wasn't unduly worried, however. Hart, the star prosecution witness, had traded his conscience for freedom, and had proved at the Bow Street committal hearing that he didn't give a toss for the truth. But my counsel had reserved my defence, and not one of Hart's damning false allegations had been challenged yet. Now, before an Old Bailey jury, the gloves would be off: Vowden would be the aggressor and every one of Hart's lies, every careless slip of the tongue – not only by him, but by all the prosecution witnesses – would be seized on and torn apart.

I honestly didn't think Hart's evidence would affect me too much. He had a grudge against the twins, may have hated them even, but I'd never done anything to make him want to frame me. He'd lied in the lower court but surely under fierce cross-examination he would crack and admit I wasn't involved in disposing of McVitie's body.

Standing in the famous No 1 Court at the Old Bailey that first morning with the nine other accused I felt supremely confident. For at the end of the day the charge against me *was* unfounded. That night in 1967 I had not even seen McVitie's body, let alone got rid of it. And anyway, as Mr Vowden had explained, if the impossible happened, if the preposterous lies *were* believed, the onus was still on the prosecution to prove I was guilty, not on me to prove I was innocent.

I looked confidently at the jury. They all appeared to be intelligent human beings, capable of distinguishing between fact and fiction, simple truth and barefaced lie. I looked at the judge – Melford Stevenson, the epitome of justice. Experienced, knowledgeable, wise. He, too, looked as if he would be eager to protect an innocent man from the falsehoods of his corruptible accusers.

The cases against the twins, their so-called Firm and me went on for thirty-nine days. The popular papers labelled it the Trial of the Century and the financial cost of the whole affair – over £150,000 – earned it a place in the *Guinness Book of Records* as the most expensive criminal hearing ever. If you want a strictly accurate, blow-by-blow account of all that went on, the statements of claim, the pleadings and submissions, wrapped up in colourful and complicated legal mumbo-jumbo, plus all the heated exchanges between accusers and accused that made the headlines, your local library will probably be able to provide you with details. Certainly I'm not going to attempt to do so here. The whole business, from the moment of my early-morning arrest on 8 May 1968 to my sentencing on 5 March 1969, was the most nerve-racking, nightmarish experience of my life, and at the end of it all I was in no position to remember much about the proceedings except what had directly or indirectly affected me. Everyone there, from the judge and jurors to the men in the dock, the barristers in their wigs and gowns and the spectators in the gallery, saw the trial differently. For me it was a mixture of highs and lows, from times when I was amused, hopeful or quietly elated, to others when I was worried, acutely disappointed or hurled into dark despair. Since this is my story, these are the moments I shall concentrate on.

The basis of Ronnie Hart's evidence against me was that I had driven with him in his mini to Freddie Foreman's pub, the Prince of Wales in Lant Street, Southwark, in the early hours of Sunday 28 October. The purpose of the visit, said Hart, was to tell Foreman to get rid of McVitie's body. This was, of course, a blatant lie, which I thought was made clear when Harry Hopwood, another prosecution witness, told the truth, which conflicted with Hart's claim. Hopwood told the jury, quite rightly, that I had indeed gone to his house but had set off home alone about half an hour later. Moreover, he added that Hart himself had not left the house. Men have been acquitted on less corroboration and my hopes were high. But I did not realize then that this was more of a political trial than a criminal one. In case the jury were having thoughts of believing Hopwood, Mr Justice Stevenson pooh-poohed his evidence. 'In things like this, people *do* get mixed up,' he told them. 'It must have been a bit of a shock for him; he must have forgotten. But at least he is telling the truth, or so he thinks. He's just mixed up. We have the proof from Ronald Hart.'

It was at that moment, I think, that I glanced up at

Mum in the gallery. Throughout my life she had drummed into me how important it was to tell the truth. How I wished right then that I could have done just that, backing up Hopwood's accurate statement and redressing the balance in my favour after the judge's appallingly biased comment. My fears that my fate was in the judge's hands rather than the jury's grew when he unexpectedly called an adjournment thirty minutes early – at a crucial moment in Hart's evidence.

Hart had been telling the court about a visit he allegedly made with me to Foreman's pub a week after McVitie's murder. He said he remembered Foreman leaning over to me and saying, 'When I found that body it was all glistening, like he had Vaseline on him.' The pub was noisy and Hart said he couldn't hear anything else. Just that sentence! It was all too pat and I was sure the jury would not believe it. Then, during Vowden's cross-examination, Hart made a slip that sent my pulse racing with excitement. Having just stated that I was with him that day he then said in a loud voice that I wasn't. As Hart was about to get himself deeper into trouble, however, Mr Justice Stevenson interrupted the cross-examination and said the court would adjourn for lunch. It was 12.30. The court normally rose at 1 P.M.

During the break I was very worried, sensing trouble. The judge had been so biased against all the defendants that I felt sure he had called for an adjournment early to protect Hart. Vowden told me I was being over-sensitive. The slip was significant, he said, and the judge, realizing this, had called for an early lunch because the case against me would be thrown out that afternoon.

I was not convinced, and no sooner had Hart got back on the stand than the judge reminded him, 'You said earlier that you weren't with Mr Kray that day.'

And, of course, dear old Ronnie had had a change of heart!

He had been thinking about it over lunch and was now sure that I *had*, indeed, been with him. Vowden couldn't believe it, but I could. I may not be as eloquent or as academically brilliant as a university-educated barrister but I am sharp-witted, and astute enough to know when the dice are loaded. No one will ever convince me that Stevenson didn't save the prosecution that day, or that its star witness was not given a gentle prod in the right direction over lunch.

Even with Hart giving an Oscar-winning performance to try to convict me, there was so much doubt clouding my case that I should have got off. One of the twins' Firm, Scotch Jack Dickson, for example, was hopelessly trapped by Vowden, only to be saved by the judge who excused his mistake.

Dickson was adamant that he had been with me in a Mile End café owned by Terry Pellicci the morning after McVitie's murder. He claimed I had told him the twins had killed McVitie, and that I knew all about it. Something bothered me about his testimony. Apart from the fact that it was all a load of cobblers designed, like Hart's, to plunge me deeper into the prosecution net, there was something else, something not right. I thought long and hard about it that night in my Brixton cell and finally it hit me.

It was impossible for me to have been in the café with Dickson. It was impossible for anyone to have been in the café at all that day . . . because it wasn't open on Sundays!

Again, my heart beat a little faster. Surely this was important. Surely a prosecution witness lying on oath was good for my case. Surely all that Dickson had said, whatever it was meant to imply, would have to be struck from the record, or the jury told to disregard it.

In his cross-examination, Vowden let Dickson go on and on about his café conversation with me. Was it Sunday? Yes. Are you quite sure about that? Absolutely. Is there just a chance, a mere possibility, that you're mistaken; that it was another day, the Monday morning, perhaps? Not a chance, sir, it was a Sunday. I remember it clearly. Thank you. Mr Dickson. That is all.

Enter Terry Pellicci for the defence. Now, Mr Pellicci, did Mr Dickson and Mr Kray come to your cafe? Yes, sir, I saw them together several times. Was one of those times Sunday 28 October? No, sir. Are you quite certain of that, Mr Pellicci? Yes, sir. How can you be so certain? The café isn't open on Sundays, sir, I haven't opened on a Sunday for seventeen years. Thank you, Mr Pellicci. That is all.

Dickson's jaw dropped. There was a flurry of activity among the prosecution barristers, much hurried whispering and looks of surprise and consternation. Vowden sat down, the faintest look of satisfaction on his face. I fought to stop myself grinning. It was a bombshell for the prosecution all right.

And then Mr Justice Stevenson stepped in to save their blushes again. 'It is clear Mr Dickson has made a mistake with the day of the meeting,' he said. 'As it couldn't have been the Sunday, it must have been the Monday.'

And that was that. For although Vowden made the point over and over again, it was what the judge said that in the end made all the difference.

Naturally I was gutted. But although the lies were making the case against me look very black and the judge, for some reason, seemed to have it in for me, I still clung to my strong belief in British justice. I had *not* disposed of a murdered man's body, so come what may I was not going to be found guilty of doing so.

I consoled myself that it was still early days; there

would be other ways in which the prosecution's liars could be exposed. One of these came in the shape of two honest men who ran a garage off Vallance Road. Hart's version of events during the early hours of that Sunday morning could not be right, they told Vowden, because the mini Hart said we drove in was parked in their garage all Saturday night and Sunday morning. They were not mistaken, they stressed, because the mini had blocked some taxis and efforts had been made to trace the owner. To me the men's joint evidence seemed manna from heaven, but apparently the police got wind of it and told them not to interfere. Despite the garage men's protests, they were not even allowed to appear in court.

Even so, there were other holes in Hart's testimony that should have made the jury suspicious of his motives. On his own admission he had been a witness to murder, yet I was supposed to have suddenly appeared on the scene and taken over. He said I made him stand by the mini outside the Prince of Wales at 3 A.M. while I rang the bell and woke Foreman up. On one hand he said he was too far away to hear all that was said but on the other he had no doubt that he heard me telling Foreman to get rid of the body. It did not add up.

Hart claimed the Lambrianou brothers had taken McVitie's body from the house in Stoke Newington 'over the water' to South London, but he and Hopwood said the brothers were not in Hopwood's house when I arrived. So how was I supposed to tell Foreman where the body was? Unless I'd driven around South London, found the Lambrianous and asked them, I would not have known. If I didn't know where the body was, how could I have disposed of it?

It was a dream-like experience, sitting there listening to people relating in sincere tones, as if butter wouldn't melt in their mouths, what I was supposed to have done. There

171

seemed to be so many conflicting statements that I got totally confused and lost track of the plot, as it were. Most of the time I found myself thinking: if only the twins hadn't told Harry Hopwood to ring me. If there hadn't been that phone call, none of this would have happened and I wouldn't have been in the frame. But the fact that I *had* gone to the house gave the police and their witnesses the foundation on which to build their lies.

In court there was so much happening, so much to take in and concentrate on that I had little time to feel angry. But at night, alone in my cell in Brixton, my feelings would boil up and my insides would ache with fury, not only at the twins for roping me in so unnecessarily and thoughtlessly but also at their short-sightedness and naïvety so far as their damned blasted Firm was concerned. Ronnie and Reggie had always attracted people and been surrounded by large groups who enjoyed their charisma. And they loved it, probably needing it to boost their own ideas of themselves as powerful leaders of men. But with one or two exceptions, the idiots who went around with them hanging on their every word were not worth two bob. The Firm were physically tough but not very bright characters with overblown ideas of their own importance. Having little ability themselves to make anything worthwhile of their lives they settled for a grubby twilight existence basking in the dubious reflected glory of the twins' reputation as fearless hard men, and grabbing the easy money that came from being their henchmen. Despite what Ronnie and Reggie believed then, or now, the Firm revelled in the violence and wallowed in their roles as self-styled gangsters.

In my lonely cell I often conjured up pictures of that fateful evening in Evering Road. I knew enough of the Firm's mentality to realize what had probably happened to prompt Ronnie to have McVitie brought to the flat

172

from The Regency, and I would play the imagined scene over and over in my mind, a worthless exercise in masochism that served no purpose except to make me even angrier and more frustrated.

"'Ere, Ron,' I could hear one of them saying. 'McVitie's in The Regency mouthing off again. Says he's going to blow you and Reg away.'

If that had got no reaction some bright spark – maybe even Ronnie Hart himself – would have stoked him up. 'You're not going to stand for that, Ron. You're not going to let him get away with that, are you?'

Such was the mood at that gathering that Ronnie bit on the bait, telling Tony Lambrianou to fetch McVitie – which they did, not from fear of Ronnie, as was suggested at the trial, but from a sadistic pleasure at witnessing a hated man's humiliation at the hands of a more powerful individual.

No one will convince me that the Firm that night didn't egg on the twins to sort out McVitie once and for all. If it was all Ronnie's idea, if they were worried for McVitie and wanted to spare him his ordeal, why didn't they just go to The Regency and tell him to make himself scarce? No one would have been the wiser if Chris or Tony Lambrianou had said, 'Do us a favour and go, so we can say we didn't see you.' As it was, they loved it all so much that they raced off to The Regency and gleefully brought McVitie back to meet a violent death.

In the early hours, when my fury had cooled, the irony of my own situation would hit me. I had received a phone call *after* the event, which had implicated me, but if someone had rung me *beforehand* it would never have happened, because I wouldn't have let it. Just as I had told Scotch Jack in The Starlight Club that he wasn't going to shoot Connie Whitehead, so I would have told the

173

twins and the idiots around them that it was madness to wipe out McVitie.

This is why no one even tried to suggest at the trial that I was at the party. If I had been, there would have been no murder. As it was, McVitie was lured to the flat and confronted with men in no mood for mercy. Reggie, out of his mind on drink and Valium, taunted him that he wasn't much of a man because he had thrown his wife out of a car, and that although he had had plenty to say about him and Ronnie he wasn't so big now. Reggie pulled out a gun. He fired, but it didn't go off. McVitie tried to dive out of a window but was pulled back in by the Firm. Then there was a struggle and Ronnie was holding McVitie, supposedly urging Reggie to kill him, and suddenly Reggie had a knife in his hand and was plunging it into McVitie's throat, the drink and drugs transforming him into a mindless killer with no regard for his victim or for himself.

Over the years, I've thought deeply about that terrible event and could never take in that Reggie did it. Yes, he could be violent, but, unlike Ronnie, he had always held back. Much was made at the trial of Ronnie's alleged comment, 'I've done mine. Now you do yours.' I do not know whether he did say it because neither twin will discuss it with me. They did not volunteer information at the time and when I've brought it up since then, they can't understand why I'm interested in something that happened so long ago. They say, 'What difference will it make if we tell you?' To me, it doesn't *seem* like the kind of thing Ronnie would have said; he'd always been more inclined to do things himself.

One thing is certain: if Frances had not died, Reggie would not have committed that crime, spurred on by a death-wish. If Frances had been alive and they were living a happy married life, with children perhaps, he would have been a different person. When guns had come on the scene he would have thought it through and seen the sense in getting out. As it was, Frances met a tragic end and Reggie lost all interest in life, becoming just like all the others. When those idiots who called themselves friends egged Ronnie on that Saturday night, the lethal cocktail of drinks and drugs helped Reggie enjoy it all as much as everyone else, and he was to pay the price.

Despite all the prosecution lies, all the inadmissible evidence, and my own barrister's reluctance to put me on the witness stand, I still believe I would have been cleared – or at least received a far lighter sentence – had it not been for Melford Stevenson. Before the case police and lawyers alike were saying that he was the worst possible choice for the men on trial, and I was to find this hard to dispute as the hearing went on and on. It was not just the words he used, it was his tone and mannerisms, his tut-tutting and sarcastic comments that were quite obviously designed to leave the jury in no doubt what he felt about a particular witness's evidence.

The transcript of the hearing does not tell the full story. If it had been taped and filmed, one would be able to see how Stevenson swayed the evidence in the prosecution's favour and then meted out the unbelievably harsh sentences that appeased his pals in high places but shocked nearly everyone else.

The small things drove me and the twins mad: the way Stevenson treated our Aunt May, for instance. May had never been in a court in her life, and was married to a man who had worked in the same company for fifty years and was so straight that he'd never even been given a parking ticket. She was a religious woman who went to church regularly, but Stevenson treated her abominably with a total lack of respect just because she was speaking

175

on behalf of the twins. In contrast, Ronnie Hart's girl-friend was treated like a lady by Stevenson. It really wound us up, but there was nothing we could do except sit there and take it.

We took it for thirty-nine days; days in which the smooth, efficient, well-rehearsed case against the twins, their Firm and me rolled on and on to its inevitable conclusion. Many days were filled with legal mumbo-jumbo which I found hard to follow; others were filled with stories of the twins' reign of terror, which I found equally hard to swallow. But there were moments of humour, too, like Ronnie's comment when he was charged with being involved in the McVitie murder. Warned by Nipper Read that anything he said would be taken down and might be used in evidence against him, Ronnie replied, 'I presume that your presumptions are precisely incorrect and that your sarcastic insinuations are too obnoxious to be appreciated.' As he watched a fellow detective write it on the charge sheet, Ronnie added, 'Bit hard to spell, that one, isn't it?' I'm not sure what the elaborately worded sentence meant, but Ronnie liked the sound of it as a child and had learned it parrot fashion. He said it to the police because he didn't give a damn. He was obviously philosophical; he always thought he'd get thirty years. His cheeky answer to the charge had to be read out at the Old Bailey, of course, and provided welcome light relief to the heaviness of the proceedings. I think the laughter in court even woke Ronnie up.

If there was going to be any humour, even black humour, it was bound to come from Ronnie. And he made me smile one day when he more or less ordered the judge to let him give evidence after making it clear to defence and prosecution counsels that he would not. Ian Barrie, charged as an accessory in the Blind Beggar killing, had just stepped down from the witness box and

Ronnie suddenly said loudly, 'I'm going to give evidence now.' Some bigwig – probably the judge – told him it was most irregular: Ronnie had chosen not to testify and had instructed his counsel, Paul Wrightson, accordingly. That cut no ice whatsoever with Ronnie. 'I can change my mind if I like,' he said. 'I want to give evidence. And I'm going to. It's my right.'

I couldn't help smiling at the turmoil he caused. Courts, naturally, have set rules of procedure and officials don't like the protocol being upset. But Ronnie couldn't have cared less; once he decided to do something he usually did it. He got his way that day, and the court buzzed with expectancy as he took the stand.

Prosecution counsel, Kenneth Jones, a little Welshman with a resounding Richard Burton-type voice that seemed too big for his body, couldn't believe his luck. He tore into Ronnie with relish, determined to goad him into losing his temper and, perhaps, betray signs of the violence that was an integral part of the prosecution case. Much to the eloquent Mr Jones's chagrin, Ronnie was far from intimidated by his cultured tones and cunning approach. He was in the mood to antagonize everyone and he matched Jones's skill with a cheeky arrogance.

'Among your Firm, you are known as the Colonel?' asked Mr Jones.

'I was a deserter from the Army, so how could I be a Colonel?' Ronnie replied.

'You gave money to charity,' Mr Jones said later.

'Is that a terrible thing?' Ronnie asked.

'There are stories that it might have been £10,000. Where did you get that money from?'

'I don't think that matters,' Ronnie countered. 'I had it. That's all that matters.' When that didn't seem to satisfy his interrogator, Ronnie shouted, 'If you want to know, my father gambles for me. He's up there in the gallery, so ask him. I know nothing about gambling, so there's no point in asking me. I may have clubs, but I know nothing about gambling.'

The judge broke in to tell Ronnie not to shout. But Ronnie just said 'Why? I'm here to speak. And I'm answering.'

Jones went on and on and finally Ronnie had had enough. 'Listen, you fat slob,' he said, making me cringe. 'You've been going on enough. You're Welsh, aren't you? Down the mines would have been a more fitting profession for you than being a prosecutor, I promise you that.'

Naturally, this attitude did not endear him to the judge or jury, but Ronnie was convinced, as ever, that he was going to get thirty years, innocent or guilty, and he didn't care: it had just come into his head that he wanted to say something, so he said it.

Something Ronnie did not say, however, despite my encouragement to do so, was what his so-called pals, particularly Hart and Albert Donaghue, had got up to during the twins' so-called reign of terror. These two supposedly tough individuals loved the villainy. Late one night they got drunk, forced their way into the Regency Club and demanded £50 a week from the owner Johnny Barrie. The next day, having sobered up, they were worried and went to Ronnie to own up. He went spare, wanting to know why they had done that when the Firm had a share in the club anyway. Hart and Donaghue admitted they had made a mistake but begged Ronnie to say he'd sent them round because Barrie might get the police involved. Typically, Ronnie helped them. He told Barrie he'd had the hump the previous night and had sent Hart and Donaghue round. He said he was sorry and asked Barrie to forget it.

To my disappointment, Ronnie didn't tell that story in

court. Nor did he tell how Hart and Donaghue went to Freddie Foreman's pub and tried to 'nip' him for £25. When I asked him why he hadn't seized the chance to redress the balance that was swinging ever more heavily against us all he said that nothing would ever make him sink as low as those 'rats'. He had his principles and he would stick to them.

But I know he was sick to the stomach over a blatant lie Donaghue told the police when he was trying to get himself off the hook in the McVitie case. During the meeting with Donaghue and our solicitors, shortly after the arrests, Ronnie asked for the address of Donaghue's mother, saying he wanted to send someone round with some money for her. It was a genuine offer of help but when Donaghue turned Queen's Evidence he twisted the story to put Ronnie in a bad light, claiming that Ronnie wanted the address because he was going to arrange for the old lady to be murdered. In those days, Ronnie seldom worried about anything, but that allegation hurt him. Set up an old woman to be wiped out! Ronnie used to get the hump if anyone even swore in front of women. But when his chance came to hit back against Donaghue he still chose not to.

I never found out whether that lie was Donaghue's idea or the police's. Certainly Nipper Read and his team weren't fussy about the tactics they used to blacken our names and reputations. The disgraceful lie about Reggie and Connie Whitehead's son, for example, takes some beating.

Reggie idolized Connie Whitehead's little boy – also named Connie – and used to take him to a boys' club to see Father Hetherington. When the balloon went up, Whitehead tried to get himself out of trouble by writing a letter to the police saying that Reggie had threatened his wife and son. Our solicitor heard of the allegations and

179

told the twins, but made them promise not to touch Whitehead. It was very hard for them because Reggie had stayed with the Whiteheads and had done nothing but try to help them. Ronnie seemed even more wound up about the lie than Reggie, and when he saw Whitehead in jail he said, 'I see. You wrote to Old Bill and said Reggie threatened your wife and kid.' Connie had no idea the twins knew and he went white, fearing the worst. Ronnie would have broken Connie in half if he hadn't promised to tell the truth.

Connie did admit in court that the police had made him say it, but as far as the twins and myself were concerned that did not make things right. What sort of man agrees to utter such a lie to make things easier for himself?

Most of the courtroom battles were, of course, won by the prosecution, but Reggie did score a couple of victories which, although they did not affect the outcome of the cases, did give him some satisfaction.

One was when Kenneth Jones brought up Frances. Reggie immediately got to his feet, his face white with fury. He was gripping the rail round the dock so tightly I thought he was going to break it. 'What has Frances to do with this case?' he demanded to know.

Jones made an attempt to justify bringing up her name, but Reggie interrupted him. 'This has nothing to do with her,' he said. Then he added, quietly but menacingly, 'If you continue involving her name, I'll be over this dock to you. I know all the police here are armed, but no gun will stop me.'

Reggie thought Jones was going to bring up Frances' suicide to make him look bad. So did the rest of us in the dock, and we all stood up to support Reggie's objection. It was like a scene from a film.

For several tense seconds Jones and Reggie glared at

each other. Then the barrister gulped and said to the judge, who was also shaken by Reggie's fury, 'In view of the circumstances, my lord, I think we'll move on to another subject.'

It proved the point, I think, that Jones was out of order in mentioning Frances. If he had been right, surely he would have insisted on carrying on, despite Reggie's threat.

The longer the trial went on, and the more the jury were swayed by Stevenson's interjections, the less confident I became that I would be found not guilty: all the signs pointed to the lies triumphing over the truth. My fears proved well-founded on Tuesday 4 March when the jury returned after seven hours' deliberation to find myself and everyone else in the dock guilty of their respective crimes. Sentencing was put off until the next day, probably to prolong the agony, and the twins, their Firm and I were taken back to Brixton to think about what sentences we would get.

Ronnie was still philosophical about it: thirty years was what he expected. Reggie was now thinking the same. And me? Well, all I prayed was that Stevenson, despite his biased performance throughout the whole thirty-nine days and particularly in his summing up, would see my position for what it was and treat me leniently. Many of the Brixton prison staff who believed in my innocence kept telling me I'd get no more than two years and, much as I hated the idea of doing any time at all for something I didn't do, I hoped they were right. With remission for good behaviour, that would be down to about eighteen months and since I'd been in custody for a year that would mean I'd be out in six months or so.

I was far from happy at the prospect of spending more time behind bars, but I wasn't in the depths of despair. I finally dropped off to sleep, having convinced myself that even if Stevenson did his worst I could reasonably expect nothing more than three years. I'd take it on the chin, make sure I kept my nose clean in prison, then pick up my life where I'd left off.

When we arrived at the Old Bailey the next morning, one of the officers in the cells offered me a bottle with some liquid in it. It was a tranquillizer to calm me down and he wanted me to take it before I went into the dock.

'No thanks,' I said. 'I'm quite capable of accepting anything Stevenson dishes out.'

Other officers pressed me to take some, but I still couldn't see the point. Then Ronnie urged me to take it to keep everyone happy, so I did. I can't say for certain what that odd-smelling mixture did to me. I did feel a bit strange, but then the whole experience had been strange, like a disturbing dream where all sorts of people pop up in the unlikeliest places, saying and doing the craziest things; where one minute everything is clear and certainly happening and the next, it's fuzzy like your imagination, and then you finally awake, not knowing where you are, and you can't tell the things that happened from the things that didn't.

I was sitting in my cell in a sort of trance when one of the officers came by. 'Charlie,' he called quietly, 'they've got thirty years.'

I stared at him, the dream focusing sharply into reality. *Thirty years*! It was what they had expected, what they had prepared themselves for. But it was still dreadful to hear. My twin brothers were to be caged until they were old-age pensioners, banished from the outside world until just one year from the end of the twentieth century.

It was hard to take in, and the officer's face and words began to fade behind a cloud of unreality, then I was floating and the next thing I knew I was standing in the dock looking at Mr Justice Melford Stevenson, feeling the heavy silence of the crowded court but not sure whether I was really there.

Then the judge was speaking, not so much *to* me but *at* me, relating incidents about my past that I'd long forgotten. I listened, trying to take in what he was saying, but it was as though he was talking about someone else, someone I'd known very well but hadn't seen for years; perhaps someone from another life.

He spoke for only a minute or so but it seemed like forever, and then he got to the point of his monologue, the denouement of my personal tragedy that had been played out on the greatest criminal stage in the land.

'Charles James Kray,' he said slowly, 'you have been found guilty of being an accessory to murder. It may well be that you were not a member of what, in this case, has been called the Firm, but I am satisfied that you were an active and willing helper in the dreadful enterprise of concealing traces of the murder committed by your brother . . .' Stevenson paused. He looked down at Kenneth Jones. 'For accessory after the fact the maximum sentence, I believe, is . . .'

My breath caught in my throat. I could see the word forming in his mouth, grotesquely enlarged like some surrealistic painting. Was this all happening, or was it a dream? Was I here? Or was someone pretending to be me?

And then he said it and I swear my heart stopped. . . . 'life.'

Jones sprang to his feet. 'No, m'lud' he corrected. 'The law has been changed. The maximum sentence for accessory after the fact is ten years. And I don't wish . . .'

Then my heart pounded. Don't wish what, Mr Jones? Say it. Go on, tell him you don't wish to press for the maximum sentence. Tell him you don't believe all the lies

183

nor do you wish for a man to get ten years for something he didn't do. Go on, Mr Jones, tell him . . .

But the judge was motioning to him to sit down. 'That's enough, Mr Jones,' he snapped. And he turned to me. 'I sentence you to ten years' imprisonment.'

I stared at him, suddenly understanding, even in my dreamlike state, the meaning of the phrase 'absolute power'.

'Take that man down.' The words seemed to come from a long way off and I was floating again and the next thing I heard was Ronnie banging on the door of the first cell, asking what had happened.

'I got ten years,' I said.

Ronnie went mad. He started kicking the door, then he began shouting. 'Ten years! The rats gave you ten years!'

There wasn't much else I could say. I was taken to my cell, where I sat, saying over and over in my mind, 'Ten years. Ten years. Ten fucking years!'

Then Freddie Foreman and Connie Whitehead were put in the cell with me. Freddie had got ten years for disposing of McVitie's body. Connie had got nine; two for having a gun and seven for complicity in the McVitie murder.

I could hear Ronnie still creating in his cell. An officer passed by and motioned towards the first cell. 'He's making more fuss over your ten than his thirty,' he said.

Shortly afterwards the officer came back. 'Charlie,' he said. 'Ian Barrie's got twenty years. He's in a state. I can't pull him out of it. Can you have a word and try to calm him down?'

I did my best. I told him I was sorry but he had to calm down. There was an appeal coming up; his sentence was bound to be reduced. I didn't really believe it, but it was all I could think of to quieten him down. Hope was all I could offer.

When I went back to my cell Connie was sobbing. 'Nine years,' he kept saying.

'Connie,' I said as gently as I could, trying to hide my irritation, 'Freddie and me have got ten years for doing nothing. How do you think we feel?' I sat down on the cell bed and put my head in my hands. Reality was forcing through the numbness as the effects of the tranquillizer began to wear off and I found myself trying to get to grips with what ten years meant. I was coming up to forty-three years old. Even with full remission I was going to be more or less fifty when I came out. Fifty!

I looked at Freddie. What had happened to bring us here? What hand of fate had decided to make us the fall guys? Why us? With the daunting prospect of spending vital middle-aged years incarcerated behind bars hitting home to me now, I was at my lowest ebb, frail and weak from nearly a year in custody, drained dry from hearing my reputation blackened in thirty-nine dizzy days of courtroom drama. And then the cell door opened and my solicitor Ralph Haeems walked in. Detectives Read and Cator were upstairs and they wanted to see me, he said.

My heart leapt. Maybe, I thought, they were shocked at the severity of my sentence; maybe they were going to make a submission for it to be reduced. Crazy thoughts, I know, but I was so low I was ready to clutch at any straw. I looked at Ralph hopefully, but his face was grim. 'What do they want to see me for?'

Ralph looked down, shamefaced, embarrassed. 'They're going to charge you again with the murder of Frank Mitchell.'

I froze.

Ten years for something I hadn't done was terrible enough. But to face a life sentence for a murder I had nothing to do with . . .

* * *

185

The previous summer the murder charge against me had been dropped through lack of evidence without the case going to trial. But since then a law known as a Voluntary Bill of Indictment had been passed, which meant that I could be charged again. The new legislation made it possible for the prosecution to put the accused straight before a judge and jury without bothering with committal proceedings in a lower court.

I looked at Read and Cator with contempt, but they couldn't bring themselves to look at me. They knew full well I had had nothing to do with Mitchell's murder. They charged me and asked if I had anything to say but I said nothing. What was there to say?

That night in Brixton, I learned from prison staff that it was common knowledge in the nick that the police were determined to stitch me up on the Mitchell case. They had not liked the charge against me being dropped at Bow Street the previous July. I ached with despair. Was there no end to the police vendetta? Wasn't ten years enough? Did they really want me to go away for a lifetime too?

I was standing on a chair in the security wing looking out of a window when Tommy Cowley called up from the remand block below. 'Charlie, I know how bad you feel. But there's no way you can be found guilty on this Mitchell thing.'

I grunted sarcastically. 'You all said they wouldn't be able to get me in the McVitie trial, but I ended up with ten years so please don't say anything now.'

Tommy simply repeated that I couldn't possibly be found guilty. I thanked him for trying to make me feel better, and I hoped he was right, but I felt it was a useless, stupid thing to say. If the police wanted to get someone they had plenty of ways of doing it.

I had learned my lesson from the Bow Street hearing

and I was going into the witness box, come what may, to say my piece. I had nothing to lose. At the committal proceedings I'd listened to Vowden's advice and it had rebounded on me: by not going into the witness box I'd left myself open to all sorts of allegations which, because of my silence, must have been believed. The most outrageous of these, which would have been funny in less dire circumstances, concerned Leslie Payne's accountant friend, Freddie Gore, whom the twins and I had had some dealings with during the Great African Safari.

The only harsh encounter I'd had with Gore had been when he walked into an office I shared with Payne in Great Portland Street and interrupted a conversation we were having. I didn't approve of his manners, but let it pass. About ten minutes later, however, he came back and did the same thing.

'Mr Gore,' I said angrily, 'don't do that to me again. It's an insult. Remember, you work here and can be sacked. If you must say something privately, do it outside.'

After our arrests, when they were holding us on all sorts of weird and wonderful charges, Gore walked into the witness box at Bow Street and was asked by the prosecution, 'Have you ever been threatened by anyone?'

'Yes – one person.' Gore replied.

'Do you see that person anywhere in this court?'

Gore looked at the twins and me and the others in dock and pointed. I looked around to see who he was pointing at, but Ronnie nudged me and whispered, 'He means you.'

Shocked, I stood up. 'I threatened you?' I said. 'I've never threatened you in my life.'

During the lunchtime adjournment I told Vowden about the incident in the office – the only time I'd said anything remotely harsh to Gore – and said I wanted to go into the witness box to set the record straight.

Vowden would not hear of it. 'Don't worry,' he said. 'Wait till we get to the Old Bailey. We'll get him there.'

'But at least ask him how I was supposed to have threatened him,' I pleaded.

Vowden would not budge. He did not want to commit himself, he said, in case we gave something away that might be useful to the prosecution.

I argued with him. Since there were no reporting restrictions Gore's allegation was going to be all over the papers, with no response at all from me. To people who didn't know me, it would look as though I was admitting the threat, and I was sure that would be bad for my case. But Vowden told me I must be guided by him in matters of law, so I swallowed it. The next day, the papers made a meal of it: 'GANG BOSS THREATENS WITNESS!' screamed the headlines.

Nice! I was choked, and I couldn't resist asking Vowden if he'd seen the papers. 'Unfortunately, I have,' he replied, embarrassed.

When I appeared at the Old Bailey on the McVitie charge Vowden was again against my going into the box, repeating that if I didn't say anything, nothing could be used against me. My gut reaction said he was wrong, but I went along with him because he was the legal expert.

As it was, the decision *not* to give evidence was disastrous for me. In his summing up, Melford Stevenson made an issue of it, saying, 'If Charles Kray was innocent, would he not have gone into the witness box?' He made it look as if I had made the decision not to give evidence!

Afterwards I told Vowden I'd been made to look an idiot. He tried to console me by saying that it did not matter and that Stevenson should not have said what he did. Sadly, that didn't do much for me.

Barristers are very highly trained but they are not very worldly. I don't think Vowden was 'got at', either at Bow Street or at the Old Bailey, but I do think he gave me bad advice (albeit in good faith) in a case that was to ruin my life. So when the Mitchell trial opened at the Old Bailey in April 1969, I made the point strongly to Vowden: I was not going to be set up twice; I was going into the box, come what may. And I did.

I'm sure that giving evidence helped me, particularly since the judge Mr Justice Lawton was fair-minded, totally aware of what was going on and, unlike Stevenson, eager to see that justice was done. For example, when the prosecution counsel – Kenneth Jones again – tried to belittle me over my earnings as a theatrical agent Lawton stepped in to let everyone know what was right.

Jones, who obviously knew nothing about the theatrical agency business, implied that I was trying to cover something up concerning a bank statement, which the judge then asked to see. Within seconds he said the statement was in order and he understood it perfectly. Jones was angry at being put in his place and tried to take it out on me. He quoted five people who had given a different version of events from the one I had sworn, and said, 'Come, come, Mr Kray. What reason do you give for their telling lies? All five of them?'

'That's quite simple,' I said.

'Oh, is it?' Jones replied. 'Why is that?'

'Because they are sitting there and I am standing here,' I said.

He did not have an answer to that. I sensed the judge nodding in agreement. He seemed to be aware of who was telling the truth – unlike Stevenson whose preoccupation, it seemed, was to find people guilty. Lawton appreciated very early in the trial that the case against me was extremely slim. One particular piece of evidence, concerning where I had been on two days in December 1966, was vital, and thankfully I was able to prove that I was not where the police said I was because I was at home in bed with quinsy. Fortunately, a Dr Morris, a child psychiatrist with a practice in Wimpole Street, came to my home to visit my son Gary, who he was treating for suspected rheumatic fever, and he wrote to the court confirming I had been in bed. Lawton told the jury that a letter from such a professional gentleman should be accepted, and from then on I was home and dry.

It was the judge who actually led the prosecution into dropping its case against me. After hearing all the evidence he ordered the jury to leave the court while he had a discussion with Kenneth Jones.

'Regarding Mr Charles Kray,' said the judge. 'Four people have testified that he was at a meeting to kill Frank Mitchell. A lot of things have been said at this trial, but let us say they were right: he was there and they all discussed it. He could have said, 'No, thank you, I want nothing to do with it.' Because we don't hear very much about Charles Kray afterwards, do we? Whatever they say, it is not very safe at all, is it?'

Mr Jones agreed it wasn't.

'Do you want to carry on with the case against him?' asked the judge.

'No, m'lud.'

'Then I am stopping the case against Mr Kray,' said the judge.

And in the dock I found myself weeping with relief. I was too caught up in the emotion of the moment to be embarrassed or ashamed of my tears. Anyone who has been in a major court, fighting to prove their innocence will appreciate my feelings. The relief was indescribable, and at last I felt that the nightmare of the Axeman was over.

I was wrong.

The police, not satisfied with my ten-year sentence in the McVitie case, had another card up their sleeves: if I didn't actually help to murder poor Frank Mitchell, they argued, then I had helped plot his escape from Dartmoor and had harboured him in London. More rubbish, of course. But more agony, too. I was beginning to feel that their persecution was endless.

Thankfully, this case was eventually thrown out too, but not before I'd been reduced to tears again in the witness box.

Fuelled by more and more lies from Albert Donaghue, Billy Exley and Harry Hopwood, the persistent prosecutor hammered away at me, insisting that I must have known about the arrangements for springing Mitchell. I took it for what seemed an age, and then the terrible injustice of having to defend myself against lying idiots finally got to me, overwhelming me, and I cracked. Trembling with emotion, I said: 'I didn't have anything to do with it. They did. You have to remember, my name is Kray and if anyone makes a statement and puts the name Kray on it, they are believed by the police.' I gripped the frame of the witness box tightly as I felt my voice going. I fought in vain to control it. 'I'm doing ten years for nothing because of all these lies,' I choked.

And as I wept again with the frustration and injustice of it all, Mr Justice Lawton adjourned the court.

The high tension of the Old Bailey saps one's energy; adrenalin starts to flow as soon as the building comes into sight. I had had more than 300 tortuous hours which had done my brain in, leaving me mentally drained and ragged, my nerves in tatters.

When they finally took me back to Brixton and opened my cell, I walked in with my shoulders hunched in dejection, what little pride I'd clung to in court all gone. I fell on the bed and curled myself into a tight ball, enjoying the silence and the solitude.

I think then I knew how a fox feels when he finally shakes off the hounds.

Chapter Twelve

The full weight of what had happened hit me when I walked into the security wing at Brixton that evening. I went into the room with four cells, and the Governor, assistant governor and chief prison officer were standing there, solemn-faced, like a bizarre welcoming committee. They were not sure what to say, but they knew enough about convicted men not to be flippant or sarcastic. On a table in front of them were cardboard boxes for our clothes. For eight months on remand and for more than a month of the trial we had worn our own clothes, but now we had to exchange them for prison issue. We put our clothes in the boxes and knew it would be a long time before we saw them again. They took away the boxes and banged us up. I wanted darkness to cover me, so that I could be alone with my thoughts, but we were all A-Category – maximum security – men and a red light was left on all the time. I didn't feel suicidal. But I *was* depressed. The prison clothes felt awful, the atmosphere in the cell was terrible, and all the time that red light was on and the prison officers looked through the flap in the cell door, invading my thoughts. I thought again of Mum and the old man and the rest of our family and wondered how they were taking the sentences. I sat there, my eyes closed to that insensitive red light, trying to work out how it had all happened. Ten years! It sounded like a lifetime. And for what? Just for keeping my mouth shut. I fell asleep through sheer exhaustion. I felt as if I'd been digging a road all day.

That first terrible night as a convicted criminal was worse than anything I'd experienced in my life.

In the morning the red light had gone out and the wing was bright with March sunshine. Ronnie came out of his cell and clapped his hands. He looked at the prison officers. 'Good morning, gentlemen. What a lovely morning.'

The officers looked at him strangely.

'There's no point being downhearted,' Ronnie said. 'We've got to carry on.'

One officer turned to me and said, 'He's something else.' I said he'd always been like that and would never change.

The cheerful banter continued while we had our breakfast and then it was time for exercise. As we were on our way out Ronnie was laughing with one of the officers, a tall, heavily built bloke in his early forties.

'What I'm going to do today,' Ronnie said, 'is write off for a world cruise because that's one thing I want to do when I get out.'

The officer was half-laughing with Ronnie and before he knew what he was saying the words had slipped out. 'Oh, well,' he said. 'You've got thirty years to save up for it.'

He knew he had said the wrong thing. But it was too late. Ronnie went white and moved forward threateningly.

'Ronnie,' said the officer quickly. 'I'm so sorry. I apologize. You were larking about and I forgot and said it without thinking.'

I believed him. So did Ronnie. He calmed down immediately and told the officer to forget it. But, he said, it wasn't a nice thing to say. After exercise, the officer came to my cell and asked if Ronnie was still upset. The incident was still playing on his mind, he said, and it was such a stupid thing to say. I said Ronnie had forgotten it, but I don't think the officer believed me, because he went up to Ronnie at lunchtime and apologized yet again.

Later that day Ronnie sent off for some brochures.

That officer's slip of the tongue was sparked off by the tension that surrounded the twins. And that tension was not helped by some idiots in a cell about fifty feet away on the opposite side of the square; a section full of drunks doing a month, or creeps finishing six months or whatever for petty crimes.

One day, as we were exercising in the square, two chaps – young by the sound of their voices – called down mockingly, 'I've got another ten days to do – and you've got thirty years. How do you feel about that?' Then they laughed.

The taunts went on and on for a couple of days. Finally Ronnie could stand it no longer; the tormentors were probably cowards who would have topped themselves if they had been given thirty years and he wanted them silenced. He asked the security wing's chief prison officer to tell whoever was responsible to shut up.

The Prison Officer was delighted to step in. He thought it was unfair when Ronnie and Reggie were taking their punishment so well; also, he would have to deal with the problem if Ronnie lost his rag. Later that day, he told them, 'By the way, I found out who it was. I don't think you'll be hearing any more from them.'

While we had all been in the square on exercise the officer had stood in a cell, waiting and watching. When the two idiots stood up and started their cowardly shouting, he noted their cell and went round. 'Hello, you brave little pair,' he said. 'Those blokes down there are doing thirty years, but I'll tell you something – at least they're men. You snivelling idiots are causing us problems by upsetting them, so I'll tell you what I'm going to do. If I hear one more peep out of you I'll bring Ronnie and Reggie through here on our way somewhere and leave them with you for five minutes. I'm warning you – one more peep.'

The two guys, in their mid-twenties, were the type who would mug old ladies, or pick on victims who couldn't fight back, the type who tease animals through bars, the type with no bottle. Not surprisingly, we didn't hear another word from them.

One day the twins and I were staring at the security cage and saw three guys taunting a tall, spindly, ginger-haired bloke who looked like an office worker. The three bullies just wanted to have a go at someone and we were not going to stand for it. We shouted out to them that they were nothing but cowards, that they were brave only because there were three of them. The men took one look at us and decided to leave it out. As they walked away, the weak-looking 'office worker' looked up and nodded his thanks. We discovered later his name was Paddy Sullivan and he was a major in the IRA. He was waiting to come up for trial.

Six months later I got a message from Freddie Foreman. His son, Gregory, had been called in by the headmaster at his public school and asked to give his father the message: 'Paddy Sullivan sends his regards and best wishes to Charlie.' Apparently the headmaster knew Paddy well and had been to visit him in Wormwood Scrubs.

Paddy was obviously one of those people with a long memory.

* * *

When I got sentenced it seemed like the end of the world. But I never thought of trying to escape. When the Mitchell case was thrown out, it helped me come to terms with the ten years. It was still terrible being punished so severely for something I didn't do, but at least it was not a life sentence. I figured I would be out in seven years if I kept my nose clean: short of being beaten up and forced to retaliate I reckoned I could keep myself under control.

But if I had been sentenced to life on the murder charge I do think I would have changed – and tried to escape at every opportunity. I would probably have been killed, but what would it have mattered? The twins know that they did certain things and they do not cry about their sentences, but I would not have been able to accept it like that, because I was innocent. I dread to think what sort of twisted, hateful character I would have turned into had that Mitchell rubbish been believed.

As it was, I did my best to accept that what was done was done, and nothing was going to change it. It would have been easy to give in to my hate and bitterness, to lose control and smash things up in frustration, but I knew that could destroy me. So, as the days and weeks and, eventually, the months wore on, I gritted my teeth and battled to keep myself under control.

It was not easy though. And when I was finally moved from Brixton to Chelmsford in Essex thirteen months later, I still had not come to terms with the fact that I was caged like an animal for something I did not do.

My world at Chelmsford consisted of just ten other A-Category prisoners in a small, maximum-security block with cameras watching every move. We were treated like children. Normal prisoners walked freely to their work but we were led everywhere and led back; we would have to wait for prison officers to fill in the pass book and to log the time. When we left for lunch we had to wait for someone to escort us fifty yards or so. It was frustrating beyond belief.

There were thirty cells for just ten prisoners, and my fellow inmates got so bored that they would move from one cell to another for something to do. Because we were in such a confined space we were allowed certain freedoms to save us going out of our minds. If you wanted to work, you did; if you didn't, no one made you. I felt I needed to keep myself busy; one week I would go into the workshop and saw iron for traffic triangles; the next I would wash the rubber floors. I even got into cooking: the kitchens would send the food to us and we would try to make it appetizing.

But it was the outside exercise I lived for. We played volley-ball – every day for two years – and football. The exercise period was one hour, and cameras in the four corners of the playing field watched us all the time while a helicopter hovered overhead. Such expensive security was senseless – one needed to be Superman to clear the wire and barbed wire on the high walls behind the playing field. The prison officers were hand-picked and as good as gold, and I'd ask them about the vast amount of money being squandered unnecessarily. They would merely shrug and say, 'Don't ask us, Charlie, we only work here.'

On Mondays we were taken into the main prison – an elaborate process in which we had to pass between electric doors and bullet-proof glass windows. But it was worth it. The library was there and we were allowed to spend fifteen minutes picking books. It was like a holiday.

In the evenings, once or twice a week, a woman would come in to teach us handicrafts. She was a lovely lady, in her fifties, and we looked forward to her visits. You have to give her credit: she was very brave, although I think she knew she was perfectly safe. We all thought so much of her we would have died rather than let anything happen to her.

I told her once that what she was doing was worthwhile, and that I admired her. I promised myself I'd take her some flowers when I got out but, sadly, it was one of the things I never got round to.

Wally Probyn was a clever bloke. He was the man who arranged John McVicar's escape from Durham Prison by knocking a hole in a shower and covering it with papier mâché until it was time to go. Wally was due to escape, too, but something happened and only McVicar got away. During the riots at Durham in 1964 some prisoners locked themselves in an office and read reports written on them for the parole board. The men could not believe the terrible, untrue things the prison staff had written: it seemed incredible that a prison officer had the power to poison a prisoner's record with the stroke of a pen if he didn't like him.

Suddenly it became all-important to me to know what my report said and Wally knew an officer who promised to find out. Nothing could have prepared me for the shock of hearing what that report, which my immediate future depended on, said. The exact words were: 'Charles Kray. This is not his natural attitude. It is all a pretence. This cannot be his normal behaviour, because he is too nice. He has caused no problems since he has been in this prison, but we know this is a big act.'

I was shell-shocked. Just because I said 'Hello, please and thank you' and didn't go around hitting people, they thought something was wrong. I tried to treat the report with the contempt it deserved, but it was impossible: the injustice of it all burned into me deeply and there was nothing I could do about it.

As I entered my second year at Chelmsford, my bitterness at being robbed of important years of my life began to fade and I softened a little. I formed close bonds with some people I might not have wanted to know outside. Somehow, when people are thrown together in jail, one doesn't think of their crimes – you just get on with the business of living.

Someone I did get close to was John Duddy, a small, grey-haired man sentenced to life, with Harry Roberts, for the Shepherds Bush murder of three policemen in August 1966. It choked me one day when he told me he'd decided to tell his wife they were finished. I felt he should not do it, because they had been married many years and were still in love. But he said he knew he was never going to get out of prison and he didn't want her to waste her life. She was too good for him, he said.

His wife didn't want to know about a divorce and she told him she would still come to see him whether he liked it or not. John was pleased, of course, but insisted she should visit less frequently, to give herself a rest. He was a very unselfish man and over the next year we got very close.

One Sunday evening about 7 P.M. I was called in to see the Prison Officer and told I was being moved to another prison early the next morning. At about 8 P.M. John Duddy came up to see me. He was pleased for my sake that I was going, but sorry to see me go because 'things have been good since you've been here'. Close to tears, he said he wasn't going to wait until 9 P.M. to 'bang up', he was going in early. But he asked me to knock on his door in the morning to say goodbye. It was all rather emotional; you do get close to people in a short time in prison.

At 6 A.M. the following morning I was handcuffed and taken to a security van by six Prison Officers. My report,

I was reliably informed, read: 'We have come to the conclusion that this is not an act with Charles Kray. It is his normal behaviour.'

It had taken someone two years to work that out and now I was being transferred to Albany on the Isle of Wight, a couple of hundred yards from Parkhurst, where the twins were held.

While I was in Albany I heard that John Duddy had died of cancer.

We travelled through London on the journey to the Isle of Wight and my stomach knotted when we hit the East End. It was a weird feeling, looking through the darkened windows at all the old, familiar places: it hurt, but at the same time it was lovely. So Poplar and Bow and Mile End and Whitechapel were still there! The joke in prison is: 'Don't worry – over the wall, the world's still there.' And now I could see it for myself. The driver pulled up at some lights and I told my six guards that I'd lived only a minute away. I'd got quite close to them in two years and one of them said, 'If we had our way, Charlie, we'd nip you down there for a quick cuppa.' But, of course, the security was so tight that it was out of the question. The van was in radio contact with police stations at different points en route, as if someone expected a helicopter to drop out of the sky and pluck me to freedom. We moved away from the lights and suddenly we were in Whitechapel Road; there, staring me in the face, was my old factory with the sign, Berman and Kray, still there. What I would have given to walk along that street just then, even as a roadsweeper! But soon the van was picking up speed towards the city, pulling me away from the warmth of my nostalgia.

I got my chance to breathe fresh air when we stopped at a police station for my guards to use the toilet. I stayed in the yard, basking in the exquisite feeling of the hot summer sun and cool breeze on my face and in my hair. I stared up at the sky, marvelling at its blueness. I'd seen the sky in prison, of course, but somehow it was different looking at it on the outside. It was only a tiny police station yard and I was in handcuffs but for those few minutes I felt I was in heaven. I could have stayed there all day, but soon we were on the move again, passing through Central London and South London suburbs towards the A3. All the way through Surrey and Hampshire I talked little and just stared out of the window, drinking in the beauty of the countryside, thinking, as I had a thousand times in prison, that you don't know how much you'll miss something until it's taken away from you.

Then we were on the ferry and I was transfixed by a kaleidoscope of colour that took my breath away. In prison I'd been surrounded by dowdy greys and blues month in, month out, but now in front of me were greens and reds and yellows, all bright despite the darkened windows of the van. It was warm and sunny and there was a holiday atmosphere. I took in the men's suits and shirts and watched them drinking beer out of cans; I watched women talking casually and children running around playing. Everyone looked happy. I'd seen smiles on the faces of people in prison but, like the sky, it was different. I wanted to get out of the van, close to the children's laughter, but it was forbidden, so I stayed there looking out through the dark green glass at the unfamiliar scenes, feeling as though I was from another planet.

When we got to Albany one of the six guards unloaded my box of gear and we waited in a little room for the prison staff to take me to my cell. When the time came one of them said, 'Well, that's it, Charlie. You're here. They'll be giving you something to eat in a minute.' And then they all shook my hand, promising to give my regards to all the people who had become my friends in Chelmsford. The Albany staff looked shocked: a Kray brother in the nick, shaking hands and exchanging good-natured pleasantries! They could not be blamed for being surprised. The publicity about the family would have made anyone expect the worst. In my case, they were to discover that the image bore little resemblance to reality.

Within a few minutes my cell was full of people wanting to say hello. I was pleased and was polite, but after a short time I wanted them to go: I had been in a world of just nine other inmates for two years and the talk and noise sort of did my brain in. I wanted to be on my own, to shut my eyes and think about the countryside and the ferry and pretend I was going on holiday. Slowly, agonizingly slowly, they drifted back to their own cells. But one bloke, a Scotsman, hung on, and when the others had gone and we were alone he started telling me how he had stabbed and killed someone. We were similar, he said, we were both doing ten years.

We were about as similar as Jekyll and Hyde!

He loved talking about his violence, thinking I would enjoy it, but it sickened me; violence always has. He was one of those idiots who have wanted to be in prison all their life. He loved it. But I was doing ten years for nothing, and all I could think about was getting out. Finally I could stand him no more and told him to go.

Alone that night, I thought back over my day. It had been an enjoyable trip: it had done me good, put me in a better frame of mind. I lay on my bed and brought the colours of those holidaymakers into focus, filling my head with the laughing faces of those happy children.

Oh, yes, over the wall the world does exist, I thought, my eyes full. I'd seen it.

* * *

For a while, Ronnie had been alone in Parkhurst, on the Isle of Wight. But Reggie was moved from Long Lartin Jail, in Worcestershire, to calm him down.

Ronnie has been taking four different tablets every day since his breakdown in the fifties. He understands that they keep his paranoia and uncontrollable temper at bay and insists he has the prescribed dosage four times a day. One day in Parkhurst a new officer in charge of the high-security wing chose not to understand Ronnie's problem.

When Ronnie went into the office and asked for one of his tablets, the new man was difficult. He was on his own, in the middle of a shift change, he said, and Ronnie's request would have to wait.

Ronnie, who knew his body's danger signals well, told him the matter couldn't wait: he was due a tablet now and he had to have it.

The officer checked his records. Yes, he agreed, Ronnie was right: four tablets a day and one was due now.

If he had simply taken out the appropriate pill and handed it to Ronnie, all would have been well.

As it was, the officer seemed anxious to prove a point. 'I'm afraid I can't give you the tablet,' he said.

'Why's that?' asked Ronnie.

'Because I don't know which one you're supposed to have right now.'

'It must say which one in my records,' said Ronnie.

The officer shook his head. 'It doesn't.'

'Don't give me that.'

'You'll have to wait until my relief comes back.'

'I'm telling you, I need to take that tablet. I know I have to have it.'

'You'll have to wait till the other officer comes back,' said the new man. And he added cockily, 'And I wouldn't bank on him giving you a tablet anyway.'

Whether it was the bloke's arrogant attitude or the

urgent need for that tranquillizing tablet I don't know, but Ronnie snapped, as anyone who understood him would have expected. He felled the unsuspecting officer with a right hook, then picked him up and vented his anger and frustration in a severe beating.

Ronnie's polite request for a tablet landed him in the chokey block for fifty-six days – with a diet of bread and water on and off for fifteen days.

When he came back to the maximum-security wing, he was very disturbed. Bobby Welch, one of the Great Train Robbers, was standing at the top of the stairs and said something. Ronnie told him to get out of the way, then picked up a chair and proceeded to smash everything he could see: lights, tables, other chairs, and the glass on the inside of the barred windows. When his frenzied moment of madness was over he turned to watching prison officers and said, 'You'd better take me to the chokey block again.'

I heard the story from Welch when he was transferred from the security wing at Albany. He said it was awful; he couldn't believe what they had done to Ronnie.

Obviously someone did. For Reggie was quickly brought down from Long Lartin and asked to tell Ronnie he would be allowed out of the block the next day if he promised to behave himself. It did the trick. Ronnie got it all off his chest and said he'd had enough of the screws treating him badly. He knew he needed tablets to keep him calm.

Perhaps next time they would believe him, he said.

I had come to terms with being robbed of my freedom. But I was becoming more and more bitter about being on the A-Book and all the stringent security that went with it. To be regarded as a constant threat, someone to be watched twenty-four hours a day, is bad enough when

205

you've done something to deserve it. When you have done nothing and are non-violent and easy-going it is terrible, and impossible to accept. What made it worse for me was that all the prison officers could not understand why I was on it in the first place. My case kept coming up, of course, but I was always turned down. Someone somewhere very high up had clearly made a decision about me. My name was Kray and that was that.

The attitude of Home Office officials did not help my mental state either. After seven months at Albany I had served a total of three and a half years, qualifying for parole. I was taken upstairs to a cell where a young man in his middle-to-late twenties was sitting at a desk, ready to interview me. There was a young woman there, too.

I sat down and he said, 'Kray?'

'Yes,' I replied.

'Ten years,' he said. 'Well, you aren't going to get parole, you know.'

'Oh, I'm not,' I said, failing to keep the hard-edged sarcastic tone out of my voice. 'And who are you to judge that?'

He said nothing, just looked at me.

'Why are you wasting my time bringing me up here for an interview if the decision's already been made?' I said. 'You give all the sex cases, all the perverts who are a real danger, parole. But normal people don't get it.' Before he could say anything, I went on. 'Anyway, if the decision has been made in my case, I don't see any point in talking to you.' And I got up and walked out.

I was seething. All right, it was my first interview for parole and I didn't expect to get it. But why build me up then put the knife in before I'd been asked one question?

Later the Chief Prison Officer said he would try to get me another interview, but I told him not to bother; it

206

would be exactly the same, and I didn't need the mental strain of false hope.

A few weeks later I was given the job of helping an officer with the inmates' workshop time sheets. When we were on our own he said, 'I wish you weren't on the A-Book. I could give you this job; it would be a bit of extra money for you. You could work up to being in charge of the workshop.' He paused and grinned. 'We could have a coffee together and a bit of the wife's cake.'

In the outside world that would be nothing. But after three and a half years in prison on the A-Book it seemed everything. I could think of nothing I'd like better than to sit down with a nice bloke and share some of his wife's cake over a coffee, without a camera watching my every movement.

'That would be lovely,' was all I said.

He said he would have a word with someone because there was no logic in keeping me on the A-Book. I didn't hold my breath, which is just as well because I didn't hear anything for about twelve months. Then one day the maximum-security wing's Prison Officer called out, 'Charlie, I want to talk to you!'

I walked over, wondering what stroke they'd pulled now. But he was grinning; maybe he'd picked a winner and won a few quid.

'Charlie,' he beamed. 'You're off the A-List. I've got the papers. You're a normal prisoner.'

He shook my hand. 'I'm so pleased,' he said.

I was delighted, of course I was. And relieved. But I couldn't resist a sarcastic jibe. 'Thank you,' I said. 'But I wonder if you can tell me how the Home Office can decide overnight that I'm no longer a threat to society when I'm no different from when I came in?'

The P.O., I must admit, was sympathetic and understanding. 'Don't ask me, Charlie. *They* make the decisions.'

Perhaps the workshop officer had put in a good word,

for within a couple of weeks I got the job in there working out the timesheets. I did them every Friday and I felt amazing; it sounds so little, so unimportant and menial, but it was a huge triumph in my life. No longer did I have to go to work with someone escorting me, opening and locking doors all the time.

I was still an inmate, deprived of my liberty. And I was only halfway through my sentence. But for the first time I felt normal, a member of the human race, if still an imprisoned one.

Now I began to enjoy my visits. It was a long haul from London, involving train, boat and taxi, and I was grateful to my parents, Dolly and the kids for making the effort. Those two hours every fortnight were a highlight of my existence and I treasured them. Sadly, though, my cell always seemed lonelier than ever after I'd said my good-byes and was sitting there thinking over what had been said. After one particular visit by Dolly and Nancy I was feeling more depressed than ever when I heard some news that sent me into a wild panic.

An Isle of Wight ferry had overturned outside Portsmouth harbour. A TV news report said that a woman and a little girl were among those missing. My world seemed to stop. The time of the tragedy fitted in with when Dolly and Nancy would have been on board. I was inconsolable, convinced they had drowned, and it was all my fault for being the reason for their visit. I begged the prison authorities to make inquiries to find out if that woman and little girl were Dolly and Nancy. Things had not been perfect with Dolly and me, and, yes, I had been thinking of leaving her to live with another woman. But in times of extreme crisis you push these things to the back of your mind: she *was* still my wife, and we *had* had some marvellous times together, and she was the mother of my lovely children; I couldn't bear the thought of her and my darling Nancy ending their lives so horribly. I waited and hoped and prayed, then finally, hours later, someone came and told me that Dolly and Nancy were safe.

They had not been on that fateful ferry. They had missed it – just.

I thanked the prison officer for telling me and added, 'Thank God.' I couldn't trust myself to say more: the feeling of relief was so exquisitely warm and spine-tingling that it coursed through my entire body and tightened in my throat, leaving me choked with emotion.

Not all the people who came to see us were family and friends. We had visits from an American judge – and even half a dozen monks. The judge was travelling all over Europe inspecting the jails and when he visited Albany he asked to speak to me. Of course I was delighted to talk to someone like that and was introduced to him in a little room the authorities made available. He was in his late fifties and informally dressed in a lounge suit. He arranged two cups of tea and we started talking.

At first I felt a little strange talking to a judge, but after a while I relaxed and started to enjoy telling him what life was like for me in prison. He asked about my case and I explained that I was serving a sentence for something I didn't do. I don't know whether he believed me, because prisons are full of people who claim they are innocent, but he seemed genuinely interested and sympathetic. He echoed my own thoughts when he said that the laws in Britain are antiquated. They can say one thing and mean another, and can be bent and twisted by clever lawyers to suit their case. In America, the judge was quick to point out, the laws are not so wishy-washy; they are black and white and it is clear what is meant. I didn't want to make a big thing of my case but, since he asked me about it, I went into some detail. He listened then said that if I'd been in America I could have pleaded the Fifth Amendment, i.e. I could have refused to give evidence against the twins because I did not want to implicate myself.

I amused the judge when I told him that the conversation we were having could not happen with a British judge. They were not living in the real world, I said, and I made him laugh when I recounted the story of a judge who made the headlines by asking in the middle of a major High Court case, 'Who are these Beatles?'

After we'd talked for an hour or so, the American thanked me for agreeing to see him. But I said it had been my pleasure: apart from being highly intelligent, the judge's views were refreshingly democratic, and his opinions had had a striking effect on me. I went back to my cell feeling pleasantly high on having had a conversation of real substance with a humane gentleman who felt genuine compassion for people who had fallen foul of the law.

The judge left the prison that day, but the monks who came to visit stayed a week to see what it was like to be a prisoner. They ate the same food as we did and slept in two cells on opposite sides of the wing. I had a chat with one of them, a charming young man in his middle twenties, and told him I admired him for what he was doing. 'At least you know how we feel,' I said.

'Yes,' he replied, 'but only up to a point.'

I looked puzzled.

'If I wake up at two in the morning and decide I don't like being caged any more, all I have to do is ring a bell and ask to be let out. You can't do that.'

I smiled. How right he was.

I wondered later whether anyone thought of searching the monks when they came in. I decided that someone probably did: no one is trusted in jail. They would probably frisk the Archbishop of Canterbury.

Chapter Thirteen

During Christmas 1972 they told me I was being moved on again. Someone somewhere, some faceless civil servant who had never met me, had decided that one year in the hard, high-security island prison had changed me, that I'd learned from the tough oppression and constant vigilance, and that the threat I'd posed had passed, and I was ready for some rehabilitation to prepare me for my return to the outside world.

The establishment they chose for this worthy exercise was Maidstone Jail in Kent. I welcomed the move; it was a more relaxed prison, and would cut out travelling problems for my visitors. Chatting in unnatural surroundings, conscious all the time of prying eyes and cocked ears, is bad enough, but it is even worse when your loved ones and friends are whacked out by a five-hour trek over land and sea. Maidstone, in contrast to Albany, was a comfortable hour's drive from London.

Quickly, my world became brighter. I was given a job in the kitchen in charge of the hotplate, took French lessons, organized volleyball competitions, kept in shape in the gym and generally made the most of prison life. But, like everyone else, I lived for my visits and when Dolly and Nancy arrived, and Nancy ran to me and I took her on my knee and held her close, it hit home to me how much I'd missed.

Spring came to Maidstone and I started counting the months to my release. I had kept my nose clean from the moment my sentence began and I worked out that, with full remission, I would be a free man in January 1975.

The thought was warm and comforting. But it led me on to think about Dolly and the children, and what our life would be like. I was far from happy. I had to face facts: Dolly and I had gone from bad to worse and it was unlikely to be any better on my release. I was going to need a lot of help to adjust and Dolly, neurotic and unstable, was not the supportive kind. I had to be careful not to stick my head in the sand and pretend our problems didn't exist. Having been unjustly robbed of precious years I wanted to come out and make the most of life with someone who cared about me. I had two years to think it through and to work out what I really wanted to do with the rest of my life. I was determined there would be no more mistakes.

It was not long before Diana came into my mind again. She had rarely been out of my thoughts, but her lack of contact had made me think that, sadly, the relationship was dead. What was she doing? Where was she working? Had she left her husband? Was she happy? The questions filled my head night after night, and I decided it might be a good idea, with my release date looming nearer, to ask a departing inmate to try to track her down. Yes, I know it was a wild, crazy idea. But after five years in prison wild, crazy plans seem perfectly logical and sensible. I began keeping my ear to the ground for Leicester-bound inmates.

On 2 May 1973 George Ince appeared at Chelmsford Crown Court accused of murdering Muriel Patience at the Barn Restaurant in Braintree, Essex, the previous November. Seven days later the jury returned saying they could not agree and a retrial was ordered. It began on 14 May, still at Chelmsford but with a different judge – Mr Justice Everleigh. As the second trial got under way, the newspapers started running stories of a 'mystery witness'.

I knew immediately who it was but when Dolly visited me I didn't say a word; nor did she. Then the papers started referring to a Doris Gray – the name to which Dolly had changed by deed poll three years before – and I knew for certain I was right. The mystery woman, it seemed, was going into the witness box to say that George Ince could not have been at the Barn Restaurant in the early hours of 5 November because all that night he had been in bed with her. Reading that, I went cold. My stomach knotted in fury, and I paced up and down my cell, my mind running hot with vivid, masochistic imaginings of the man walking into my home, talking and playing with my children before climbing into bed with the woman who was still my wife.

Suddenly my brighter, more hopeful world was shrouded in a gigantic black cloud of despair. I fought to control my self-torture, but agonizing thoughts kept invading my mind. How often had Ince been to the house? Had little Nancy been encouraged to call him Daddy? Did he walk about the house half-naked like I'd done? Did she . . . did she see or hear her mother moaning in ecstasy as Ince made love to her in my bed?

It was a terrible, terrible experience and I was impotent in my frustration, unable to vent rage on anything except my cell wall. And then I was told Dolly was coming to see me.

The prison promptly ordered six extra officers to be present at the meeting. After more than five years, they still didn't know me; they had no idea how I thought or how I reacted to situations.

'Nice,' was all I said to her as she sat down.

She started gabbling on nervously about it. I cut her short. 'All I want you to tell me,' I said curtly, 'is whether Ince has got something on you to make you give evidence. Or did it happen? Were you with him?'

'Do you want someone to get thirty years, like the twins?' she said.

I ignored the fact she had avoided the question.

'I don't want anyone to go down for anything,' I said. 'I just want to know, Dolly.'

She opened her mouth again, but I shut her up. '*I just want to know, Dolly.*'

She was quiet for a few seconds. Then she looked down. 'He *was* with me,' she said softly.

I didn't say anything. Silence was a massive wall between us. Then, deciding attack was the best form of defence, she started to get hysterical.

'What do you expect?' she screeched loudly. 'You've been away all these years!'

'That's not the reason,' I said, still calm. 'It happened before, I know.'

'Not like you think,' she snapped. Then she started blaming me. 'It's your fault. You went away. What do you expect me to do, sit indoors all my life?'

'I didn't expect you to take him home. I didn't expect you to screw him in front of Nancy.'

'Anyway, he *was* with me. And I *am* going to give evidence. How can I let a guy go away for thirty years?'

I took in what she said. I didn't like what I'd heard, but I felt she had no choice. 'Quite right,' I said finally, amazed at my tight self-control. 'If that's the truth, go and give evidence.'

I meant what I said. I knew Ince *could* get thirty years and I didn't want to see that happen to an innocent man. Not even Ince. 'I don't like it,' I added. 'But you have to do it.'

With it all out in the open Dolly started running off at the mouth. 'I couldn't help it . . . all the problems I've had . . . It's been one thing after another . . . I had to do something . . . you don't know what it's like . . .'

214

'Don't make excuses,' I broke in. 'You've done it. You've probably been doing it for years. The thing I can't stand is that you've let him in our house with Nancy there. With me here and him there it's blowing the kid's brain.'

She didn't say anything. There wasn't much she could say. We talked about it a bit more, then I said I wanted to be alone to think what I was going to do about her now.

It didn't take me long. Dolly hadn't reached her Poplar love-nest before I decided that I didn't want to know; our marriage had run into stormy waters long before and it was now lying smashed to pieces on the rocks. Divorce was going to be painful for Gary and Nancy, but that was the price that would have to be paid.

Dolly did give evidence and George Ince walked out of Chelmsford Crown Court a free man. I hated the idea of seeing Dolly again but I had to because of the children: we needed to talk about what was going to happen to them after the divorce. On her next visit I told her we were finished, but she refused to accept it.

'Why?' she asked. 'Everything is going to be all right now. It's over between George and me. We'll go away when you come home. It'll be nice.'

'What?' I said incredulously. 'We're not going away anywhere. I don't want to know. It's over. End of story.'

But still she couldn't believe I meant it. 'I got twenty thousand from a newspaper for my story of my affair with George. I can put some of it away till you get home. We can go away somewhere.'

'Listen,' I said. 'I don't need holidays or anything else with you. I don't want to know about that money. Give Gary some and keep the rest. As far as you and I are concerned, we talk about the kids and that's it.'

Over the next few months, she kept trying to make me change my mind. Once she brought a friend with her, who said I really should forgive Dolly and make an effort to patch things up.

'I don't really want to discuss it any more,' I said.

'The thing with George is over,' she told me. 'Dolly isn't seeing him any more.'

By then Ince had been arrested on a charge involving a gold bullion robbery and was in Brixton awaiting trial. News travels fast on the prison grapevine and during the next few days I heard that Dolly had visited him. So much for it being finished, I thought.

Dolly's friend came again. 'I know what you're going to say,' she began.

'Well, *did* she see him?' I cut in brusquely, not wanting to waste time on it.

'Yes,' the woman replied. 'But it was the last time.'

'Do me a favour,' I said. 'Tell her to come and see me. I want this over. Now.'

The following week Dolly arrived with Nancy and Gary. She looked dreadful: thin, with bags under her eyes, untidy make-up and her hair a mess.

'What's the matter?' I asked. I meant it. I'd never seen her look like that.

'Why should I look well?' she replied defensively. 'All the problems I've had.'

I almost choked. '*You've* had problems!'

She talked rubbish for about two minutes. I looked at Nancy, then Gary. I felt for them, but I couldn't stand it any longer.

'Do me a favour,' I said quietly. 'Get out of here. Now. And start divorce proceedings. I can't do it from in here.'

We sat there glaring at each other. Nancy and Gary were quiet. They didn't know what to say; I suppose they were frightened.

216

Finally Dolly said, 'I will do that.' And she took Nancy's hand and half-dragged her out of the hall, leaving Gary sitting there with his eyes full of tears.

I put my hand on his. 'I'm sorry about that, Gary.'

'I'm not,' he said. 'I'm glad you said it.'

We sat there for a few seconds, not knowing what to say. My heart went out to him.

Finally I said, 'You'd better go. She'll leave without you.'

'I don't care,' he said. 'I don't care any more.'

We sat there and finished the visit. When Gary left he found his mother waiting in the car for him. The journey back to London must have been awful.

That was the last time Dolly visited me.

My darling, adorable Nancy, just eight years old and so lovely and innocent. How I idolized her! The thought of her being hurt cut through me as I sat in my cell that evening, but I knew there was nothing I could do, especially from prison. It really was all over with Dolly, and the sooner the break was made, the better. Nancy would come to terms with it, I consoled myself: kids always do.

But later that night the pain was deep as my mind ran back over all the precious years I'd missed of Nancy's growing up. She had been three when I was arrested. One minute I'd been free to come and go as I pleased, to take my child wherever I wanted and care for her like any normal working father, the next I was caged like an animal, stripped of all parental rights except an unnatural, stilted chat in a sombre prison visiting room a couple of times a month. Five years I'd missed, years that should have been carefree and fun-filled, lovingly memorable. And I was to miss more. Even if all went well and I was released in January 1975, Nancy would be coming up to ten. Another two years and she would be in puberty, then a teenager. Before I knew it, she would be asking me to give her away in church.

Sitting in my cell, alone yet again with my thoughts, I concentrated on memories of Nancy until I could summon up a mental picture of our holiday together in Sitges. How pretty Nancy had looked that April, her blonde hair bleached even lighter by the Spanish sun and her little body bronzed deep brown. She was a water baby, always in the hotel pool – only two years old but totally fearless, running and jumping into the safety of my arms then, as her confidence grew, jumping into the deep end on her own. When I reprimanded her with fatherly concern she would climb out then leap straight back in, going under and coming up again, clinging to me and giggling with childish joy as she rubbed the water from her eyes.

Yet, as always when I thought of Nancy, the doubts surfaced in my mind despite my attempts to push them away. That night after I'd seen Nancy dragged from the hall without a chance of a loving goodbye kiss the doubts stared me in the face, again, and this time I had to accept they were real. Deep down I knew Nancy was not my child.

It wasn't easy to accept, of course, and for a long time I'd refused to believe it. Not mine! That laughing, giggling, squealing, shrieking little ball of wide-eyed innocence, that cartwheeling bundle of energy, that adorable impish little girl? Not mine!!

As a loving father it was something I had never ever questioned or considered. Cradling Nancy as a new-born baby, watching with pride as she tottered on her first unsteady steps, holding her hand as she toddled along East End streets, talking to her softly as she lay in bed exhausted after a play-filled day . . . the very idea that the little girl I worshipped might be someone else's flesh and blood was absurd. No, impossible. And then I had

218

heard it from the mother of the child herself and for six years the horrible haunting question had hung over me like a thunder-cloud.

Dolly told me during a row when Nancy was two. I was getting ready to go to Leicester on business and Dolly didn't like it. 'You think more of that bloody club than you do of me,' she said.

I groaned inwardly. This was an old chestnut and I wasn't in the mood for it. I wanted to get on the road. 'You know I've got to keep an eye on things,' I said, fighting to keep the exasperation out of my voice.

But Dolly *was* in the mood for a row. She'd been tense all day, building up to it. 'It's probably not the only thing you keep your eye on,' she sneered.

'What do you mean by that?' I snapped.

'You certainly don't seem interested in me. You don't want to know.'

I ignored that and carried on dressing.

'You don't want to bloody know!' Dolly raised her voice, trying to provoke.

'Leave it out, Dolly.' I said calmly. 'Not now. I'm late.'

'Business. Bloody business. It's business all the time. When's the last time you took me out?'

I felt it best to ignore her and not rise to the bait.

'Come on,' Dolly persisted, more loudly. 'When's the last time?'

'Keep your bloody voice down. What's the matter with you?'

And then she went into one, shrieking hysterically, accusing me of ignoring her, not wanting her any more, moaning that I let the twins run my life. Her voice got louder and louder and then she shouted, 'It'd serve you right if I found someone else while you're enjoying yourself up there.'

219

I snapped. 'Shut your mouth, for Christ's sake!' I said fiercely. 'You'll wake Nancy.'

'Why should you worry about that?' Dolly bellowed.

I didn't understand what she meant, so I said nothing.

'I don't see why you should worry about someone else's kid.'

Silence. Then I said, 'What are you talking about?'

'What I say. Nancy's not yours, you know.'

I froze, then just stared at her, searching her hard green eyes, unblinking now in blazing hatred.

'She's not, you know.' Her mouth curled and twisted with arrogance, enjoying my pain.

What she had said roared in my ears, deafening me with its implications. I felt suddenly weak. A thousand responses hammered in my head but my brain was too numb to make sense of them, then one single thought forced its way to the front of my mind, pounding and pounding away: 'Don't let it be true. Don't let it be true. Please, please don't let it be true.'

But Dolly, cocky in her desire to hurt, just stared at me in silence, enjoying my anguish.

Later, days later, she took it back, said it was a lie dreamt up in the heat of the moment. But it was too late. She had sowed that seed of doubt and it was to grow and grow until it was always there in the back of my mind.

And now in my cell, swimming around in a sea of warm memories of little Nancy, Dolly's damning declaration began to dominate my thoughts. I remembered all the odd coincidences, the strange happenings that somehow didn't add up, and I remembered, too, the innocent slips of Nancy's tongue telling me 'George' had been round.

All those wasted, precious years when my little girl had needed the influence of a caring father. Well, I had to stop tormenting myself. For my own sanity I had to accept once and for all that Nancy had indeed had that father's influence all the time I'd been away.

His name was George Ince.

Mum and the old man were not surprised, of course, by my decision to divorce Dolly. When the papers revealed the affair with Ince Mum admitted she'd known about it for some time but hadn't said anything because she felt it was not her business. 'I didn't like it,' she said, 'but I felt you had enough problems. I knew you'd have to decide for yourself one day.'

Dolly, ever ready to see the worst in people, always blamed Mum for telling me about Ince, but that simply wasn't true. Mum was not the sort of lady who liked making waves and causing problems. When the mystery witness story broke I told Mum I hoped Diana would read it and get in touch with her, in which case she was to be sure to bring her to see me. I was tempted to ask Mum to try to find Diana herself, but decided against it because she had enough on her plate earning a living, taking care of the old man and visiting the twins and me in different parts of the country. I'd been keeping my ears open for departing inmates going to Leicester but had not heard of any so far.

I'd spent hours describing Diana to a little Jewish man called George who was in for fraud. He often said I talked about her so much that he felt he knew her personally, and he told me nothing would give him greater pleasure than to go to Leicester to try and find her. But of course that's easy to say when you're locked up more than 150 miles away. George was coming up for release and due to be given a little job in a hostel to prepare him for life outside.

One day he came looking for me, beaming all over his face. 'Charlie,' he said, excitedly, 'I've got the hostel.

They're offering me London.' He paused, then grinned. 'Or Leicester.' He stood there, waiting.

I didn't know what to say; it's difficult to ask someone to organize their life in a certain way just to help you find a lost love. But it was as if George was reading my thoughts.

'Charlie, I've got no family to worry about. It makes no odds to me where I go. I'd love to go to Leicester to try to find Diana.'

I was lost for words. Prison life is not known for its generosity of spirit, for humane gestures that demand nothing in return. Finally I said, 'That's really nice of you, George. I'd love you to try to find her.'

George beamed. I think it made his day.

Sadly, George had no luck. The club in Leicester had closed and he could not find anyone who had worked there. He did the rounds, asking in pubs and so on, but drew a blank. I was disappointed, naturally, but told myself it was probably for the best. If Diana had got her marriage sorted out she certainly wouldn't need an ex-jailbird knocking on her door and asking her to renew a romantic relationship with someone she had probably forgotten long ago.

And yet, as the months towards my release wore on I could not get Diana out of my mind. She had been so beautiful, so kind, so loyal; so much the woman of my dreams. I knew I was still in love with her and had never stopped loving her.

And I knew, despite everything, that I would not be able to stop myself trying to find her to tell her so.

Chapter Fourteen

I could see the road from my cell. Day after day I would gaze out, lost in thought about the horrors of yesterday and the hopeful tomorrows waiting for me on my release. I would watch the cars on that road and think of the people in them, trundling along in comfort, peace and freedom. One day, I thought, I'll be on that road. One day, I'll be free; free to prove to my captors, my prosecutors, my friends even, what a terrible wrong I had suffered in the name of justice. One day . . .

At Maidstone there is a reception area where inmates arrive and depart. One morning I had to go there for something connected with my job in the kitchen and I found myself staring at four cubicles, each with a prisoner's name on the outside. I peeked into one of them: there was a long mirror, and a jacket and trousers hanging on a hook. There was also a clean white shirt, some socks and on the floor were some shoes. The cubicles were for inmates leaving for good or for a pre-release weekend. I looked at the clothes, then at the names on the doors. One day it will be my clothes hanging there, I thought. One day it would be my name on the door. One day . . .

Two or three months later, in July 1974, a prison officer told me to go to reception again. It had nothing to do with the kitchen, so I guessed it was about my pre-release weekend. A wave of excitement surged through me; I felt like a schoolboy being given an unexpected day's holiday. Sorting out the clothes I needed for my weekend was a tingling experience: nylon socks, not coarse woollen ones, white cotton pants, not drab prison issue, a blue blazer, and neatly pressed light-brown trousers. I didn't need to try them on, but I did, even the socks. Then I looked in the mirror at myself. It was an indescribable feeling, the first time in more than six years that I'd worn normal clothes.

They told me I was being released on Friday 23 August for three days and I went back to my cell, walking on air. Over the next few weeks I could think of nothing else but putting on those clothes and walking out of the door, breathing the sweet, fragrant scent of freedom. And then it was the Thursday before the Friday and I was so excited that I felt I'd never drop off to sleep. But I did and slept wonderfully peacefully. I was woken twenty minutes before other prisoners so that I could get washed and shaved. I could not do it all quickly enough: I was quivering all over with excitement like a child on Christmas Day.

There are many people in prison who are not worth two bob, but there are others who are genuinely sincere and really care about people other than themselves. I'd struck up friendships with several people and later that morning as I sat around waiting to be called to reception they came over to me. 'Have a lovely weekend, Charlie ... Enjoy yourself, mate ... Don't do anything I wouldn't do, my old son ... Don't forget to come back, Charlie ...' They were all pleased for me and I didn't hide my excitement, then someone was calling my name and I was on my way to reception, half-running to taste the freedom I'd dreamt about for over six years.

A prison officer told me there were some people waiting outside, reporters and photographers mainly, but I couldn't care less. My day had come and I would talk to anybody about anything. Not for long, however, because Mum was meeting me to drive me to London and I was going to make the most of my three days, squeezing the maximum enjoyment and pleasure from my short-lived liberty.

The Press were great, as they always had been to me, then I was in the car and Mum, bless her, was putting fifty pounds in my hand and we were driving away from the grim establishment that had been my home for the last eighteen months.

I glanced back and caught a brief glimpse of my cell. Yes, I would be back there on Monday, I knew that. But for the next seventy-two hours I was going to push my hatred for that lonely cage out of my mind. My 'one day' had come and I was going to think of nothing but catching up with the world that had left me behind so cruelly on 8 May 1968.

That evening, Mum and the old man suggested going to the Blue Coat Boy pub in Bishopsgate; just a quiet drink, they said – there were a couple of old friends who were dying to see me again. We walked into the downstairs bar and chatted to a few people. I was a little baffled; I certainly knew the people there but only to say hello to – they were hardly old friends. But I was enjoying myself anyway, so I didn't say anything.

Then Mum said casually that we ought to go upstairs where there was a bigger, more comfortable lounge.

And I nearly fell over.

There were not a few friends who wanted a quiet drink with me, there were over two hundred! Everyone I'd known down the years, it seemed, was standing there waiting for me, wanting to shake my hand and say how good it was to see me again. There was a beautiful buffet laid out, the drink was flowing, and all the time I was being taken from one person to another, exchanging a piece of news here and enjoying a bit of nostalgia there. Suddenly, around closing time, I started feeling dizzy: I'd spent more than six years with just a handful of people –

sometimes only one or two – and the hustle and bustle and heady party atmosphere was getting to me.

As if by magic, the chap who owned the pub came over and asked me to go downstairs with him; he had something important to tell me. The pub had now closed, and in the welcome tranquillity of the downstairs bar he sat me down and grinned. 'I haven't got anything specially important to tell you, Charlie,' he said. 'Your mum saw it was all getting a bit much for you so she asked me to get you away for a few minutes. She could see it was doing your brain in.'

I laughed. It was typical of Mum; she didn't miss much.

After I'd got my breath back we rejoined the fray, and the drinking, eating, laughing and joking went on until 4 A.M. I was so high on excitement and joy I was neither tired nor drunk, and when some of us went back to Braithwaite House I happily sat there, drinking one gin after another, with no thought of going to bed. We talked about prison but it seemed a long way off. It was as if those six years had never happened.

I spent the whole weekend in the East End, strolling around to see how much of the old place was still standing, and chatting to other people I'd known before I went away. They were a highly charged, emotional few days for me and of course they couldn't last. Before I knew it, it was Sunday night and I was making plans to return to the prison at 10 A.M. Mum wanted to come back with me, but I did not want her to have the upset of seeing me walk back through that door again. So, around 8 A.M. the next day, it was my old mate Tommy Cowley who drove me through South London and on to the A20 to Kent.

The Press were there in force, not so much to record my arrival, I think, but to be on the spot if I failed to turn up; that would have been a far better story. Tommy and I sat chatting until a couple of minutes to ten, then I walked to the gate and pressed the bell. The cameras clicked and I forced a smile I didn't feel. 'Fooled you, didn't I?' I cracked. 'Bet you thought I wouldn't be back.'

The newshounds liked that.

It was weird being back inside. It was as if I'd never been away and those three marvellous days as a free man had never happened. But they had, of course, and my friends wanted to know all the details – what I'd done, who I'd seen, whether things had changed, and whether I'd enjoyed myself. They would not taste that freedom for many years, so I drained my seventy-two hours of every little detail and they hung on every word. What I told them could have been put over in five minutes; I made it last a week.

Of course, one of the things they wanted to know was whether I'd slept with a woman. Like any normal man I'd missed sex desperately and had thought of going to bed with someone – probably a professional lady – on my first day out. But when it came to it, so much had been arranged for me, so many people were wanting to see me, that I simply did not have time. And anyway, deep down, the only person I wanted to go to bed with was Diana and I didn't even know where she was.

My mates in prison thought it hilarious that I'd been too busy for sex.

Everything, they say, comes to those who wait. And the one thing I'd been waiting for – my full release – finally arrived on 8 January 1975. My name was on one of those reception cubicles again and I changed out of my prison gear for the last time. All the excitement I'd felt five months before was still there, but this time it had a hard edge to it, tinged with a fierce determination that once I was out of prison I would begin a campaign to prove I should never have been jailed in the first place.

Several days earlier I'd been told that, despite our divorce, Dolly had rung the prison governor asking for details of my release. No doubt she wanted to make a big show of meeting me to squeeze some more money out of a newspaper. Fortunately, the governor had told her she had no rights, and the only people who met me that nippy winter's morning, apart from the Press, were Mum and two dear friends, George and Sue Dwyer. Driving down that road I looked back at the retreating prison wall, then up to where my cell was. For a few brief seconds memories of my prison existence swam around in my mind: the boredom and frustration, the anger and bitterness of maximum security, and the joy of coming off the A-List; the callous prison officers who loved making life difficult, and the sympathetic ones who bent the rules; the stupid inmates who drove me mad by talking rubbish and the mild-mannered ones who became my friends. These memories sped through my mind like a fast-forward video and then suddenly seemed to switch off. As on my pre-release weekend, it was as if those years, all that never-ending forever, had never happened.

As we left the town and headed towards the A20 and London, I sank back in my seat and closed my eyes, trying to take in that from that very moment I could do precisely what I wanted when I wanted with no questions asked, no permission to be sought. I was a free man, and it was a blissful, blissful feeling which sent a shiver of exquisite pleasure through me.

I cannot remember a more enjoyable hour's drive.

One of the first things I did was persuade Mum to give up her office cleaning job. On my pre-release weekend I'd been shocked to learn that she was getting up at four in the morning for this, then waiting on tables at the Blue Coat Boy at lunchtimes. She said she needed the money to be able to afford to go on prison visits, but it made me ill to think about it. All the people who had had money from us over the years! You would have thought somebody would have helped her out with a few quid. I didn't mind her doing the pub work, because she was an outgoing type who enjoyed company but I hated the idea of her getting up in the middle of the night to clean bloody offices. So when I was home for good I told her that that was the end of it. Mum, bless her heart, said she couldn't give it up – the cleaning company boss was a lovely man and she did not want to let him down; but I persisted and eventually she rang him and said she was quitting. He was very understanding and thanked her for all she had done.

Mum had started with nothing, suddenly had everything, and now she was back to nothing again. Yet she never complained, never moaned. I was so pleased for her and the old man that they still had that flat in Bunhill Row. When we bought the house in Bildeston, people suggested we should sell the flat, but I said: supposing something happens and we're not around, what would they do? Well, something *did* happen, and the house had to be sold. But Mum just went back to living in the flat and took on two jobs to make ends meet. Living the high life in the West End or on the breadline in the East End, she was still the same lady.

Money was a nightmare. I'd gone into prison with a lifetime's experience of threepenny bits, tanners, half-crowns and ten-bob notes, and I came out to the complexities of decimalization. The old half-crown had bitten the dust and the much-loved half-a-quid note was now a fifty pence piece.

For a while it was like a foreign currency and, on my second night home, it hit me just how much I had to re-learn. I was staying with George and Sue at their home in Orpington and while I was in the local pub I decided to ring Gary. Without thinking too much about it I went to the phone, but I couldn't work out how to use it. Coping with the new money was bad enough, but the phone system had changed too. I went back to George and Sue, feeling pathetic. 'I can't do it,' I said, like a child. They fell about.

Once I had picked it up, I seemed to be on the phone all the time, trying to pick up the threads of my life as fast as I could. I was always flying about, always in a hurry, I couldn't bear the thought of standing still; I'd idled away nearly seven years of my life, and I was determined to make up for lost time.

For two weeks I didn't think of driving, even though my licence was up to date. But then, after a night at Mum's, I asked George if I could drive us back to Orpington. Like swimming, or riding a bike, driving is something you never forget, and I drove the twenty miles as safely as if I had never been away from the wheel. After that, I was eager to drive everywhere. But I was still in a hurry: if I needed to stop for a paper or cigarettes, I'd see a shop then think, 'I'll wait for the next one.' Then I'd do the same at the next shop. It was as if I felt I'd be missing something, losing my place in the queue of life, if I allowed myself to pause. The changes took a bit of getting used to: I lost count of the number of times I took a sharp turn into what I thought was a traffic-beating back-double, only to find myself facing a block of flats or a one-way street that had not been there before. Then when I did calm down and took Shanks's pony I'd find the traffic had increased so much that crossing the road was a major, life-risking event.

There were people who were wary of me because of my name, but on the whole I found nearly everyone very friendly. I never took anything for granted, however, and was always on my guard. One night in the Chinbrook pub in Grove Park, South London, I was aware of a man at the next table staring. Then he said something to his wife, who looked over; it was obvious they were discussing me.

I felt a bit awkward – rather like an animal in a zoo – but ignored them and carried on chatting to George and Sue. The man continued to stare and I began to feel uneasy: the Kray trial had affected a lot of people and even though seven years had passed one couldn't be sure of people's reaction to meeting one of the convicted men.

Finally, George, Sue and I got up to leave. The man got up too, and walked towards me. He was about sixty, but huge – about six foot six. I tensed inwardly. This is it, I thought. He's going to take a pop at me, or slag me off. He certainly didn't look the type who wanted my autograph.

The gentleman looked me in the eye, but instead of giving me a load of abuse or even a right-hander he merely extended his hand and said, 'I hope you don't mind me asking, but how are you?'

I replied, 'I'm very well, thank you.'

'Oh, that's good,' he said. 'I'm so pleased. I'd like to wish you all the very best for the future.' And then he shook my hand warmly.

He was a middle-class, confident sort of man who, I believe, said what he meant and meant what he said. I left the pub with Sue and George, feeling buoyant. The encounter boosted my confidence no end.

* * *

231

I decided I had to talk to Dolly. Even though I knew Nancy was not my child I still wanted to see her; the upset of that last prison visit when Dolly had half-dragged her out still bothered me and I was missing her more than ever. I went to the flat in Poplar, which I had handed over to Dolly along with everything else, and discussed visiting arrangements. Dolly agreed it was best if I popped up whenever I liked and for the next few weeks I did that. For a while it was quite friendly; Dolly often cooked a meal and I looked forward to the visits, which I found rewarding and enjoyable.

Suddenly everything changed, however. For some reason Dolly decided she didn't want me to see Nancy any more and I got a summons ordering me to go to court to fight over custody. I was shocked then angry, thinking this is all I need – court! I could not understand what it was all about. I didn't want Nancy to leave her mother and live with me; I just wanted to see her once a week or so. Surely that could be arranged without the hassle and expense of going to court?

I started wondering what possible legal argument could be put forward to stop me seeing Nancy whenever I wanted. Surely Dolly wasn't going to come clean and tell the truth about Ince? When Dolly's solicitor eventually told me, I burst out laughing. 'One of the points we shall be making,' he said pompously, 'is association.'

'Oh, yes,' I said. 'And what do you mean by that exactly?'

'That it is not in the child's interests to be associated with you, a convicted criminal.'

I laughed in the solicitor's face. Well, what a joke! Dolly knew full well that I had served a sentence for something I didn't do, and here she was, living with a man who had done time for something he admitted, yet it was me who was not a good influence on Nancy.

The court case went ahead. I won the right to see Nancy once a week and did so for a while. But it became clear that Nancy was not bothered about seeing me and gradually I stopped going round to the flat altogether.

Once I'd got back into the swing of normal life again, I turned my mind to tracking down Diana. The first weekend I could, I drove to Leicester. But seven years is a long time and I couldn't find anyone I knew who could give me some leads to try to trace Diana. George, my old Maidstone mate, had discovered that she and her husband had once owned a pub, so we did the pub circuit again, but with no luck. Leicester is a fairly big city and Diana could have been anywhere. On the other hand, she may well have left the area entirely. I returned to London none the wiser.

George and I agreed to try again the following weekend, but during the week I got involved in some work that made it difficult for me to get away. George rang me and I explained that our private detective business would have to wait a week. An hour after I put the phone down, George rang back. 'I bet you'll come up now,' he laughed.

'Why?' I asked.

'I've found her,' George said.

Suddenly I found myself short of breath.

George had discovered Diana's pub was called The Carousel and had rung there. He had learned she was still married, and was ready to put the phone down if her husband answered, but luckily it was Diana who picked it up. When George told her he had a message from a 'mutual friend' Diana, who later said she knew that the 'mutual friend' was me, was pleased, but also wary; she had been questioned by the police after my arrest and didn't know if what she'd read about the murders was true. Anyway, she told George, she didn't like talking to

233

strangers on the phone. George immediately went to the pub, discreetly introduced himself to Diana and told her that I'd been thinking about her for nearly seven years. Diana was not totally convinced but agreed to go to a Leicester hotel a couple of days later to meet me again. The agreed time was 8 P.M.

As a boxer, I never suffered from butterflies. I knew I was good and could handle myself, and always walked from the dressing room to the ring with no tummy rumblings at all. But waiting for Diana in the hotel room that evening I went slowly but steadily to pieces. By 8 P.M. I was almost a nervous wreck. Seven years was a long time, I kept telling myself. Things change; people change. Before the arrest, I'd been a happy-go-lucky man about town – a wealthy businessman with a neat line in chat to match my expensive clothes, not bad-looking for my forty-four years, and supremely confident in myself because of my business success. In short, a winner. But I knew that prison had changed me. Seven years for something you did was hard enough to take; seven years for something you didn't do was a knockout blow that was bound to take a heavier toll. I looked at myself yet again in the mirror. Yes, I had lost weight, and I was seven years older. But would Diana detect something lacking in me? Would she feel that the happy-go-lucky spirit that had attracted her all those years ago had died? That my eyes had lost their sparkle? That the effervescence and cavalier approach to life had been replaced by a quieter, almost inhibited, shyness? That seven years locked away from society had robbed me of my personality, leaving me a shadow of my former self? Would she see not the winner she had once admired, but a loser to be avoided?

In the end, I bottled it. After all the build-up, I couldn't face the confrontation and the accompanying possibility of rejection. Not in the hotel foyer, anyway. If the reunion was not to be how I had imagined and dreamt throughout all those imprisoned years, I wanted it to take place in the privacy of the room, where we could at least be polite and brief and make small talk, then go our separate ways without too much hurt and certainly without any fuss.

So, at 8 P.M., I asked George to go down and bring Diana to the room. As I started on yet another packet of cigarettes new worries started banging away in my brain. What if she was scared to go to a hotel room with a man she had met just once? What if she wasn't just scared, but mightily offended? What if she just walked out? What if . . . ? I was piling one obstacle on top of the other when the door opened and there she was standing before me, blonde and beautiful, just as I remembered her. As we stood there looking at each other, smiling shyly, I knew it was going to be all right, and I walked over to her and gave her a kiss.

'Well, I think I'll be going,' said George, bless him. And he went out, closing the door quietly behind him.

Diana and I talked and talked. She was eager to tell me how much she had wanted to get in touch; how many letters and cards she had written, only to tear them up because she didn't want to cause me problems. In the end, she said, she reluctantly decided that she would leave it to me. She was so pleased that I'd tracked her down and had felt confident that I would do so. For my part, I was eager to tell her that I felt the same about her as I had done before I went away, but I stressed that if everything was all right in her life I didn't want to spoil things and cause her problems. She immediately reassured me that I'd come back at the right time. She had left home once while I was away, but had returned; now she was so unhappy with her husband that she was on the point of leaving again. When she had read that I'd been out for a pre-release weekend she'd considered ringing, but had feared that I'd be too busy.

The talking went on and on, and then, quite naturally it seemed, we went to bed. I would like to be able to describe the sheer joy of holding, caressing and making love with a woman you adore after nearly seven years without any female contact whatsoever, but it is beyond me; I would think it is beyond most people.

There is only one word to describe my feelings that night – they were wondrous.

Life as a free man was wonderful. But there was always something nagging at me that would not allow me to enjoy it to the full. It was that unfinished business of injustice.

I started to pop up to Leicester regularly, and eventually Diana decided to leave home. It was a difficult decision for her because her daughter, Claudine, was only twelve, but she felt it was best for everyone involved, so she moved in with a girlfriend in Beulah Hill, at Crystal Palace in South London.

Diana was so good with people, particularly the elderly, that I couldn't wait to introduce her to Mum and the old man. I felt sure they would adore her as much as I did, and I wasn't disappointed. The old man did not make friends easily, but he took to her at once; Diana really cares about people and the old man quickly realized this. They got on really well. Mum thought she was great and said it was a pity I hadn't met her years before. Mum never spoke badly of Dolly, but she went off her after the shabby way she behaved over the Ince affair. More than once Mum said my life could have been so much happier if I had met Diana first.

A friend of mine, Wilf Pine, former manager of the hugely successful rock band Black Sabbath, kindly loaned me a house, and Diana and I moved in together. Imme-

236

diately after the breakup Claudine and her brother Ian stayed with their father in Leicester, but it wasn't long before Diana and her husband agreed that it was best for the children if they moved to London. Some loyal pals made sure I had a few quid to help put me back on my feet and I was able to buy a flat in Worcester Park in Surrey. The kids came down and soon we were all living happily under one roof.

Sleeping had never been a problem for me. I'd always had the knack of being able to cut myself off from the hassles and aggravation of everyday living, and I managed this in prison, despite all the problems. But when I started living with Diana I would wake up in the middle of the night, shouting at the top of my voice. A dream would set me off and I'd wake up in a sweat but I could never remember what the dream was. It did happen once in prison – at Maidstone – and I woke myself up shouting. When it happened at home I would get up and have a coffee then go back to bed but then I'd have to get up again, and it would be backwards and forwards like that all night. Diana was worried, and a little frightened to begin with, but as soon as she senses the build-up now she shakes me and I slip back into a peaceful sleep.

I found I could go on television to talk about the past and my time inside, but in one-to-one situations – particularly with women – I'd find myself stumbling over my words with embarrassment. So you can imagine how awkward I felt when people actually wanted my autograph.

I'd got a job working on a big cutlery and silverware stand at the Ideal Home Exhibition at Olympia and attracted a lot of publicity. Around 80,000 people passed through the Exhibition each day and after a while I started feeling as though many of them were looking at me and pointing me out to their friends. One day a couple of girls asked me for my autograph.

Not knowing what to do, I said, 'You must have got me mixed up with someone else. I'm nobody famous.'

One of the girls laughed. 'We've seen your picture. And read about you. You're the Kray twins' brother, aren't you?'

Of course I signed my name for them, but I did feel funny doing it. And then it happened again, and again. A *London Evening Standard* reporter must have noticed, because he came up for a chat. He mentioned I was working, as though it must be a new experience for me. I told him I'd always worked, despite the notoriety.

'But ten hours a day?' He was shocked.

'I like it,' I said.

The next day I picked up a copy of the *Standard*. The reporter had written an article saying Charles Kray was working at Olympia and signing more autographs than he was selling cutlery. I thought it hilarious.

Communication with Dolly became cold and casual. We only spoke to each other about our son Gary but I knocked even that on the head when she did something I'll never forgive her for. Dolly would be the first to admit that she is a hard, unemotional individual, but what she did to my family, particularly Gary, was quite spectacular in its selfishness and brutality.

When George Ince had been released from prison, Dolly had decided it was not convenient for Gary to live with her. She did not discuss it with him but waited until he went out one day, then packed all his belongings in a suitcase and left it on the doorstep for Gary to find when he came home that night. He went to live with Mum and the old man in Bunhill Row. But I always made sure he kept in touch with Dolly.

I had always got on well with Dolly's mother and was

very upset one day to hear she was ill. She was staying at the home of Dolly's elder sister, so Gary and I went round there with some flowers. She was a lovely woman of about seventy and thought the world of her grandson. We had a nice chat and before we left she whispered, 'Just because I'm getting old, they think I'm senile. But don't worry, I know exactly what's going on.'

I smiled and took her hand. 'Well, you know what we think of you,' I said. 'I'll be running around, but I'll be back to see you in a couple of weeks.'

Early one morning, about ten days later, I was going on a visit to Parkhurst and left a note for Gary reminding him not to forget to ring his mother.

When I came back from Parkhurst around 7 P.M., an awful atmosphere hit me as soon as I walked in the door at Bunhill Row. Mum and the old man were in tears. I wondered what the hell had happened, then Mum said, 'Charlie, I've never said anything about Dolly, but I think this is terrible. After you left this morning, Gary phoned her.'

I nodded. 'I told him to.'

'He asked how she was, and said can I come and see you today? She didn't want him to. Then . . .' Mum was finding it hard to speak through her tears. I put my arm round her. '. . . then Gary asked how Nana was.' Mum couldn't speak for a few seconds, then she said, 'Dolly just told him, "Dead and buried," and put the phone down.'

I went numb. Then cold fury swept through me. How could Dolly not tell us her mum had died? How could she not give us the chance to pay our respects at the funeral? It was almost unbelievable.

'That's it,' I snapped. 'That's the end.'

Seething, I got on the phone and rang one of Dolly's brothers, Raymond. 'Dolly's taken a right liberty,' I said, and told him what had happened.

'Charlie,' he said sympathetically. 'We never thought our sister was that bad. We thought she'd let you know.'

'Somebody should have rung, Ray,' I told him.

'We thought you were away.'

That didn't cut any ice. 'I respected your mum, Ray. If I'd been in China, I would have come home. It's bad enough me not being there, but Gary . . .' I was so angry I couldn't speak, then finally I said, 'Anyway, that's the end for me. It's the most terrible thing to do to anyone.'

After that I told Gary I didn't want to have anything to do with the family.

Dolly felt guilty about Gary. For the next few months, she would ring him a couple of times a week, but it was purely because she felt she had to, not because she wanted to. She is incapable of feeling much for anyone other than herself. I would have expected Dolly to take Gary home to her flat, but she never did. I would have thought she could have taken him to see Nancy; after all they grew up as brother and sister. But she never did. Perhaps I should not have been too surprised. Dolly was jealous of Mum's popularity and stopped Nancy from visiting because she knew the child loved her. Every one of Dolly's relations said it was a bitchy, hurtful thing to do but Dolly didn't care. She was the only person who didn't like my mother. And the reason? She knew she couldn't compare with her in any respect as long as she lived.

At one time both Gary and I missed Nancy terribly, so when a young bloke I knew said he often saw her, I asked him to set up a meeting with her for us. I told him to let us know if he wouldn't be seeing her so we wouldn't be waiting unnecessarily. Well, we waited. Nancy didn't turn up, and neither did the bloke who was due to see her. That was the end for me and I decided not to bother any more. It was painful because I'd thought the world of her. Even though she was another man's child.

Chapter Fifteen

I started visiting the twins while they were together in Parkhurst. I didn't moan to them about my ten years because they were sentenced to three times that. We did discuss the events that had put us away but neither Ronnie nor Reggie wanted to know about the problems I had faced because of the Kray notoriety. I was out and they were still inside, they said; they would love to have my worries.

I did mention that I'd warned them not to trust those idiots, the so-called Firm, particularly Hart and Donahue, but the twins, as usual, took the view that it wasn't worth talking about: it was a thing of the past, finished; nothing could be done to change what had happened so best forget it.

For two criminally minded people, the twins are strange in that they do not like talking about crime, or violence. As young men they never discussed it and in prison all the talk of villainy and boasting drove them round the bend. Because of their name and reputation other inmates used to seek them out to try to impress them, and it bothered the twins so much that they would ask to be put in cells on their own. For years they were marked men, as they had been on the outside. And sometimes the pressure got to such a pitch that they exploded.

During the first few months of my freedom Mum phoned me, saying that there had been an upset in Parkhurst: Ronnie, it seemed, had gone into one and belted a couple of prison officers. They had injected him to sedate him, and chucked him in the chokey block. Mum and I were on our way to Parkhurst at once.

They told us we would have to see Ronnie in his cell, because he wasn't well enough to go to the visitors' room. That surprised us, but it was nothing to the surprise we got when we saw the state of Ronnie – and the cell, which was filthy and stank to high heaven. Even I, who had spent years inside, was shocked, and it knocked Mum bandy. I couldn't believe the authorities had allowed us to see the state of it; I suppose they felt it better to let us see Ronnie in those conditions than stop the visit altogether, in case we thought something was wrong.

There was just an iron bed in the cell and Ronnie was sitting on it. He looked awful: his eyes were lifeless, with bags under them, his skin sallow, and his normally neatly combed hair was dirty and straggly.

The twins and I were never demonstrative towards Mum, despite our deep love and respect, but that day, as Mum leaned towards him, Ronnie grabbed her by the arms and kissed her warmly on the cheek. He was ashamed of the cell and upset that we had been brought there. Mum said that it was terrible to see him looking so dreadful in a place like that, but Ronnie just said, 'Mum, I had a fight. I hit a couple of screws. What do you think they're going to do? Give me a medal?' He always took what they dished out without moaning or complaining.

We sat at the foot of the bed talking to Ronnie for nearly two hours and at the end of the visit Mum said that, despite everything, she felt better for having seen him. Ronnie replied quietly that he was pleased we'd come; he had needed to see us. It was an emotional and highly personal visit, and a prison officer sat behind us all the time listening to every word.

* * *

Mum's stamina was amazing. She hardly missed a visit, every week, winter or summer, from the moment we were arrested and on remand in Brixton, to the time when we were sent to far-flung prisons in Durham, Leicester and Chelmsford, then Albany, Parkhurst and Maidstone. It was a feat that only a deeply caring, loving mother could have achieved. Remember, she was getting up at 4 A.M. for her office cleaning job then working in the pub at Bishopsgate.

Thankfully, in 1979, Ronnie was transferred to Broadmoor, the hospital for the criminally insane, in Crowthorne, Berkshire, and, later, Reggie was moved to Long Lartin prison, in Evesham, Worcestershire.

For Mum, not having to catch a train to Portsmouth, a ferry to the Isle of Wight, then a taxi to the prison, made a huge difference and she continued to visit the twins regularly, with never a word of complaint.

There was one visit I insisted she didn't make, however – to Long Lartin, after she received a distressing phone call from the prison. I told her the visit would be awful and would make her ill.

For Reggie had tried to kill himself.

Early one morning in February Mum had rung me in tears at my home in Crystal Palace. 'Reggie's tried to commit suicide,' she sobbed.

'What!' I couldn't believe it. Ronnie had told me he had a feeling all was not well with Reggie, but I put it down to the change of jail; he would get used to Long Lartin after a few weeks.

'He tried to slash his wrists,' Mum said. She was in a dreadful state.

'I'll be right over,' I said. 'I'll ring the prison from your place.'

I covered the fifteen miles in less than half an hour and rang the prison. It was true, they told me: Reggie had tried to slash his wrists. It was a nasty incident, but he was recovering and everything was under control.

I was not convinced. I asked if I could visit him that day and they agreed. Mum wanted to come with me, but I felt it better if I saw Reggie's condition first. Obviously things were bad and I didn't want her upset more. Also, I sensed trouble and I wanted someone other than family with me, someone honest and trustworthy with no criminal record who would be a reliable witness. I chose an East End mate, Laurie O'Leary, and we arrived at Long Lartin that afternoon.

Reggie was in the hospital wing. He had been feeling depressed and wanted to be on his own, we were told. Ah, I thought, so they knew he wasn't well. What else did they know about my brother that had led him to try to take his own life? As we followed a prison officer to Reggie's cell I wondered what state he was going to be in. Nothing could have prepared me for what we were about to see.

Like our father, Reggie had always been fussy about cleanliness. As a young man he kept himself spotless: you rarely saw Reggie unshaven or with untidy hair, and he was always dressed in clean, neatly-pressed shirts and suits. So the sight that greeted me when I looked through the flap on Reggie's cell door jolted me. He was sitting on his bed, his clothes creased as though he'd slept in them, his uncombed hair standing on end, and with two or three days' growth of beard. He looked like a raving lunatic who had been locked up for twenty years.

Laurie and I went in and, after the usual pleasantries, I motioned towards one of his arms, which was heavily bandaged. 'Why did you do it, Reg?' I asked. There was no point in beating about the bush.

Reggie shook his head. 'I don't know.'

'There must be a reason,' I persisted.

'I don't know what's wrong with me,' he said. 'People keep saying strange things to me. They keep taking a pop at me.'

I looked at Laurie. It did not sound like the Reggie we knew and I didn't know what to do for the best. I looked at his arm again. 'How on earth did you do all that?'

'With my glasses,' he replied.

Apparently he broke his glasses in half and used a piece of a lens to saw into his wrist. Listening to him describe it made me go cold. He had been alone in his cell and no one had seen him until an officer had spotted him covered in blood. I stared at Reggie as he talked. I could not get over the state he was in. I'd never seen him like that in my life and all I could think was that no one in their right mind breaks their glasses and saws into their wrist. I had to ask him, again. 'But why, Reg?'

It's strange with people who have gone over the edge: when we had arrived, he was reasonably okay, although not like the Reggie of old, of course. Then suddenly when I asked him that question he seemed to break up in front of our eyes, and finally cracked. Close to tears he told us that he'd been depressed because he was causing everyone so many problems, and had decided that if he was out of the way it would make life easier for everyone, particularly Mum and me, what with the visiting and everything. 'It seems it will never end,' he said quietly.

I told him not to be so stupid, not to think like that. No, the visiting was not much fun for Mum, who wasn't getting any younger. But she wasn't complaining; she could cope. Hadn't she always? 'She loves you and wants to see you,' I insisted. 'And Ronnie. You'd break her heart if you did yourself in.'

Reggie listened, but I could see he was not convinced. There was a dullness in his eyes, a look of defeat. I asked

245

him if he had been taken out of the cell. He nodded.
'They've just brought me back up.'

'From where?'

'The chokey block,' he said.

I stared at him disbelievingly. He'd sawn his wrist, lost
a lot of blood and they had put him in the chokey! I knew
that people were stripped naked and left on their own in
there with just a blanket. Sometimes there wasn't even a
bed, just a mattress or a sheet of canvas.

I knew Reggie was not himself, so I asked him if he was
sure. Then I left the cell and demanded to speak to the
Chief Prison Officer, who confirmed that Reggie had
spent the maximum twenty-four hours in the chokey
block. I went spare. The block was meant for normal
prisoners who went off the rails and needed time on their
own to quieten down. Why, I wanted to know, had Reggie
been taken there and kept there all day and all night in
his condition?

'He was put in the chokey for his own protection,' the
P.O. said, 'so he couldn't do anything else.'

But that didn't wash with me.

'You didn't have to put him in the strong box for that,'
I protested. 'Someone could easily have watched him in
his own cell.'

But the P.O. did not want to know, saying the prison
was not to blame for Reggie's condition. He felt Reggie
was in a perfectly balanced frame of mind and had
probably cut his wrist deliberately to cause trouble. He
even suggested Reggie was trying to 'nut himself off' so
that he would be certified insane and sent to Broadmoor
where Ronnie had been transferred three years before. I
lost my cool and told the P.O. that he was out of order.
Reggie did not want to go to Broadmoor; he had always
said that once you go there, you're in for ever. After a

heated exchange I went back to the cell, seething. The whole thing was a disgrace but what could one do?

When I told Reggie what had happened he didn't take much notice and didn't seem with it at all. Then he said something that convinced me I had to take the matter further.

'That bloke who found me in my cell,' Reggie said. 'He asked why I'd cut my wrist. He said people usually hanged themselves with a piece of sheet or something.'

Dora Hamylton is a Leicester magistrate who has taken an interest in the twins' cases. After meeting them several times and starting work on a biography of our mother she had become a friend of the family, and I rang asking her to come to Long Lartin with me to see Reggie and the prison authorities.

She could not believe what she saw. Reggie had been cleaned up but he was still in a terrible state, nothing like the person she had seen when she had last visited him. The chief male nurse asked to speak to Dora alone, which made me suspicious, but there was nothing I could do about it. I learned later that he told her he thought Reggie was putting on an act. She said he could not be serious: she had visited Reggie many times and knew him well enough to know that he certainly wasn't acting; he had gone over the edge. Whether the nurse was convinced I don't know, but some good came out of the talk, because he promised Reggie would not be put in the chokey block again.

We then went to see the assistant governor. I demanded to know why Reggie had been driven to cut his wrist and why he had been treated the way he had. The assistant governor went round and round the houses before saying that he wasn't sure whether Reggie knew what he was doing. I cut him short by telling him I knew what was on his mind: he felt Reggie was trying to work his ticket to Broadmoor to be with Ronnie. He admitted that I was right.

'Well, you can forget it,' I said. 'Ronnie or no Ronnie, that's the last place Reggie wants to go. He's always said so.'

The assistant governor simply looked at Dora and me with a total lack of concern.

'You don't seem at all bothered that one of your inmates has tried to commit suicide,' I went on. 'Have you seen what Reggie did to himself?'

He said he hadn't.

'He broke his glasses and actually sawed into his veins with the lens,' I told him. 'Do you think anyone could do that as an act?'

The assistant governor did not have an answer to that.

'Would you have been happy if he'd managed to kill himself?' I asked.

'No, I wouldn't,' he replied casually.

Getting angrier by the second at the man's offhand attitude, I told him that the prison staff should have known what was happening to Reggie to make him so depressed and should have been aware of the pitch he was reaching. The assistant governor mumbled some stock reply but I knew from my own experience what had gone on. Prison officers are not aware of such things because they think there's a hidden ploy behind everything. They write reports on people every minute of the day but they don't seem to notice the things that matter.

Then Dora put her bit in. Reggie was not at all well, she said. She had not liked what she had seen, nor what she had heard, and she trusted something would be done about it.

I let a couple of weeks go by before I took Mum to the prison. Reggie was a little better but still not right, and the sight of him really upset her. I'm glad I didn't take her with me on that first visit or she would have collapsed from the shock.

Reggie continued to progress. And then one day I got a phone call from the prison authorities, saying they wanted to see me because he had got out of control and attacked four officers. I went the next day and asked Reggie what it was all about.

'They're driving me mad,' he said. 'I ran into them and they all jumped on me.'

It didn't make sense to me. He had had no problems in Parkhurst but Long Lartin was bringing out the worst in him. I'd been dubious at first, but now I believed Reggie when he said that the officers there provoked him. In the end it all worked out well for him because Long Lartin said they couldn't handle him and he was sent back to the Isle of Wight. Reggie was delighted and relieved.

After he had been at Parkhurst a couple of days, I went to see the Chief Prison Officer, who told me that Reggie still wasn't one hundred per cent but they would have him back to normal in a few days.

Within a week, Reggie was as right as rain and able to talk coherently about what had been a four-week blitz on his brain. He said the move to Long Lartin had unsettled him and he had never been happy there. His letters had either been late or stopped altogether and officers tried generally to provoke him, as if they were seeing how far they could go and how much he could take.

And he remembered being told that people 'usually hang themselves with a piece of sheet or something'.

'That was a very irresponsible thing to say,' Reggie said. 'Or maybe they really did want me to top myself.'

Ronnie had known before any of us that Reggie was heading for a crisis. Reggie did not talk about his problems in his letters but Ronnie picked up that something was wrong. Even if Reggie had not written at all Ronnie would have sensed the trouble ahead, for the amazing telepathy they shared as children was still there.

Mum never ceased to be amused by it, even though she had grown used to it over the years. Ronnie, for example, would write to her from prison saying she should go on holiday for a couple of weeks, then Reggie, from a different prison hundreds of miles away, would write saying the same thing, even though the twins themselves had not discussed it. She would go to see one of them and talk about a certain subject, then when she visited the other one, he'd bring up the same subject, and Mum would find herself having an identical conversation. She would come home and laugh. 'Would you believe it, it's happened again!'

So it was hardly surprising that Ronnie knew Reggie was suffering in Long Lartin. One thing is certain: Ronnie would have understood Reggie's desire to be left on his own to avoid listening to all that talk about violence from idiots. For Ronnie had gone through the same problems himself, first in Durham then in Parkhurst. He liked being on his own so much that I'm sure it wouldn't have bothered him to stay in the chokey block for six months, not twenty-four hours. Broadmoor is perfect for him: most of the inmates there are in for domestic crimes and not caught up in the supposedly glamorous side of villainy. The novelty of having a notorious Kray twin in their midst has worn off and Ronnie can now go off and sit on his own for an hour without being bothered. It took him a long time to get to this comfortable stage, though. After he arrived so many people from other parts of the hospital wanted to chat to him that it got on his nerves and he didn't go out for two years.

One would have thought that after all the medical reports on Ronnie the staff at Broadmoor would understand that he doesn't need people nor does he want to buy friendship. But they are still puzzled by his charitable nature.

The Superintendent called me in once, a concerned look on his face. 'Ronnie keeps giving things away,' he said. 'What do you think the motive is?'

I smiled to myself. I knew he kept half his ward in tobacco, and at the last count he'd given away thirty watches. 'He likes giving things away,' I said. 'He's done it all his life.'

The Superintendent was not convinced.

'What possible motive could there be?' I asked.

The Superintendent shook his head. 'I don't know. That's why I asked you.'

'If you think he's bribing people so they'll be on his side, so they'll help him in some way, forget it. You should watch and see what sort of people Ronnie picks out. You won't find any tough six-footers, I can assure you.'

It was true. All their lives the twins have had an overwhelming compassion for the underdog – the little man who can't protect himself from the bully, the old lady who is ill or down on her luck. Often I've been sitting in the visiting hall at Broadmoor when Ronnie has spotted an old lady he's never seen in his life. 'Look at that old lady, Charlie,' he'll say. 'Bless her. Get her a box of chocolates, will you?'

I do it for him because I believe in it. I've always been soft-hearted too.

I realize that I knew this side of Ronnie for more than thirty years before our arrest, but one would expect an institution that has supposedly been monitoring his health and behaviour to understand that acts of good-natured charity are part of Ronnie's character and nothing to get

251

worked up about. In Broadmoor, he gives away so many watches that he is nicknamed 'the watchman'. Wilf Pine gave him a watch on one visit which Ronnie immediately sold for £50, giving the money to someone who was having an operation for throat cancer.

Once he gave away a chain which I had just given him. I was quite angry and said, 'I didn't buy you a present to give away.'

'If you gave it to me, it's mine,' Ronnie replied. 'So I've got the right to do what I like with it.'

'But I expect you to keep it,' I told him. 'I bought it for *you*.'

'If it gives me pleasure to give it away there's no harm in that, is there?'

There was no harm in it, I suppose, but it was galling to think that a chain I wanted Ronnie to wear was being worn by someone else who I had not even met. 'Anyway,' I said, 'I'd prefer it if you didn't give my presents away.'

Ronnie assumed that look of determination, the look that said: Don't you argue with me. If I want to do something, no one is going to stop me. 'If *I* want to give them away, I think it's better that I do,' he said. 'I would accept it if you did it. Why can't you?'

And Ronnie *would* accept it. But then he can go one way or the other.

Other inmates must think the world of Ronnie. He will give away half his tobacco allowance, borrow some back when he runs out then buy them some more. Sometimes inmates are allowed to buy meals and Ronnie will pick ten people he feels are in need and treat them. Once Wilf took him in a platter of seafood and Ronnie immediately said, 'We'll have a party tonight.' If he gets money, he'll buy a dozen steaks and share them round. It goes on all the time. He'll never change.

I had had six years and eight months taken off my life for something of which I was totally innocent. I'd sat in jail seething with frustration at the injustice of it all. I'd driven myself almost round the twist discovering people who had received far lighter sentences after pleading guilty in similar cases. But I'd resisted the temptation to write letters because I felt them to be a waste of time. However, something had to be done about it and I decided to wait until I was out then go to the International Court of Human Rights in Strasbourg. If there was one place that could put right the wrong that had been done to me and mete out the justice I'd been deprived of all those years before, that was it.

Day and night, night and day, throughout the agonizing, mind-numbing tedium of prison existence, I had thought and dreamt . . . and fantasized about the wonderful moment when the truth about me would scream across the pages of the British Press and people would know they should not tar me with the same brush as my twin brothers.

Then, three months after my release, a visit to Ronnie, in Parkhurst, led to me having an emotional talk with an eminent psychiatrist, Dr Klein, and abandoning all those dreams. Ronnie wanted to know the truth about his mental state and needed Dr Klein's help. He'd known him for many years before our arrests and felt he could rely on him to get accurate information from the prison's medical staff.

I fixed an appointment to see Dr Klein at his Harley Street office. We were talking about Ronnie, but also about me, and after a while it dawned on me that Dr Klein was analysing me. I asked him if this was the case and he admitted it, saying he found it worrying that I seemed so full of hate and anger, even though I had served my sentence.

'Wouldn't you be if you'd been jailed for something you didn't do?' I said.

He had assumed I'd helped dispose of Jack McVitie's body, so I put him right as succinctly as I could. He sat back, behind his desk, deep in thought. Then he leaned forward and looked at me. 'Charlie,' he said earnestly. 'Don't waste your time trying to prove your innocence.'

'What!' I snapped. 'I've thought of little else for nearly seven years. I'm taking the case to Strasbourg.'

Dr Klein shook his head slowly, sadly.

'No matter what you do, you won't be allowed to win.'

I didn't understand.

He explained. 'Even if you did succeed in getting the case to Strasbourg and the court did agree you were wrongly convicted that doesn't mean the British Government would do anything about it.'

'They would have to,' I said.

He shook his head again. 'It would cause some embarrassment, but that's all. They certainly wouldn't issue a pardon.'

'But it's the principle,' I insisted.

'Even if the principle's right, the whole exercise would be futile because you've served your time. You can't get back those seven years.'

I said nothing. I stared back at him, unable to think of anything except that his last point was spot on. Nobody could give me back seven years of my life.

He let the silence continue, allowing the profundity of what he had said to sink in. Finally he said softly, but very warmly, 'After being away so long, don't you think you should just enjoy your life? Don't you think you owe that to yourself?'

'Of course I do,' I said quickly. 'But I'll enjoy my life more if I can clear my name, make people aware I didn't do what they believe I did.'

Dr Klein shook his head. 'If you carry on your fight, it will become a full-time occupation that would ruin your life. It could ultimately destroy you.'

I didn't reply, and he asked me if I respected him and his advice. I told him I did.

'I know you will never completely forget the injustice,' he said finally. 'But try to put it to the back of your mind and put all your energies into living. That is the best advice I can give you because you will never be allowed to win.'

As I walked out of his office and along Harley Street I thought of what he had said. I hated the idea of not going through with what I'd promised myself, but there had been something in Dr Klein's warm sincerity that warned me I should consider his advice very carefully indeed. I was no fool. I knew no one was going to admit I was wrongly convicted, because that would throw a huge question mark over the whole case. The authorities had been given all the evidence they needed to release me when Ronnie Hart tried to kill himself and left a note admitting that he had lied about me in court. But even that had made no difference to my appeal.

Over the next few weeks I pondered Dr Klein's advice: it dominated my thoughts, nagging away at me as I tried to get back into the swing of daily working life, hammering inside my brain as I fell exhausted into bed at night. And then, one day in the summer of 1975, one lovely day when the sun was shining and the East End was bustling with happy, smiling, contented people, I knew what I had to do.

Dr Klein was right in everything he said; I think, deep down, I knew that all along. But it was something he didn't say that made me decide to drop my plans for taking the case to Strasbourg. Life was precious, but short, and I was one year away from my fiftieth birthday.

I was fit, strong and as alert as I'd ever been – a youthful fifty – but no matter how I looked or felt, time was not on my side. As Dr Klein had said, taking on the Establishment would be a full-time occupation; to give myself even half a chance of success I would have to drop virtually everything else I was involved in, all the little business deals I was trying to pull together for Diana and me. I would have to dedicate myself singlemindedly to the whole business, think, talk, dream about nothing else twenty-four hours a day, seven days a week. And not just for a year; I'd read of human rights cases taking years. And for what? Dr Klein's words came back to me, filling my mind: '*You will never be allowed to win.*'

Did I want that? Did I want more pressure, more aggravation, more courtroom confrontations, more legal mumbo-jumbo, when the odds were stacked so heavily against me? Did I want to go through yet again all the mental anguish of trying to convince people of the truth of that terrible October night when they had had enough facts to convince them already, and had chosen to come to the wrong conclusion?

Did I really want all that in my life as I approached my half-century? And, just as important, did my darling Diana?

On that sunny day, with the East End and its people so full of life, I decided once and for all to stop dreaming about getting a pardon or even a court victory for wrongful conviction. I would take Dr Klein's advice and I would take it from that very minute.

I would never be able to forget the trauma and indescribable agony of it all. But at least I could try to push it further and further back into my mind until it was just a memory, not a crusade. I would not allow the Establishment another victory by destroying myself. I would rediscover my zest for living and get back into the business of making money to provide for the woman I planned to marry.

After the darkness of prison, where nothing is easy, I would revel in the sunshine of a free life, where everything is possible. I would throw myself into it with all my heart, determined to try to catch up with my lost years by making every moment count.

Chapter Sixteen

I cannot thank Maidstone Jail enough for teaching me artificial resuscitation. I passed the elementary exam so well one morning that I was asked if I wanted to take the advanced test in the afternoon, and passed that with honours. This was great for me but even better for Diana a few years later. For it helped me to save her life. Three times.

Diana suffers from asthma, and towards the end of an evening at Joe and Rose Rankin's pub in Hackney she suddenly found it hard to breathe. I suggested we leave, and soon we were heading down Kingsland Road on the way to Ewell in Surrey. I did not realize how serious Diana's asthma attacks could be until I looked at her in the passenger seat and realized she was passing out. I needed to get her home as fast as possible so I put my foot down, assuming that if I was stopped the police would be sympathetic. Fortunately, there were no police cars to be seen that night and I got her home in double-quick time. Without a booking.

I helped Diana out of the car and sat her in an armchair while I made some coffee. When I came back she was on the floor. Out of my mind with worry, I picked her up and put her on a settee.

I felt for her pulse. There was none.

I felt to see if she was breathing. She wasn't.

I picked up the phone despairingly. It was out of order.

Trembling with panic, I moved Diana gently back to the floor. She was lifeless. And she would stay that way unless somebody did something quickly. Well, there was nobody else. Only me. I knew I had to find out just how well I'd learned artificial resuscitation in jail and I prayed I'd learned it well enough.

My Diana was not going to die on me.

I took a deep breath, filling my lungs with as much air as I could, and blew into her mouth – first one big blow; another deep breath; another blow, then another. Next I hit her on the sternum to start the heart.

She didn't move. Didn't breathe.

Another deep breath. More air, more life-giving air. I hit the sternum again, harder this time.

Come on, Diana, come on!

But nothing.

And then again, and again and yet another rib-crushing thump on the sternum. Come on. Come on. COME ON! Breathe, my darling. BREATHE!

And then, finally, she did. She took in the air I'd given her and started breathing it. From an inert, lifeless body, she started coming back to me again.

I got up and dashed across the road. I knocked on a door urgently and a young girl of about fourteen opened it, alarm on her face at the sight of a strange man on her doorstep at 11 P.M.

'Don't worry, darling,' I said, not wanting to frighten her. 'There's a lady across the road having an asthma attack. She's in a bad way. Can you ring for an ambulance?'

I left her to it and ran back into the house. Diana's breathing kept stopping then starting and I prayed I could keep her going until the ambulance arrived. Just then the girl came in, looking terrified. The ambulance was on its way, she said. At that moment the ambulancemen came running into the house, carried Diana out and put her on oxygen. I jumped in the ambulance and we were racing to the hospital with someone radioing ahead to tell them

259

to prepare for a major emergency. And all the time Diana's breathing was stopping and they had to keep starting it again.

At the hospital they put her on a machine, then on to a bed which turned upside down so that a pipe could be put down her throat. It seemed like hours before the ambulancemen came out and told me I could relax because Diana was breathing normally.

I thanked them for all they had done, then, as they started to leave, one of them turned to me and said, 'By the way, you saved that lady's life. Where did you learn resuscitation?'

I shrugged, embarrassed. Somehow, the place did not seem right to get involved in a conversation about prison. 'It was years ago,' was all I said.

Diana was told she was being kept in overnight but I was allowed to see her once she was settled. She was sitting up, looking perky and right as rain.

'How do you feel?' I asked.

'Like a fool,' Diana replied. 'I feel perfectly well enough to go home.'

'Well, you're not,' I said. 'We're not taking any chances.'

I told her how the whole business had opened my eyes: I hadn't realized asthma attacks could be so lethal. 'You were completely out,' I said.

Diana smiled. 'I know. They told me who saved my life.'

'Well, now you're in my debt,' I joked. And we both laughed.

I left her at 3 A.M. and suddenly remembered my car was at home in Ewell. I got a cab easily in Epsom town centre, but I was so brimful with relief I could happily have walked all the way.

* * *

In 1984 we had another drama while at a wedding. Diana swallowed a couple of mouthfuls of brandy, then felt so ill that we decided to leave for home, which was now in Crystal Palace, South London. Diana's brother, John, and his wife Dede, who were over from Canada and staying with us at the time, were surprised to see us home so early. But it was nothing to the shock they got when Diana slumped in an armchair and stopped breathing.

Dede went into a panic. John told her to quieten down: he had been a medic in the Navy and was now medical director of a hospital. He was calm; he knew what had to be done.

What a relief! I thought. My memories of the first crisis were still quite fresh and quite honestly I didn't want the responsibility of trying to pull Diana through again: the thought of failure petrified me. Thank God this time someone was on hand who knew more about medicine than I'll ever know.

But when I saw what John was preparing to do I knew Diana's life was in my hands again. He was taking a carving knife out of a drawer, saying that Diana needed a tracheotomy.

'What are you doing?' I asked, shocked.

'It's the only way, Charlie,' he replied. 'It's the only way to make her breathe.'

'No it's not,' I said sharply, my panic and concern for Diana giving a rough edge to my tone. I knelt beside her and took a deep breath, then I whacked her sternum hard, probably harder than necessary but I was taking no chances.

Looks of relief swept our faces as Diana started to breathe again. Dede had called an ambulance and I went with it to the nearest hospital. I told a doctor what had happened, but he was very offhand and seemed to think

Diana had been drunk and it was all a waste of time. After a check-up she was allowed home.

The next day, her doctor hit the roof. He rang the hospital, demanding to know why Diana had been treated so shabbily, despite her medical history, in such a dangerous situation. He asked Diana for the name of the doctor who had treated her so that he could take it further, but she persuaded him to drop it.

Things go in threes, they say, and we did not have long to wait for Diana's hat-trick of crises. We were having a meal at a Crystal Palace restaurant when Diana said she was going outside for some air. She promptly collapsed on the pavement.

The first I knew about it was when a girl came running in, saying a lady had fallen down, hitting her head. I dashed outside while someone rang for an ambulance. Diana's breathing had not stopped this time but she was out cold so I turned her over and started giving her the kiss of life anyway. I didn't manage to bring her round, but then the ambulancemen arrived and took over. Diana finally came to fifteen minutes later and was soon feeling well enough to insist that she was okay and did not want to go to hospital. To this day, we don't know what brought that attack on.

I was getting quite a dab hand at the kiss of life. And my prison training in medical crises was to come in useful again, in tragic circumstances.

During the early eighties the twins' telepathy was working strongly. In their letters to each other neither had mentioned confessing to their respective crimes, yet they both did so at roughly the same time. I don't know the reasons; they haven't told me and I haven't asked. I think, perhaps, they both decided they had served so many years that it didn't matter any more.

They owned up in front of a panel reviewing their cases for parole, and one of the questions each twin was asked was: 'Do you feel any remorse?'

Ronnie decided he could not lie just to get parole. He said he was unable to feel remorse because of the situation behind the killing: he knew George Cornell was going to kill him, so he killed him first. And, he said, he would do the same again in similar circumstances. He accepted that the panel would not agree with him; they would probably let the other person shoot. But that was not his nature, he said.

Reggie said he *was* sorry about what had happened. But it did not do him any good. He was told his parole was being turned down and he would not be released until the 1990s..

I was bitterly disappointed at that decision, but delighted that Reggie had confessed to the McVitie murder because it meant, at long last, that I could tell the truth about my involvement that fateful October night. Family loyalty means everything to me – no matter how terrible the circumstances – and all the time the twins denied killing McVitie I had to pretend I hadn't gone to Harry Hopwood's house. However, with the admissions came my chance to get the truth out in the open and clear my name once and for all.

My first thought was to seize the chance quickly with both hands. I remembered my anger and bitterness throughout my years in captivity, my fantasy about seeing my reputation redeemed in blazing newspaper headlines. Well, here was the perfect opportunity to hit those headlines and make all those pompous prosecution legal eagles see that, in my case at least, they had got it wrong.

It would not give me back six years and eight months of my life; it would almost certainly not win me an official pardon. But it would make me feel better and make the rest of my life taste sweeter. I thought and thought about it, trying to convince myself I should go against Dr Klein's advice, but in the end I didn't. His words, *'They won't let you win,'* hammered away inside my brain and convinced me that no matter how much I wanted the world to know that 'Charlie Kray is innocent, OK?' the battle was not going to be worth it – even though Reggie had confessed.

Dr Klein is more experienced than me. He has studied for years and years and knows about life. I am positive he was right in everything he told me and I am so, so glad I decided *not* to go back on his advice.

Chapter Seventeen

Just before 9 a.m. on Tuesday 5 April 1983, the phone rang at my home in Crystal Palace. It was Gary, calling from the flat in Bunhill Row, where he was living with the old man. Gary was sobbing. He had woken up and found the old man lying at the bottom of the stairs. I told him to ask a neighbour to ring for an ambulance; I would get over as fast as possible. As I got ready, I knew what had happened and, ten minutes later, an ambulanceman phoned to confirm it. The old man was dead.

The ambulanceman was kind and gentle and told me to take my time; there was nothing anybody could do and he didn't want me to have an accident. He and a colleague would wait until I arrived.

On my way through South London to the City I saw a crowd of people standing round a man on the ground. They were just staring at him, not knowing what to do, so I stopped the car and ran over. I suggested someone rang for an ambulance, then I loosened the man's tie and checked his pulse and breathing. They were fine – the man, who was a postman, had just fainted. I put him in the recovery position and told the crowd that he was going to be all right, but I couldn't wait because I had an emergency of my own. I got back in the car and carried on to Bunhill Row.

Five days later, we buried the old man next to his beloved Violet in Chingford Cemetery. The prison authorities made it clear the twins would be given permission to attend the funeral, but neither Ron nor Reg asked for it.

The old man had said he did not want another circus. Neither did they.

I went to the graveside at least once a fortnight, often more. Like visiting the twins, it was something I felt I had to do. If the weather was bad, I wouldn't go, but then I felt guilty. It is lovely and quiet in that cemetery and I'd go there with Gary to put flowers down, clean the stone and sort it all out. I'd read the stone for the millionth time – 'May you both rest peacefully. Our love and memories are always with you. May God bless you both' – and I'd talk with Mum and the old man as though they were there. Afterwards, me and Gary would go to the car and I'd look over and say: 'We're off now.' Driving away I always felt better for having gone.

By 1986, my relationship with Diana had changed dramatically. It was nearly nineteen years since we had met at that club opening in Leicester, and although we still loved each other, we had fallen out of love and now had an unspoken understanding that each was free to have flings with other people, as long as we were discreet and did not get heavily involved.

I had to admit I had my cake and was eating it, too; I could treat our lovely flat as home; at the same time I was able to go off in search of female company, with Diana's agreement, if not her encouragement. I didn't always know what Diana was doing; I never asked. We had become like brother and sister, and certain things, like outside relationships, were better kept private. Then, that summer, something happened to me that would disrupt my cosy life and make me face some harsh realities.

I fell in love again.

Her name was Judy Stanley. She was a bright, articulate, strong-minded woman of thirty-five and the mother of three children, a girl of seven and two boys, aged six and three. We met in a restaurant in Surrey on the day Judy was officially separated from her husband – and we clicked immediately. I was not sure whether Judy would welcome starting her newly acquired liberation with a date with a man twenty-five years older than her, but I asked for her telephone number anyway. To my surprise and delight, she gave it to me and, several weeks later, we began a relationship that would grow and grow until we became what was unacceptable to the understanding Diana and I had – 'heavily involved'.

I did not like cheating on Diana, but I could not help myself – I really couldn't. I became obsessed with Judy and would make all sorts of excuses to ring her. For the previous years, my life had been chugging along in a low gear, but now, overnight, it seemed, I had changed up and was motoring. I'd always been what my friends called Champagne Charlie, always ready for a good time, but Judy had given me an even keener zest for life.

To start with, however, we were on different wavelengths, out of sync, if you like. Maybe I was out of practice; maybe Judy was too important to me. I was terrified of making the wrong move and scaring her off. Whatever the reason, I never seemed to ask the right questions. I wanted to take her to a wine bar in Croydon I knew she liked, but instead of coming straight out with an invitation, I'd say: 'Are you going to the wine bar tonight?' Mostly, Judy had no plans to go there, so, naturally, she would say no. I learned later that if I'd invited her to go there with me, she would have said yes. So our relationship got off to a slow start.

Thankfully, we found ourselves in the wine bar on the same night a month later and I seized the opportunity.

'I've got this friend in Suffolk, Jeff Allen,' I said. 'Lovely fella, with a beautiful house. Would you like to go there for the weekend with me?'

I knew it was a long shot; even if Judy did fancy the idea, finding someone to look after her children might be a problem she could not overcome. But I did not want to risk being seen with her in Croydon by anyone who knew Diana.

To my delight, Judy said she *could* make arrangements, and would like to come.

We travelled by train from Liverpool Street and had lunch in the buffet car on the way. What an experience that was for Judy. She had led such a sheltered life that, to her, travelling on a train was merely a means of getting from A to B; she had never dreamed of having a cup of tea on one, let alone a four-course lunch with wine and liqueurs.

We had a lovely weekend with Jeff and his wife, Ann. They liked Judy immensely; the four of us got on great. I did feel guilty about Diana, because my feelings for Judy were different from those I had had for any woman other than her, but I have to admit it did not stop me enjoying the weekend. When we stepped off the train at Liverpool Street, though, I was far from relaxed. I was getting near home territory and could be spotted by anyone.

I was terrified of Diana finding out about Judy: taking an attractive woman away for the weekend was definitely not part of our arrangement.

Judy was like a drug to me: I had to see her as often as possible. But it was not easy. Diana and I had been through a lot together, one way and another, and the last thing in the world I wanted to do was hurt her.

It was vital to me that she never had an inkling about Judy. I feel now that I was less than fair to Diana, but, when it comes to facing up to things, I'm an emotional coward and I took the soft option. I wanted to protect Diana's feelings at all costs, and, at the same time, I did not know how far my relationship with Judy would go. I wanted to be with her as much as possible, but I had no idea where our affair would lead us. Certainly moving in with a mother and her three children was not part of my plans and, just in case Judy was thinking in this direction after our weekend in Suffolk, I made it clear I wasn't. I don't know whether it was the adoring look in her eye, or simply that, subconsciously, I felt my future lay with her, and I was frightened of commitment, but when I saw her next, at her home, I told her: 'I'm not getting married, you know.'

I blurted it out five minutes after sitting down and it tickled Judy. 'That's a relief,' she said. 'I'm only just getting divorced, thank you!'

And so the affair began in earnest, with both of us knowing the ground rules. I would have loved to roll out the red carpet for Judy, because she had never had that treatment in her life, but money was a major stumbling block. The odd deal here and there came off, but I did not have the cash to wine and dine Judy the way I wanted.

The only big pay day likely at that time was a film about the Krays. Roger Daltrey, who had made millions as the singer with the rock band The Who, was fixated with the idea. He felt it was the only British gangster film worth making and was convinced that, handled the right way, it could be a powerful blockbuster, as good, if not as financially successful, as *The Godfather*.

Very early in the negotiations, Roger said he was going to Parkhurst to talk things through with Reggie and asked me to go with him. I always travelled from Waterloo to Portsmouth, then took the ferry to the Isle of Wight, so I said we ought to meet at Waterloo.

'No,' said Roger. 'I'll meet you at Battersea.'

I was confused. 'The Portsmouth train doesn't stop at Battersea, Roger,' I said.

'Who's going by train?' he said. 'We're flying there in my helicopter. Is that okay?'

'Suits me,' I said. And it did. It certainly beat a five-hour round trip by trains, ferries and taxis. And since the millionaire rock 'an' roll star would be picking up the bill, it would be cheaper, too.

Naturally, Roger needed special permission to land near Parkhurst, but he had all this sorted. His pilot brought us down on the landing pad of a hotel a couple of miles from the prison, where a taxi was waiting to pick us up.

We spent the whole two-hour visit talking about the film and what the twins and me wanted as an up-front payment. Then, as we prepared to leave, Roger said: 'Reg, ask permission to watch us fly over the prison. We'll give you a wave.'

Reggie did get permission and he admitted later that the 'fly past' gave him a real gee. Well, it's not every day of the week that someone serving thirty years for murder gets a personal cheerio from a rock 'n' roll millionaire from the clouds, is it?

Roger piloted the helicopter home himself, and as we hovered over his home in Sussex, he called out: 'Look, Charlie – my trout lakes.' As I looked down, trying to spot them, I heard him and the pilot laughing. I couldn't see what the joke was but a second later I felt it! The helicopter suddenly turned on its side and dropped out of the sky, leaving my stomach several hundred feet behind.

We landed in Roger's grounds and he jumped out, telling the pilot to drop me back at Battersea Heliport, as one might order a chauffeur to give a lift in a car. Watching the helicopter soar off back to Sussex, all I could think was how nice it would be to have bundles of money and live like that.

All the money in the world does not guarantee realizing one's dreams, however, and pulling everything together to make the film happen proved a headache for Roger. He had paid for not one, but three scripts to be written. He even had similar-looking actors lined up to play the twins – Hywel Bennet as Ronnie and a less well-known actor, Gerry Sunquist, as Reg – and an up-and-coming East Ender, Billy Murray, to play me. I was particularly thrilled at the prospect of being played by Billy. He came from Canning Town and was a genuine bloke, as well as an accomplished, brave, young boxer.

Roger saw Jean Alexander, who played Hilda Ogden in *Coronation Street*, as our mother, Violet, but he did not want her to have a big role. Nor did he want violence to be a major force in the film. He was fascinated by the twin element, and the fatal power of one brother over the other. The film he had in mind was about the bond between the twins more than the fear they instilled in people. This, naturally, would come into it, but the proposed movie would not be a cheap, blood and thunder adventure, more an atmospheric and profound thriller, where words, for once, spoke louder than actions.

Sadly, Roger's dream of producing the movie came to nothing. Despite having the rights to John Pearson's bestseller, *The Profession of Violence*, and a binding agreement with the twins and myself, he could not seem to make it happen. And when two other film producers, Dominic Anciano and Ray Burdis, came on the scene, saying they were going to make their own film about the Krays without our permission, Roger decided it was time to bail out. Anciano and Burdis had the financial backing of a company, Parkfield, which was prepared to buy all the rights Roger owned. Albeit reluctantly, he decided that, if he could not make the film he wanted, it made financial sense to get back all his investment and let someone else have the headache of getting the Kray story on the big screen.

It was a disappointment for the twins and myself; we all liked Roger and would have liked him to make the film. But, to be truthful, it didn't really matter to us who was behind it, as long as it happened and we all made some money. And money we did make from Parkfield: a quarter of a million pounds, split equally among the three of us, to be precise. By current Hollywood standards, it may not sound a lot of money for the rights to one's entire life story, but, to the twins and me, in 1988, it was a fortune.

The year before Judy and I started going out, Ronnie had surprised everyone by popping the question to a big, buxom lady in her mid-thirties, who had been encouraged to visit him by Reggie, to whom she had written, then visited, at Parkhurst. Her name was Elaine Mildener, and she came from Islington, in North London. She had two children from a previous marriage, but, when Ronnie asked her to marry him, she agreed immediately.

The Press, naturally, made a big deal out of the wedding, on 11 February 1985, and the cynics called it a sham, saying that Ronnie, a homosexual, had married Elaine purely to get £10,000 from the *Sun* for the exclusive rights to the newlyweds' story.

Actually, the truth is that Elaine was one of those lovely, gentle-natured creatures it is impossible to dislike, and Ronnie took to her at once; he loved the idea of being a father figure to her two children. Despite being an inmate of Britain's most famous hospital, he never found it difficult to get money and he honestly felt he could help Elaine and her kids.

And he did. Whatever deal he pulled off, courtesy of his many pals on the outside, Elaine always got a share. She was an uncomplicated person, and Ronnie liked her for it. She liked him, too, and respected him for the courtesy and kindness he showed her.

Everything seemed fine for a couple of years, but then, one day in the autumn of 1988, I visited Ronnie and he told me he was divorcing Elaine.

'What on earth for?' I asked. 'You both seem to get on so well together.'

'It's not fair, Charlie,' Ronnie said. 'What sort of future has she and her kids got? She's too nice a person to be married to a bloke like me, who's likely to be locked up for the rest of his life. I'd like her to meet someone outside, a normal guy, and enjoy her life.'

I said Elaine would not be too happy and he agreed. But his mind was made up and, as was usual with Ronnie, there was no way anyone was going to change it.

So Ronnie started divorce proceedings. And I have to say it was the biggest mistake he made since that Saturday night in October 1967 when he triggered the terrible events that ended in Jack McVitie's murder. It left the door open for a tubby, bleached-blonde to become Mrs Ronald Kray No 2 and eventually make his life a misery.

I met her in the Broadmoor reception area on one of my visits to Ronnie later that year. She introduced herself as Kate Howard and explained that she had been visiting Ronnie for several months. I had heard about Kate, but had never met her. She seemed a pleasant enough young woman, if a little brash and over-confident about herself, but I did wonder – as I did when I encountered other women on Ronnie's visiting list – just why she was there.

I learned that it was, in fact, Reg who had arranged the visits. Kate, it seemed, had written to Reg in Gartree after reading a book about the twins' lives. There was something in her letter that made Reg think he could do some business with her and he agreed to see her. At the time, one of Reg's closest friends on the outside was a lively young guy in his twenties, named Peter Gillett, who had got to know Reg well in Parkhurst Prison, while serving time for armed robbery. Reg put Kate in touch with Peter in July 1988 and, although Kate was married, the two quickly became lovers.

Kate had big ideas about living with Reg and Peter in a country mansion when Reg was released. But her plans were dashed one afternoon when she was in bed with Peter. She let slip that her husband, Harry, was dying from multiple sclerosis and there was no way she could, or would, leave

273

him. Appalled that Kate was sharing his bed while her husband was so ill, Peter ordered her out of his house. A few days later, he took her to Gartree with the object of convincing Reg that he should not have any more to do with a woman he felt was lacking in sensitivity and principles. Reg did not want to kick Kate into touch totally, because he was worried she would go to the papers with embarrassing letters he had written her. So, to keep Peter happy, he asked Kate to meet Ron.

I did not have any reservations about Kate on that first meeting, nor on subsequent visits. She was a bubbly, cheerful, chatty girl and seemed to make Ronnie happy; that was all that concerned me.

The money from the film changed my life dramatically for a while. Ronnie, of course, could not wait to give most of his share away and Reg put his into deals with people he had met in and out of prison over the years. For me, it was party time. I had been without serious money for more than twenty years and now that I had some, I was going to enjoy spending it, particularly as I had two women in my life to enjoy it with.

I got a kick out of introducing Judy to the high life. Before she met me, she was in a family set-up and unable to go to restaurants without thinking carefully what she ordered; usually she would only be able to afford the main course. With me, however, I made it clear that she should go through the card and hang the expense.

Throughout her married life, going to the local Beefeater or Berni Inn was something of an event, so you can imagine her delight at getting dressed up to the nines and having cocktails at the Hilton Hotel, and dinner in a fashionable Soho restaurant, before going on to some swish Mayfair club for a nightcap or three.

Judy enjoyed all we did so much she said it was as though

I had waved a magic wand and transported her out of her run-of-the-mill, fairly dull and humdrum life into a glittering and expensive world where anything was possible and only the best would do. I could not do enough for her and kept telling her how much I wished I'd had her with me in the sixties when money was around all the time and the twins and me thought it would never dry up.

I've always enjoyed giving more than receiving, and Judy was a joy to treat. Once, we were strolling around the West End when Judy spotted a beautiful jacket in a leather shop. I knew she had always wanted one, so I took her inside. The jacket looked fantastic on her and there was a skirt to go with it. Judy looked at me, a little embarrassed, unsure what to do, but I told her not to worry – to try the skirt on, too. It was a perfect fit and looked terrific. I handed over £250 without batting the proverbial eyelid and gave Judy a big smile. It gave me a thrill to buy her something she liked so much.

If I had not needed the money so desperately, I would not have signed the film contract. And I would have advised Ronnie and Reg not to, either. One look at the script told me it was the total opposite of the fascinating movie Roger Daltrey had had in mind. There were so many inaccuracies and omissions, it was as if the writer was talking about different people, not me and my brothers. I did tell the producers that certain incidents they were planning to film never happened, but my protests fell on deaf ears. It was a case of he who pays the piper calls the tune: the people putting up the money – Parkfield – wanted the film made a certain way and that was that. I was given the title 'technical adviser' which sounds grandly significant, but, in reality, it meant very little: all I was asked to advise on for the sum of £4,000 was the look of Vallance Road and the clubs we had owned, and the scenes of violence.

Watching the film being shot, mainly around the Rotherhithe area of South London, I could not help feeling that the producer had missed a great chance. There were so many highly dramatic incidents in the twins' lives which did happen that there was no need to embellish anything: that legendary Wild West-style fight at the Coach and Horses; the time Reg posed as his twin so that Ronnie could escape from a mental home; and the terrible night Ronnie was driven to the edge of madness and did not recognize Reg or me as his brothers. By sticking to the facts, the producers could have made a spectacular, compelling – and, more importantly, realistic – movie. As it was, they toddled off into fantasy land and made a ludicrous one.

So many things were wrong, but the worst, by far, was the way our dear mum, Violet, was portrayed. Very early in the film, she is shown in an East End hospital, where Ronnie, as a child, is in bed with rheumatic fever. Our 'mum' feels Ronnie is pining for Reg and she wants to take him home. A doctor does not think it is a good idea, and 'Mum' has a row with him, during which she bellows, 'Bollocks!' If Mum, or the old man, come to that, had lived to see that stupid scene they would have been furious. For a start Mum never swore – not even 'bloody' – but, even if she did, she would never in a million years have had the impertinence to swear at a doctor; she held them in too high a regard for that.

Violet was played by the lovely actress, Billie Whitelaw, and she knew the scriptwriter had got the character wrong. One day, early on, we were introduced and she asked if she could have a quiet word with me in her caravan. We chatted about this and that and, all the time, she was holding my hand. After a while, she said: 'I'm psychic, you know, Charlie. I can feel your mother through you. You were very close to her, weren't you?'

'Very,' I said.

'I'm sorry,' she said. 'I know this isn't Violet in the film. But, unfortunately, I've no choice. I have to say what is in the script and play the part to suit the director.'

I said I understood that, and it was enough for me to know that she was aware that my mum was nothing like the person the public was going to see.

It wasn't only Mum who was portrayed badly; the old man was, too. The film made him out to be an idiotic drunk, a nobody, but he wasn't; he was a good, straight man, who worked all his life for an honest living. Those who saw the film can be forgiven for thinking he was so frightened of going to war that he went on the trot from the Army, but that's not true, either. He was very smart and very clean and would have made a great soldier if he had put his mind to it. Unfortunately, he hated authority; he could not stand being told what to do. That's why he spent the war years on the run from the police – not because he was a coward.

From a personal point of view, I was acutely embarrassed at one scene in which I am seen running away from a boxing booth where the twins are in the ring trying to punch lumps out of each other.

The twins did volunteer to fight each other, but they were only ten – not young men as the film portrays them – and had no intention of hurting each other. That was not what embarrassed me, however: it was the sight of me running away from the booth crying out for my mum to come and tear the twins apart. What a joke! I was not even there at the time and, if I had been, being seven years older, I would not have needed any help to split them – I would have done it myself.

All this had been in the script, of course, so I should not have been surprised. But somehow it came over so much worse watching the scenes being acted out.

*　　*　　*

277

Ronnie was divorced from Elaine in June 1989. On a visit shortly, afterwards, he told me he was getting married again – to Kate. No alarm bells rang in my head, but I have to admit, deep down, I did wonder what her motive was.

There was something that was not quite right about Kate: she seemed a nice enough girl, but there was something about her, and her brash, cocky approach to life, that made me feel a touch uneasy. It would take me a few years to find out what it was.

The wedding, on Monday 6 November, 1989, was a more relaxed affair than the first one. I was surprised just how well it went: more guests were allowed in, the food was superb and Ronnie was even allowed a glass of champagne for a toast. Kate had laid on a reception for a hundred or so guests at a nearby hotel, which, obviously, Ronnie was not allowed to attend. He wasn't bothered in the slightest. As the wedding guests left the hospital for the reception, Ronnie took me to one side and said: 'Enjoy yourselves. Have a good night and give my regards to everyone. I can go back now and sit and think about what a nice time you're having. I can be there in my mind.'

He asked me to go with Kate in her Rolls-Royce to protect her from newspaper photographers he knew would be waiting outside, which I did. On this occasion, thankfully, the gentlemen of the press behaved impeccably. They took the photos, asked a few questions, then left Kate alone to enjoy the rest of her wedding day.

The Krays was released the following spring. The weeks leading up to it should have been an exciting time, but I had nothing but problems – between me and Judy and me and the producers.

The premiere, at the Leicester Square Odeon, on 26 April, promised to be a glittering occasion, guaranteed to attract a number of showbiz celebrities and, naturally, Judy wanted to go. I could not risk it, however. The press photographers and TV cameras would be out in force and, as the only Kray brother able to be there, I could expect a lot of attention, particularly with an attractive young woman on my arm.

When I told Judy I wasn't taking her, she was put out.

'Would you prefer it if I didn't go?' I asked.

'Would it make any difference?' she said.

'Yes,' I said. 'If you don't want me to go, I won't.' I didn't mean it. I desperately wanted to go; I love first nights and dressing up in black tie and dinner jacket.

But Judy called my bluff. 'Okay, I don't want you to go,' she said.

In the end, the film producers made a difficult decision easy for me. They wanted me to pay for tickets for myself, Gary and a couple of close friends, and I took the huff. I felt it was a right liberty. If Ronnie and Reggie had been free and able to go, can you imagine them being asked to send off a cheque for tickets to attend a film about themselves? I'm an easy-going bloke who, normally, is easily pleased, but I was incensed and decided to boycott the premiere altogether on a point of principle.

I also snubbed the party after the premiere. Instead, I had my own party at Browns, a fashionable nightclub in Mayfair. The guv'nor there laid on an invitation-only 'do' after hearing I was giving the official one the elbow. I'm grateful he did: loads of friends turned up and we had a great time. The official party could not have been much cop, because, shortly after midnight, several of the film's stars – including Martin and Gary Kemp, the former pop stars, who played Ronnie and Reggie – joined us at Brown's.

The party was terrific. Shame about the film!

The twins did not get around to seeing it until after it was released on video the following November. When they did, the 'technical adviser' was in the firing line. It's a long-standing problem that whenever I do anything right for Ronnie and Reg, I never get the credit, but if anything goes wrong, I always get the blame. The film was no exception.

I saw Ronnie after he had seen it, and he had the right hump, particularly at how our parents came across, but also at how he was supposed to have cut someone's face with a sword, stabbed another geezer on a snooker table and run around the East End with Reg, armed with a machine gun.

'I'm not an angel, but I wasn't the idiot that film's made me out to be,' Ronnie ranted. 'I was capable of a lot of violence, but the sort of things in the film were over the top.'

Reg was so disgusted with the inaccuracies he did not want to talk about the film at all; to him, it was negative rubbish that was best forgotten. But he did give me an ear-bashing for letting the film portray Mum so badly. He seemed to think I should have insisted on changing things because I was on the outside, representing them. We had a scream-up and I pointed out that there was no point going on and on at me, when he and Ronnie had signed away their rights to any control in the film long before I added my own signature. Even if they had been free, they would not have been able to do anything because they had signed on the dotted line and taken the money. I think Reg thought the ridiculous script was down to me; but I had nothing whatsoever to do with it. I wish I had.

I could not begin to count the number of people who have come up to me and said how much they enjoyed the film: nearly all believed it was a true account of the twins' lives. But, believe me, it was a load of rubbish – one that certainly would not have been made the way it was, had we not needed the money so desperately. We put our signatures to a contract that allowed the film-makers to do what they liked. The result, I'm sorry and rather ashamed to say, was embarrassing and did none of us any good at all, least of all Reg, whose chances of early parole must have been damaged by what appeared on screen.

The three of us were left thinking what a pity Roger Daltrey had become so disenchanted and abandoned the project. It was dear to his heart and he had so much faith in it. At least he would have kept to the facts and ensured that his film reflected the true Kray twins, not farcical figments of a young scriptwriter's vivid imagination.

Chapter Eighteen

It was only a matter of time before Diana found out about Judy and me. And when she did, in the autumn of 1991, she was, understandably, furious. We were leading virtually separate lives, but she hated the idea of me living in the flat while seeing someone else on a regular basis. I had broken our pact not to get 'heavily involved' and she was not going to put up with it. She suggested we went out to dinner for a 'summit' meeting. And she laid the law down.

'We need a rest from each other, Charlie,' she said. 'I would prefer you to leave, but, if you're not going to, we have got to distance ourselves from each other.'

I was in a quandary: I did not want to leave the flat; but I could not bear the thought of not having Judy in my life, either. In the end, I stayed in the flat, but the atmosphere between Diana and me was ice cold. Even the brother and sister relationship had vanished. When we were in the flat together, we rarely talked. When we did, we were merely polite, not loving. After all we had been through, it was awful. But I could not see a way out, without throwing in my lot with Judy and asking to move in with her, which I did not feel was right. Apart from anything else, she had three children, which meant that space at her semi-detached was tight. I did stay there at weekends, however. I would pack my bag on Friday and stay with Judy in Sanderstead until Sunday night. By now, all the money I had had from the film had gone, but having little money to go out on the town did not bother me. When two people are in love, they can be happy just being together, doing nothing in particular. Judy and I did go to a nightclub in Croydon some nights,

282

but we were at our happiest staying in, watching all the new movie releases on video, with a bottle of wine. Judy had always been a white-wine person, but I had introduced her to red, and, now she drank it all the time.

Despite her own love for me, Judy did try to help me sort it out with Diana. She even wrote to her, stressing that I still felt a lot, and urging us to resolve things between us. Judy, bless her, said she would disappear from my life if I felt Diana and I could make a go of it, and we did have a break from each other for a while. But I knew it was over with Diana. I was even more deeply in love with Judy and knew I wanted to spend the rest of my life with her and her children.

Sadly, I didn't have the courage to make a choice, preferring to let the women make it for me. I was weak and I regret it, because all it did was leave us all in a miserable limbo, each realizing that something must be done, but none of us knowing what.

My son, Gary, knew and liked both Diana and Judy and would have been embarrassed by the situation. But he was in Blackpool helping out at the Verona Hotel, run by friends of ours, Paul Jonas and his wife, Susie. Paul and I had got on well from the moment we met at Chatterly's Club, in Mayfair, in 1982, and when he and Susie bought the Verona six years later, there was an open invitation to Gary and myself to stay there whenever we wanted. I did not take up the offer very often because I was happy enough living the high life in London, but when Paul suggested my son stayed at the hotel long-term, helping out with the chores in return for board and lodging, Gary jumped at the chance.

What a haven Blackpool was for him: after we all saw in the New Year at the hotel in 1989, he stayed there, on and off, for three years. Paul and Susie liked Gary's gentle nature and willingness to do whatever was asked of him and they insisted on throwing a party for his fortieth birthday in July 1991. I'm sure Gary was at his happiest up north. The clean, fresh sea air was an obvious attraction for anyone who has spent most of their life in the smoke and grime of London, but for Gary it was more than that. Paul and Susie, and their son, Nikki, treated him as one of their own, and Gary revelled in being part of a warm family environment. When he wasn't changing beer barrels, cleaning bedrooms or waiting up to let in late arrivals, he was drinking Bacardi and Coke in the hotel bar with all sorts of people, including showbiz personalities, such as Frank Carson, Brian Conley and the Nolan Sisters, and it suited him down to the ground.

For a couple of years, Ronnie's marriage to Kate was fine. She visited him regularly and, like the dutiful wife, did her best to make him as happy as she could. She was always on time for visits, stayed the allocated two hours and was meticulous in relaying all kinds of messages to Ronnie's friends and acquaintances beyond Broadmoor's walls. She had even brought her sister, Maggie, to Broadmoor to meet Ronnie's closest friend there, Charlie Smith. And they had got on so well, a romance blossomed that led, eventually, to marriage. But then, during one of my visits just before Christmas that year, Ronnie admitted he was beginning to see a side of Kate he had not seen before – a side he did not like.

'What exactly do you mean?' I asked.

'She seems very money conscious,' he said.

'Aren't we all?' I said.

'But it's all she ever thinks about. Every time I see her, it's money, money, money all the bleedin' time.'

I didn't know what to say. We all like money; all need it. And, to be fair, Ronnie liked it as much as anyone, even though he was locked up and didn't need it as much as the rest of us.

284

'What do you think of her, Charlie?' Ronnie asked.

I wasn't going to be drawn into that one. Whatever I said was bound to be wrong; after all, Kate was Mrs Ronald Kray and it wasn't for me to criticize another man's wife, even if she was my sister-in-law.

'I don't really have an opinion, Ronnie,' I said. 'I don't know the girl well enough.'

'I'm wondering whether she doesn't really care for me and only went through with the marriage to cash in on the publicity, or to get some kind of reflected glory.'

Again, I said, I didn't know; it was their business. But what I did know, was certain of, driving up the M3 towards London that evening, was that Kate spelled Trouble with a capital T.

In many ways, Broadmoor was good for Ronnie, and he was happy there. But there were times when he was treated in an off-hand manner, as though he was still a violent gangster, not a sick patient; as though they could do anything they liked and to hell with what he or anyone else thought.

One morning, we greeted each other in the visiting hall and I knew at once he was upset.

'What on earth's the matter?' I asked.

'They're trying to drive me round the bend, Charlie,' he said.

'Who are?'

'The screws,' Ronnie said. 'They keep coming into my room in the middle of the night, waking me up. I know what they're up to. They're trying to push me over the edge.'

'Don't be silly,' I said. 'They wouldn't do that. Nobody would do that.'

'That's what the doctor said when I told him. But I know they are.'

That night, Ronnie put a huge hardback book against the door of his room, thinking that if anyone came in, the book would fall over and wake him, and he would be able to catch whoever they were in the act. Nothing happened that night. Nor the next; nor for the next five nights. The following night around 3 a.m., Ronnie heard a loud bang and jumped out of bed, ready to confront the intruders. But there was no one there. The door was shut, the big book still in place. And it dawned on him that he had been imagining the intruders all the time.

Ronnie always admitted when he was wrong, so, the next morning, he apologized to his doctor, who said: 'I knew it was all in your mind, because the treatment for the mastoids in your ears meant we had to cut down on your medication, and that caused you to have delusions.'

Why, I wanted to scream, could the doctor not have told Ronnie that before; then he would have known what to expect and would not have got wound up. It seemed the same old story: He's only Ronnie Kray; it doesn't matter about him. We don't have to tell him anything.

Perhaps I should not have been surprised. Throughout Ronnie's time in Broadmoor, they carried out all sorts of experiments on him, gave him all types of drugs, without once telling him, Reg, or me what they were for or why. I suspected what was going on because I never knew what mood Ronnie would be in from one visit to the next. Ronnie suspected too. He'd say: 'They *do* try me out in here, Charlie. They're always pumping me full of different things. But I take them because they might do me some good.'

That was Ronnie all over. He disliked drugs and hated people talking about them, but he took his medication religiously, because he knew he needed it. He knew that, sometimes, he felt different from other people.

In the main, the Broadmoor staff respected Ronnie and never took liberties with him or wound him up. There was

286

one occasion, however, when a couple of idiots did try to take advantage.

Ronnie had been to an outside hospital for an operation to cure his ear problems. When I visited him in the Broadmoor infirmary, I found him sitting alone in a ward with five other beds. He could barely hear me, but I sensed something was wrong besides the pain.

'You don't look too clever,' I said. 'What's the matter?'

'Two screws in here keep having a go at me,' he said.

He must have detected a disbelieving look cross my face, because he added, quickly: 'And this time I'm *not* imagining it, Charlie. I started eating an orange and they came and took it away. One of them started eating it in front of me and they both stood there laughing.'

He went on to tell me that he had not been allowed a cup of tea since the previous night, and had to go to the toilet for a cigarette when everyone else was allowed to smoke in the wards.

When I confronted the two young male nurses, they laughed in my face.

'I don't find your attitude funny,' I said. 'Do you realize that my brother has just had a serious operation and you can't even give him a cup of tea?'

One said the tea was their business, not mine. Then they started laughing again. I freaked.

'I want to see your guv'nor,' I snapped. 'Go and get him. Now. And don't laugh at me or my brother any more, because I'll give you both a good hiding.'

That wiped the smiles off their faces. They went off and came back, minutes later, with two of their superiors, who knew me. They expressed their surprise at seeing me so agitated.

'I think I'm entitled to be when I have these two idiots standing in front of me laughing when I'm trying to get some decent treatment for my brother,' I said.

I poured out my fury, even threatening to tell the papers and get all our friends to parade outside the hospital with protest banners.

Ronnie was sitting in his bed, saying nothing; he did not want any trouble. But after a while, sick as he was, he couldn't stand it any longer. What should have been a calm visit was ruined. 'Don't worry, Charlie – leave it out,' he shouted. 'You'd better go.'

He was right: me making a scene was only going to wind him up and that's the last thing he needed after what he'd been through. So, reluctantly, I left, warning the hospital bosses that if they antagonized Ronnie and he got violent, I would hold them responsible.

I went back early the next morning to find Ronnie all smiles.

'After you left yesterday, everything changed,' he said. 'They took those two slags off the ward and replaced them,' he said. 'I got a cup of tea immediately.'

'Good,' I said. 'That's how it should be. I can't understand why they can't treat you like any other person, and not make a big deal out of it all the time.'

I meant it. He had just come round after an operation and was not well. He did not want to cause any problems and was not going to. Yet two idiots, who were not physically capable of standing up to him, decided to take a liberty just because he was vulnerable. Thankfully Ronnie was sedated and responsible for his actions, so all was calm. But what would have happened if he hadn't been and was provoked into hitting out at those insolent, unprofessional nurses? No doubt, he, not them, would have got the blame.

In the summer of 1992, Ronnie was pleased when Kate told him she had been asked to write a book about her life as a Kray. He was working with a ghost-writer on a book himself, *My Story*, but that was concerned mainly with the past.

What Kate had to say would be about the present, and Ronnie liked the idea of the public being told what he was like now by someone who spent a lot of time with him.

The offer to Kate was made by John Blake, a tabloid pop reporter who had started a publishing company with his brother's money, after being sacked from a newspaper. The book he had in mind would make more money from newspaper serialization than over-the-counter sales, but Kate did not mind: it gave her licence to say anything about the twins – and me – whether it was true or not. Much to our dismay, she took full advantage of it.

Over the new few months, Kate asked Ronnie if he wanted to read what she was telling her ghost-writer – a woman named Mandy Bruce – but Ronnie said no; he had no worries. Why should he? He had always treated Kate as a lady; he was certain she would have only good things to say about him, the family in general, and our friends.

How wrong he was. The following year, when he learned what had been written, he was so upset he became emotionally unstable and his paranoia returned. What did not help was that the ghost-writer working on *My Story* – a TV presenter named Fred Dinenage – misinterpreted certain points, leaving Ronnie desperately unhappy at the finished product.

A warning of the emotional turmoil that would affect Ronnie's mental and physical state drastically came that summer when doctors reduced his medication level – as another experiment presumably – and he attacked another inmate, Lee Kiernender. I never got to the bottom of what happened exactly, but apparently, Lee irritated him so much one day that Ronnie grabbed him by the throat and tried to strangle him. Feeling Lee's body go limp in his arms, Ronnie was convinced he had killed him and he was filled with remorse.

He poured out his sorrow to Charlie Smith, vowing that he would never carry out any act of violence again. All he wanted now was peace and quiet.

This was the frame of mind Ronnie was in when he received a hardback of the Sidgwick & Jackson book, *My Story*. After reading it he hit the roof, claiming that Dinenage had attributed certain things to him that he never said and were not true anyway. Stressed out, Ronnie asked me to go to Broadmoor and, in a highly emotional visit, he told me he was going to ask Robin McGibbon, a journalist and mutual friend, to set the record straight by writing a story for a national newspaper, denouncing the book.

What followed is, I believe, an indictment of Broadmoor for the cavalier manner in which they treated my brother. In just fourteen days, Ronnie wrote sixteen letters to Robin – letters that bore all the hallmarks of a deeply disturbed man suffering a mental breakdown. All inmates' letters are censored, so why, I'd like to know, did someone not pick up that Ronnie was going through an emotional wringer and needed help?

The first letter, on 11 September, said: 'Can you put in the papers that the book, *My Story*, that has just come out is a lot of lies that Reg never said, nor did I. One has only to use their common sense to know we would not put all the lies and rubbish in it.'

Ronnie's mind was in such turmoil that he wrote another letter the same day, repeating his request. Three days later he wrote two more, saying the same thing. In the second of those letters, Ronnie showed his paranoia by saying all letters should be sent by registered mail, because he was not receiving all the letters he felt he should.

By 16 September, he had got worse. Robin rang me, very worried, saying Ronnie had written the most poignant cry for help: 'Take no notice of anyone, only me. Try to come to see me as soon as you can. I *must* see you, Robin. Believe me, I'm not mad. I must see you – it's urgent. Take no notice of no one only me. I *must* see you.'

Robin had tried to arrange a visit, but was told that the number of people on Ronnie's visiting list was so high that it was being cut to ten: the hospital would be in touch to say if Robin could be one of them.

That night, I tried to put Ronnie's anger and frustration out of my mind as I took Judy to see an old flame of mine, Barbara Windsor, in the famous Joe Orton play, *Entertaining Mister Sloane*, at the Ashcroft Theatre in Croydon.

When we went backstage afterwards, I sprang a surprise, which backfired on me, giving us all a giggle. After giving Barbara a hug and a peck, I pulled up my jacket sleeve and showed off some gold cuff-links I knew Barbara had bought me during our affair more than thirty years before.

'Bet you can't remember these, Barbara,' I said.

She took one look, then gave me one of those famous cheeky looks. 'Remember them, Charl!' she screeched. 'How can I forget? I bought those cuff-links after you told me you loved me so much you were leaving your wife for me.'

We both roared.

The following week, Ronnie was in an even worse state: he had received a copy of Kate's book, *Murder, Madness and Marriage*, and had gone off the dial. She had written certain things he felt embarrassed and humiliated him, and he wanted me to go to Broadmoor immediately to discuss what we should do about it.

I bought a copy of the book and could see why Ronnie was upset. I was shocked at basic inaccuracies that not only Kate but the ghost-writer and publisher had allowed through, but it was Kate's vitriolic personal attack on me and brazen admission of her infidelity that stung most.

In a chapter, ambiguously titled 'Friend or Foe?', Kate

291

says Ronnie was so angry about what I wrote about him in another book that he had disowned me.

She said that '. . . no one could believe that Charlie had been so disrespectful and so disloyal to his own brother.'

And she claimed that Ronnie said: 'I never want to see Charlie again and I'll never forgive him. He's no longer my brother. I don't have two brothers any more. Just Reggie.'

If I had not been so angry at the stupidity of the woman, I'd have laughed. If Ronnie felt so bad and never wanted to see me again, why was I the first person he turned to in his fury over her book? And why was I on my way to Broadmoor to talk to him about it? Perhaps I shouldn't have been surprised: Kate had even got the title of my book wrong. It is *Doing The Business*, but she called it: *We Did The Business*. As she gets the little, but very important, things wrong, her so-called revelations lose their credibility.

Kate claims I betrayed Ronnie by stating that he was once intimidated by Mafia bosses and frightened for the first time in his life. The truth of the matter, quite simply, is that this remark was wrongly attributed to me – and Ronnie knew that. The real issue, however, is not what I did or did not say – it is Kate's appalling hypocrisy in accusing me of betrayal when she herself was guilty of treachery on a far grander scale.

She knew – as, indeed, all of us close to Ronnie knew – that he did not expect her to live the life of a nun: she was a youngish, reasonably good-looking woman, with a bubbly personality, and Ronnie understood that a certain type of man might want to get her into bed. He told her she had his blessing to go out and enjoy herself, within reason, as long as she never flaunted whatever sexual encounter she had. This was terribly important to Ronnie: although he was locked away, his pride and self-respect were very much intact and the worst that anyone could do was embarrass him – or mug him off, as they say down the Mile End Road. Kate was fully aware of this: indeed, she admits that Ronnie told her, 'If you *do* have a relationship don't flaunt it.'

Well, sadly, Kate showed her true colours in her book. She did not merely flaunt one of her sexual relationships and mug Ronnie off – she humiliated him. In a tacky chapter, 'Sex And All That', she made me squirm as she devoted nearly 4,000 words, over eleven pages, describing her lust for a tall, half-Spanish car dealer she called Pa, and what they got up to when they saw each other several times a week over more than two years.

Ronnie knew Kate was seeing this guy: she had shown him a photograph and he nicknamed him 'gypsy boy'. What Ronnie did not know was that Kate saw the relationship as far more than merely a sexual fling; she viewed it as some predestined romance that was written in the stars. As she writes: 'With Pa it was different. Sometimes in life I'm sure you're fated to be with someone and that's how it was with me and Pa.' Can you imagine how Ronnie felt reading that? This was *his* wife gushing, not about some fancy-free bachelor who had swept her off her feet, but a married man – with a wife and child!

By exposing herself as some sex-starved bimbo with little regard for anything but her own sexual gratification, Kate ridiculed not only Ronnie but herself. How many other prisoners' wives, I wonder, would have had the gall to talk publicly, and in colourful detail, about adulterous trysts in out-of-the-way restaurants and sexual romps in hotels? Kate seemed positively proud and unconcerned about the effect it would have on Ronnie.

I could hardly believe it when I read: 'We didn't rush into bed with each other. We wanted it to be special ... we booked into a hotel in Brighton ... but didn't pounce on each other, we wanted to save it. We didn't want it all over in a few minutes ... I was excited. Everything in me wanted this man, Pa picked me up his arms and laid me on

293

the bed ... then, very slowly, he undressed me and we made love all night. The next morning I felt great ... I would have been happy to stay in that bed for a week ...'

What was it Ronnie had told her? Don't flaunt your relationships. Kate was not merely flaunting, she was revelling in it, gloating almost, in every sexy memory. And to make matters worse, she was happy to see the more salacious bits of her book serialized in a national tabloid newspaper.

Kate rubbed Ronnie's nose further into it by revealing she went to California on holiday with lover-boy and took him to a marriage guidance counsellor to try to cure his jealousy. But it was Kate's graphic description of her own appalling, maniacal behaviour in the middle of a busy street that caused Ronnie to flip.

According to her book, Pa was drunk, and infuriated her by breaking a pair of sunglasses and chucking them out of the car Kate was driving. She screeched to a halt, went round to the passenger side, opened the door, then kicked Pa in the face. He got out, forced her against a van, and she stabbed him with her car keys. She drove off, but was so angry she turned round and drove into him as he walked up a hill. Apparently, that was not enough, because she turned round and drove into him again.

'Then I went really mad,' she writes. 'There was a wooden stake lying by the side of the road. I picked it up and began to beat him ... I'm not a violent person, but something in me snapped. By now, the police had arrived and they pulled me off him. Good job, too. I think I could have killed him ...'

Kate says she was arrested and taken to a police station. But she gave a false name because she did not want Ronnie to hear about it. 'He would have been livid at me for making such an exhibition of myself,' she says.

Oh, really! If she was worried about upsetting my brother,

Kate could easily have kept quiet about that degrading episode and neither Ronnie, nor anyone else, would ever have known about it. As it was, she wrote about it in detail for book buyers and millions of newspaper readers to see.

Not surprisingly, Ronnie had made his own mind up what to do about a woman he now viewed as a tart.

'I knew I was right – the girl's a wrong 'un,' he said, as soon as we'd sat down in Broadmoor's visiting hall that afternoon in September 1993. 'I'm divorcing her.'

I just sat there, saying nothing, just trying to keep the smile off my face. Ronnie had been stewing on what was in the book and wanted to get it all off his chest.

'She's taken a right liberty. I'm in here and she's out there and I told her I was happy for her to go out and enjoy herself. But she's showed me up and made me an idiot – a laughing stock.'

What bothered him most was not getting rid of Kate, but what she would say if she saw any pound signs.

'She's the type of girl who'll tell more lies if there's money in it,' Ronnie said. 'She doesn't care. God knows what she's going to say next.'

He said he was writing again to Robin and, the next day, another letter went off, pleading: 'Can you ring my doctor to arrange to see me. Unless Kate stops her book that is diabolical I'm going to divorce her.'

Robin rang me to say that, at last, he had been given a date to visit Ronnie – the following Friday 29 September. But, two days before, he received another letter – the seventh in just two weeks – that was extremely worrying. Ronnie's paranoia was such that he genuinely believed someone at the hospital did not want the visit to go ahead and was planning to sabotage it.

The letter said: 'If anyone rings you and says I've cancelled the visit, believe it only if it is Stephanie . . .'

(Stephanie King is a Nottingham housewife, who was acting as a sort of unpaid secretary to the twins.)

In the event, the visit never happened because, the very day Ronnie's letter arrived, he was taken to Wexham Park Hospital, in Slough, suffering from what was thought to be a mild heart attack. He was still anxious to put right the two books, however, because he wrote to Robin again: 'I am in hospital. Can you come to see me next Wednesday morning. I may have angina.'

The next day, Ronnie wrote yet again, and this time the plea was desperate: 'Can you come to see me any day, any time . . .'

Ronnie was taken back to Broadmoor on the Saturday and insisted on seeing Robin the next afternoon. Robin got a shock when he saw Ronnie. He was normally immaculate in a pressed suit and tie, but this day he was wearing ill-fitting jeans, a rumpled green and mauve rugby-type shirt. He apologized for being scruffy, saying his best clothes hadn't been sent over from the special care unit, where he had been sent after attacking Kiernender.

When Robin phoned me, my first question was: 'What about Ronnie's heart attack?'

'The doctors told him his heart is okay – very strong in fact,' Robin said. 'Apparently, Ron had all the symptoms of a heart attack, but it wasn't. He hasn't even got angina.'

'What's his mood now?' I wanted to know.

'He's very positive. He's always bounced back when his health has gone down, and he says he'll bounce back this time. But he told me the thought of death did occur to him when he collapsed. He said he felt terrible.'

'Was he scared?'

'He said he'd never been scared of dying because he believed in reincarnation and often dreamed of who he was going to be in future lives.'

Something that was bothering Ronnie, however, was a

296

rumour that he was so depressed he had lost the will to live. That was rubbish, Robin said; although Ronnie was bored stiff at the moment, he said he still found life interesting and always managed to enjoy himself.

Ronnie was at pains to stress he was not going 'all nutty and religious', but he was convinced God had saved his life in hospital.

'How come?' I asked.

Robin said: 'All Ron said was that God performs miracles – like a baby coming out of the womb, and a caterpillar changing into a butterfly – so who is to say God didn't perform a miracle and deem he should recover?'

I had to smile; that was a side of Ronnie the public did not know. All the tabloids ever talked about was the evil gangland killer with a thirst for violence.

'What does he want you to do about Kate?' I asked.

'Make it public that he was divorcing her because of the way she had embarrassed and humiliated him,' Robin said. 'And to make it clear that he is a humble man, with principles, not the flash, arrogant, rude, ignorant idiot she's made him out to be.'

I could understand Ronnie's anger. Contrary to what many thought, he was very considerate about other people and their feelings. And he did care about what people thought of him. In his eyes, Kate had betrayed his trust and made a fool out of him. The marriage had been going downhill and her tatty, downmarket book, with its even tattier content, was the last straw.

He was definite he wanted nothing more to do with Kate and asked Robin to tell Stephen Gold, the family solicitor, to start divorce proceedings immediately. I was euphoric. I had reached a point where I couldn't stand Kate. I'd thought she was genuine and she had turned out phoney. I'd thought she was good for Ronnie, and she had turned out bad. Like Ronnie, I wanted nothing more to do with her.

297

SEP. 16TH THURSDAY 1943. MON / CARY

AIRDOOR
MY DEAR FRANK WARD

MOTION . XXXX NO
MORE OF ANY KIND,
ONLY ME

TRY TO COME & SEE
ME AS SOON AS
— CAN.

I MUST SEE —

MOTION BELIEVE

ME. Y AM

NOT MAD.
PD

y MUIT SEE —

IT IS ENGET

last FAKO

AND MOTHE OF

no all

ONLY AN
___

y MUIT SEE —

God Bless Armstrong

The mistake Kate made was thinking she could manipulate Ronnie into shoving Reg and me aside so that she would have him all to herself. She believed she was clever, one step ahead, but she was stupid to think that. Blood, as they say, is thicker than water and in times of crisis a family sticks together, no matter what rows they may have had. Ronnie was incensed about her behaviour, but he was beside himself with rage that she had belittled me in such a cruel, unjust manner.

During the marriage, our friends were nice to Kate, but she has lost the respect of everyone. No one has any time for her.

She revelled in being Kray, basked in the limelight the name gave her, and spoke, seemingly with authority, about the family in general. But, really, she knows nothing about us.

I often think what our dear mum would have made of her and her avaricious ways, but Kate was not the sort of girl you take home to mother. She wouldn't have been mum's cup of tea, in any situation, but as a daughter-in-law – forget it. As for the old man, he had a very strict Victorian outlook and he would have gone spare at the damaging drivel Kate was allowed to get published.

As anyone who has met me knows, I'm an easy-going guy who tries to be friendly and respectful to everyone. But I have to admit I would find it hard to have anything pleasant to say to my brother's ex-wife should I be unlucky enough to set eyes on her.

As 1993 drew to a close, I had little time to dwell on Ronnie's troubled mind; my own emotional and financial crises were building up. Some business deals I'd been counting on had broken down and I was strapped for cash. To make matters worse, Diana could not tolerate our domestic situation any longer and was making it clear she wanted me out of the flat and her life so that she could make a fresh start.

Things came to a head in December when we had a blazing row and she insisted I left. I told Judy and asked if I could move in with her. She would never have been the first to suggest it, but she wanted me under the same roof and readily agreed. Like me, she felt a sense of relief now that the move had been forced on us.

Those first days in Limpsfield Road, being part of Judy's family, were very strange. I didn't know what to talk to her children about, but I wanted them to accept me into their home so much that, whenever I went out, I would come back armed with all kinds of sweets, chocolates and Cokes. When Judy came home and we sat down on our own to watch the telly, I would start chatting non-stop. It was a sort of nervousness, I suppose, and, finally, it got up Judy's nose.

'For goodness' sake, Charlie,' she said one night. 'Stop talking so much. You don't have to talk all the time. Relax.'

It gave her the opportunity to get something else off her chest, too. 'Charlie,' she said, gently but firmly, 'something else you don't have to do, and what I don't want you to do, is spoil the kids. I don't want you buying them everything they want all the time.'

I saw her point immediately. The relationship was very important to both of us and she felt it essential to lay down certain ground rules to prevent problems arising later between us. Having just got out of an unhappy marriage, she did not want to waste time on another relationship if it was not going to work. And I felt the same, for different reasons.

Two of those ground rules were (a) that we would both be faithful to each other and I would never lie to her; and (b) that the children's discipline was Judy's responsibility, unless their behaviour directly affected me, in which case I would be expected to reprimand them.

It was a calm, clear-the-air discussion that made us both feel better. And, after a lovely, relaxing stay-at-home Christmas with the kids, Judy and I celebrated the arrival of 1994 with optimism for our future together.

I did not feel good about the way I had handled things with Diana. All I could hope was that time would heal the hurt and bitterness she felt at my betrayal.

Chapter Nineteen

One evening in March 1995, I got a phone call that frightened the life out of me: Ronnie had collapsed and had been taken to Heatherwood Hospital, in Ascot. I asked what was wrong, but nobody knew.

The following morning, as I was preparing to leave for the hospital, someone rang me to say that Ronnie had been taken back to Broadmoor. I couldn't understand it; if he had been ill enough to be rushed to hospital, why had he been taken back to Broadmoor so quickly? Surely the doctors had not had enough time to determine what was wrong with him?

A couple of days later, I was given even more cause for concern: Ronnie had taken another turn for the worse and had been taken to hospital again. I drove to Ascot immediately, with Laurie O'Leary, one of Ronnie's dearest and much-respected childhood friends.

We found Ronnie in bed in a tiny room, now watched by not two male nurses, but three. Some joker obviously thought that, after twenty-seven years, Ronnie had hatched an escape plot!

Typically, Ronnie said he was all right, but would we, please, take all the medical bits and pieces off him.

'You have to have them,' I said. 'They're there for a reason.'

He looked at a monitor, registering his heartbeat. 'I suppose that's really a tape recorder as well,' he said.

'Don't be silly,' I said. 'You're unwell. No one is recording what you're saying. They just want to find out what's wrong with you.'

'All right,' he said, not very convincingly.

We talked for about an hour, but Ronnie was getting tired, so we got up to leave, saying we would be back in the morning.

As I walked out, I noticed Ronnie pull Laurie towards him and whisper something in his ear. When we were in the car, Laurie said: 'You want to know what he said?'

'Yes,' I replied.

'He said: Look after Charlie, Lol. I don't mean physically, you know what I mean.'

Laurie did *not* know. Neither did I. But I'm convinced that Ronnie's weird, but amazingly accurate, sixth sense had told him he would not be seeing us again.

For the following morning, 17 March, Ronnie was dead.

I was told, not by Broadmoor medical staff, but by my friend Robin McGibbon, who had received a call from a TV news reporter, asking if it was true that Ronnie Kray was dead.

When Robin rang me, I was shocked, but refused to believe it. It's just another Kray rumour, I told myself; if Ronnie had died, I would be the first to be told. If not me, it would be Reg, who would have contacted me before anyone else.

But Broadmoor confirmed that Ronnie was, indeed, dead. 'Oh, yes,' I was told, matter-of-factly. 'He died at 9.07 this morning.'

I was devastated. Then I was angry. 'Are you telling me my brother died this morning and I wasn't notified?'

'I am very sorry, Mr Kray. The news was put out before we had an opportunity to call you.'

'That's terrible,' I said. 'What's Reg going to do now?'

I put the phone down. There was nothing more to say. No matter how bad I felt about not being told, it was not the point right now. I had to speak to Reg. Fighting back my tears, I dialled Maidstone Prison.

The usual procedure is to leave a message for the prisoner, who rings back on his phone card, but when I explained why I wanted to speak to Reg, someone fetched him from his cell and he took the call in an office. He was so choked, he could barely talk.

'I've heard,' he said.

'How?' I wanted to know.

'I was walking along the corridor just now and one of the cons said he'd heard it on the radio.'

I didn't know what to say to that. What *was* there to say?

'Wouldn't you have thought they would have told me if anything happened?' Reg said. 'I asked Broadmoor on Thursday morning if I could visit Ron because I had a feeling something was wrong. But they told me he was all right and not seriously ill enough to warrant me going. They said if anything changed, someone would ring Maidstone.'

'I know how you feel, Reg,' I said. 'I feel the same. I was just getting ready to go to the hospital when Robin rang to tell me.'

'How did he know?'

'A TV station rang him.'

'Jesus Christ! I think it's disgraceful. We should have been the first to be told.'

'There's nothing we can do about it now.'

'Poor Ron. Do you know how he died? Was it natural causes?'

'I don't know, Reg.'

'I need to know how he died, Charlie. Anything could have happened. They could have done anything to him.'

Suspicion about Ronnie's death was not something we needed right now. We were both too emotional.

'We'll have to talk about it later,' I said. 'Now isn't the time.'

I didn't want to speak any more. I wanted to be alone with my thoughts. I knew Reg did, too.

'Reg, go and do your own thing,' I said. 'I'll be down to see you tomorrow. We'll talk about it all then.'

I put the phone down and poured a large measure of whisky into a tumbler. I drank it down fast and then the tears started to fall.

I could not stop crying for two hours.

The following morning, I drove to Maidstone Prison with Laurie and Robin. We were shown into a private room, where we waited for Reg to be brought up from the cells. When he came in, he and I fell into each other's arms. Neither of us said a word, we just stood there, hugging each other, crying quietly.

After half a minute or so we sat down and, astonishingly, Reg's mood lifted. He is a great believer in positive mental attitude and he was anxious to let us all know he was not going to allow himself to get too depressed at Ronnie's death.

'I was bad yesterday,' he admitted. 'I was refused permission to visit Ron in hospital and I felt I'd been deprived of comforting him as his life ebbed away. But I was granted a few privileges last night and I feel in a better frame of mind today. I woke feeling at peace. I know Ron is. He's free at last. And he beat the system, didn't he? He didn't die in Broadmoor, as everyone expected him to.

'I didn't sleep much last night, but I forced myself not to think back over all the years, because it would have been too hurtful. During my sentence, I've learned to switch off and keep my emotions under control – be dispassionate about things.

'You know, Ron had a premonition of his death three weeks ago. He told me: "I'm not long for this world."

'I had a premonition, too. Only a few days ago, another con asked me if I had a suit I could lend him for a wedding he was being allowed to go to. I gave him a black suit willingly, but as I handed it over I had this strange feeling I would be asking for it back before too long. And I was right. Ron died two days later.'

Then, businesslike as ever, Reg turned to me and said: 'Now, what about the funeral? Ronnie wanted six black horses, you know.'

I did know. I remember him saying to Mum, as a kid: 'When I die, I want my coffin pulled by six black horses with plumes.'

Mum was horrified. 'For goodness sake, Ronnie. You're a young man. It's silly talking about things like that.'

'I mean it, Mum,' Ronnie said. 'I want horses at my funeral. Black ones.'

'I don't think it'll be possible, Reg,' I said. 'The cemetery is in Chingford. It's six miles from Bethnal Green. It'll take all day. The police won't allow it.'

'Ron wanted horses. And he'll have them.'

I knew better than to argue. Reg was a persistent so-and-so when he wanted to be. Not as insistent as Ronnie, but still a formidable force. I knew he would have his way. 'I'll look into the horses,' I said.

'No, I want to do it,' said Reg.

'Leave it to me, Reg,' I said. 'Ronnie will have the best. The funeral will be exactly the same as Mum's and the old man's.'

'Charlie,' he said, 'if it's okay with you, I want to deal with the arrangements. I've got all the time in the world in here to sit and think about what to do for the best.'

I could see the sense in that. Ronnie was my brother and I hurt badly; but being one half of a twin made it worse for Reg, and it would help him overcome his grief if he occupied his time organizing the funeral.

'Okay, Reg,' I said. 'Do what you want to do. If you need any help, just call me.'

307

'I'll make sure Ronnie has the best send-off possible. I want twenty Rolls-Royces and Bentleys for all our friends. And we *will* have those horses. And they *will* take Ron all the way to the cemetery.'

That was Reg all over. And he knew that if it had been the other way round, Ronnie would have done the same for him.

Reg wanted to get on with the arrangements, but there were two things worrying him. One was the cause of Ronnie's death; the other was whether he would be given permission to say goodbye to his twin in the Chapel of Rest at English's, the funeral parlour in Bethnal Green Road.

The cause of death really bothered Reg. On the Monday, he came on the phone to me, really wound up, saying he had heard the autopsy had taken only a few minutes, and he was far from happy about it.

'They could fob us off with any old rubbish, Charlie,' he said. 'I'm not going ahead with the funeral until we've got some answers.'

He instructed Stephen Gold to look into it, but, by Thursday, we were no wiser. Ronnie had died of a heart attack, and that was that. If Reg or I suspected there was more to it, something sinister, we were never going to find out what it was. So, somewhat reluctantly, Reg gave the go-ahead for the funeral to be held the following Wednesday, 29 March. He asked me to organize everyone involved in the funeral arrangements to meet him at the prison the next afternoon. We had five days to get it all together.

Happily, Reg's second worry was dealt with easily and without any fuss. There is a lovely married couple working at Maidstone Prison – Chris Rogers, the head of security, and his wife Debbie, who is a senior officer. They had had a lot of dealings with Reg in the year he had been there and knew he was a model prisoner.

I contacted them and said it would be marvellous if they could arrange for Reg to be escorted to the East End to pay his final respects. If they wanted me to be there, I would; but if they felt that, in the interests of security, it was better if I did not know when he was going, that was okay, too. I just wanted Reg to be allowed to say a final farewell.

Chris, bless him, spoke up for Reg, saying he posed no security risk at all, and, one afternoon, three days before the funeral, Reg was driven up the A20 and into the East End with hardly anyone knowing about it. His handcuffs were taken off and he was allowed fifteen minutes or so alone with his twin. I do not know what he said or did in that time, but what I *do* know is that being allowed to see Ronnie that last time gave Reg a big gee, as we say in the East End. As one of Britain's highest profile prisoners, he knew it was far from certain he would be allowed out and he was thrilled when he was. It made a huge difference to his mental state and he told Chris and Debbie how much he appreciated their compassion. To be perfectly truthful, at that harrowing time, it was the greatest gesture they could have made for Reg and I know he will never forget it.

The funeral was a cross between a West End film premiere and a Wembley Cup Final: the crowds that Wednesday morning brought the East End to a virtual standstill.

I'd expected a big turnout, especially outside English's, but the amount of people lining both sides of Bethnal Green Road amazed me. Fortunately, the police, and security guards laid on by Reg, had foreseen what chaos could be caused, and had cordoned off the area outside the funeral parlour with steel barriers so that invited guests could get through.

Reg had not arrived when I walked into English's, an hour or so before the procession was due to leave. I took the opportunity to go into the Chapel of Rest, with my son

Gary, to spend a few minutes with Ronnie. I went up to the coffin and found myself talking to him, as though he were merely resting.

'You're all right now, Ronnie,' I said softly. 'It's the end of all the misery for you. You did it the right way, you got out. You're with Mum and the old man now.'

No sooner had Gary and I left the Chapel of Rest than Reg arrived. He was brought to a reception room down the narrow corridor where sandwiches had been prepared for specially invited guests. He was pale and red-eyed, and dressed in a dark suit, white shirt and black tie. He was handcuffed to a Maidstone Prison officer, with another officer and Chris and Debbie Rogers standing nearby.

Reg and I embraced and I said: 'We'll go in and see him in a minute.'

I looked at Chris, who nodded to the prison officer. Reg's handcuffs were unlocked and we were escorted out of the room and along the corridor to the Chapel of Rest. We were allowed in on our own and, as soon as the door closed and we were alone with our brother, we both began to cry.

Reg walked to one end of the coffin and looked at Ronnie's face. He started stroking his forehead, then his shoulders, saying over and over again: 'You're all right now, Ron, you're at peace.' He couldn't take his eyes or hands off him; it was as if he were trying to get in touch with Ronnie's soul to help him in some way. I did not know what to say; I just watched Reg breaking his heart and all I could think of was all those wasted years when destiny had parted them.

We were in that little room for ten minutes. Finally, I had to tear him away.

'Reggie,' I said gently, 'we've got to leave him sometime. It's time. We've got to go now.'

Reluctantly, Reg forced himself away from the coffin and we went out into the corridor. The handcuffs were slipped back on and we were escorted to another, larger room where friends from Reg's past had gathered to pass on their condolences.

Those ten long, emotional minutes watching my brother's heart break was the most moving experience of my life since the Friday morning thirteen years before, when I had stood in a similar room at English's funeral parlour in Hoxton, weeping beside my mother's coffin.

Reg and I had not spoken again of our suspicions surrounding Ronnie's death; seeing him lying so peacefully, dressed lovingly in a new white shirt and dark tie, we felt everything was as it should be.

How wrong we were.

Those beautiful black horses led a procession of twenty-six limousines up Bethnal Green Road, past where our house used to be, in Vallance Road, to St Matthew's Church, in St Matthew's Row, where the crowds were even bigger. Hundreds had come to pay their respects to Ronnie, but others, mainly young people, were there only to catch a glimpse of Reg, and, as he was escorted, through the crowds, ten deep in places, they chanted: 'Reg-GIE! Reg-GIE!' as though he were a soccer hero. It was comforting, even a little flattering, for him to know he had such support, but both of us would have preferred a quieter, more dignified greeting, in keeping with such a solemn occasion.

For the hundred or so relatives and friends in the limousines, getting into the church was a battle. Reg's security men thought they had done the right thing, wearing badges to identify themselves to police, but looking back, the people who should have been identifiable were those entitled to be in the church. Sadly, it was such a mad scramble at the door that several we wanted there did not make it.

One who did, I gather, was Ronnie's ex-wife, Kate. Why did she turn up? There was no money in it for her, now that Ronnie was dead. Maybe she just wanted her picture in the papers.

Ronnie would have been proud of his twin brother for the way he organized his final farewell. The service was carefully thought out, touchingly simple, yet poignant, and it went off without a hitch.

Reg had a brilliant idea, that the pallbearers should represent the four areas of London in a symbol of peace. He chose Johnny Nash, from North London, Teddy Dennis, from West, me from East, and Frankie Fraser from south. Frank dearly wanted to be a pallbearer but, as he pointed out, he was only five feet four and would make the coffin lopsided. So, reluctantly, he declined, and on the day, Freddie Foreman represented South London.

The four of us, plus Laurie O'Leary, carried the coffin into the church a few minutes after midday, to Frank Sinatra's hit record, 'My Way' – the song Reg felt typified Ronnie more than any other.

After Father Christopher Bedford had read out the names of certain prisoners Reg wanted included in the service, we sang the hymn 'Morning Has Broken', then Robin McGibbon's wife, Sue, read 'Invictus', William Ernest Henley's classic poem about impending death.

I was standing a few feet to Reggie's right, on the other side of the aisle, and I could not stop myself glancing at him to see how he was taking it. He was staring at the coffin a few feet in front of us, his eyes seemingly trying to penetrate it, as if he wanted to be in there, in spirit at least, with Ronnie. The service meant everything to Reg and the paleness of his face betrayed the tension he felt, wondering whether it would all go precisely as he planned.

Sue then read 'A Message from Charlie and Reg':

'We wish for only good to come from Ron's passing away, and what is about to follow is our tribute to Ron. It is a

*symbol of peace in that the four pallbearers, each rep-
resenting an area of London, will encircle Ron's coffin in
a minute's silence.'*

Reg was allowed to join us for this tribute and he stood
next to me, at the foot of the coffin, his left hand cuffed to
a prison officer.

After a full minute of absolute silence – not one person
among the 300 packed in the church so much as coughed
– we returned to our seats and listened to Sue read a short
message in Reg's own words:

*'My brother, Ron, is now free and at peace. Ron had great
humour, a vicious temper, was kind and generous. He did
it all his way, but, above all, he was a man. That's how I
will always remember my twin brother, Ron. God bless.
Affection. Reg.'*

As Sue finished and stepped down from the lectern, Reg
gave her the briefest nod of approval and mouthed the
words: Thank you. The crucial part of the service was over
and it had been faultless. The anxiety that had been etched
in Reg's face was gone and colour had come back in his
cheeks. As we all stood to sing the hymn 'Fight the Good
Fight', I could see him visibly relax.

And so to some lovely, honest words about Ronnie from
Father Christopher, the Final Commendation, and a final
poem read by Sue: 'Do Not Stand at my Grave and Weep'.

As the pallbearers lifted the coffin and carried it to the
door, the most beautiful sound broke the silence: it was the
ideal song Reg had chosen to conclude the service – Whitney Houston's 'I Will Always Love You'.

It is a memorable song, a fitting finale to a memorable
service, and many of the 300 mourners were in tears as
they filed out of the church towards the crowds, press

313

photographers and TV camera crews milling outside in the bright spring sunshine.

The collection that morning reflected the respect Ronnie commanded. It totalled an astonishing £850, more than had ever been given in the church since it was built a hundred years ago.

My own tears and Reg's would come later. Now, we had to face the toughest part of the day – the six-mile drive to Chingford Cemetery, where we would lower Ronnie into a grave beside that of our beloved mum and dad.

The six black horses clip-clopped out of the East End leading an incredible cortege that stretched almost half a mile. Frankie Fraser had given a radio interview that morning, likening Ronnie's funeral to the State occasion given to Sir Winston Churchill, and he was spot on. Obviously, many of the people were there out of curiosity; few wanted to miss out on the East End's biggest, most publicized event since the time the twins were allowed to attend our mother's funeral thirteen years earlier. But I have to stress that the majority of the thousands on the streets that day were there out of respect for Ronnie and the Krays in general. People find it hard to understand, but my brothers *did* have a lot of respect in the East End. The Krays had a good name and, after the twins were jailed in 1968, it was passed down to children not born at the time of our heyday. Good, straight people, not villains, remember the twins as much for the help they gave less fortunate folk as for the murders that led to their demise. These people laugh at some of the ludicrous tales of terrifying violence that have been exaggerated over the years.

The cheering seemed to go on and on: 'Reg-GIE ... Reg-GIE ... Free Reggie ...' Following in the car behind his, I could see young kids, no more than fifteen, running alongside the car, pushing their hands through the driver's

314

window, trying to touch him, saying: 'They should free you Reg, it's time they let you out . . .' Reg did not take this as hero worship; he preferred to think of it as respect for his dead brother.

The kids even ran alongside my car, in which I was travelling with Judy, and begged me for autographs.

It was more like a wedding than a funeral.

The farther we got from Bethnal Green, the more the crowds tailed off. But they increased the moment we hit the hill at Chingford that leads up to the cemetery, and, of course, the graveside was packed, not only with mourners, but reporters, photographers and TV film crews.

As soon as he got out of the car, Reg was handed three beautiful bouquets of red roses. He was allowed to go first to our parents' grave. Gently, he laid one bouquet at Mum's headstone and another by the old man's. He put the third bouquet on Frances's grave, then stepped back and bowed his head. My heart went out to him: over the years I have had every opportunity to go to the cemetery, but that Wednesday afternoon was the first time Reg had seen the graves of his loved ones for thirteen years.

Reggie and I and our closest friends gathered round the open plot where Ronnie was to be buried. Watching the coffin being lowered into the ground, I moved close to Reg and said: 'He's at peace now.'

'Yes,' Reg said, quietly. 'He is.'

'Part of you is with him.'

'Yes it is,' he said.

'You'll be down there with him one day.'

'Half of me is with him now.'

The prison officer handcuffed to Reg allowed him two minutes looking down on the coffin, then indicated that it was time to head for the car waiting to take them back to Maidstone. Reg said: 'Rest in peace, Ron; see you one day.'

Then he was escorted to the car and driven away. God knows how he felt.

Some people had asked me if I was worried that Reg might be so overcome with grief that he'd do something silly, like throw himself into the grave. I was not worried in the least; I knew Reg's pride, his strength of character, would not have allowed him to behave in any other way than Ronnie would have wanted.

For me, those moments at the graveside brought back all I had gone through at Mum's funeral and the old man's. Although time is, as they say, a great healer, I miss them both terribly and think of them constantly. Reg and I will be buried on the same plot and I'm sure he, like me, takes great comfort in the thought that, one day, we will all meet again. I can't think of anything nicer.

The TV that night, and the papers the next day, were full of the funeral. I was grateful for that, because, to be truthful, I was out of it on the day, floating in a sort of limbo, and I had very little idea what was happening around me. My deepest thoughts were for Reg, and how he was going to get through it, and I'm proud to say that he handled himself impeccably.

Ronnie would have been so, so proud of him.

Chapter Twenty

The following Christmas Day, Judy's children were with their father – her ex-husband – so we decided to go to the Croydon Park Hotel with Gary for lunch. The quality of service from the friendly staff matches the exquisite food and we had a lovely time. The only worry I had as we left was Gary; he wasn't feeling very well and, to be honest, he didn't look too clever.

Over the next few days he seemed to perk up and said he was going to see the new year in with a friend of ours, Roy, at his home in West Norwood. But when I got a phone call from Roy on 2 January, saying that Gary's back was so painful he was taking him to his doctor, my heart sank; I had a feeling that something was dreadfully wrong.

The doctor arranged for Gary to have an X-ray and when we went back for the results the next day, Gary was so weak, he couldn't walk. The doctor immediately called an ambulance to take him to King's College Hospital, in Camberwell, where he spent the next seven days. He was allowed home for the weekend, but had to go back on the Monday. He was given all sorts of tests, but nobody was saying what was wrong with him. Finally, the following Friday, 19 January, a doctor called me into his office and confirmed my fears.

'Mr Kray,' he said, gently, 'I'm sorry to have to tell you that your son has lung cancer.'

All I could think to say was: 'How bad is it? Can you operate?'

'I'm afraid not,' he said. 'It has gone too far.'

317

'How long are we talking about?' I asked. I was hoping for a year, possibly two, but knew in my heart it was unrealistic. What that doctor told me, however, knocked me sideways.

'Eight weeks,' he said. 'At the most.'

I walked out of the office in a daze. My Gary. My poor Gary, who had never done anything wrong, never hurt anyone in his life. All I could think was: why can't it be me? I'm coming up to seventy. I've had my life. Why does it have to be him? He's only forty-four. He's in the summer of his life.

I made a decision then and there that Gary would not be told the truth; he was not a strong boy and would not be able to handle it. I told Judy and said I had to let Dolly, Gary's mother, know, even though she had not set eyes on him for years. I went to a pine furniture shop in the East End, where Dolly's sister, Elaine, and niece, Pat, worked, and broke the tragic news.

'Would you tell Dolly that Gary is in King's College, and she can visit him if she wants,' I said.

'Is it all right if I tell Nancy?' Elaine asked.

I didn't know what to say to that. Neither Gary nor I had seen Nancy for nearly twenty years; I did not know how she would react to hearing that her brother was dying. I knew that Gary would love to see her, though, so that solved my dilemma.

'Yes, Elaine,' I said. 'Please tell Nancy.'

Later that day, I got a call saying that not only did Nancy dearly want to see Gary, she was going to visit him that very evening. Sitting in a communal TV room with Gary later, I said: 'You've got a surprise visitor coming tonight, Gal.'

'Who is it?' he asked.

'Your sister, Nancy,' I said.

Gary's face broke into a wide smile; he was thrilled, really made up.

318

'That's lovely, Dad,' he said, 'I'd love to see her.'

Half an hour later I spotted a beautiful blonde at the far end of the corridor and knew at once it was Nancy. She was with Pat. I walked towards them and hugged Nancy tightly.

'Hello, darling.'

'Hello, Dad,' she said.

'Come on,' I said. 'He's waiting to see you.'

'I'm so pleased you let me know. It's been so long. I should have tried to contact you both before.'

Now wasn't the time for recriminations. 'We're to blame, too, darling,' I said. 'It's the way of life.'

If Nancy was shocked to see her brother in a wheelchair, looking terribly frail, she didn't show it. She walked straight up to him, bent down and cuddled him. Gary's face lit up; it was the happiest I'd seen him since Christmas Day when he first complained of being off-colour.

Nancy, it was clear, was a very tactile person: she kept touching Gary, couldn't leave him alone the whole hour she spent with us. It was a joy to see.

What made the visit so good was that Nancy made a determined effort to be as natural as possible. When Gary asked her to get something for him, for example, she laughed: 'Hey, stop bossing me about, just 'cos I'm your little sister.' When he asked the time, she pointed at the clock and said: 'What time does it say up there?'

I hadn't seen Gary laugh since Christmas, but Nancy brought a smile to his face. He thought she was fabulous; he liked everything about her.

When it was time for us to leave, Nancy told Gary not to worry, she would be back the following night.

Walking away from the hospital, she looked at me, sadness clouding her eyes. 'What a waste, Dad,' she said. 'All the years we've been kept apart. We could have had a marvellous time together. And now he's going to die. What a terrible waste.'

With Gary so desperately ill, I did not want to dwell on the past; there was no point. I wanted to see the positive side of Nancy turning up in his life, no matter how late.

'Seeing you together, so happy, pushed all those years away, darling,' I said. 'You made up for all those missing years just by being there tonight.'

And I meant it. One only had to look at the sparkle in Gary's eyes to know that seeing his sister again made his day.

It was not possible for Gary to stay at King's indefinitely; on the other hand, it was a non-starter for him to go home to his flat. The obvious answer was for him to move in with Judy and me at Sanderstead, but how could I expect a mother of three teenage children to help care for a dying man in our crowded home as well?

I had to ask Judy, though; I didn't have a choice. To her great credit, Judy's reaction was positive and immediate.

'Of course, Gary can stay,' she said. 'I'll convert the downstairs front room into his own bedroom.'

What a blessed relief that was. Having Gary with me twenty-four hours a day would give me the opportunity to make sure his last weeks were as comfortable as possible. My respect for Judy, which was sky-high anyway, soared. With a full-time job to hold down, plus three children to bring up at crucial and difficult times in their lives, she could have been forgiven for saying she could not cope with Gary as well. But she didn't, and I shall be grateful to her for ever for that.

We turned that front room into something resembling a hospital ward and looked after Gary there for the next three weeks. I hardly slept; I would lay awake upstairs, listening for the slightest sound from Gary, then get up to tend to him as necessary. Judy, bless her heart, would often get up even though she had to be up early for work. Her children were as good as gold, too, always popping in and out of the room, when they were home, asking if Gary wanted anything. He was in good hands and I know he appreciated what everyone was doing for him, because he would often say: 'They're lovely people, aren't they, Dad?'

I was so pleased that Nancy had come back into both our lives, but I did worry that she might not make contact, given that we were many miles apart – she in north London, on the borders of Hertfordshire, and us in Surrey. My fears were unfounded: no sooner had we settled Gary into his 'hospital ward' than the most touching card from Nancy arrived, assuring Gary that 'I Am Thinking of You'. The words on the front, written by Susan Polis Schutz, read:

> I have no definite purpose
> for writing to you
> other than to say that
> I am happily thinking
> about you right now
> and when you read this
> I know I will have captured
> a small part of your day,
> causing you to think about me.

Gary was very moved by the sentiment, but what Nancy had written inside brought tears to his eyes. And mine, I have to admit. She wrote: 'It was so lovely seeing you again. Where have all the years gone? You would think that we had never been apart – God only knows what happened. Time goes by so quickly. I have always thought about you, but I suppose thinking is not enough. I SHOULD have made the effort to get in touch with you – there are no excuses. But now you've got me and I'm not going to let you go again! You've had too many years without your 'pest' of

321

a sister driving you mad!! Gary, I love you so much, and to see you again made me SO happy. I'll always be here for you. I'm just sorry it took so many years. Love always, Nancy.'

Gary put that beautiful card in pride of place on the mantelpiece beside his bed. I lost count of the number of times he read it.

Nancy came regularly to be with Gary. She always arrived laden with little delicacies; salt beef, bagels, cakes, fruit – anything that might tempt him to eat. I'd take the opportunity to get out and run some errands, knowing Gary was safe in his sister's loving care. But no matter how much we all did for Gary, it was painfully obvious he was slipping away fast: he had never been a strapping lad, but now he was nothing more than skin and bone, and unable to do anything for himself. Steroids prescribed by King's combated his pain and gave him an appetite for a while, but it was short-term relief. My son was dying before my eyes and, as much as I did not want to believe it, I knew he would not last as long as we had been told.

I had to take Gary to Maidstone Prison and I dreaded it: he was so frail that even the shortest journey was a painful effort, but I feared for Reggie, too. He knew Gary was very, very ill, but had no idea how bad he looked, and I was worried he would be shocked at what he saw. I asked our dear friend Laurie O'Leary to drive us down and we set off in his white Mercedes, just after midday on Monday 5 February. Gary's wheelchair was in the boot and he lay, stretched out, on the rear seat with me, his head in my lap. He was in great pain, but never once complained, and whenever we hit a bump in the road and I looked at him, concerned, he gave me a little smile to let me know he was all right. I was taking him to see his Uncle Reg for what I

322

knew was the last time and it was all I could do to stop myself falling apart in front of him. Funerals apart, it was the saddest journey I'd ever made.

I had notified the prison about Gary's condition and we were allowed a special visiting time, so that the four of us could be alone. We still had to have a security check, however, and were asked to walk through one of those invisible screens that detect metal objects. I followed Laurie, then turned to push Gary through. What I saw made my blood boil: a prison officer had an arm down Gary's back, searching him.

I could not believe it. They knew how ill he was. Did someone seriously think a dying man would be smuggling something illegal in to one of the highest profile prisoners in the country?

All the emotions I had been fighting to keep under control, for Reggie's sake as much as Gary's, came gushing out in one long agonizing scream and tears started rolling down my face.

'Take your hands off my son, take them off NOW. My son is very ill. You know that. You've been told that.'

I was shaking and my fists were clenched. 'Lay one finger on him and you'll have me to deal with,' I yelled.

Dear, dear Gary. He looked up at me, shaking his head. 'Don't get upset, Dad,' he said. 'I'm all right.'

Fortunately, the security man saw sense and allowed me to wheel Gary through the screen without further physical searching. As we waited to be escorted over to the visiting room in Weald Wing, Gary said: 'Dry your eyes, Dad. Don't let Reg see you've been upset.'

Which, of course, nearly set me off again: Gary, just skin and bone, wasting away, but thinking of me.

Reggie was sitting in a chair when we walked in. He got up and came over and put both arms round Gary, fighting to hide the sadness he felt. 'How are you, Gary?' he asked

– a ridiculous question, but what else do you say in such tragic circumstances?

We sat there, the four of us, chatting about this and that, nothing very important, and all the time Reggie was rubbing Gary's shoulders and stroking his hair. After just half an hour, though, I could see that Gary had had enough; the strain of the journey was beginning to show.

'Well, Gary, I think I should be getting you back home now,' I said.

'Yes, Gary,' Reg said. 'Don't tire yourself out too much.'

All Gary did was nod in agreement. He was exhausted. He just wanted to get home and get back into bed.

As we prepared to leave, Reggie hugged Gary's tiny shoulders. 'God bless you, Gary,' he said. 'Hope to see you again soon.'

I wheeled Gary to the exit door. Waiting for it to be unlocked, I turned round to give Reggie a farewell wave. Tears were streaming down his face.

He knew he would not see his nephew alive again.

It was at this time that a close friend told me about St Christopher's Hospice, at Crystal Palace. Until then, I had no idea there were establishments that cared for terminally ill patients. I am so relieved I was put in touch with St Christopher's, because the lovely, caring people there made Gary's last days peaceful, comfortable and, although it may sound strange, enjoyable.

From the moment he went there, on 12 February, those kind, unselfish people loved Gary; they said he was one of the nicest people they had ever met – so polite and appreciative of all they were doing for him. After eight days, we took him home, knowing that, when the end was in sight, we would have to take him back.

He loved the idea of being at home, fussed over by all of us, but St Christopher's was so wonderfully peaceful and efficient he would not have minded staying. In fact, after a week or so, something happened that made me feel he would be better off there. He woke in the middle of the night, all hot and bothered, saying he had had a strange feeling, which he couldn't explain. I sat him up in bed and told him to take deep breaths. It was nothing to worry about, I assured him. But I *was* worried, because I was not a nurse and had no idea what to do in an emergency. When I suggested we ought to consider getting him back in St Christopher's, he seemed relieved.

'I don't mind going back, Dad,' he said. 'I love it. I love them up there.'

My concern at not being equipped to deal with a crisis was genuine, but if I'm honest, I seized on this as an excuse to get Gary back into St Christopher's: I wasn't blind; I could see the end was very close.

The hospice confirmed that I'd done the right thing: Gary had only a few days to live. He went in there on 1 March and I let all those close to Gary know that, if they wanted to see him, it would have to be sooner rather than later.

With all the stress that lay ahead, the last thing I needed was another emotional trauma. But I got one the following Sunday when I opened the *News of the World* and saw a huge headline across two pages that screamed: THE GREAT BRAIN ROBBERY, and a sub-heading below shouted: DOCS HAVE PICKLED RONNIE KRAY'S BONCE IN A BOTTLE – NOW HIS WIFE HAS HALF A MIND TO SUE.

The jocular cynicism of that last line made me think it was some sort of sick send-up – a mickey-take, based on Ronnie's notorious insanity and schizophrenia. But the story was deadly serious. Apparently Broadmoor's top medical staff had secretly ordered Ronnie's brain to be removed before his funeral, and sent to a laboratory in Oxford for scientific examination. The results, it seemed, could be of vital interest to scientists who believe criminal behaviour may be brought on by chemical imbalances in our little grey cells.

The horrific revelation came to light, the story claimed, after a tip-off to Ronnie's ex-wife, Kate, who, it was clear, had wasted little time in making money by passing the information to the newspaper. She accused Broadmoor of theft and said she was contemplating legal action. In the meantime, she wanted Ronnie's brain returned for burial with the rest of his body. She was outraged, so the story said, to learn that there was part of Ronnie imprisoned in a jar with a little paper label.

If the former Mrs Kray was outraged, I was beside myself with fury, and so was Reg when he heard. He rang me, shattered, and wanted to know if anyone had asked my permission for the bizarre operation. I told him No, and he said: 'How can people do this without asking permission from the deceased's family?'

I said I didn't know. But I did really. So did Reg. It was the same old story: if your name is Kray, they can do what they like with you – without fear of any come-backs. Hadn't the hospital authorities – Broadmoor and Heatherwood – allowed the media to hear of Ronnie's death before having the common courtesy, let alone the decency, to notify Reg and me first?

Proof of the latest couldn't-care-less attitude became evident a few days later when Reg asked his solicitor to contact Broadmoor to find out (a) who gave the go-ahead for Ronnie's brain to be removed; and (b) why the next of kin had not been asked to give permission. The solicitor got nowhere.

The same week a Tory MP, Peter Cohen, took up the case, describing Broadmoor's action as 'gruesome'. But he got nowhere, too.

I found the whole business unsavoury and disgraceful –

and, more importantly, hypocritical. If Britain discovered Saddam Hussein was experimenting on dead people behind their families' backs, we would be the first to condemn him as a monster.

How would other people in this country feel if they picked up a paper to read that their dead parent or brother or sister had been buried without their brain? To realize suddenly that all the time they had been praying their loved one would rest in peace, the deceased relative was lying there with part of their body stolen?

It's inhuman, isn't it?

My mind went back to when Reg and I spent those quiet, private moments alone with Ronnie in English's Chapel of Rest. I could see Reg, stroking Ronnie's face and shoulders, saying over and over again: 'You're at peace now, Ron, you're at peace.' And I felt quite sick, knowing that Ronnie, after all those nightmarish traumas caused by an appalling sickness, was *not* at peace; and that we had been deceived – no, duped! – in the most cynical, callous, uncaring manner possible. It is a terrible memory to have.

Ronnie's brain was eventually removed from that Oxford laboratory by a representative from English's, who put it in a casket and buried it beside Ronnie's coffin at 7 A.M. on 23 February. I would have liked to have been there, but I had no idea it was happening.

One of those who wanted to see Gary was his mother. She had not been to the hospital or Judy's house, but she turned up at St Christopher's unexpectedly one day. I walked in to find her sitting at Gary's bedside with her sister and brother-in-law. After a few minutes, they all got up and left.

'I don't know why she came,' Gary said. 'She hardly said a word to me.'

We should not have been surprised. The few times she phoned Judy's house, it seemed she couldn't wait to get off the line. Always, Gary would look at me, confused, and say: 'What did she ring for?'

I didn't tell Gary, but I knew why: it was a guilt thing. When Gary was gone, she didn't want people accusing her of not making contact with him. That was Dolly all over.

She turned up again a couple of days later. There were half a dozen of us around Gary's bed and when Dolly saw us all she collapsed on the floor outside the ward. She made it look as though she had fainted, but a nurse told us she had fallen on the floor deliberately. It was her guilt complex again: she knew what she had done to Gary all those years ago and she knew he knew. What she couldn't handle was coming face to face with people who might know, too. Hence the dramatics.

She was taken to a room at the end of the corridor and asked a nurse if she could see Gary on her own for five minutes. Nancy was with us that day, and we all went to the tea room, while Dolly sat with Gary. After about fifteen minutes, Nancy could stand it no longer. She marched into the ward and said: 'I think you've had long enough. Charlie is here every minute. So is everybody else. Charlie wants to come back now. I think you should go.'

Dolly did not want to go, and there was a bit of an argument. But she did leave in the end and we all went back in with Gary.

When Gary heard that Diana, and her daughter, Claudine, were coming to visit him, he admitted he was worried that there might be friction between them and Judy. But there wasn't: all three ladies put whatever feelings they may have had to one side and thought only of Gary, not themselves. I will always respect them for that: it was difficult enough for Gary without having to worry about an 'atmosphere'.

For most of those awful weeks since January, I believed Gary had no idea how seriously ill he was. But I now know

328

Above Welcome home: me and my beloved mum and the old man at Vallance Road in 1975, on the first day of my release from jail

Left Me with Mum and Gary on the same day

Starry-eyed: Mum and the old man at Vallance Road when actress and family friend Diana Dors and her husband Alan Lake dropped in with a copy of Di's autobiography, *For Adults Only*

Me with Diana at the launch of the first edition of my autobiography in 1975

Above Farewell my lovely: me at Mum's graveside, with Diana on my right and Gary, in glasses, on my left

Right Security circus: Reggie arrives at the funeral amid a costly police operation

Me with Barbara Windsor, on the night she jogged my memory about those cuff-links

Posing with the Kemp twins – Martin, left, and Gary – who played Ronnie and Reggie in the dreadful film *The Krays*

Centre of attention again: me with snooker stars Jimmy White and Steve Davies

funeral cortege that brought the East End to a standstill. Ronnie would have been
tickled, but the spectacular turnout could not have done Reggie's parole chances much
good

Reggie, in spectacles, heads a gesture of peace around Ronnie's coffin in St Matthew's Church. Facing me are John Nash and, on his left, Freddie Foreman

Reggie, as the strain of wanting the perfect farewell to Ronnie begins to show

United in grief: me and Reggie at Ronnie's burial service at Chingford Cemetery, March 1995. Behind us, with the shaved head, is Steve Wraith, a nice guy from Newcastle, who became a good friend

Big man, big heart: Me and my great friend, Albert Chapman, during another enjoyable night in his Birmingham club, The Elbow Room

Cheeky chappie: My loyal pal, Dave Courtney, and me outside Maidstone Prison, in Kent, after visiting Reg in the mid-nineties

Above A picture I shall treasure: one of the last ones taken of me and Gary before his tragic death at forty-four

Left Model mate: me with lifelong, loyal pal, Maureen Flanagan, at the opening of unlicensed boxer Lennie McClean's East End pub, Guv'ner's [sic], in 1996. Sadly, Lennie died of cancer two years later

Below Me with Robin McGibbon, my ghostwriter, after a book-signing session at Murder One bookshop, in London's Leicester Square, in 1988

he did. Once, when Di was with him, he suddenly said: 'Will Dad be all right?'

Di could not bring herself to ask him what he actually meant; she just assured him that, of course, I was going to be all right.

Then, on the evening of 7 March, a friend of ours, Alan Land, was with Gary when I had been delayed.

'What's the time, Alan?' Gary kept saying.

'Don't worry, Gary, he'll be here. You know he's always here around this time.'

'I know,' Gary said, 'but I'm a bit worried about him really.'

'Why?' Alan asked.

'I don't think he knows how ill I am,' Gary said. 'I'm worried about what will happen, what he'll do, when he finds out.'

I walked in a few minutes after that conversation. Gary just said, 'Hello, Dad,' the same as usual. There I was, worried about him and all the time he was worrying about me and not wanting me to know. I found that deeply touching.

The following day I was at Gary's bedside with Judy, Diana, Nancy and Dolly's sister when a nurse called me outside into the corridor.

'I think he's got about three hours, Charlie,' she said.

I went back into the ward and looked at Gary; his eyes were closed and he looked as if he were in a deep, peaceful sleep. I told the others what the nurse had said and we all just sat there, looking at Gary, not really knowing what to say to each other.

We sat there for two hours and then I had to go to the toilet. I was walking down the corridor when I heard Nancy's voice: 'Quick. Tell Dad.'

I ran back into the ward. I got to Gary in time to hold him as he took his last breaths.

All of us held him in turn and no one wanted to leave. Finally, after about half an hour, a nurse came in and said, softly: 'Of course, you can stop as long as you like, but we feel it best if you leave Gary with us. We must see to him now.'

She was right; there was nothing more we could do for Gary. We had done all we could, given him our love, let him know he was a special person, but it was over now.

All I could think, leaving St Christopher's and the lovely people who work there, was: I wish it could have been me, not him.

You don't expect to have to bury your children, do you?

Three days later, the phone rang at Judy's. It was Dolly. And she wanted a row over an article in an East London newspaper about Gary's funeral.

'Dolly,' I said. 'Gary is lying dead at the moment and I don't want to argue with you.'

'Your feet won't touch the ground when I've finished with you,' she yelled.

'Listen,' I said. 'Gary is lying dead. Do you think I want all this? I don't need it. I'm shattered.'

I honestly didn't want a row, but she said something – I forget what – that wound me up.

'You want to remember something,' I said. 'You threw Gary out of the house years ago for no reason whatsoever.'

'No I didn't,' she screamed.

'You know you did,' I said. 'He came home one night and his bags were packed. You threw him out so George Ince could move in.'

Dolly just screamed down the phone, denying what everyone who knows her knows is true.

'Your son was a great kid,' I said. 'He knew what you did to him. And so do I. I will never forget it. Without my mother, whatever would have happened to him? Don't ring me. I don't want to talk to you. Ever. I don't want to know you.'

And I slammed the phone down.

I couldn't handle it. Gary lying dead in the Chapel of Rest and his mother screaming at me, wanting a row, when all I wanted was a miracle that would open my Gary's eyes and bring him back to me.

As Reg had lost part of himself when Ronnie died, so I had lost part of myself with Gary's death. The unexpected suddenness of it slaughtered me, to be quite truthful. All I could think was: he was such a lovely, gentle innocent, and I'm not going to see him again.

I dreaded the funeral. It was less than a year since Ronnie died and we would all be gathering at the same funeral parlour, watching the coffin being carried into the same church and driving to the same cemetery. It was going to be an eerie experience and, quite frankly, I was relieved when Reg asked if he could, again, make the funeral arrangements. The way I was feeling, weighed down by a crushing, exhausting emptiness, unable to think of much except my grief, I was going to find it tough enough just getting myself to St Matthew's Church.

Reg did a good job. He organized a short but moving service in which the packed congregation heard his voice on tape, reading an appropriate poem by his favourite writer, Kahlil Gibran, and some lovely hymns.

I knew that the Reverend Ken Rimini was going to say a few words about Gary before the Final Commendation, but I had no idea what they were. What he said knocked me out, and because he seemed to sum up Gary so perfectly that sombre day, I have reprinted some of what the packed church heard:

331

'When we recount the life of someone who has died we often tend to emphasize the great achievements they have attained: running the fastest mile, climbing the highest mountain, sailing the widest ocean. But the human race is not made up solely of superstars and heroes. On the contrary, the world is actually made up of ordinary people going about their ordinary business, living their own lives.

'Gary was a bit like that. He never sought the limelight. He never wanted to be front page news. No, Gary, in many ways, was just one of those ordinary people. But ordinary people are capable of extraordinary deeds and they manifest themselves at times of crisis.

'A couple of months ago, crisis struck the life of Gary Kray when he was diagnosed as having cancer. Now, an ordinary man would have fallen apart, devastated at the news. But Gary's acceptance and courage were stunning, a shining example to all the "superstars" that surround our lives.

'His courage made the pain of those who loved him and cared for him somehow easier to bear, particularly the staff at St Christopher's Hospice, who immediately fell in love with this polite, gentle man. That ordinary man, whose extraordinary courage makes him a 'superstar' in his own right and an inspiration in our lives, will live forever in our memories.'

Sue McGibbon read a hymn, then Diana's daughter, Claudine, bravely battled through her tears to read Henry Scott Holland's famous and poignant 'All Is Well' and, almost before we knew it, we were all filing out of the church to the same record that had accompanied Ronnie's exit twelve months before – Whitney Houston's 'I Will Always Love You'.

Hundreds of people had been drawn to English's funeral parlour, because of publicity nationally and locally, but the crowds were nothing compared to Ronnie's amazing turn-out, and the cortege of seven limousines arrived at Ching-

332

ford Cemetery just forty minutes later. Six of them carried lifelong friends, such as Billy Murray, my old Canning Town mate, who is now one of the most popular actors in *The Bill* TV series. But there was one empty car – the one travelling directly behind the hearse. That was Reg's idea: a symbolic gesture that he was there in spirit, even though the prison had refused him permission to attend the funeral.

Someone who *was* there was my old mate, Patsy Manning, from Birmingham. He had been driven down in a Jaguar owned by Joe Sunner, an Indian pal, who runs a bustling general stores in Snitterfield, a village just outside Stratford-Upon-Avon, fifteen miles from Birmingham.

Indian Joe, as he was called, did not use his regular chauffeur for the trip; he called in someone else – a shortish, stocky guy in his mid-thirties, with thinning hair and a week's growth of beard.

He was introduced to me only as George. He seemed a nice enough bloke and I thanked him for taking the trouble to come, particularly as he had never known Gary.

Four months later, I would learn why the trip was so important to him.

We buried my lovely, innocent, gentle son, in the rain. I thanked our many friends for coming from all parts of the country to pay their respects. I couldn't thank Dolly. She wasn't there. Too heartbroken, I've been told.

Then I went home to be alone with Judy and her children, Nina, Glenn and Sean. Still, all I could think was that I wasn't going to see Gary again. Not ever. And it hurt.

It did for many months afterwards. I would be overcome with the most stressful panic attacks at the oddest times – either in bed in the middle of the night, sitting on my own having a cup of coffee, or driving the car in the middle of the afternoon. The finality of death – as far as we know anyway – will suddenly swamp me and my heart starts pumping and I break out in a sweat. The thought of never seeing Gary again is too horrible to contemplate and I sit where I am until the panic is over, trying to convince myself that I *will* see him one day.

I will never know for sure, but I'm convinced Gary's cancer was triggered by a traumatic experience that shocked and upset him deeply two years before his death.

He had come back from Blackpool and was renting a little flat in Crystal Palace, just round the corner from where I had lived with Diana.

One night in May 1994, he was walking home with a Chinese takeaway when two, possibly three, young blokes jumped him from behind. They knocked him to the ground, kicked him in the ribs, cut his eye, then snatched a gold chain from his neck, a wallet containing £70 and his watch.

A passing police car found Gary lying on the pavement, dazed, but thankfully not seriously hurt. He was taken to nearby Gipsy Hill police station, then driven home in a police car.

Gary had done nothing to warrant such a cowardly attack. He was a quiet, peaceful bloke who never invited trouble. He had such a nice way with him. He never spoke badly about anyone and no one had a bad word to say about him. He was liked by everyone who met him.

Please God I will see him again when it's my turn to go.

Chapter Twenty-one

Big Albert, we call him. He's a huge bear of a man, about 6ft 3in. and broad with it, but it's his heart, as much as his physical presence, that makes his nickname so appropriate. He is a warm, generous man and has been a good, loyal friend to me for more than twenty years. So, really, I should not have been surprised, a few days after Gary's funeral, when Albert rang, inviting Judy and I to spend a couple of days in Birmingham.

'After all you've both been through, you need to get away from London and relax,' he said. 'When can you come up?'

'It's really lovely of you, Alb,' I said. 'But to be quite truthful, things aren't too clever at the moment. I can't afford to come up just now.'

Albert laughed. 'Who's asking you to pay?'

I had a word with Judy. She was able to get the following Friday off. She sorted out Nina, Glenn and Sean for the weekend and we got an early coach from Victoria, arriving in Birmingham at midday on Thursday 28 March. Big Albert had booked a double room at The Novotel Hotel, in the city centre, and waiting for us there was a bottle of champagne.

It was the start of what turned out to be a most wonderful weekend. As tour manager of the hugely successful rock band, Black Sabbath, Albert had a few bob and, where I was concerned, he didn't mind spending it. He told us to order anything we wanted in the hotel and, that night, when he took us out to dinner, then on to his club, The Elbow Room, in Aston, the drinks continued to flow. I don't mind admitting I got well and truly smashed. I think I needed to.

For three months, while my heart had been breaking, I had forced myself to be stoical for Gary's sake. But now that the terrible, tragic, inevitable end had come, I needed a release from all the anguish I'd been holding in check.

Through Patsy, I'd got to know a lot of people in Birmingham and I felt comfortable – safe, if you like – in their company. I didn't need to look over my shoulder. I was among friends and able to get as drunk as I wanted without worrying what anyone thought. Towards the end of the evening, however, I found myself getting emotional: being back in The Elbow Room again brought back memories of Gary, because he had been there with me, in May the previous year, celebrating Patsy's sixty-fifth birthday. But it was a wonderful night nevertheless.

Judy and I got the coach back to Victoria around lunchtime on the Sunday, and were back in Sanderstead by teatime. We were tired, but happy, having been thoroughly spoiled by a lovely, gentle-natured man, who always puts others before himself. Big Albert knew how much Gary meant to me and recognized the pain I'd been going through. I'll always be grateful to him for providing that bolt hole for me at a time when I needed it most.

Money was always the problem, but I never lost faith in Ian Walsh and in the oil deal he was setting up. I was confident he knew what he was doing and that, eventually, he would pull off something that would solve my financial worries once and for all. But waiting for it to happen was becoming more and more frustrating and, not surprisingly, the cash problem caused tension between me and Judy. Most of her £14,000-a-year salary went towards the mortgage, household bills and upkeep of three youngsters at expensive times of their lives. I would have liked nothing more than to have a windfall and taken the financial pressure off her, but, apart from the six-monthly royalty cheques of a few hundred pounds and the odd loan from friends, I had nothing coming in; not a penny. I felt ashamed that I did not even have enough to pay for Gary's funeral; I had to ask Reggie to deal with that.

I hated being in a situation where I had to rely on Judy for money, but I felt there was nothing I could do but wait and hope that the oil deal would come off. With money so tight, we did not go out socializing much. To be honest, I didn't mind: there's nothing worse than being in the company of people with money when you haven't got any to stand your own corner. And, anyway, I preferred to stay at home with Judy and the kids, watching telly and talking about Gary.

On the few occasions when we did go out, that April, I discovered that drink was now having a different effect on me. Before Gary's death, it had always made me happy and sociable, the life and soul of the party; but now, the more I drank, the more sad and emotional I became. People would be talking to me, but my mind would be elsewhere. Everyone around me would be laughing and joking and I'd be conscious, suddenly, of my eyes filling with tears. I'd try to cover this by faking a smile, but I never fooled Judy. When she saw the signs, she would give me a nudge, or tap me on the knee, to bring me out of my mood. It may seem off-hand of her, uncaring even, but it was just the right attitude. If she had been more demonstrative, hugged me and tried to comfort me, I'm sure I would have broken down and howled my eyes out, which would not have been too clever in public.

This was the frame of mind I was in, when Patsy rang, saying Big Albert was throwing another birthday party for him at The Elbow Room, on 9 May. As politely as I could, I said I didn't think I would go up this time; I didn't feel in the mood for partying and, in any event, it would all be too emotional for me.

337

Perhaps, I would have felt differently if Judy could have gone with me, but the party was on a Thursday and getting time off work was out of the question for her. I felt bad about not going, however: apart from snubbing Patsy, I was concerned about offending other friends up there who had been very supportive over Gary's death. I tried to excuse myself, saying I could not afford to make the trip, but Patsy knocked that one aside: a friend of his owned a hotel in Moseley, about four miles from the city centre, and Patsy was sure he'd let me stay there for nothing. And the party at The Elbow Room would be free, he reminded me, courtesy of big-hearted Albert.

I talked it over with Judy, who felt I should make the effort. Yes, it would be an emotional night, with people who had known Gary all around me, but, maybe – like the previous trip in March – it would do me good.

Patsy was true to his word. The friend who owned The Wake Green Lodge Hotel, in Moseley, was a charming Tunisian in his thirties, named Fethi Torki, and he made it clear that I was to be his guest for two nights. What a relief that was: I hadn't a bean in my pocket and one look at the wonderfully extensive menu in the hotel restaurant, Medallion Vert, told me that this was a high quality establishment with prices to match. Dover sole, for example, was just 50p short of twenty quid and lobster in brandied tomato sauce was verging on thirty. For connoisseurs for whom money was no object, Fethi's wine list offered everything, from basic German hock at £8.50 a bottle, to classic Chateau-Lafite Rothschild at £150.

Later that Thursday afternoon, I was shown to my room and had a shower and a brief nap. A couple of hours later I put on fresh clothes and went downstairs to meet Patsy. He was standing by the bar at the far end of the restaurant about to buy drinks for two smallish, stocky guys he introduced as George and Deano. I recognized George from

338

Gary's funeral; he was the one who had driven Patsy down in Indian Joe Sunner's Jaguar. While I was chatting to them, and a girl they introduced as Lisa, another bloke came through the restaurant towards us.

I was wondering who the guy was when George said, 'I'd like to introduce you to my friend, Jack, from Newcastle. Jack – this is Charlie Kray and this is his mate, Patsy.'

We shook hands and smiled at each other. Jack was a tall, well-built, good-looking guy and really pleasant; he seemed pleased to meet me.

After a few minutes, Deano called out, 'Best of order for one minute.' We all went quiet. 'This is just a little token from me and our kid, Georgie, and Jack and Lisa. I know all you southerners call us northerners tight, but we've all clubbed together. We've got Patsy this lovely present and I hope he likes it and appreciates it. Happy birthday.'

Everyone clapped as Deano handed Patsy a smallish package. He opened it and took out a CD.

'*Simply Red*,' he said. 'Thanks a million. It's me favourite music.'

'No, no,' Deano interrupted with a jokey speech. 'What we've got for you, you know what you could have won . . .'

Someone shouted, 'The Star Prize!'

Deano handed Patsy a very large package. 'It's from me, Jack, Georgie and Lisa,' he said.

'Christ Almighty,' Patsy said as he took the package.

'Unfortunately, we haven't got a receipt for it,' Deano said, and everyone laughed.

They had bought Patsy a fabulous music centre.

It was obvious they had bundles of money. They would not hear of me or Patsy buying any more drinks, and on Jack's left wrist was a Rolex watch, which I suspected was worth around twelve grand.

We stayed at the hotel until around 9 P.M. when Patsy

339

said it was time to move on to his party at The Elbow Room. Jack promptly told the barman to charge all the drinks we'd had to his room. Thank God for that: it must have come to over a hundred quid.

Before we made a move, I decided to pop into the loo. I hadn't been in there long when Deano came in.

'Lovely night, eh, Charlie? We're going to have a great time at Albert's.'

'Yeah,' I said. 'Mind you, I haven't got the money to keep up with you guys.'

'Don't worry about it, old mate,' he said.

And he slipped me fifty quid.

I was pleased I'd decided to come up to Birmingham. These guys were the business. Who knows, I thought, some of their wealth might rub off on me. We might be able to do some business.

When we arrived at The Elbow Room, I was far from sober, but not in one of my depressions, thankfully. Whether it was because of the company, I don't know, but I felt great and determined to enjoy myself. When I rang Judy, drunkenly, at midnight, I told her about Jack and his pals, and the money they were flashing around. I said they were really lovely, genuine guys who liked me. She said she hoped something might come from the new friendship.

Over the next couple of weeks, Jack kept in touch on the phone. And when I told him that a friend of mine, John Corbett, was holding a charity evening at his pub in Kent to raise money for St Christopher's Hospice in Crystal Palace where Gary had died, Jack was enthusiastic.

'I'll get you a football signed by the Newcastle United team, which you can raffle,' he said. 'I'll pop down with a pal of mine, Ken, and give it to you and John.'

They came on 23 May and I arranged for them to stay at The Selsdon Park Hotel, near our home in Sanderstead.

340

John and I took them to a couple of nightclubs in Croydon, ending up at The Blue Orchid, and, once again, Jack would not let us put our hands in our pockets. He was such a lovely guy; so generous.

When I told Jack that another friend of mine, Laurie O'Leary, was putting on a variety show at The Mermaid Theatre – in memory of Gary – he was as enthusiastic as he had been about John's pub charity.

'Ken and I would love to come down, Charlie,' he said. 'It would be nice to show support and meet some of your friends.'

I thought it would be nice, too.

That Sunday evening, 2 June, was a roaring success. An Elvis Presley lookalike called Liberty Mountain was top of the bill and very good. But, for me, the star was Brian Hall – the East End actor who played Terry, the chef, in *Fawlty Towers*. He performed an hilarious skit on the famous *Cabaret* number, 'If You Could See Her Through My Eyes', using a pig puppet for a prop, and had everyone in stitches. It was a terrific, professional performance by any standards, but what most of the 300 people in the audience did not know was that Brian should not have been on stage at all. Only a year before, he had had his left kidney removed after doctors discovered a cancerous growth, and now he was suffering from a tumour behind his left eye. He should have been at home in Sussex, looking after himself and his lovely wife, Marlene, but he chose to honour his commitment to Laurie. That says it all about Brian Hall.

After the show, certain guests were invited upstairs for drinks. There were people from all walks of life, including Billy Murray, my old mate, Freddie Foreman, and his actor son, Jamie, and of course, Big Albert.

And there was Jack and his sidekick, Ken. They were keen to meet as many people as they could and I obliged.

I was happy to. They had been good to me and had travelled a long way.

I introduced my new-found friends from Newcastle to dozens of people that bitter-sweet night. One of them was Ronnie Field. Another was Bobby Gould.

My hopes that some money might be forthcoming from the Newcastle connection rose a couple of weeks later when Jack rang, suggesting that I fly up for a meeting. He said, 'We might be able to get some business sorted between us.

'And bring Ronnie,' he told me. 'Don't worry about money – I'll arrange for two tickets to be left at Gatwick. It's easier and quicker to fly.'

I couldn't believe my luck. 'Some business sorted between us.' After all the disappointments with Ian and the oil deal, maybe these wealthy Geordies were going to come up with something that would end my financial misery.

Ronnie and I flew from Gatwick on Wednesday 25 June. Jack and Ken picked us up at Newcastle Airport in a Range Rover and drove us to a five-star hotel, The Linden Hall, on the outskirts of the city, where Jack introduced us to another of his friends. He was a hulking great geezer, dark haired, six foot and pushing twenty stone. He had a goatee beard and Jack said his name was Brian.

Once again, Jack proved a faultless host, plying us with drinks the moment we walked through the door. It was the night England were playing Germany in the semi-final of the European Championship at Wembley and the Geordies were keen to watch it. I was, too, although I must admit I would have preferred to talk about the bit of business Jack had in mind before settling down to watch a football match, no matter how crucial it was to the country.

Later that afternoon, I rang Judy at work to tell her that we had arrived safely and were going to eat in the hotel restaurant before watching the match.

'Jack is looking after us brilliant,' I said. 'They're really lovely people.'

And I meant it.

I lost count of the number of Scotch and cokes I had, and by the time we went to bed I was so drunk I could not find my room key. I staggered downstairs to ask the girl on the reception desk if I'd left it there. I can't recall what she said, but the key must have turned up somewhere, because I woke up in the right room the next morning.

The trip was pleasant enough; I'd drunk myself silly and it hadn't cost me a penny. But I still had not solved my financial worries.

That July, another emotional period was looming: what would have been Gary's forty-fifth birthday on Wednesday, the third; and my seventieth on Tuesday, the ninth. Big Albert insisted on throwing a party for me in Birmingham on Thursday, the eleventh, and I, in turn, insisted that Judy got time off from work, so that we could go together. Seventy years is a significant landmark in one's life and it promised to be quite a night, if tinged with sadness over Gary.

Money, though, was now a critical problem. I didn't even have enough for a packet of fags, let alone a coach ride for two to Birmingham. When Jack rang, the Sunday afternoon before my party, I took the opportunity to ask him if he would lend me five hundred quid.

'That's no problem, Charlie,' he said. 'I mean, I know it'll be safe.'

I was embarrassed. 'But I need it, like, well tomorrow, sort of thing. I know you can't get it tomorrow, but I was wondering if you could put it in the post tomorrow morning early. I'll get it Tuesday morning, 'cos I need it before I go to Birmingham.'

'Ain't a problem, mate. I'll get that in the post for you.'

'I appreciate it, Jack,' I said.

And I was very grateful to him.

The cash arrived in a Jiffy bag by registered mail on Tuesday morning. It was a life-saver: it helped reduce Judy's bank overdraft, bought some essentials for the house and left us a little bit of spending money for Thursday.

Again, I found myself thinking: what a lovely, generous fella Jack was.

As luck would have it, Fethi was holding a spectacular VIP dinner/buffet at his hotel that Thursday, to launch officially his Medallion Vert restaurant after extensive refurbishment. He had hired a huge marquee for the grounds and the food that kept coming out of hotel kitchen would have graced a State banquet.

Again, Fethi allowed Judy and I to stay at the hotel for nothing – as a birthday present for me, presumably. Jack and Brian were staying there, too, and we all met up at the bar, preparing to enjoy Fethi's hospitality before going on to The Elbow Room. With Jack and Brian still eager to get the drinks in, the evening was a wonderful curtain-raiser to my own party, and it was made even more special when Jack handed me a little package, neatly wrapped in colourful paper.

'Happy birthday from Brian and me, Charlie,' he said.

When I opened it and saw a beautiful gold-plated cigarette lighter, I was lost for words. What lovely guys, I thought: they've only known me eight weeks, but they must think a lot of me to buy me a birthday present. I did not have much time to dwell on what to say to thank them, however, because Jack was back at the bar again, ordering more champagne.

Around 10 P.M., me and Judy went on to The Elbow Room, leaving Jack and Brian at the hotel. They re-joined us around midnight, by which time I was feeling no pain – and certainly not my age!

We all rolled out of the club at around 3.30 A.M. Me and

Judy took a taxi to The Wake Green Lodge. Jack went back, too, but not Brian: he had struck lucky with an attractive blonde and, it seemed, was going back to her home.

I did not hear from Jack again until Saturday 20 July, when he phoned, asking me to tell Ronnie to contact him. Four days later he rang again to say he was coming to London the next day, the 25th, and would I book him into the Selsdon Park again. I wondered why he couldn't ring the hotel himself, but I did it anyway. On the afternoon of the 25th, I was at Robin McGibbon's home, near Bromley, in Kent, working on the revision to this book when Judy rang, telling me that Jack wanted me to pop into the hotel and have a drink with him, Brian, Ronnie Field and Bob Gould.

I did not really want to go, but as I had to pass the hotel on the way home, I decided to pop in for a quick whisky. Typically, Jack tried to twist my arm to have a double, but I insisted on just a single. I was whacked from working on the book and all I wanted was to get home to Judy and the kids and put my feet up.

The following Wednesday morning, I drove to Kent again to work on the book. I spent from 11.30 until 4.15 reading the completed up-date, then left to pick up Judy from work at 5 P.M.

I was in a good mood. I was still as broke as ever, but my account of all that had happened since *Me and My Brothers* was published in 1988 read well and I was confident that sales of the new edition would help ease my financial worries.

How wrong can you be! What happened two hours later not only put the block on the book, but put me behind bars.

Judy had cooked dinner and, at 7 P.M., we were settling down to watch television when there was a firm knock on the front door. Judy answered it then came back into the lounge, followed by four policemen – two uniformed bobbies and two plain-clothed detectives. As they walked in, two other detectives came into the room through the patio doors.

One of the detectives gestured for me to get up, then told me I was being arrested on drug charges. All the time he was cautioning me and advising me of my rights I was in a daze; seeing six policemen in that tiny lounge seemed unreal and I had no idea what it was all about.

The detective in charge asked me to go upstairs with them because they needed to search the bedroom. I assumed they were looking for drugs, but they found none because there were none to be found. It was all very calm and civilized, while the detectives went through the rest of the house. A very subdued and confused Judy made cups of tea for the uniformed guys, who sat making polite conversation with her and the three children.

I was asked to sign for various papers the police were taking with them, then, at 9 P.M., I was asked if I wanted to change out of my tracksuit bottoms into something more appropriate.

Judy was shocked. 'Are they taking you away, Charlie?'

'Yes, darling,' I said. 'They've arrested me.'

Judy was crestfallen. She assumed I would merely be asked to report to a police station with my solicitor the next day.

I kissed her goodbye, then went with the police to a car waiting outside to take me to Ilford police station. As we drove off, I looked at Judy in the doorway, her face creased with worry. I felt my eyes filling up. Just what did all this mean?

I found out the next day when the full story was outlined in the presence of my solicitor. And at 10 P.M. that evening, when Judy was allowed to see me, bringing fresh clothes for my appearance in court the next day, I broke it to her as gently as I could.

We were allowed to spent five minutes alone together in an interview room. As she came in, I got up from a chair, and took her in my arms and hugged her.

'I'm so sorry, darling,' I said.

Then, my voice choking with emotion, I whispered, 'That lovely guy, Jack. He's an undercover cop. He's been tape recording me talking about cocaine.'

Chapter Twenty-two

There were twenty tapes in all: some were recorded from transmitters concealed on Jack's body, others on the phone. On most of them, I was told, me and Ronnie Field could be heard offering to supply Jack and his two mates, Brian and Ken, with five kilograms of cocaine every two weeks for two years.

After Judy left, I sat in my cell and let my mind drift back over the summer months to that Thursday evening in May when I'd met Jack for the first time in The Wake Green Lodge Hotel. I needed to know why the police had slipped Jack into me to set me up, and who had helped them.

My old mate, Patsy, had made the introduction at the hotel, but he would not have known Jack was old Bill, I could bet on that: we went back more than thirty years; and anyway Patsy had no reason to cause me any aggravation.

I could picture the other two guys with Patsy that night, but, for a while, I couldn't remember their names. Then they came back to me: George and Deano. Funny, I thought now: neither Patsy, nor I, had thought of asking their surnames. And, on reflection, Deano was an odd name. Why wasn't it just Dean? That night was the first time I had met him, but I'd met George at Gary's grave. I vaguely remembered Patsy saying that George had driven them down in Indian Joe's Jaguar. Now, sitting in my cell in Ilford nick, I started wondering what that had all been about. George had never known Gary. Why had he made a two hundred-mile round trip to be at his funeral? And, by the sound of it, he had never met Patsy before, either.

And what about Deano, who was supposed to be George's

brother, slipping me that fifty quid. It hadn't struck me as odd at the time: I thought he was just a lovely fella with bundles of money, who liked me. But now, trying to piece it all together, it sounded iffy.

Patsy's birthday present, for instance: Jack had met Patsy for the first time that Thursday night and George and Deano had known him only a matter of weeks, yet they had splashed out on a music centre that must have set them back two hundred quid, not to mention the *Simply Red* CD. In view of what had happened, it did not take me long to work that one out. They had massaged dear old Patsy's ego to get to me. The fifty quid from Deano was just a little taster to whet my appetite; I would soon be getting a birthday present, too. My mind went back to the same little hotel, almost two months to the day later. George and Deano were off the scene by then and Jack was there with Brian, another mate he'd introduced me to along the way. I remembered Jack handing me the gold cigarette lighter, neatly wrapped in colourful paper, smiling: 'Happy birthday from Brian and me, Charlie.'

At the time, I was flattered.

Now, I felt sick.

My mind was in such turmoil that Friday morning of 2 August that I did not fall asleep until the thin grey light of dawn began to brighten the darkness of my cell. I kept thinking over and over again about all the meetings I'd had with Jack and his pals over the past two and a half months: The Wake Green that May, the Selsdon two weeks later, the Mermaid 'do' on 2 June, the trip to Newcastle later that month and the Selsdon again on 25 July. It had not crossed my mind that he was an undercover cop, taped up to record anything that might incriminate me in something unlawful. All he seemed was a wealthy wheeler-dealer with a bottom-less well of cash; a soft touch who might be able to solve my desperate financial problems.

What was on those tapes? I wondered.

And what price would I have to pay for all that free champagne Jack and his pals had poured down me since that fateful meeting on Patsy's sixty-sixth birthday?

Later that morning, I was taken to Redbridge Magistrates' Court in Ilford, but it all felt so unreal it might just as well have been Mars. One minute, I'd been settling down to watch telly with the woman I loved; the next, I was standing in a crowded court, with a mass of newspaper, radio and TV reporters staring at me as though I was an alien from outer space.

I looked towards the public seats and was relieved to see Judy, with a couple of our friends, who had travelled with her from Croydon. It was a hell of a journey, particularly in the morning rush hour and I was so grateful for the support. I gave her a brief, faint smile, trying to convey, in a fleeting second, that I was sure everything was going to be all right. Bad as I was feeling, my heart went out to her; she must be worried sick. At the end of her row, nearer the dock, was an old man, with a copy of the *Sun* on his lap. On the front page was a photograph of me, under the headline: CHARLIE KRAY IN £78 MILLION COCAINE STING. My mind flashed back to the sixties when me and the twins were pulled in. The newspapers had had a field day then, too, making it seem like we were all guilty of the most heinous crimes before we'd even been charged with anything.

There I was, standing in a court, with holes in my shoes, wearing a ten-pound watch and not a penny in my pockets, and I'm supposed to be involved in some multi-million pound drug operation.

Still feeling removed from what was going on around me, I stood in the dock with Ronnie Field and Bobby Gould. The three of us were each charged with conspiracy to supply two kilos of cocaine, worth £63,000, and conspiracy to supply 520 kilos of the drug. Me and Field were also accused of conspiracy to supply 1,000 ecstasy tablets worth £20,000.

Next on the agenda was bail. Not surprisingly, it was refused. I was seventy years old with no money or assets and no risk to anyone, but my name was Kray. Guilty or not, I was going to be treated as if I was a dangerous terrorist, evil killer and ruthless rapist rolled into one. I was convinced I'd be holed up in a top-security prison and I was right. They chose Belmarsh, near Woolwich, in South East London, where they cage callous IRA murderers. I thought I'd be put on Category A security, but I was wrong about that. The powers-that-be felt I was such a danger they put me on an even higher security.

In case anyone missed the point that the police had nailed one of the most dangerous men in the country, armed police in flak jackets manned the rooftops of Barkingside Magistrates' Court – the venue for the next committal proceedings on 9 August. And I was driven there from Woolwich at high speed, with police motorcyclists riding ahead to clear the traffic. The only parts of the circus missing were the deafening klaxons and circling helicopters that had accompanied me and the twins and their so-called Firm to the Old Bailey in 1969.

Thankfully, someone saw the stupidity in carting me from South East London to Essex, and arranged for the next committal hearing to be held at Woolwich Magistrates' Court, which is on the same complex as Belmarsh prison. Instead of having to be driven through South London, under the Blackwall Tunnel and through a busy part of East London, all I had to do was walk along a tunnel – escorted by prisoner officers – and up into the court. It took about twenty minutes, compared to more than an hour on the road to Essex.

Despite offering to be electronically tagged on both feet,

not just one, I was still considered too much of a risk to be allowed home. Where they thought I'd go, with no money or passport, no one was saying. If it wasn't so awful, I'd have laughed. Could the magistrate have really believed in the Kray fantasy; that I was some superhuman being with hidden millions and the contacts to spirit me away at the drop of a generous backhander? As it was, I had no inclination to try to escape. I'd thrown in my lot with Judy and the kids and I was not going to abandon them now.

One of the reasons they felt I might try to escape was that, at seventy, I would not want to risk a long jail sentence. That showed the ignorance of the police and judiciary. Anyone who knew me was aware that, despite having a name synonymous with all that is evil, I am a man of principle, who faces up to his accusers and does not run away from them.

I was warned that my trial would not start until the following summer. That September, summer seemed light years away. I wondered how I would get through it.

The three of us – me, Ronnie Field and Bobby Gould – were locked up in the High Security Unit, Category A, with IRA hit men, PLO terrorists, ruthless Yardie killers and a gold bullion robber.

There was another gentleman in there, too: David Courtney, a bubbly Cockney in his thirties, who had been on remand for two months, awaiting trial on an alleged drug smuggling charge. Me and the twins had known Dave for about twelve years: he ran a security company, employing heavies, who manned the doors of nightclubs. We had used him to take care of security at Ronnie's funeral. I was pleased when I met Dave in Belmarsh: he has an agile brain, a sharp wit and a positive attitude, and I knew he would be good for me; a loyal ally.

Dave told me that when he was sent to Belmarsh, a prison official had told him, 'Mr Courtney, I don't care who you know outside, what finances you've got or what you think. This place is designed to break you.'

Dave laughed. 'Wait a minute,' he told him, 'you don't even know me. This place isn't going to bend me a little bit, let alone break me. I'm going home in a few months. I'm going to use this as a learning experience and have a good time.'

And that's what he did. He took it on himself to be the court jester for the whole unit and tried to make each day memorable by getting up to the most outrageous antics to give everyone a giggle. Once, as an ironic gesture to the prison's Fort Knox-like security, he stripped naked, wrote his address on his stomach, stuck a stamp on his forehead, then lay in the mail tray, waiting to be posted. The prison's writing paper gave him an idea for his own headed note paper. At the top of the prison paper, where it left a space for the prisoner to write in his relevant wing, Dave wrote 'Commander', and had some fancy letter-heads made up, saying, 'Wing Commander David Courtney', with his cell as his office number. Then he started sending off to companies, asking for sales literature on dozens of bizarre products, because he knew that all his mail went to the Home Office and had to be read before being forwarded to him. The thought of someone having to plough through hundreds of pages of literature that he had no intention of reading himself gave Dave a buzz, and helped break up the monotony of hum drum prison life.

Dave, more than anyone, helped me adjust to life in that claustrophobic, security-conscious unit. But there was someone else I turned to in order to keep my sanity – Gary. Even now I could not bring myself to accept that he was gone, and I would look at his photos in my cell and talk to him as if he was there with me.

What, I'd ask him, do you think of the mess I've got

353

myself into? What do you make of this tiny, spartan cell that's going to be my home for the best part of a year? It was roughly ten feet by six: the bed was a metal slab jutting out of the wall and the mattress and pillow, flattened by dozens of prisoners before me, were not worth having. A table and chair, also metal, were attached to the wall and another piece of metal, highly polished admittedly, served as a mirror. In Category AA, no one was taking any chances that anything in the cell could be broken and used as a weapon on himself or a guard.

The doors of the twelve cells – six opposite each other in a rectangular block about twenty yards by twelve – were opened at 8 A.M. Half an hour later we had breakfast: cornflakes, porridge, one rasher of bacon, or one fried egg.

At 9 A.M. we were allowed to walk around an exercise yard, which was about a quarter of the size of a football pitch, for an hour. I wanted to see the sky, but it was blotted out by a roof made of bomb-proof wiremesh, designed to make it impossible for a helicopter to drop down and pluck a dangerous undesirable like me to freedom! In case someone thought of a way round that, the exercise times were staggered with those of the other thirty-six prisoners in the other three high-risk units, so that no one with ideas of escaping could be sure he would be in the exercise yard at a set time.

Such was the paranoia over security that, while we were on exercise, all twelve cells would be searched and anything we'd written down – particularly pertaining to legal matters – copied by a prison officer on a portable photocopier. I'm not sure whether the authorities wanted to keep this secret, but the cells were so tiny and sparse that most of us could tell at a glance whether anyone had been in there. And, besides, the smell of the photocopier – and the paw-prints of the officer's dog, used for sniffing out possible drugs – was a giveaway!

By the time we had been through the electronically-controlled doors and strip-searched, it would be around 11 A.M. We were normally allowed to watch TV or make phone calls until midday, when the caterers came in with lunch. We would collect our meals and we were then banged up until 2.30 P.M., when we were let out again for three hours. At 5 P.M. we were banged up for the night.

Cameras were on us twenty-four hours a day – even in the toilet – but we would regularly be moved from one cell to another. If a prisoner had the inclination to try to dig a tunnel in his cell, it would be pointless; he'd never have time to finish it before he was moved to another.

There was even less privacy on the phone. I was allowed to make calls at certain times of the day, but the phone faced a bullet-proof screen, behind which a prison officer watched me as he tape-recorded every second of my conversation.

I would long for visiting times.

Only Judy, Robin and John Corbett were cleared to see me – once a week – in the first six months of my remand. I wished away the days to their visits so that I could have what I call a 'normal, everyday' conversation, without reference to prison or anything criminal.

Getting to the visiting cubicles took half an hour, which was tedious. I had to go through all the doors again and be strip-searched, but it was always worth it because I'd go back to my cell, feeling more positive about things. It didn't matter that the hour-long visits were filmed and taped, because nothing remotely dodgy was ever discussed.

I was determined to keep myself fit by going to the gym regularly for a work out. Prisoners are allowed fifteen minutes every day, which can be enough if you're doing the right things. But getting to the gym was a drag. Each time, I had to go through ten electronically-controlled doors, taking my clothes off twice to be searched by guards with metal detectors. It took three times as long to get to and from the gym, as the time I spent there and, in the end, it gave me the hump and I knocked it on the head.

That was my life on remand until 14 April this year, when, at long last, my trial was due to begin next door. Thankfully, the charges had been significantly changed: I was now accused of offering to supply cocaine and supplying two kilos of the drug.

I was relieved that the time had come, but I was not without a few nerves. I had read and digested all the incriminating tapes and was under no illusion that I had a huge battle on my hands.

I was confident, however, that I had one of the country's top barristers in my corner, who was going to fight my case as vigorously as he could. His name was Jonathan Goldberg. He had been called to the Bar in February 1971 and made a QC in April 1989. He was a dapper, elegant man, just turned fifty, with close-cropped steel-grey hair, and an abrasive manner, bordering on rudeness. That bothered me little. What he lacked in bedside charm, he made up for with a brilliant legal brain, gritty determination and an impressive track record of dazzling courtroom triumphs against the odds.

I felt in the best possible hands. Whether Mr Goldberg believed my version of what had happened between meeting Jack on 9 May and my arrest on 31 July, the previous year, I didn't know. But he seemed to like me.

I had faith in him.

Chapter Twenty-three

The prosecution claimed that the curtain went up on my personal drama in The Elbow Room on 9 May, when Jack told me he had been left 'a bit dry' after a guy he was trading with had been 'topped' in Amsterdam.

I knew he was talking about drugs, it was alleged, because I told him I had a mate who could supply him with large quantities of cocaine on a regular basis. Two weeks later, Jack and a pal, named Ken, came down to London with a football – signed by the Newcastle United team – to be auctioned at John Corbett's pub, in aid of St Christopher's Hospice.

I arranged for them to stay at The Selsdon Park Hotel and met Jack and Ken there to talk further about supplying cocaine. It was claimed that I told Jack that I never went near it and only put people together, ''cos I've too many eyes on me'.

Nine days later, I introduced Jack and Ken to Ronnie Field and Bobby Gould at The Mermaid Theatre, where drugs were discussed. On 18 June Jack invited me and Ronnie Field to Newcastle and paid for us to fly there on the following Wednesday.

On Thursday 27 June, it was alleged, me and Field agreed to supply Jack with five kilos of cocaine every two weeks for two years and said the first exchange would take place at the Selsdon Park Hotel the following month.

On 25 July, Field and Gould met Jack and Ken at the hotel, but the exchange was aborted and re-arranged for the following night at The Swallow Hotel, at Waltham Abbey.

That exchange did not happen either, it was said. But Field and Gould did hand over two kilos of cocaine to Jack at The Swallow the following Wednesday evening, in return for £63,000 – and I had set up the deal.

My defence was that the curtain went up on 21 March, when an undercover cop, called George, infiltrated my son Gary's funeral to ingratiate himself with Patsy Manning.

The point of this was to be introduced to me so that I could, subsequently, be entrapped into committing a crime. Believing Jack and his pals to be wealthy drug dealers, I agreed with Ronnie Field to pretend to be drug dealers ourselves to get some money out of them.

I was all geared up for the trial to begin on Monday 14 April but, first, vital issues of law had to be thrashed out before Judge Michael Carroll in a pre-trial hearing called a *voire dire*. If I doubted what a huge mountain I faced, that first day convinced me. The judge seemed not only heavily biased against me, but anti Mr Goldberg, too, particularly on the subject of jury protection.

The Crown Prosecutor, John Kelsey-Fry, pressed for a twenty-four-hour guard on the jury because, he argued, the consequences of conviction to a man my age might prove an incentive to me – or someone with my interests at heart – to try to interfere with the jury.

To give this ludicrous idea credence, he suggested that because of the large amount of cocaine involved in the case, I had access to lots of money and could afford to pay someone to nobble the jury.

I found it hard to believe, but I shouldn't have been surprised. The notoriety of the Kray name had done me many favours over the years, but it was bound to be bad news for me in court, despite all that rubbish about being innocent until proven guilty.

Mr Goldberg showed his fighting qualities by arguing a strong case against jury protection. Quoting Lord Hailsham – 'Everyone is entitled to a fair trial by an untainted jury' – he said it was impossible for me to have a fair trial if the jury was prejudiced. And they would be if they believed they were being guarded because one of the notorious Kray family was in the dock. Quite simply, I would be starting the trial ten points down, he said.

I sat there, shaking my head. To get at the jury, a member of the public would first have to be able to recognize them, and that was impossible because the gallery is situated directly above the jury box and every juror is hidden from view. The only people able to see them – apart from me – were the lawyers, the police, reporters and court staff. What was Kelsey-Fry trying to insinuate? That some underworld pal of mine would peer down from the gallery, select a likely candidate, then try to bribe he or she to get hold of a juror's name and address? How nonsensical!

The only way to see the jury was to get into the court itself. But that was impossible: everyone going into court had to produce identification and pass through a metal detector, watched all the time by two armed policemen. Even journalists were directed to the public gallery if they did not have a valid, and authorized, Press Card. So, Joe Public had no chance of even getting anywhere near the door of the court.

Mr Goldberg fought several battles on the jury protection front, but, in the end, lost the war: the judge ruled that the twelve ladies and gentlemen would, indeed, be guarded round the clock.

The injustice of this surveillance, as the judge insisted on calling it, angered me, but I was grateful to Mr Goldberg for fighting it all the way. He was a pugnacious guy and clearly showed no fear of Judge Carroll. It bode well for the bigger battles that lay ahead.

*　　*　　*

As far as I could gather, what Mr Goldberg had to do in the *voire dire* was to persuade the judge to kick out evidence that would have an adverse effect on proceedings once the jury was sworn in and the trial proper began. He wanted all my conversations – on and off tape – ruled inadmissible, because of the way the undercover police had incited me to commit a criminal act. For me, though, I felt my best chance lay with discrediting the police with the evidence of our surprise witness, Michelle Hamdouchi, a buxom blonde in her early thirties, who had been in The Elbow Room for my seventieth birthday celebrations.

She was the woman Brian had gone home with in the early hours. What he did not know was that she had made a statement to my solicitor eight months before, in which she claimed she had had sex with Brian that Thursday night, and a further sexual encounter with him at The Swallow Hotel on 27 July.

When Brian gave evidence at the *voire dire* he denied he had sex with Michelle, and claimed her arrival at The Swallow Hotel was a 'complete surprise' to him. I was elated, because Michelle was a believable witness and if her evidence didn't brand Brian a liar, then testimony from the staff at The Swallow Hotel would. That night, I went back to my prison cell, convinced that Brian would be discredited in the eyes of the judge and that he would rule his evidence inadmissible in front of the jury.

Once again, I was totally wrong.

When the judge made his ruling at the end of the *voire dire*, he said he was 'unsure' of what had happened between Michelle and Brian; that, even if he felt he was lying, he would not exclude his evidence, because the relationship was unrelated to the conversations between me and the undercover police. He went on to rule that all taped and untaped conversations were admissible and that, indeed, the whole prosecution, as presented at the *voire dire*, would go before the jury.

If Mr Goldberg was disappointed, I was mortified. The judge, I felt, had trumped our best card.

Before falling asleep that night, however, I consoled myself that everything would be different in front of a jury. Twelve ordinary men and women could not fail to be impressed by Michelle's honesty and see through Brian's lies.

The following Wednesday morning, 14 May, the twelve who were to decide my fate were sworn in: seven women and five men. As each stepped forward to take the oath, mid-morning sunshine brightened the modern courtroom. The silence was deafening. Sitting in the dock in my navy-blue suit, light-blue shirt and dark tie, I clenched my fists at my sides and looked at each person closely, trying to read them. What backgrounds did they come from? What were their beliefs? Were they intelligent people, able to take in and understand a trial likely to last six weeks? Were they capable of judging me on the evidence? Or would they prejudge me on my name alone?

Of course, it was impossible to know, but all those thoughts raced through my mind in the fifteen minutes or so it took to swear them all in. They were the people, chosen at random, to decide whether I would walk out a free man or be locked away. All I could ask for, that dramatic morning, was that they were honest citizens who would take their roles seriously. And that they would believe my version of what happened the previous summer. Not the prosecution's.

As Mr Kelsey-Fry rose to outline the prosecution case, I glanced up at the public gallery to my right. Judy was not allowed to attend because she was due to be a witness, but I expected certain friends there that first day. There were none. The gallery was deserted, except for Robin and a woman who had become fascinated with the Krays' exploits after reading *Me and My Brothers*. How times change! When Ronnie, Reggie and me went on trial at the Old Bailey in 1969, queues for the gallery formed two hours before the court opened.

Nothing Mr Kelsey-Fry said that first morning shocked me. I'd been warned to expect the worst and I was long enough in the tooth to know that the prosecution would paint a black picture.

There were two sides to my character, he said. One was an affable, slightly down-at-heel, but popular, character. The other was a man prepared to be involved in the drugs trade, a man who said he would never physically handle drugs, but who pulled both ends of a deal together.

I was pleased to hear Mr Kelsey-Fry tell the jury, up front, not to let my name influence them, even though the fact that I was the Kray twins' brother may explain some of the facts of the case. 'No man is his brother's keeper,' he said. 'Whatever his brothers may or may not have done thirty years ago cannot, in any way, adversely reflect on this defendant. Their actions can't help you determine this man's innocence or guilt on these charges.'

I steeled myself not to glance at the jury for their reaction. It was vital that they separated me from the twins. I stared straight ahead. I knew Mr Goldberg would have a lot to say on that subject. All I could do now was sit there and listen to how me and the other two were arrested; how Jack and his pals were not all they were supposed to be.

'Jack was an undercover police officer,' said Mr Kelsey-Fry. 'As you will know ... it is a legitimate weapon in their battle against serious crime for the police to attempt to infiltrate the underworld, posing as part of that world to attempt to expose criminals. And when they are successful ... it is no defence for those caught to say, "If I'd known

362

they were police I wouldn't have supplied them with drugs." '

I shook my head. No defence! I believed I was enticed into a crime that night in The Elbow Room. All the talk I gave Jack on the tape the following morning was rubbish. If he hadn't followed it up with a phone call the next week, we'd never have seen each other again, I'm sure of that. As it was Kelsey-Fry spelled out the financial aspects of the cocaine deal and the reporters rushed for their calculators and worked out that five kilos of cocaine every two weeks over two years, at £31,500 per kilo, had a street value of £39 million. My whack, they reckoned, was £8 million. Predictably, the next day's papers, under headlines like: 'CHARLIE KRAY OFFERED COPS £39M COCAINE', had me as the mastermind of a deal that would make me a multi-millionaire.

If it had not been my neck on the block, I'd have laughed. How ridiculous!

For the next two days, barristers on both sides, the jury, me and even the judge, put on headphones to listen to the tape recordings on which me and Ronnie Field had allegedly incriminated ourselves. When I'd read the hundreds of pages of transcripts while on remand, I could not believe them. Jack and his pals had seemed so genuine it made me sick to realize they were phoney and had been secretly and deviously taping us all along. Now that I was going to have to *listen* to everything – all the drinking and laughter and joking – I felt worse. I'd been duped.

The first tape was recorded in The Wake Green Lodge when Deano gave Patsy his birthday present, but the prosecution wanted the jury to know only about the next morning when Jack brought up the subject of Amsterdam again.

'I got let down badly . . . my guy got taken out,' I heard Jack say.

'Did you really?' I said. 'And you're looking for some more, or you wanna buy some more?'

'Yeah, yeah. I'm looking for some more.'

'You're looking for some to buy?'

'Yeah.'

'Well, I'll tell you, a mate of mine might be home this weekend. I know someone who's got five hundred.'

'Yeah?'

'Five hundred. And the paperwork. In and it's paid for. It's there.'

'Yeah?'

'So they're very good and they want the transport. I'll get that anyway. I've got the transport.'

I went on, 'My people just go, do it . . . a lot is happening at the moment, but once something happens, I'll let you know.'

Jack said, 'Sweet,' then added: 'I do "charlie" and I do the smoke.'

'It's gonna be another, I think, three or four weeks. Regular, regular, regular, a lot of it, you know what I mean?'

'Are you in a position to talk a price, or will I have to talk to him?'

I said, 'Well, we'll wait till we know.'

'Okay.'

Later on the tape, Jack asks about the 'charlie', and I'm heard saying, 'If anything happens, oh that, that won't be for I think another three or four weeks. Then, when it starts, it will be regular all the time.'

A minute or so later, Deano is driving me from The Wake Green Lodge to the coach station. I'm heard giving Jack my phone number and arranging to see him when he comes to London. Then I say, 'I'm just waiting now. But that other thing will be . . . home grown, a lot of it. It'll be good, I'll tell you, and that should be regular.'

I took off my headphones and glanced at the jury. From my point of view, what we had all heard sounded awful. What were they thinking? I tried to push negative thoughts out of my mind. I had my answers to everything said on those tapes. When it was my turn to speak, they would hear why I said what I did.

The prosecution then covered my meeting with Jack and Ken at The Selsdon Park Hotel on 23 May, and I'm heard saying, '. . . it's a bit embarrassing to fucking go and admit it, like, when I was up there last time, but what's happened, you know, I lost about fucking a hundred grand on a deal.'

Jack said, 'No, I didn't know.'

'Well, I did, and, er, it put me on the floor, 'cos I got money coming to me, but it don't come in, 'till, like certain times.'

'Yeah?'

'But, yesterday, things came together, like, didn't have to, some people and, er, things they came together. I set it up.'

'Yeah?'

'And this was . . . the awkward thing.'

'Uh, uh.'

'But I've put fucking five grand up yesterday. And that was it as far as I'm concerned.'

'Yeah?'

'Until I get this, mind you. It's only gonna take a couple of fucking weeks, it'll be done, but, and it's knocked me bandy.'

'Yeah,' Jack is heard to say.

'But there you go, you have to do these things if you're going to get anywhere. You know you gotta do something about it.'

'Yeah.'

'So, fucking, if it comes, that's why I lost all that money. It's so good and if it comes, like well, it will now, it will happen, so outstanding, so like now, it'll be done, it's, if it does and it goes steady and fucking.'

'Yeah.'

'Like you had a chance with this . . .'

'Yeah?'

'It's the other gear, obviously, you know.'

'Which?' Jack is heard to ask. 'The smaller gear?'

'No, the other.'

' "Charlie"?'

'Yeah,' I said. 'We'll know more. It's going to be a lot and it's going to be regular . . .'

'Yeah?'

'Be the right price as well.'

'Yeah? What are they talking about?'

' 'Cos I don't want to meet . . .'

'Obviously.'

'I don't never get near it, and they all know it.'

'Yeah?'

'I put people together and do this and running about. I ain't . . . I said it won't be my partner, it's me fucking make a big business out of it. It wouldn't be true and my brother, it'll affect him in the nick . . .'

'Yeah?'

'Right, I've done it all, I've committed all these things in my life, so I now have to take, steady on, you know, 'cos I've too many eyes on me.'

I have to admit I squirmed when I heard myself, not so much what I was saying, although that was bad enough, but the swearing. Anyone who knows me is aware that I *never* use foul language. I can't understand it. I must have been drunk.

We talk about the signed football Jack has brought for John Corbett's charity evening, then I'm heard saying that we'll go to The Blue Orchid, in Purley.

The next morning, Jack rang me, and I'm heard saying,

'Went for a little drink, didn't we? My pal, Steve, wasn't there, he had to go do something. But we had a good night anyway.'

Kelsey-Fry seemed to place a lot of significance on Steve. I would learn why later.

The next stage in the scenario was The Mermaid Theatre variety show, on 2 June, which Jack invited himself to when he stayed at The Selsdon Park Hotel. There were a few hundred people from all walks of life at The Mermaid and I introduced many to Jack and Ken. The only two the prosecution wanted the jury to know about, however, were Ronnie Field and Bobby Gould. Jack claimed I took him into a corridor to introduce him to them, and we talked about drugs.

Three weeks later, Ronnie and I were royally entertained, no expense spared, at the fabulous Linden Hall Hotel, just outside Newcastle, and this is where Jack came on strong. The morning after a heavy drinking night before, he invited us into his hotel room and quickly got down to business. It was all recorded.

He started off, 'Well, the reason we're here, I suppose, is the "charlie" . . . we want to do the business with that . . . we want to know how much regular and, obviously, how much, you know.'

A few seconds later, I was heard to say, 'At the moment we're guessing, but we know it's gonna, it'll be all right, it's just we ain't got it. I mean, we know it will be all right.'

Ronnie said, '. . . it's like good, like good gear. We know we can come to an agreement on the price.'

After a brief discussion on price and delivery, I'm then heard speaking in a low voice, 'I'm not exaggerating, but if you had a ton tomorrow, we've got people who've got the readies *immediately*.'

Brian replied, 'Well . . . we're not going to be introducing to somebody else. We'd rather just . . .'

Ronnie broke in, 'You won't see no one else.'

And I said, 'No one else? Only Bob. You know he's working now. That's it.'

Ronnie repeated, 'You won't see no one else.'

'No one else,' I echoed.

Seconds later, I was heard saying, 'What we're talking about now, we got people that do hundreds a week . . . now he can do, he can do, forty a week . . . easy.'

'I can do forty of this a week,' Ronnie agreed.

'What, the blow?' Jack asked.

'No,' Ronnie said. 'The "charlie".'

Jack is heard to question whether he should ring me and Ronnie says, 'Charlie don't know where these boxes are.'

And I say, '. . . I don't want to know and he does it, and that's how we do it all the time.'

Later, on the tape, talking about another meeting at The Selsdon in a few weeks, I say, '. . . 'cos we don't know when we'll see Steve. He might say, hold up, it ain't gonna be here till Monday, then . . .'

Ronnie describes how the cocaine will be delivered, '. . . it'll be wrapped. Comes in like a, erm, rubber wrapping, like a bag . . . vacuum sealed. Then it's wrapped up in tape and it's got another bag around the outside of it.'

And I said, 'Will it be wrapped in, or should it be wrapped the same as our one?'

I would later regret chiming in with that comment.

Over the next two weeks, the tape recordings proved that Jack rang me five times pressing me to ask Ronnie to contact him about the deal. And on the third call, on 2 July, he invited himself – with Brian or Ken – to my seventieth birthday party at The Elbow Room on 11 July.

On the Sunday before the party, Jack phoned me and asked me to call him back because he was in a phone box.

I'm heard asking if Jack had spoken to Ron, then saying, 'I've been told it could be tomorrow or Tuesday.' I then ask Jack to send me five hundred quid as a loan because I've not got enough money to get up to Birmingham for the party. When he hears I'm staying at The Wake Green Lodge Hotel, he says that he and Brian will stay there, too. Then, in a phone call on the Wednesday, Jack asks if Ronnie is going to Birmingham.

'No,' I'm heard to say. 'He can't 'cos he's waiting for something.'

Nine days after the party, Jack rang me again and I'm heard telling him, 'We're on the verge, but not there.'

'Okay, mate,' he said.

'You know what I mean?'

'Yeah.'

'I spoke to Ron this morning.'

'Yeah.'

'You know, 'cos he rang.'

'Uh, uh.'

'And I said, fucking drag, innit.'

'Yeah.'

'Waiting. Gets on your nerves, don't it?'

On Wednesday 24 July, Jack rang Ron, who is heard telling him, 'You can put your name to how many you want. We got hundred here at the moment.'

'A hundred?' Jack asks.

'Yeah.'

A meeting is then arranged at The Selsdon Park Hotel at 6 P.M. the following night, when Jack will buy five kilograms of cocaine for £157,500.

Four hours later Jack rang me to say he had spoken to

'our friend' and would I book two rooms at The Selsdon for the next night.

Mr Kelsey-Fry told the court that I visited the hotel that Thursday evening, but stayed only fifteen minutes or so. During that time, drugs were not mentioned.

Then the jury was told of another recorded phone call Jack made to me on Friday morning. After asking if I had spoken to 'our friend', Jack said, 'There were some problems last night.'

'Held up was it?' I asked.

'Pardon me?'

'Was it held up?'

'Yeah, there was a problem with it.'

'Oh, I see,' I said.

'Our friend was going to sort it out for eleven o'clock this morning.'

Jack suggested re-arranging the meeting with Ronnie and Bobby Gould for 6 P.M. that evening at The Swallow Hotel and asked me to contact Ronnie to tell him.

I was heard agreeing to do that.

Then Jack said, 'Ronnie will tell you, it went a bit fucking horrible last night . . . there was a couple of clowns came on to the plot.'

At 11.58 A.M. twenty-three minutes after Ronnie had called him, Jack phoned me again to tell me 'everything's sorted', and to ask me if I was going to The Swallow Hotel myself. I said I was not.

The jury then heard this conversation on tape:

Jack: 'Okay mate, did he tell you about the disaster last night?'

Me: '. . . tell me like, yeah.'

Jack: 'What a muppet that guy was. I mean, I couldn't believe it, walking in, he's just off his face with it, you know.'

Me: 'Oh, yeah, yeah, yeah. What, the big guy?'

Jack: 'The big guy, yeah.'

Me: 'Oh, yeah, I know. I'll have a word with someone today.'

It was another conversation I would regret.

That Friday afternoon, Jack rang again, worried that Ronnie had not phoned at 1 P.M., as promised.

I said on tape, 'No, no, he said he's waiting, 'til he gets that thing and then, when he's got it in his hand, then he's going to ring you immediately . . .'

In the end, the scheduled exchange at The Swallow never happened. But something else did, which would embarrass the police greatly. Michelle Hamdouchi, who claimed to have had sex with Brian at her home after my birthday party, arrived at the hotel around 1 A.M., and enjoyed Brian's company again. Her evidence at the *voire dire* had rocked the undercover men's superiors, who knew nothing of Brian's indiscretion and felt they should have. Hopefully, when she went into the witness box again, she would expose Brian – and possibly Jack – as liars. At best, this would discredit them as reliable witnesses and get the case against me thrown out. At worst, it might persuade the jury to take what they claimed I said with a pinch of salt, particularly when it was backed up only by their handwritten notes, often written many hours after an alleged conversation had taken place.

When Mr Goldberg got up to outline the defence case, he said he faced a 'unique difficulty' as far as his career was concerned. He was defending someone called Kray before a jury under round-the-clock surveillance. He urged the jury not to fall into the trap of thinking the surveillance was because they were trying a top-class gangster, despite the fact that I'd been put on AA security, the highest possible. The guard was merely a part of the hype created in my case.

'It is nothing other than the fact that his name is Kray,' were his actual words.

I steeled myself when he began describing the 'defendant'; he had warned me what he was going to say and I knew I wasn't going to like it. I sat there, squirming with embarrassment, at the sad picture he started to paint of me.

'Charlie Kray is nothing more than a pathetic, skint, old fool, who lived on handouts from pals,' he told the jury, in his opening address. 'Because of the hand-to-mouth existence he has been forced to lead, he has become an expert at "bull". He's been doing it all his life. It's the only way he's been able to earn a living, because nobody would give him a job.'

The reason Mr Goldberg took this tack is that, in law, simply offering to supply cocaine – even if you had no intention of doing so – is a criminal offence. And I could be heard on tape doing just that.

The only possible defence – and it was a long shot – was to convince the jury that I was conning the police with a load of bull, in order to get some money out of them. I promised cocaine, but I would have promised scud missiles and gold bars if I thought it would help.

Mr Goldberg told the jury to disregard the tapes on which they had heard me speaking of bribing police, their detection methods and phone taps, my contacts with the Israeli secret service, and even my boasts about having killed a man. It had all been nothing but invention, designed to impress people I thought were wealthy drug dealers.

'You will hear that the defendant has never been a drugs dealer in any way, shape or form,' he said. 'Have you ever heard of a drugs baron who lives like a pauper, cadging fifty pounds here, twenty there? He doesn't even have a bank account. All you have in the dock is a charming, but gullible, old man, who doesn't know his limitations, who does not recognize where his charm and bull ends and where the reality of life begins.'

Despite the hurtful personal attack, I thought Mr Goldberg's address was brilliant. His subsequent attack on the police echoed my own sentiments precisely.

He said, '. . . the undercover officers should be ashamed of themselves for carrying out a deeply offensive operation. With the help of seemingly bottomless expense accounts, they acted as devious *agents provocateur*, even using Gary's death to infiltrate into Charlie Kray's circle of friends. No doubt it was a feather in the caps of several of the officers to have nicked the last of the Kray brothers, but the way they went about it was deplorable.

'They targeted Charlie Kray . . . and breached flagrantly their own instructions – not to solicit a person to commit an offence or one of a more serious character than they would otherwise have committed,' said Mr Goldberg. 'They lured a foolish and vulnerable old man with no money into a carefully prepared web. They would not leave him alone. They made all the running.'

The tapes the jury had heard of me speaking about tons of cocaine and millions of pounds was nothing more than 'absurd exaggeration' as any fool of a detective should have seen, and probably did – but didn't want to admit it for obvious reasons, said Mr Goldberg. The police must have realized that I was not a big-time criminal with wealth behind me; otherwise why would one of their undercover officers have given me fifty quid for nothing? If you genuinely believe someone is a drug baron, you don't insult him by giving him that sort of money.

That fifty quid Deano slipped me in Birmingham was the key to the case, Mr Goldberg suggested.

I had mixed emotions when Jack came into court. Part of me was full of loathing for the insidious way he had deceived me; another part pitied him for having to prey on vulnerable old men to earn a living. How, I wondered, did he sleep at night when he spent all day under-cover living a lie?

He stood to my right, behind a screen, hidden from everyone but me. This was ordered by Judge Carroll under a court ruling called Public Interest Immunity, to keep the undercover cop's identity – and his methods of operation – secret. I did not like it; nor did Mr Goldberg and his team. It gave Jack, Brian and Ken *carte blanche* to refuse to answer critical cross-examination questions that might jeopardise the Crown's case.

Jack, the prosecution's chief witness, wasted no time clutching that cloak of secrecy.

'When did you meet George?' asked Mr Goldberg.

'Can't answer that,' replied Jack.

'You told Kray and Patsy Manning on tape that 9 May at The Wake Green Lodge was the first time you met George. True or false?'

'Can't answer that.'

'You say on tape that you and Deano are firm friends. True or false?'

'Can't answer that.'

'Did Lisa pose as Deano's girlfriend?'

'Can't answer that.'

And so it went on. It was frustrating for Mr Goldberg because he, like me, believed that the first act in this sad scenario was played out before 9 May, and he wanted the jury to know why.

After a while, I couldn't bring myself to look at Jack as he ducked and dived his way out of Mr Goldberg's reach. He denied he was party to Patsy's birthday present and knew nothing of his musical tastes. But he is on tape, drinking Patsy's health, when Deano made the presentation of the music system.

374

An important conversation in the prosecution case was the one I had with Jack shortly after midnight in The Elbow Room on 9 May. He denied that his remark about a guy being 'topped' in the 'Dam' was an attempt to bring drugs into the conversation. He denied he had breached his instructions – not to incite or procure a person to commit an offence. But if he wasn't trying to do that, why not mention another city and something less gruesome?

Surely he knew that nothing would have come of that drunken nightclub conversation if he had not contacted me the following week and insisted on meeting me in Croydon?

I don't know who was more pleased to see the back of Jack – me or Mr Goldberg. Hopefully, the jury, who knew nothing of the judge's PII ruling, would have been concerned at his refusal to answer all those questions. If they weren't, perhaps big, fat Brian would do the crown case some damage when he squeezed his nineteen stones into the protected area.

Brian had got his act together after being caught with his trousers down at the *voire dire*. He now admitted he stayed the night at Michelle Hamdouchi's home after my birthday party, but denied they had sex. He also denied that he knew she was due to turn up at The Swallow Hotel in the early hours of 27 July, and that she gave him oral sex in his hotel room.

Having heard Michelle's excellent evidence at the *voire dire*, I could not wait for Mr Goldberg to start his cross-examination of Brian. I felt that whatever he said, or refused to say – there was only one person the jury would believe. And she didn't have a Geordie accent!

No doubt in an effort to save himself as much as destroy me, Brian quickly accused Michelle of trying to involve him in a mortgage fraud soon after they met in The Elbow Room. But Mr Goldberg dismissed that, telling the court that Brian had not mentioned that point at the pre-trial hearing.

'It's a late invention, designed to blacken Miss Hamdouchi's name, isn't it?' he challenged.

Brian said it was not. But it was an early own goal. I could tell it didn't go down well with the jury.

After that, it was downhill for Brian. He denied this, he denied that and he denied his bit of the other. All not very convincingly.

To the barely disguised delight of the court and the public gallery, Mr Goldberg called Michelle Hamdouchi. I leaned forward in the dock so that I did not miss one word. At that point, I felt my best chance lay with her doing a demolition job on Brian. She did not disappoint.

In a very soft, husky Cheshire accent, Michelle, a respectable mother of three daughters, told the jury she had travelled down from Birmingham 'to do what was right'. She said Brian kept asking her if I could come up with a cocaine deal. This was helpful to me, because of the entrapment angle, but it was Brian's sexual indiscretion that would be the most damaging to the prosecution.

Her account of what happened on 11 July left no one in doubt, I'm sure, that Brian and she had full sex, no matter what he claimed. And when she came to the night of The Swallow rendezvous, she had witnesses to back her up.

Brian denied Michelle's story that he and Jack – who had been drinking in the hotel bar with Spice Girl Victoria Adams – were expecting her to arrive at the hotel. But Jacqui Cave, a bar supervisor at the hotel, told the court that she had overheard them discussing Michelle – and they even passed Brian's mobile phone to her to give Michelle instructions on how to get to the hotel.

Brian said he was totally surprised when Michelle arrived and ignored her. But Jacqui and two other hotel staff told the jury that the undercover men were *not* surprised when she turned up and that Brian was, in fact, very chatty with her.

376

Michelle's compelling truthfulness spoke for itself when Mr Kelsey-Fry said he would not be enquiring about her love life and had only one question to ask.

'Would you agree that Brian was a bit of a plonker?' he asked.

Michelle smiled: 'Yes.'

Chapter Twenty-four

A plonker, eh?

Well, if fat Brian was a plonker for indulging in two nights of lust with a sexy blonde, what did that make me? I'd put myself on offer, simply for free booze and the cheerful company of guys I assumed liked me, and now I was going to pay for it with my freedom and – who knows? – maybe even my life. If anyone was a plonker, it was me.

In my cell, lying on the metal slab they called a bed, the thought that had been nagging me was there again: Why had I fallen into the trap so easily, willingly almost? Why, oh, why, had I been so trusting, thinking Jack and his mates wanted nothing more from me than my company? As they say, there's no such thing as a free lunch, is there?

When it hit the papers that I'd been pulled in, Reg had been quick off the mark, as usual, slagging me off for getting involved in drugs and jeopardizing his parole chances. He said I should have been on my toes, seen the set-up coming, and, for once, he was right. Bells should have rung when I saw Patsy Manning being handed an expensive birthday present by someone he barely knew. And they should have rung louder when I received a gift, myself, then was given money by a guy I'd only just met.

I could understand Reggie's anger, but, then, neither he nor Ronnie had ever appreciated how their notoriety had destroyed my life, shattered my confidence and self-esteem, and made me more susceptible than most to flattery and generosity.

The effect of the twins' murders and general violent life-style hit me soon after walking out of Maidstone Prison that January morning in 1975. My aim was to pick up where I left off, get on my feet, financially, and restore my pride – a pride that had been swamped in shame by my unjust conviction.

I didn't expect it to be easy, but nothing could have prepared me for the wave of distrust, bordering on hatred, my name now inspired. The dramatic headlines and long-running stories of violence and terror that followed each day's Old Bailey evidence seemed indelibly printed on everyone's mind. In restaurants and bars, people stared at me warily, their expressions full of curiosity, disgust – even fear. Acquaintances who, before, were only too pleased to offer help were now 'unavailable'. Business contacts who once saw me as a reliable, skilful operator now didn't return phone calls. The name Kray, spelt NO in giant capitals, not only in London, but the whole country.

What made my blood boil was not so much that I'd been locked up for something I hadn't done – although that was bad enough – but that people refused to give me a chance. They assumed that what they had read or heard must be true, and that was that. People who'd never even met me took it for granted that, because I was the Kray twins' brother, I was a ruthless, nasty piece of work who should be avoided at all costs.

I had to try harder with everything. And I did. I battled to revert to my former self, to recapture some of the good-humoured personality and energy that had endeared me to many people and helped make my businesses successful. I even tried to win over the doubters by telling them precisely how the twins had dragged me into the McVitie murder. But, in the main, people didn't want to know.

Several friends suggested that the simplest solution was to change my name. But that was something I'd never do. I've always been proud of my mother and father, and the name they gave me and my brothers, and I remember being

379

so proud, seeing Kray on my boxing trophies, before and after my Navy life. The mere thought of going through a legal process to rid myself of that name would make me feel quite sick. It would be a betrayal of the dear mum we loved so much. And I couldn't bear that.

Once I'd decided not to fight a legal crusade to prove my innocence, I did become a happier, more contented, person. It still bothered me, though, that people could hate and distrust me without knowing me and I found myself wanting, needing, to be liked. I didn't go out of my way to be popular or win approval and I certainly didn't beg for it, but it became very important that people liked me for myself – cheerful Charlie, a fun-loving party animal, always up for a laugh.

It was this insecurity that made me so vulnerable to Jack and his sneaky mates. They gave me the impression they didn't give a monkey's what my name was, or what had, or had not, happened in the past. They liked me for myself, I was sure of that.

Why else would they push the boat out so grandly on Patsy Manning's birthday at The Wake Green Lodge? Why else would one of them slip me fifty quid in the toilet? It was not as if I was some influential businessman they needed to impress, whose palm they wanted to grease. It was as plain as the nose on your face that I had nothing to offer. Honestly, I felt the same about them as I did with Big Albert. He treated me to this and that all the time, with no strings attached, simply because he liked me and could afford to.

Looking back, of course I'm angry with myself for falling for all the bullshit, for guzzling Jack's champagne with not a thought that he and his cronies wanted something from me; that there would be a price to pay. But unless you've been tainted in the papers and on TV as an evil criminal, who got rid of the body of a man, murdered by one of his equally evil brothers, it will be difficult to understand.

Someone who did understand was Dave Courtney. When Reggie decided he needed someone on the outside to help pull the funeral arrangements for Ronnie together – particularly the security – he called Dave, not me. Unfortunately, like many others who provided services that day, Dave is still counting the cost. The funeral gained him a lot of kudos for his security company, but there's no doubt in my mind that the Kray association also led to his wrongful arrest – and put him in Belmarsh on remand with me – for importing drugs illegally. Fortunately, he was acquitted and released from prison early in 1997.

At the time, I was hurt that Reg wanted me to have nothing to do with the funeral. But, watching Dave in action during the build-up, I knew I would not have handled it so well. The discussions with the police over crowd control, for example. The Commissioner of Police, Sir Paul Condon, who came to Bethnal Green himself, clearly had no idea how big the funeral was going to be, but Dave and his security guards had seen the huge numbers wanting to see Ronnie's body and knew it was going to be colossal – far bigger than even our mother's funeral in 1982. And that had brought the East End to a standstill.

The three of us met at English's funeral parlour in Bethnal Green Road and Sir Paul made it clear he wanted his men in sole charge of the operation, from the time the funeral cortège travelled from English's to when it left St Matthew's Church for Chingford Cemetery. But Dave was having none of it, and said he had 150 very big, very tough, experienced security guards who would be more of a deterrent to troublemakers than young PCs more used to controlling pop fans.

'You just get your lot in the street and do the holding hands bit and leave everything else to me,' he said, in his usual cocky manner.

Sir Paul thought about it then agreed. 'Okay,' he said.

381

'But I think your men should wear coloured bibs to distinguish them from mine.'

Dave nearly choked. 'My little band of men will be wearing £2,000 overcoats, mate. They won't want to be wearing any bibs – fancy coloured or otherwise.'

'But I insist your men wear *something* that identifies them,' Sir Paul said.

'Okay,' Dave said. 'I'll have some little red badges made, saying Courtney Security. Will that do?'

Sir Paul agreed, albeit reluctantly. 'I'll allow you to do the security, Mr Courtney. But not everyone is a Kray fan, you know. A sniper attack or assassination has not been possible for thirty years because the twins have been locked up, but, the Krays being driven at ten miles an hour, who knows what might happen. Something we've got that you haven't is a firearms' unit.'

'Sir, the one thing you've got that we haven't is a firearms' *certificate*,' Dave said. 'We've all got fucking guns!'

Sir Paul's face was a picture: if he could have nicked Dave there and then, I'm sure he would have. I found it hilarious, but, in the light of what happened to Dave later, I wonder whether his cockiness that day did him any favours. Policemen, particularly high-ranking ones, do not like being made fun of. And they never forget. I told Dave that his association with the Kray name would affect him badly for the rest of his life, like it had with me.

I never thought there would be any trouble at the funeral, but we did get a scare the day Ronnie's body was taken to the undertaker's. One of the staff there told a newspaper she had received a phone call from someone threatening to break in and desecrate Ronnie's body – and Reggie went spare: he told Dave not just to guard the funeral parlour itself, but to sleep next to Ronnie's body in the Chapel of Rest.

Easier said than done: Dave's band of hard nuts may

have been fearless in the line of strong-arm duty, but not one of them was brave enough to sleep in that room on his own – Dave included! In the end, he had to persuade three to do it – and, as he said afterwards, it was harder finding them than the 150 he needed to handle the funeral security.

'A ghost is scary enough, but imagine the ghost of Ronnie Kray,' Dave admitted to me. 'I slept in there a couple of times myself and don't mind admitting I was scared shitless. I can imagine how frightening Ronnie was with the hump when he was alive, because he looked scary enough when he was dead. But I'm pleased we did it, to put Reg's mind at rest.'

I hope Reggie was as grateful as me for the work that went into that funeral. From the outset, Dave said he wanted to organize a State-like occasion, fitting for Britain's criminal monarch, a flamboyant affair that would show the world what England could do for its most famous gangster. He succeeded spectacularly, but, unfortunately, ended up £14,000 out of pocket. Dave didn't believe Reg's promise to cover all costs – such as wages, travelling expenses and walkie-talkies – but went ahead anyway because he felt the international publicity would be good for his security company and eventually earn him more than what he was laying out.

Unfortunately, Dave never got paid and, worse, his connections with the country's major villains – most of whom were employed for the funeral – brought him to the attention of the authorities and he has had all sorts of aggravation ever since. The curse of the Kray name again!

That night before going into the witness box, I found it hard to sleep and started wondering about my decision to talk directly to the jury. It hadn't once crossed my mind not to. After what had happened at the Old Bailey I was taking no chances. What had I to lose? One had only to listen to those incriminating tapes to know I was certainly going to be found guilty, at least on the first charge of offering Jack cocaine. My only chance of getting a lenient sentence was to let the court see the real me, no matter how degrading and humiliating that would be; to stand before the jury and convince them that I was, indeed, a pathetic, if likeable and charming, old man, not a top-class gangster, so dangerous and well-connected that I needed round-the-clock surveillance.

The thought that had been nagging me most of the time since my arrest was there again: was I right to plead not guilty in the face of such crushing evidence? Mr Goldberg had told me the judge had indicated I'd get a much lighter sentence if I did admit the charges – six years, probably, seven at most. With parole, which I'd certainly get, being a model prisoner, and less the time I'd been held on remand, I'd be out in three years or so. It was tempting, because Mr Goldberg said I could plead guilty without compromising Ronnie Field and Bobby Gould, which obviously I wouldn't want to do.

But I could not plead guilty unless I was prepared to betray Reggie and lose the respect of all those people who'd kept me going all these years. It was the East End code: always keep your mouth shut and admit nothing. And I was trapped by it, no matter how much I wanted a lighter sentence. With everything else in my life in shreds, the respect of my friends was something I could not, would not, throw away.

Not for the first time I found myself wishing Dave was in the next cell. How I'd love to hear his cheeky banter now! Dave wasn't everyone's cup of tea: he was loud, brash, talked at a hundred miles and hour, and was very much in your face. He didn't suffer fools – gladly, or otherwise – and I'm sure people were in awe, if not frightened, of him. But I'd known him for years, even been on holiday to

Marbella with him, and wouldn't hear a bad word said about him. We'd got close when he was organizing doormen for London clubs, and he'd given me a job as host at the London Hippodrome, off Leicester Square. Someone told me later that he saw me as the perfect man for the job because of my 'charm and impeccable manners'. That pleased me, as you might imagine. I was only there a couple of weeks, but it was the closest I'd come to a proper job, since coming out of prison, and I revelled in it. A shame it couldn't have lasted longer; maybe then I wouldn't have attracted the attention of those Geordies.

In our time on Cat A, Dave was a diamond who knew who I was – the *real* me that is – and what I was going through. There were times, during those six months, when I was so low I could barely open my eyes and get out of bed, but Dave's fast wit and general good humour always lifted my spirits. Despite my anxiety at what lay ahead, he had me in stitches and brightened most days. Behind the wisecracks, though, Dave is nobody's mug: he's a clever, very intelligent, guy, quick to cut to the chase and size up situations for what they were, not what they appeared to be.

He's honest, too, and always tells it how it is: he gives people the truth, not just what they want to hear. That's why I liked talking with him. He was the only one in that high-security wing I'd have dreamt of opening up to the way I did. The others in there didn't have a clue what I was all about, but Dave knew the full SP. He knew what rubbish I'd had to endure because of the Kray name. And he understood, more than most, why, even as I faced another prison sentence, I felt compelled to uphold that name, keep the legend going. I was the Kray flagship, he'd say. And he was right: as the only Kray brother free, I'd been the one that all those people fascinated by the twins could look at, speak to, touch even; the one the twins were judged by.

It sounds pathetic, but that's all I've had to do in the last twenty-two years – be a sort of ambassador for my brothers, so that they can continue to sell their books and get fan mail from all those thousands of strange gangster groupies.

With all doors to a respectable job locked, money became a big problem, which was hard to take, because I've always been a sociable animal and I loved having a few quid in my pocket to enjoy myself. This is why, I think, I started accepting offers from people on the strength of my name. As is clear from those incriminating tapes, I love a good drink and, to be frank, if someone was prepared to get them in for me in return for a few stories about the twins, who was I to refuse?

In the late seventies and eighties, when I was living with Diana in her flat near Crystal Palace, I didn't have to prostitute myself in this way: Di was hard-working and always made sure I had money in my pocket to pay my way. But when she kicked me out and I threw in my lot with Judy and her children, my life changed significantly: with all the money from the film long gone and Judy having next to nothing from her £14,000 a year salary to spend on socializing, I started living on people's generosity more and more and very soon it became a way of life, with me going more or less anywhere, provided it didn't cost me anything to get there, and I didn't have to put my hand in my pocket. I've got to be honest: in this respect, the Kray name worked for me and provided an enjoyable social life I wouldn't have had otherwise. There was the odd business opportunity, too: all sorts of strangers would worm their way into my company, with various weird and wonderful schemes, so that they could bask in that inane, reflected glory of being seen with the Kray twins' closest living relative. Of course, I loved it, didn't I? When you haven't got two bob, and there are holes in your shoes, a bit of hero-worship does wonders for one's morale and self-esteem. I found I became all things to all people, telling them what they wanted to hear.

Now, in my cell, thinking about my appearance before the jury, I thought back to those long months on remand, when Dave made me laugh at the image I'd invented for myself. He'd say: 'If someone asked you if you could get a bright pink Scud missile delivered to Peckham the following Saturday, you'd say: "I'll see what I can do – get us a brandy and coke ... Someone wants a combine harvester, painted yellow, driven by a black man – I'll have a chat – mine's a brandy and coke ... Madonna tickets? Singing on stage with her? I'll make a phone call. Brandy and coke? That'll be lovely." '

It sounds ridiculous, but Dave was spot on: I found it impossible to say No – to anything, or anyone. Even if a guy asked me if I could arrange to have someone hurt, I'd say, 'I'll see what I can do.' Then, the drinks would continue to flow and the subject would never be mentioned again. It was all about keeping the Kray legend going: I couldn't admit I was unable to do something, give the cold shoulder – in the same way I couldn't admit I was skint.

It doesn't please me to admit it, but throughout the nineties I was – no two ways about it – a ponce. And it was that lifestyle that landed me in this mess. I remember opening my heart to Dave, saying how much I wanted to talk to the jury as I was talking to him; how much I wanted to tell them: 'It's my name. It's the second time I'm going to prison because of my name. There's no £39 million cocaine deal. I have no money, not even a home of my own. Look at the holes in my shoes, my worn-through suit. All I have done is talk a load of rubbish to someone because he gave me loads of booze. Yes, I *am* guilty of that. Sentence me for *that*. But not for being a drug dealer, because I'm not.'

I don't mind admitting it, I cried in Dave's cell more than once; and when he saw my look of defeat, and I told him I was going to die in prison, his eyes filled with tears, too. Dave, more than most people I know, could identify

387

with what I'd gone through. He had image problems, too: because he's publicly loud and brash, oozing self-confidence, people assume that's the real person. But there's more to Dave Courtney than meets the eye and he was a good understanding friend to me. More than once, it had crossed my mind that we were both in the position we were because the circus that was Ronnie's funeral had drawn the attention of more than just the public and media.

Quite honestly, I don't know how I got *any* sleep that night before my evidence, and, shortly after nine o'clock the next morning, I was walking robotically along the tunnel to the court. It was the day the Press had been waiting for; the moment when the evil Kray twins' older brother spoke up for himself. What were the reporters and jurors expecting? I honestly didn't know. Would I appear to be everything they thought I'd be, or a bitter disappointment? All I *was* sure about, as I stepped from the dock and walked to the witness box, was that I had to be myself. Everyone close to me had told me that. Let those twelve jurors see the real you, they said. Tell them how different you are from the image they have of the Krays; let them see you have not got it in you to deal in drugs. That was the easy part. What I was going to find more difficult was swallowing my pride and self-esteem and admitting how shabby and shallow my life had become. And, more important, what I really was.

A plonker.

Chapter Twenty-five

Standing in front of Mr Goldberg answering his questions was easy, rather like a gentle game of tennis: he would lob the ball mildly so that I saw it clearly and whacked it back strongly; every one a winner.

'What is your attitude to drugs?' he asked.

'I've always been anti-drugs. And everyone knows it,' I said. 'I saw the terrible effect they had on my brother Ron, over the years. If I'd been involved in drugs, people would have known it. I can't buy a newspaper without people knowing it.'

'What do you think of people who sell drugs?'

'I despise them. I wouldn't touch them with a barge pole.'

'Why did you have anything to do with Jack, who you suspected was a drug dealer?'

'Because I felt I could get money out of him by pretending to be a drug dealer myself. I had no compunction about conning people like him.'

'Did you tell Jack you had access to drugs?'

'Yes, I said I could get him tons of puff. But it wasn't true. It was just a story to get money out of him.'

'Did you say you had seen a ton of cocaine?'

'Yes. But that was a story, too. There isn't that amount in the country, I shouldn't think. Jack must have known I was spinning him a line.'

And so it went on, with Mr Goldberg skilfully pointing me in the right direction to help explain why I said what I did on those incriminating tapes. To me, it all added up: I was telling Jack and his pals everything they wanted to hear merely to get some of the 'wads of money' Patsy had told me they had. I just hoped the jury saw it that way, too.

I felt composed and sure of myself under Mr Goldberg's questioning, but when he brought up The Mermaid Theatre I felt my throat tighten: the mention of it naturally made me think of Gary and that usually set me off. I fought to keep my emotions under control as I heard Mr Goldberg ask why Ronnie Field and Bobby Gould were at the show, on Sunday 2 June.

I told him that I bumped into them at East Croydon Station and they had said that they might come.

'The Crown's allegation is that, at The Mermaid, you drew Jack into a corridor to meet Field and Gould and you talked about drugs,' said Mr Goldberg.

And that tipped me over the edge.

My eyes filling with tears, voice shaking with emotion, I told him that was untrue. 'I would not insult my son's memory by talking about drugs there.' And I meant it. Gary was everything to me and, that Sunday, he had been dead only three months. I was still in deep, deep grief and missing him more than words can say.

Jack had made a big deal out of me introducing him and Ken to Field and Gould. But I told Mr Goldberg that the place was teeming and, as Gary's dad, I was moving around the room, introducing lots of people to each other. Yes, I introduced Ron and Bob to Jack, but I left them speaking together and had no idea what they talked about.

Mr Goldberg was taking me through the whole sequence of events slowly. But I was ahead of him. I'd had nine months on remand to think about Jack's treacherous behaviour and I knew the scenario backwards. After The Mermaid, I did not speak to Jack for more than two weeks. I had no reason to: I had nothing to say to him. It was *him* who contacted *me*. Why? To get me and Ron up to Newcastle to talk about drugs.

390

He rang on Tuesday 18 June. The conversation, which he taped, went like this:

'Well, how's you?' Jack asked.

'All right, thanks. How you been?' I replied.

'Oh, we've been busy ... Ken and I were across in Brussels for a few days.'

'Oh, have you?'

'Getting some business sorted out.'

'Oh, good, good ... the lottery have you, mate? How you been, all right otherwise?'

'Yeah, yeah.'

I laughed. 'See you soon and have a drink or something.'

'Yeah, that's what I was ringing you for actually ... what I was thinking of doing was, if you were okay for next week.'

'Yeah.'

'I was going to invite you and Ronnie up, just the two of you.'

'Yeah.'

'See if we can get some business sorted out.'

'Yes.'

'What I was thinking was maybe Wednesday next week.'

'Yeah.'

'I'll sort you a couple of tickets out.'

'Yeah.'

'And just fly up. We'll meet you. We've got somewhere nice and quiet lined up where we can maybe get some business sorted between us and yourselves.'

'That'll be nice, mate,' I said. 'Very nice of you.'

Jack told me he would arrange for two airline tickets to be left at Gatwick for me and Ron, then he said: 'So, yeah, then stay over and we'll get some business sorted.'

'Oh, that's smashing, mate.' Then I laughed. 'I could do with it.'

'Yeah.'

'To be quite truthful, at the moment, you know, after

391

Gary and all that . . . I've not done nothing for fucking four months, have I, you know?'

A few minutes later, Jack rang back asking what names me and Ron wanted to use at the hotel where we would be staying.

'Normal names,' I said, '. . . Field and Kray.'

What names did we want to use? I didn't know what he was on about.

Being guided by Mr Goldberg, I found it easy to bring all that happened then into focus. Three days after I'd squeezed £500 out of Jack, he rang, anxious to know if Ronnie was coming up to Birmingham for my birthday party. Ten days later, on Saturday 20 July, he rang again, wanting me to ask Ronnie to contact him. The following Wednesday morning, he called again, asking me to book him and Brian into The Selsdon Park Hotel for the next night, because he was meeting Ronnie and Bob there.

I agreed to book the rooms, although, once again, I wondered why he did not pick up the phone and do it himself. Also, I said I'd pop in for a quick drink early in the evening.

By now, I told the court, I'd decided to confess to Jack that I was not really a drug dealer, and that it had all been a con to get money out of him. Although Ronnie had yet to get any money, he was, as far as I understood, going to own up and get out of the relationship himself that night. I did pop in for a drink, as arranged, and stayed just fifteen minutes.

What happened after I left, and what I said on the phone the next morning, would not do me any favours.

I had listened in some awe to Kelsey-Fry's questioning for several days. An urbane, courteous gentleman – in his late thirties, I guess – he had an enviable courtroom presence, with an eloquence other barristers, I'm sure, would kill for.

In cross-examination he would not be taking prisoners. I'd have no easy tennis match with him; he was bound to have some aces up his sleeve.

He was particularly keen to know about my relationship with Ronnie Field. How long had I known him? How often did we see each other? Was he a close friend? I told him what I felt was the truth: that Ron was someone I'd seen only occasionally, perhaps three or four times in the past couple of years or so.

With barely concealed delight, Kelsey-Fry asked me to look at BT bills, listing the number of calls in and out on the phone at Judy's house in Sanderstead. I was amazed to be told that, between 23 November and 2 June, I had spoken with Ronnie Field more than fifty times.

'Quite a lot for someone you did not know all that well and hardly ever saw, wouldn't you say, Mr Kray?'

I just shook my head disbelievingly. I was genuinely shocked. Worse was to follow, however. Reminding me I claimed to have told Field and Gould about The Mermaid after bumping into them in Croydon, Kelsey-Fry told the jury that BT's records showed that I spoke to Field the day before the show. And on the Sunday itself.

I didn't know what to say. What I *did* know was that it did not look good to the jury.

Kelsey-Fry reminded me that I had denied knowing Bob Gould, then invited me and the jury to turn to a transcription of a conversation with Jack, Brian and Field in The Linden Hall Hotel.

He read out:

Brian: 'Well ... we're not going to be introducing you to somebody else. We'd rather just ...'

Field: 'You won't see no one else.'

Kray: 'No one else.'

Kelsey-Fry seemed to think it was a significant conversation.

393

My pal Steve Grant was the person on whom Kelsey-Fry placed most importance, however. Steve had gone to The Selsdon Park Hotel with a 6ft 3in. car dealer, named Warren, on Thursday 25 July, and met Jack and Brian, with Field and Gould.

I said I knew two men had gone to the hotel, but understood they were friends of Ronnie. He told me he had phoned them, asking to borrow some money.

Kelsey-Fry produced the phone records again and asked me whose number I had called a couple of minutes after Jack told me about the problem at the hotel.

It was Steve's.

He also inferred that because I'd responded to Jack's comment about 'the muppet . . . off his face' by saying: 'What, the big guy?', this indicated that I knew it was Warren.

And that, in turn, proved I must have known all about that meeting.

I left the witness box and walked, as elegantly as I could, across the courtroom to the dock, mentally drained. What would the jury have made of that? I wondered. I felt an urge to look at them, to try to see the answer in their eyes, but resisted it. I was on a loser, wasn't I? If I smiled, they might think I was confident at having conned them; if I merely stared, would they think I was trying to intimidate them? And, anyway, even if I did look, and detected they believed all I said, what would that prove? My voice on the tapes was going to decide my fate.

That night in my cell I played it all back in my mind. To be truthful, I wasn't happy with the way it had gone: I didn't think I'd done myself justice at all. I'd been given the chance to address the jury, tell them about the real me. I'd even worked out a little speech, explaining exactly how the unjust McVitie sentence had destroyed my life; how I'd always suffered because of the crimes of my brothers; how

Gary's death had shattered me, causing me not to think clearly. I'd had the chance to tell those twelve jurors what an idiot I'd been – and, crucially more important, why. But I'd blown it. Goldberg had done his best with his questioning, but I hadn't picked up his lead, hadn't let the jury see the real Charlie Kray at all. And then, of course, there was Kelsey-Fry, with all those damn – and damning – questions. I'd been made to look a plonker all right. But it was my answers to those questions that had done it.

I stretched out on my metal bed and looked at Gary's photo on the wall and thought, yet again, what a blessing it was that my poor boy wasn't around to see his old man humbled and humiliated the way I'd been that day. 'Well, Gal,' I said. 'What do you think? I let myself down in there, didn't I? I had so much to say and I didn't say it, did I?'

It's difficult to explain, but I'd found it hard appearing as the pathetic human being Goldberg had described. Yes, I knew I *was*. And, yes, I knew it was crucial to my case that the jury saw me as someone incapable of masterminding a drug deal. But I've always been proud and dignified, and I suppose my pride kicked in when I stood before the jury. It's stupid, I know, particularly when my liberty – indeed, the rest of my life – was at stake, but I found it impossible to let those people see a broken man, getting through the last years of his life on handouts. Perhaps, I should have put on an act, maybe shed a few tears at my desperation. But that was against my nature: I've always tried to be straightforward and genuine and, in that box, I honestly thought that simply telling the truth about myself would see me through. Why, oh, why hadn't I just talked to those jurors the way I'd talked to Dave Courtney on remand? Opened up and bared my soul and let them see precisely how the stigma of the Kray name had destroyed my life. Who knows, I might have managed it if The Mermaid hadn't been mentioned. That had really done me in.

That magical day in June had been just like the old days when me and the twins put on charity events in the East End. The day had been about Gary and those caring nurses at St Christopher's. It was all about raising money for the hospice, not about putting people together for a drug deal: the only drug I'd have had on my mind that day was the morphine those girls had given Gary to ease his pain. I told the court I wouldn't insult Gary's memory by talking about drugs on such an occasion. And I meant it.

I was so proud to be doing something to repay St Christopher's, to thank them for making my son's last days bearable. I told everyone I knew about the show. People close to me knew how much I loved Gary, and the theatre was packed.

Whatever was raised during that emotional evening, I would loved to have been in the position to give more to St Christopher's. I'd willingly have nipped to the bank and increased our donation to a nice ten grand – or even more – but, as I'd made clear on the tapes, I didn't have two pennies to rub together. In fact, apart from the proceeds from the Kray movie, I never had a lot of money after my arrest. It always made me laugh that people thought the twins salted a fortune away when the writing was on the wall. What rubbish! They did earn a lot, it's true, but certainly not a fortune. And what money they did get, they spent – or, in Ronnie's case, gave away.

If there was a lot stashed away, do you think I'd have had to rely on the fifty quid Mum gave me when I came out of nick? Do you think we'd have allowed her to move back into a council house and do, not one, but two, jobs to make ends meet? If there'd been bundles of money around you can bet your boots that the woman all three of us adored would have lived like a queen. Because that's what she deserved. Neither Ronnie, Reggie nor I can speak too highly of our mum. In the face of the worst publicity imaginable

– nationwide shame, in fact – she never lost faith in us. And only twice in the nightmare that followed our arrests did she allow us to witness the anguish that was tearing her apart.

The first time was in 1968, when the three of us were in Brixton, awaiting trial. A bloke told a newspaper he'd overheard someone saying that the twins were arranging for Princess Margaret's son, Lord Linley, to be kidnapped and held until we were released. The twins were slaughtered. And our mild-mannered mum, who rarely raised her voice, went spare. She wrote to the Queen, saying that the story was a load of rubbish, that never in a million years would the twins dream of involving a child in any sort of trouble, let alone a royal one. The newspaper printed the story as though it were true and Mum was horrified that millions of people might believe it.

The other time she cracked in front of us was when she came to the cells below the Old Bailey after our sentences. We were allowed to talk to her, one at a time, through a glass wall, and it broke Mum's heart. She kept sobbing, saying over and over: 'That's it. That's the end of the story. Thirty years. I can't believe it.'

We all did our best to comfort her; told her not to worry, we'd be released on appeal. But we knew it wasn't true, and she wasn't fooled. 'How can I not worry?' she said, through her tears. 'It's the end of your lives.'

In those emotional moments, I'm sure Ronnie and Reggie came the nearest to feeling regret – if not remorse – for the murders that brought them to justice and broke the heart of the woman they worshipped. For they, like me, held her in such high esteem that they couldn't bear the thought of hurting her.

If I was disappointed with my performance in the witness box, my solicitor, Ralph Haeems, was livid. Why hadn't

I said all that we, and Jonathan Goldberg, had agreed before-hand, he wanted to know? Why hadn't I seized the chance to try to save myself? I looked at him and shook my head, sadly. 'I honestly don't know, Ralph,' I said. 'I was over-whelmed, I guess. And embarrassed.'

'I don't know why you didn't just tell the jury everything you've been telling Dave on remand.' Ralph knew all about Dave Courtney, had represented him on a number of fit-up charges and got him off on every one.

I just shook my head, not sure what to say. The truth was that baring one's soul to a friend you've been cooped up with for many months was a lot easier than doing so in a packed courtroom. Ralph thought for a few moments, then said: 'I wonder if Dave will go in the box for you. Say everything about you that you didn't.'

'It's worth a try,' I said.

'It will be tough for you, Charlie,' Ralph said. 'He'll have to say a lot of things you won't want to hear.'

I forced a smile. 'It can't be any worse than what Mr Goldberg has said already.'

'I'll make contact and ask him,' Ralph said. 'He may not want to put himself in the frame again, having been released.'

And he may not want to be associated with a Kray trial after the aggravation Ronnie's funeral caused him, I thought. But it was worth a try because Dave was one of those super-confident guys who would say what he wanted to say, and wouldn't be fazed by the solemnity of the court, a biased judge or a tricky barrister. After all, he'd had plenty of experience!

I was fairly sure Dave wouldn't let me down – and he didn't. But, before he went into the witness box, close on twenty friends and acquaintances of mine were preparing to do so, too, either to speak about my character, or confirm or refute allegations by the prosecution, particularly about my Gary's funeral and the two parties in Birmingham.

Nothing could have prepared me for the bumpy roller-coaster ride of emotions as these people went into the witness box to tell why their own impression of me backed up the sad, pathetic picture painted by Mr Goldberg. Their evidence took five days, and in that time I learnt a lot about myself. I learnt that for all my carefree bonhomie and good-natured charming bullshit over the years, I had not fooled anyone. All those who came forward so loyally in my hour of desperate need had always seen through me, seen the hapless dreamer I really was. And what touched me deeply, reduced me to tears at times, was that they did not care a jot. They liked me – loved me, perhaps – for myself, not for what I pretended to be. That's why they were there, telling the truth, no matter how painful I might find it, to convince the jury I was not the despicable person they might think I was.

With all the frightening hype surrounding my appearance in the dock the jury could be excused for thinking they might be murdered in their beds, Mr Goldberg had said. They needed guarding round the clock, because I was, supposedly, so dangerous I'd been locked up in the country's highest security prison.

But those lovely people who knew me told a different story and, no matter what happened, I'd never forget them. Diana, as elegant as ever, whose flattering description prompted Goldberg to say: 'Many distinguished men have not had a testimonial like that'; Billy Murray, the Canning Town kid, now a famous actor, who did not forget his past; Albert Chapman, the Brummie with a big heart; Flanagan, the Cockney sister I never had; my ghostwriter Robin McGibbon, Steve Wraith, my young friend from Newcastle, Father Christopher Bedford, who had conducted Ronnie's funeral, and, of course, John Corbett, whose support had never wavered.

'Mad' Frankie Fraser also spoke, but, like Goldberg's junior counsel, David Martin-Sperry, I felt it was a mistake to call him. Frank had got carried away with the fame of writing a couple of books and, I'm sure, went into the witness box as much for himself as me. He showed off too much for my liking, and was stupidly cheeky to the judge, which I didn't think went down well with the jury.

Dave Courtney, on the other hand, was a real star for me – even though I squirmed with embarrassment when he described me as a desperate pauper, with holes in my shoes, a faded suit and fake watch, capitalizing on the legend of my twin brothers. 'I'm sorry to burst your bubble, mate,' he said, looking at me, 'but none of us have ever bought into what you pretend to be. You're just a nice, charming old man who really can't do anything, hasn't got anything.' As for masterminding a multi-million-pound drug deal, Dave left the jury with the impression I couldn't run a bath; and although he didn't actually use the words, he said I was like a performing seal, entertaining various groups with stories of the twins – in return for drinks – until the novelty wore off and I was passed on to the next group. I was always promising to help people, never ever saying NO, he said.

I was proud of Dave that day: of course my ego took a battering, but what did that matter if it meant the jury saw the real me, and the reason I went along with what Jack and his pals were suggesting?

Dave's magnetic, cabaret-style evidence was a breath of fresh air in that solemn court, but it had a down side for me and my defence team. The following day, one of the male jurors told a court official that he knew of Dave through a cousin, and wondered if it compromised his role. Much to Goldberg's annoyance, the judge felt it did, and dismissed him.

Far worse was to follow: I'd always pinned a lot of hope on Ronnie Field giving evidence; he could have answered a lot of questions that would have helped me. But, during the *voire dire*, he was advised by Judge Carroll to seek counsel's advice before doing so. The result was that Ronnie refused to speak on my behalf.

Mr Goldberg was furious. He accused the judge of putting pressure on Field and said I could not have a fair trial if I had a reluctant witness. The point of it all was that, by pleading guilty, Ronnie had been promised a more lenient sentence than he would otherwise have got. And, according to Mr Goldberg, the judge was giving a clear message to Ronnie: If you give evidence I don't like, you'll get a longer sentence. Mr Goldberg was so angry he actually asked the judge to disqualify himself. Predictably, the judge refused.

If it was a slap in the face for Mr Goldberg, it was a crunching uppercut to me. I wanted the jury to hear what Ronnie had to say in my defence, but we were prohibited from telling them we wished to call him.

If that's not an injustice, I don't know what is. But, then, I had not seen much justice where the name Kray was concerned.

I can't – and won't – make excuses for what the twins did to George Cornell and Jack McVitie. But I do want people to know – whether they were around at the time, or have only read about those awful crimes – that we were all victims of parliamentary pressure. Someone high up in the corridors of power had decided that the Kray brothers had become too powerful, too influential, knew too many powerful and influential people, and should be removed from society for a long time. The outcome of the case was worked out before it even got to court; you only have to consider the antagonism and unforgivable bias, and downright bad judgement of the trial judge Melford Stevenson to appreciate that. No matter what was said in the twins' favour – no matter if they got a glowing testimonial from the Pope! – they were going away for thirty years.

People talk about justice in this country. We hold Britain up as shining example of democracy and fairmindedness, and the symbol of this is there for all to see in the scales of justice above the Old Bailey. How damned hypocritical! Ronnie got thirty years for murdering a gangster, who had threatened to kill *him*, yet some monster who starves and tortures a child to death gets away with a third of that. Reggie got thirty years for killing a despicable, woman-beating thug, yet an evil terrorist warrants the same sentence for killing and maiming innocent men, women and children in the name of politics and religion. Where is the democracy and fairmindedness in that?

Chapter Twenty-six

Kelsey-Fry was due to begin his closing speech on Thursday 12 June, but was ill. I wasn't happy about him doing a demolition job on me on such a notorious day as Friday the thirteenth, but I saw the positive side: the nearer Mr Goldberg's closing speech was to the judge's summing up the better. If Kelsey-Fry finished his on Friday, that would leave the weekend for the jury to forget a lot of what he said, leaving Mr Goldberg to close only one day before the judge's summing up.

As it was, Kelsey-Fry managed only the morning session on Friday before he was taken ill again. So, it was all scheduled to happen the following week: both counsels' closing speeches, the judge's summing up, the jury's deliberation and, hopefully, a Not Guilty verdict on the second charge of supplying cocaine, if not the first of offering it. After a marathon eight weeks of *voire dire* and trial proper, we were approaching the finishing line. I was exhausted. I wanted it sorted. One way or the other.

Not surprisingly, Kelsey-Fry made light of fat Brian's indiscretion, telling the jury that his credibility was less important than mine; that if they felt he had been discredited, they should ignore his evidence, unless it was corroborated by someone else. The defence said the police were cunning and devious and should be ashamed of themselves, but it was my behaviour that was shameful, he said. If I suspected that Jack's overture in The Elbow Room was all about drugs, all I had to say was: 'That's not my game – I'm going off to have a drink with my mates.' But I didn't. I saw my chance, he said.

He poured scorn on my plan to con money out of Jack, saying I had many friends who could have helped me out, but I assumed the role of a despicable drug dealer, even though one of my witnesses said I was 'a coward who would not say boo to a goose'.

But it was all the drug-related statements I'd made on tape that he asked the jury to consider. And, in case they did not know the ones he meant, he read some of them out:

'I know someone's who's got five hundred and the paperwork ... I put people together and do this and running about ... that won't be for another three or four weeks, then it will be regular, fucking hundred a week ... we're at standby ... it's going to happen next week ... we're on the verge.'

And, even more damaging for me: 'I'll get him to ring you, I don't think it will be this weekend ... you had a word with Ron, I've been told it could be Monday or Tuesday.'

Kelsey-Fry paused, letting the heavy silence hang in the air. He turned towards the dock and motioned to a detective sitting in the back row of the court in front of me. The detective handed an evidence bag to the prosecution's junior counsel, who, in turn, passed it on. Kelsey-Fry placed it on a chair, then, dramatically, pulled on a pair of flesh-coloured surgical gloves and opened the package.

Inside was a black rubber container covered in tape, stuck to a plastic bag – the same packaging Ronnie Field had described to Jack and Ken at The Linden Hall Hotel on 27 June.

Kelsey-Fry reminded the jury of what Field had said in the transcript: '... they will give this to you. It'll be wrapped. Come in like a, erm, rubber wrapping, like a bag ... vacuum sealed. Then it's wrapped up in tape and it's got another bag around the outside of it.'

I needed no reminding that I'd chimed in with a comment of my own about that wrapping.

And then, lastly, he left the jury with the impression that my pal Steve Grant was a significant figure in the whole scenario. I had denied that Steve knew Ronnie Field, but Steve had gone to The Selsdon on 25 July for a meeting with Field and Gould and the undercover police.

I had intended to introduce Steve to Jack at The Blue Orchid and was on tape referring to this. I was also on tape at The Linden Hall Hotel, saying: 'We don't know when we'll see Steve, it may be held up.'

And Kelsey-Fry made a big point about me ringing Steve on 26 July after Jack told me about the 'clowns on the plot'.

If I believed Field was going to confess all to Jack that night, the first person I would have rung the next morning, having learnt he hadn't, surely would have been Field to ask: 'What are you playing at?'

Kelsey-Fry closed his speech, telling the jury Steve Grant had been arrested in January of this year and was serving six years for laundering drug money.

I knew Steve was in prison on a charge involving money, but I had no idea it had anything to do with drugs. I had no time to dwell on that, however, because my mind was now on how my defence was going to counter what Kelsey-Fry said was overwhelming evidence against me.

Mr Goldberg told the jury that my trial 'was one of the great cases of the decade', then, reminding them of my autobiography, said: 'You are writing the last chapter ... it's a mind-blowing decision you have to make.'

I wanted him to stress the appalling way the police had behaved since slipping George into my Gary's funeral, and he did not let me down.

An elaborate and expensive operation had been launched 'by career-hungry police who saw feathers in their caps by arresting this old man', he said. The undercover officers who carried it out lived the life of Riley for two and a half months at the taxpayer's expense: bottle after bottle of champagne, £2,000 on booze from Fethi Torki's cash and carry, £1,000 on air tickets and a loan to me, rooms for five at a five-star hotel, birthday presents for me and Patsy.

'They were spending money like crazy, because they were Kray-fishing,' said Mr Goldberg. 'Other police officers might say, "If this is undercover work, give us some any day of the week." ' And he added: 'Jack and his pals started to behave like the people they want to put away. The protective screen they have hidden behind is a cloak for their accountability.'

Just twenty per cent of their tape recordings were decipherable; the rest were useless, said Mr Goldberg. The only other evidence was in their notebooks, but who was to say *when* they had written in them? One had only their word that what they had written was true – and the prosecution had chosen to accept it.

That Jack had breached his instructions was blatantly clear. His superior officer, Detective Inspector Michael Allen, had specifically told him not to indulge in talk about criminality, but, Mr Goldberg argued, that is precisely what Jack did in The Elbow Room on 9 May, by telling me someone he knew had been 'topped' in Amsterdam.

Jack denied he gave the impression he was a drug dealer, because he knew he had breached those instructions, said Mr Goldberg. Jack stepped over the line again by telling me at The Wake Green Lodge Hotel: 'I do "charlie" and I do the smoke.'

He was acting as *agent provocateur* by inciting me to commit a more serious offence.

'What's the point in having instructions if no one pays any attention to them and shrugs their shoulders,' said Mr Goldberg, adding: 'Poor Charlie.'

I was on tape talking of 'tons of drugs', but where was it? Mr Goldberg wanted to know. No one had gone looking for it. If the police genuinely believed me and Field were into drugs in a big way, why didn't the police put us under surveillance and catch the big fish in their net, too? As it was, we'll never know where Field got those two kilos of cocaine, because the little fish got all the attention, while bigger fish went swimming by.

The reason, said Mr Goldberg, was that there were big forces at work within the police to get Charlie Kray convicted. There was no surveillance because they *knew* he was bluffing. They could have gone for a high target and brought a charge of conspiracy to supply drugs. But they didn't want a negative result.

Why I was targeted for this elaborate set-up was not known, because the undercover police were not obliged to say, said Mr Goldberg. And he reminded the jury of twenty questions Jack had been allowed to duck, even the significant one of why George and Deano had been allowed to spend £2,000 on booze without accounting for it.

Rightly, not too much time was spent on the love life of Brian, the *undercovers'* officer. At the *voire dire* he said he could not recall Michelle. Yet, at the trial, she produced a telephone bill listing *seventy* calls between them.

'Mr Kelsey-Fry referred to Brian as a plonker, but I'd go further than that,' said Mr Goldberg.

That said it all about fat Brian.

Kelsey-Fry emphasized the point that if Field was not bluffing in being able to supply drugs, then I was not either. But, Mr Goldberg told the jury, Field became serious in his intentions without my knowledge or consent. When we were invited to Newcastle, we went along separate roads. On those incriminating tapes, Field was heard singing the song, while I provided the chorus. 'Go and ask Field yourselves,' Mr Goldberg urged the jury.

And then he advised them on a point of law which I was convinced would help me get off the charge of supplying cocaine. It was not enough for me merely to have known about the plan to supply the drugs, he said. For the jury to find me guilty, the prosecution had to have proved that I aided and abetted it.

I was in the dock, said Mr Goldberg, only because I was a broken, shambolic figure, desperate for cash, who had had to invent stories to keep up a front. If all the stories I'd told the police on tape – losing £1.25 million on a deal, contacts with Israeli secret service and the rest – were accepted as rubbish, why weren't my statements about enormous quantities of drugs?

Just when I was wondering what he would say about my notorious surname, Mr Goldberg once again told the jury that they could be forgiven for thinking, during the trial, that they were in danger of being murdered in their beds. There was only one reason why they had been under surveillance twenty-four hours a day throughout the past five weeks: the defendant's surname was Kray.

'The police claim the jury protection was the court's decision, not theirs,' he said. 'But it is the police who have created the atmosphere you feel in this court. It suits their case for the hype surrounding the name Kray to stay in place.'

It was indeed a remarkable and unique case, the like of which we would not see again, he said. 'A sad old-timer has been badly set up.'

I did not care for the first bit, but I could not agree more with the second.

I just hoped the jury did, too.

That night, thinking over Goldberg's statement that the undercover police knew I was bluffing, my mind went back to 1968 when I was arrested with the twins and all the other idiots. The police knew then that I was straight and had nothing to do with any of the murders or violence.

I wouldn't class any copper as a bosom pal, someone I'd

invite home to dinner, but I'd always enjoyed a friendly relationship with men of various ranks over the years and, while most of the Old Bill were suspicious of the twins and their friends, they accepted I was not part of the so-called Firm. If I was around when they pulled the twins in for questioning, they would say: 'Stay out of it, Charlie – this has nothing to do with you.' This was one of the reasons I felt confident then, that whatever the police had on the twins it could not have anything to do with me. I honestly thought it would be only a matter of time before I was released. But the police had been ordered to nail *all* the Krays – and no matter how much they believed I was innocent, that is precisely what they set out to do.

My name was written on a long prison sentence and the law made sure I got it – even though, a year after I was jailed, Ronald Hart swore an affidavit that his evidence was false: that neither me, nor Freddie Foreman, was involved in the killing of McVitie. You would have thought that such a turnabout would have been viewed as vital new evidence, but the legal brains pooh-poohed it and although a copy of Hart's affidavit was supposedly sent to the Home Secretary, calling for the case to be reopened, nothing happened. Later, Chris and Tony Lambrianou also made statements, confessing that they had disposed of McVitie's body. But, again, nothing happened.

I was disappointed and very bitter at the injustice of it all. And now it looked like my name was written on a long prison sentence once again.

I was sure Judge Carroll would put the boot in. He had been against me from the start and, when he summed up the case, I expected him to direct the jury towards guilty verdicts on both counts. Surprisingly, he did not. He read out what he felt were the crucial, important issues and left the jury to it. Maybe he felt I was clearly guilty and did not see the need to steer the jury. Certainly I was relieved; so was Mr Goldberg and his team. They felt it was a point in my favour.

As the jury left the court, at 12.04 P.M. on Wednesday, I looked up at the gallery. Now the trial was nearing its end, friends had turned up to give me support. I gave them a smile I did not feel, then walked out of the dock into the little room, where I'd spent so many days hanging about, waiting for one thing and another over the past nine weeks. It was out of everyone's hands now; all we could do was wait and find out who those seven women and four men believed.

A few minutes before four o'clock I was told they were on their way back. My pulse quickened. If a jury returned in anything under a couple of hours it usually meant a guilty verdict, but this one had been out four. I sat down in the dock, expectant, hopeful. But it was an anti-climax: the judge had called them back merely to ask if they had reached a verdict on either count. When they said they had not, he dismissed them until the next day.

The waiting went on all day Thursday until just gone half-past three when I was told they were coming back. I did not get my hopes up. Throughout the trial, the judge had shown a desire to pack up around four, and I felt he might be thinking of dismissing the jury until the next day again.

But when the foreman of the jury was asked if they had agreed a verdict on Count One – offering to supply cocaine – he replied: 'Yes.'

I had not felt so tense since that day in March twenty-eight years earlier when I stood in the Old Bailey, waiting for the McVitie verdict.

Everyone was looking at the foreman, but I could not bring myself to. I stared straight ahead.

'And what *is* your verdict?'

My throat was dry. I gulped. I clenched both hands.
'Guilty.'

To be truthful, I was not really surprised. My voice was there on tape, offering to get cocaine for Jack. Whether the jury believed I was bluffing or not did not matter. In law, simply making the offer is an offence.

The jury were not agreed on Count Two – supplying two kilos of cocaine. Good! It was the more serious charge and I wanted them to take their time on that one. If they considered the evidence carefully, I was sure they would believe me, not the police. I was sure they would believe I knew nothing of what went on at the Selsdon Park and Swallow hotels. I was sure they would believe I played no part in Field's supply of those two kilos.

I was sure I'd be acquitted.

I looked up at the gallery. Judy had got time off work and was there, with a couple of friends of ours. I shrugged and forced a half-smile, then heard my solicitor telling me not to worry: if I was acquitted on the second charge, I could get a light sentence – possibly as little as eighteen months – which would mean I would be released immediately, because of the time I'd spent in prison on remand.

I clung to that thought overnight.

I spent most of the next day, locked in a cell beneath No. 1 Court with Field and Gould, but would have preferred to be alone. We'd been locked up together since our arrests and there was little we had to say to each other now. With the most important day of my life ahead, I didn't want to be bothered with trivial conversation: I just wanted to lose myself in my own thoughts, and they, as usual, centred on Judy and her kids, Nina, Glenn and Sean. How I missed them; how much I wanted to get back to them, get back to normal. Thinking of Judy and her family brought Gary into focus once more. When he was dying, early last year, Judy

411

had turned her front room into a hospital ward and the family had nursed him through his final weeks. He was so appreciative: he kept telling me what lovely people they were. And he was right.

Poor Gary. What would he have made of all this? It was a blessing, perhaps, that he was not here to go through it. He was such an innocent, he would have been bewildered by all the guns and metal detector security checks, and me all over the papers and the telly, branded an evil drug baron. Once, I was with Gary at Robin McGibbon's house, having just spent five hours being questioned about a murder I knew nothing about, simply because my name was Kray. I was going on and on about the injustice of it all, and suddenly Robin and Sue and I looked at Gary, and he was crying. To him I was not the person the papers made me out to be. To him I was just his dad, and he couldn't bear to see me upset.

Now, waiting for the jury to return, I felt I'd done enough to convince them I was innocent. But, deep down, there was a terrible nagging fear that history might repeat itself. In March 1969 I was sentenced to ten years for a crime the police knew – and maybe the jury suspected – I had not committed.

Would it – could it – happen again?

We got the call just after three. No one knew if they were any nearer reaching a verdict, even though, earlier in the day, the judge had said he was prepared to accept a 10–1 majority. For all anyone knew, they were split 7–4, or 6–5, which meant a hung jury and a retrial.

My heart started racing: it was like being in the dressing room, waiting to go into the ring. I was all keyed up, knowing that where I was going there was nowhere to hide. Field and Gould were taken up with me, because they would be sentenced if the jury had reached a verdict on me. They already knew they were facing several years in prison, but I was clinging to the hope that I'd be acquitted and released that day.

I walked into the dock, leaving my co-defendants behind the locked door of an adjacent room. I was told to stand as the clerk of the court addressed the foreman of the jury.

'Have you reached a verdict on Count Two?' the clerk asked. 'Answer Yes or No.'

The court was silent.

'Yes.'

My face felt on fire. I was fidgeting with my shirt cuffs.

'What is your verdict?'

I sensed all eyes from the public gallery on me. I was too tense to do anything but stare ahead, seeing nothing, just thinking that, in the next second, I'd hear the two words that would end my nightmare; two words that would spell freedom. And then, breaking the deathly quiet:

'Guilty.'

Barristers started moving about and the judge was telling the jury something, but I just stood where I was, in a sort of trance. I was so sure I'd be acquitted I felt the jury had, for some reason, been asked to give their verdict on Count One again. I motioned to Helen Guest, one of Mr Goldberg's team, a warm, friendly lady in her thirties, with a legal brain as sharp as her wit. 'Could I have a word with Mr Goldberg, please?' I asked her.

Goldberg came to the dock. 'Was that guilty on the first charge?' I wanted to know.

'No, Charlie,' he said, his face creased with disappointment. 'It's the second. I'm sick, totally sick. But try not to be too depressed. There are grounds for an appeal.'

I was so confused that I just stood there, not taking it in, and then I was aware of Field and Gould moving into the dock alongside me, and the judge telling the court that everyone had had a long day and that he would not pass sentence on the three of us that day; he would do it on Monday.

Saturday and Sunday were the longest, most worrying days of my life. It took a long time for the jury's verdict to sink in and, to be truthful, I did not understand how they had reached it. While giving evidence, I'd sworn on oath that I'd never handled drugs, and I meant it: I would never dream of doing anything that would jeopardize me going to Chingford Cemetery to tend my Gary's grave. That is everything to me.

For comfort that terrible weekend I looked at his photo more than ever and talked to him as though he were with me. God knows what the judge was going to do on Monday; throw the book at me, I shouldn't wonder.

Whatever the sentence was going to be, I was relieved Gary would not be around to suffer it. He'd been such a soft, sensitive, innocent young man and, seeing his dad behind bars in the winter of his life would have destroyed him. I was pleased, in a strange, sad way, that my dear mum was not alive either. She had gone through enough with all that happened in the sixties, and I would not have wanted her to witness my humiliation. She was such a wonderful woman, and that Sunday I tried to keep my mind off what lay ahead by thinking about her and her lovely ways.

The next day, the public gallery was packed for the sentencing. There were the familiar faces of friends I'd seen over the final days of the trial, but there were people there for the first time. Funny, isn't it, how certain people like to be in at the kill?

I had resigned myself to a long sentence. No matter how ludicrous it was to me, and everyone who knew me, I'd been set up as the linchpin of a deal that was, supposedly, going to swamp the streets with millions of pounds' worth of cocaine. So, no doubt, I would get a sentence that would reflect that.

For an hour and a half Mr Kelsey-Fry went through the entire case again, then there were mitigations on behalf of the three of us.

Then the judge retired for twenty minutes.

When he came back, he wasted little time. Reading from typewritten statements, he said he was sentencing the three of us in ascending order of importance of our crime.

He gave Bobby Gould five years and Ronnie Field nine.

Then, turning to me, he said: 'Charles Kray, you have been found guilty on both counts by the jury on overwhelming evidence. You showed yourself ready, willing and able to lend yourself to any criminal enterprise which became known to you. There was never a real question of entrapment of you by these officers, but, when caught, you cried foul. I'm pleased the jury saw through that hollow cry: infiltration by officers is an important tool in society's fight against crime. Throughout this case, you professed your abhorrence against drugs, but the jury's verdict has shown your oft-repeated protestations to be hypocrisy. Those who deal in Class A drugs can expect justice from the courts, but little mercy. Eight years on Count One, twelve years on Count Two, to run concurrently.'

I was shocked by the sentence; but, after listening to the judge for nine weeks, I knew it was going to be severe. What did hurt, though, was being accused of hypocrisy. It's one of my pet hates; I can't bear double standards.

When asked if I had anything to say, again I failed to do myself justice. Don't ask me why, but all I could think to say was:

'All my life I have advised people, particularly young people, never to be involved in drugs. I went along with the stories, as the officers did. But they are all untrue. It was only to get money.

'I swear on my son's grave that I have never handled drugs in my life. The jury have got it wrong for me before and the jury have got it wrong again.'

And then I was led out of court and back along the tunnel to the High Security Block and to my cell and to a life of God knows what.

Chapter Twenty-seven

Back in my cell after the verdict, I looked at myself in the highly polished piece of metal that served as a mirror, and was shocked at what I saw. I didn't mind the laughter lines round the eyes; they were testimony to the fun I'd had, and, God knows, there had been plenty of that, before and after McVitie. I didn't give a toss about my sunken cheeks, suitcases under the eyes, or that my skin was prison-grey. What with being caged in a maximum security jail, and the never-ending angst of the trial, I hadn't had a decent night's kip for the best part of a year; I was hardly going to look as if I'd been on a cruise, was I? I wasn't bothered, either, at looking so old. I *was* seventy-one, for Christ's sake.

No, it was the look of defeat in that gaunt, haggard face that got to me; it was the look of a beaten man, who knew it was all over; who was resigned to spending the last years of his life, banished from everything and everyone he treasured.

Jesus Christ, twelve years. TWELVE YEARS! Even if I got full remission, which I was bound to, given that I'm a model prisoner, I'd be a year off eighty when I got out. *A year off eighty!* What life would be worth living then?

I looked away from my haunted face and stretched out on the bed, my head on the pillow that had been flattened by hundreds of prisoners before me. And, again, I was consumed with the same question that had tortured me since that July evening in Ilford police station when I learnt that Jack was an undercover cop.

Just why had I been targeted for such an elaborate, costly sting?

417

I wasn't a drug dealer, never had been. So it had to be because my name was Kray. But why had the Old Bill gone to such lengths to put me away? The only answer I'd been able to find in the year I'd been locked up was that Reg would soon be due parole, and the authorities didn't want him to get it. In 1998, he would have served the thirty years recommended by the trial judge, Melford Stevenson, and, no doubt, the Press and public would be saying, as they had been for a long time, that enough was enough.

The Establishment didn't feel that way, I was sure of that. Having witnessed the televised hero-worship of Reg at Ron's funeral, the men in suits in Whitehall would have believed he still wielded the power he and Ron did in the sixties. Watching all that cheering and chanting of Reggie's name, someone must have said: 'No way can we have a Kray in the East End again. Let's find a way to keep him inside – make him ineligible for parole.'

Think about it. Reg had kept his nose clean for years, was now likely to marry a respectable young woman, Roberta – and, more significantly, had, at last, shown remorse for the brutal slaughter of Jack McVitie. He had everything going for him. With his recommended time up and other, more dangerous, killers being given lesser sentences, the authorities would have risked a public outcry if they had refused parole. So, they had to find another way to keep Reg banged up.

What better than to discredit his elder brother? Stitch him up as a conniving drug baron with the money and contacts to flood Britain's streets with millions of pounds' worth of a Class A drug? That would do it, wouldn't it? How can we possibly let Reg Kray loose when his brother is such an evil criminal? That would quieten the Press, wouldn't it? And the noisy majority who'd been screaming for years for Reg's release.

The more I thought about it, I was in no doubt that

someone at the Home Office had sent a directive to the Met to fit me up. Anyone who'd been close to me in the last twenty years knew I had neither the money, nor the where-withal, to put any sort of big bucks deal together. But that wouldn't be a problem for a well-oiled police force adept at framing innocent people, would it? If anything, it would make it easier. I was a soft touch: not only was I desperate for money, I was well used to people I didn't know being friendly, so they could boast about having been in my company.

Anyway, there was nothing I could do now. My future was out of my hands. Of course, there was the appeal, and Goldberg seemed confident we could win one. But I wouldn't be holding my breath. Not after what had gone on in court over the last nine weeks. Not after hearing my drunken voice on those tapes. To be truthful, if *I'd* been on that jury and heard all that talk of 'charlie' and 'blow' and 'vacuum sealed' and 'regular, regular supplies', even I'd have found me guilty! It was damning stuff, so convincing I almost believed I was an experienced drug dealer myself.

I had to cling to the hope of an appeal, even if it was just against the length of sentence, but, to be truthful, the thought of topping myself passed through my mind. If I didn't win the right to appeal, or we did and it failed, what would I have to live for? I forced myself not to dwell on that morbid thought, because Judy had remained loyal throughout the trial and, despite the long sentence, I was sure she wouldn't desert me.

Apart from Judy, the one woman I knew would want to visit me was Maureen Flanagan, a lovely, blonde model, who had grown up in Bethnal Green and had been a close friend of the Kray family for more than fifty years. No one referred to her as Maureen. To everyone, she was simply 'Flanagan', or, even more simply, 'Flan', and she had a heart of gold. She'd always been a dear, loyal friend, as

419

she proved by speaking up for me in court, and the one Reg and I turned to to organize the seating for Ronnie's and Gary's funerals. She was one of the *Sun* newspaper's early Page Three girls in 1971 and I made sure the prison officers knew this when I learnt she had been cleared to visit me. She was due to come with her boyfriend, Derek Francis, but he had flu, so she brought another friend of mine, Les Martin, instead.

Knowing that being one of the first Page Three girls meant a lot to Flan, the first thing I did when she and Les sat down in the small Category A visiting room facing me was introduce her to my guards. Despite having her hair all messed up during the pre-visit security search, Flan still looked every inch the glamour model and I could see the officers were impressed with meeting her.

'Flan's the sister I never had,' I told them. I'd always said this whenever I introduced Flan to anyone and knew she loved it. In many ways, I wished she *had* been my sister. Imagine what my life would have been like if Mum had given birth to her, not the twins!

'My mother and brothers loved Flan,' I told the prison officers. 'Ronnie was always on to her to marry Reggie. He's proposed three times, but she always says No.'

One the officers laughed. 'I bet that's the first time Reggie has had a knockback, isn't it, Charlie?'

Flan and Les did their best to lift my spirits and, for a while, I was fine. But I found it hard keeping up the pretence of being good old Charlie, ready to laugh and joke, and finally took Flan's hand. 'I've got nothing left inside me to fight, darling,' I said. 'I did nearly seven years as an innocent man, and now I've got twelve. It's all over for me. I know I won't get out.'

Flan leant over the table and put her arms round me. She didn't say anything, but I'd lost so much weight I knew she'd be shocked at being able to feel my ribs.

'Remember your mum, Charlie,' she said. 'If she was here now, she'd be telling you that you must never ever give up hope.'

'I should have listened to her years ago,' I said. 'She kept telling me I was different to the twins and should not live my life around them. She adored them, as you know, but in her own way, I think she always felt they were headed for disaster.'

Suddenly, talking about my mother choked me and I started to cry, and, of course, that set Flan off, too. She held me tight for a minute or so, then, to try to lighten the mood, said, 'Now, come on, Charlie – it's not like you to cry like a baby.'

I eased myself away and looked at the bright orange sleeveless top that Category A prisoners have to wear. 'Well, I *have* got a bib on,' I said, forcing a laugh.

I told Flan and Les I'd been having chest pains and that I'd been seeing the prison doctor.

'What's the chances of you getting early parole through ill health?' Les asked.

'No chance,' I said. 'Reg has served more than his recommended time and isn't a threat. But the authorities don't want two Kray brothers on the streets. Goldberg's going to appeal, but they won't ever let me out. I'll be kept inside until I can't walk.'

I was sad when the two-hour visit was up, but relieved, too, because pains in my chest were making it difficult for me to breathe.

As we stood up, I leant over and cuddled Flan again, closely. 'You know more than anyone, I was never like the twins,' I said. 'They were strong and could handle prison. But I won't make it. I've written and told Diana I won't last two years.'

And I meant it.

Visits were always bitter-sweet. I always looked forward

to them, always enjoyed the chinwag, but always felt low when I said goodbye. The time immediately after Flan's visit was particularly distressing. Talking about my mother had hit me hard and now, alone in my cell, remembering how lovely she was, I couldn't stop the tears falling again.

What an idiot I'd been to let the makers of *The Krays* movie portray Mum the way they did. I've got a lot of regrets about the way my life has turned out and, the jail sentences apart, one of the biggest is not taking my role as consultant on that film seriously enough. How she came over was a travesty and I'm as much to blame as anyone. No wonder the twins went spare at me. Thank God Mum wasn't alive to see that load of tosh; she would have been ashamed beyond words. She never used bad language, but almost the first word she uttered on screen was: 'Bollocks.'

The twins were right to have a go at me: as the only brother free I should have made sure that, if nothing else, the woman we cared for so deeply was shown in her true light. I've always felt very, very badly about this: I let my brothers down, but I let our mother down, too, and I've never forgiven myself. To be truthful, when I signed the movie deal I was more interested in the money I was getting than in using my £4,000 consultant's role to protect the twins and our parents.

I'd signed away a big chunk of my share, in order to survive for ten years or so, but I still came out with £55,000, and having been broke for so long it was great to have money in my pocket. To my discredit, I paid less attention to the film than I did in making up for lost time – and living up to my nickname, Champagne Charlie. With my good-time girl Judy in tow, it was party time most days of the week.

As I say, I'm not impressed with my input as consultant. I was supposed to advise on the violence, but even when the twins were seen running around the East End with machine guns I kept my mouth shut. No wonder the twins didn't like the film – and heaped all the blame on me.

While on remand, I'd been such a model prisoner – 'faultless', according to an official report – that I was granted what they called an 'enhancement', allowing me to have an extra hour on my visits. This is a big deal in the prison system and I was the only one among the twelve on Category A to be given the privilege.

After my sentence I felt sure this would go in my favour, perhaps encourage the prison service to downgrade me and transfer me to a prison in the South, making it easier for Judy and the kids and all my friends to visit me. So, you can imagine my shock when I was told I was staying in Belmarsh, still the oldest prisoner in the country on Category A. I was bitterly disappointed, not just because it was such a strict regime, but without Dave Courtney I'd have no one to turn to for some humour, support and general light relief to ease the crushing boredom. I didn't have too long to be depressed: the following Monday (30 June) I was told I *was* being transferred. Any delight I felt, however, turned sour when I heard that I was going to Long Lartin, near Evesham, in Worcestershire.

The prison held bad memories for me, because it was where Reggie had tried to kill himself fifteen years before. I didn't hold out much hope of being taken off Category A and I was right: I'd been a model prisoner, but I was still a dangerous man, wasn't I? And my name was Kray, after all!

As it turned out, Long Lartin had changed since Reg was treated so badly there. I could not have been made more welcome by the other Cat A prisoners: they were quick to give me phone cards and tobacco, and assured me that, as nicks go, Long Lartin was one of the less miserable. I quickly discovered they were right: the staff were very nice to me and I was allowed on to the prison grounds to enjoy the July sunshine. What a relief that was after the claustrophobia of Belmarsh. I quickly started working on my tan, which, as a free man, had always been one of my trademarks. That and my long hair, which I always combed in the most artistic way to cover all my bald spots!

Thankfully, I was allowed more than three visitors, and, after Judy, the first ones on my list were Laurie O'Leary and John Corbett. I wanted to see Robin McGibbon and his wife, Sue, too, but he had been commissioned to write a book on Battersea Dogs Home, to tie in with a BBC TV series, and they were going to be tied up on that for the next four or five months. I was disappointed they would not be coming, but Rob had visited me every week on remand, and had been in court every day of the trial. I fully understood that he now needed to earn a living!

Naturally, I was keen to see the up-to-date edition of *Me and My Brothers*, which the publishers had rushed out within a few days of the end of the trial. But, prison rules being what they are, the copy Rob sent me had been put in my locker, with my civilian clothes and other personal possessions, until such time someone decided it was safe for me to have it. Honestly, people who've never been in jail have no idea of the idiotic rules that make life even more frustrating for prisoners. Having worked so hard on the update, covering Ronnie's and Gary's deaths, and that awful film, I was keen to read the book, but I refused to let myself get in a state about it; I had other matters on my mind, and the most important was Judy. I'd detected a change in her attitude when she'd visited me in late August and it hadn't come as much of a surprise when she wrote, soon afterwards, saying she wouldn't be coming again. I was gutted, to be honest: we'd gone through so much together and I'd believed her when she'd assured me she was going to stick by me. But I had to face facts: she was so much younger than me, she had to think of the future, not only for herself, but for her three children, too. God knows where I was going to spend my prison life. What sort of existence would it be for her, traipsing to depressing nicks in far-flung parts of the country, for just a couple of hours' chit-chat? So, much as I didn't care for the cowardly 'Dear John' manner in which Judy dumped me, I had to accept that it was over and forget about her. I didn't like it, not one bit. But I had no choice, had I? The good news was, with Judy out of my life, Diana would be applying to visit me; her loyalty never wavered.

I tried not to think about my sentence, only the application to appeal. I was told it could take up to a year. And it did. Unfortunately, though, my solicitor Ralph Haeems, for reasons known only to himself, failed to provide Jonathan Goldberg with the necessary paperwork, which put the barrister at a distinct disadvantage.

The following August 1998 we did win the application to appeal against conviction and sentence, but what hopes I had were dashed, three months later when Lord Justice Pill and two other judges turned down my appeal against conviction. I was bitterly disappointed, naturally, given that I believed I shouldn't have been found guilty in the first place. But I was given leave to appeal against my sentence and I clung to that hope over Christmas, pending the hearing early in the New Year.

When I was transferred back to Belmarsh in the last week of January for the hearing in front of the Lord Chief Justice, Lord Bingham, and Mr Justices Kennedy and Jackson, I thought it was simply to save me being driven from Worcestershire, should the hearing go into a second day. But it was more sinister than that. The prison intelligence system, it seemed, had heard of a plot to ambush the van taking me to London and either organize my escape, or, believe it or not, harm me. I was baffled then and I'm baffled

425

now. Anyone who knows me will laugh at the thought of me even considering going on the run. And as for anyone going to such lengths to harm me, who on earth would they be? And, more to the point, what motive would they have? Wasn't twelve years behind bars in my seventies harm enough? It seemed all too ridiculous for words, but Les Martin had heard of the supposed plot and alerted Jonathan Goldberg, who was interested enough to contact the Governor at Long Lartin. My transfer to Belmarsh, the Governor said, had nothing to do with my appeal hearing; it was for 'security intelligence reasons'. No one was saying what that meant, but maybe all the talk about ambushing the van might not be as ridiculous as I thought.

Thankfully, it all came to nothing, but I was grateful to Les and Mr Goldberg for making inquiries because you never know; there are a lot of idiots out there. Can you imagine the headline: PLOT TO SPRING CHARLIE KRAY? I had enough to think about without all that rubbish.

I must say that, out of all the people angry at the way I'd been set up and sentenced so severely, Les Martin was the one who seemed to be taking it particularly badly. I heard that he'd sworn to do all he could to clear my name, or at least make prison life better for me, and he was true to his word. I'm sure it was as a result of his terrier-like persistence that Mr Goldberg wrote to the Home Secretary, Jack Straw, in February 1999 about my Category A status. In his letter, while we were awaiting the Appeal Court judges' findings, he said he was 'very concerned' that I had been held as a top-security Category A prisoner since my arrest, in July 1996. It was hard, he said, to see anything in my previous record, or in the circumstances of the current case, that justified such treatment and he was asking for a review of my status 'because there is a fear that the system may have gone wrong'. He said that I was seventy-two, becoming frail, and had admitted to him that I was taking life on Category A very hard. He was certainly right about that!

Mr Goldberg's letter said that an 'impressive body' of character evidence from eighteen witnesses – unchallenged by Crown or judge – had spoken of my 'non-violent temperament, acts of kindness and decency and impecuniosity' over many years. I had to look up impecuniosity, and discovered it was educated people's way of saying broke! Mr Goldberg was right about that, too!

Mr Goldberg also stressed that I was very different from the notorious twins, but was, perhaps, being 'tarred with the same brush'. And just in case Mr Straw didn't get that last point, he enclosed a character reference from a Long Lartin prison officer, Mr A. Jenkins, who had known me since I arrived on his wing in July the previous year. Mr Jenkins's note, which I very much appreciated him writing, said:

Although I am not his personal officer, I have day to day contact with him [Kray] when on duty. Throughout his time at Long Lartin, he has been very polite and had adhered to wing regimes and expectations. He works in the Time Shop and regularly attends, appearing quite keen to do so. He is approachable to staff, had caused no problems to Discipline and has not been placed on report whilst here. I have always found Kray to be cheerful and polite, he does what is asked of him and is never disrespectful to staff.

I was delighted when I eventually saw what Mr Jenkins had written. If I ever got out, it would be ideal for a job application!

I was right not to set my hopes high on the appeal, because, three weeks after the hearing, I was told my sentence was being upheld, and I would have to serve six years before being considered for parole. No surprise there, then. And no surprise, either, that my Cat A status was not high on the Home Office agenda; it was close on a month before Mr Goldberg got a reply. Each Category A prisoner normally has his case reviewed every year and a review of mine was 'currently in progress', the Prison Service's Director of Security, A. J. Pearson, informed Mr Goldberg on 5 March. The Category A Committee was meeting on 21 April, he said, and Mr Goldberg's letter would be considered, with other representations by me, or submitted on my behalf.

That did give me a boost, I must admit, but I did wonder why – if there were annual reviews, and I'd always been such a model prisoner – I had not been taken off Cat A after my first year in Long Lartin. And would my review this time around have been quietly kicked into touch had Messrs Goldberg and Jenkins – and dear old Les – not made noises on my behalf?

The Category A Committee *did* see the sense in downgrading me and, in April that year, I was told I was on the move again. Having been a model prisoner, I was hoping to be moved to a prison further south, but was disappointed: I was being transferred further north, to an unpleasant, very old prison in Durham that I remembered one of the twins' friends, Chris Lambrianou, referring to as a 'grim, forbidding fortress'.

With such a long journey ahead of us, and no security of any kind at risk, you would have thought the most sensible, and quickest, mode of transport would have been a police car. No chance! I was handcuffed and ordered into a minibus. I seem to remember it was a six-seater, but, apart from the driver and an accompanying policeman, I was the only passenger, crammed into one of the six single compartments with my knees virtually up to my chin. It was a cold April morning, but someone had felt it necessary for me to make the journey wearing just prison paper overalls. I was freezing for every one of the four hundred or so miles and, not surprisingly, developed a chill.

Now that I'd been downgraded, I could have as many people on my visiting list as I liked, and one of the first I wrote to was Steve Wraith, who lived relatively nearby, in Newcastle. We'd met at Ronnie's funeral, in March 1995, and had stayed friends. He was well connected in the North-East, and the following July arranged for Tony Lambrianou and me to travel to Newcastle for a charity evening. It was a remarkable occasion: 700 people paid £20 a ticket to meet Tony and me and, what with the auctions and raffles etc., many thousands of pounds were raised for a family friend of Steve's who had been horribly burnt in a Bonfire Night accident. The evening doubled up as a birthday party for me, so you can imagine I had a great time. Paul Gascoigne's mum was there and she seemed as pleased to meet me as I was to meet her. She was great fun and we hit it off. Later that night, Steve took Tony and me to a nightclub on Newcastle's quayside, where everyone, it seemed, wanted our autographs and photos taken with us. We felt like celebrities and, of course, didn't have to put our hands in our pockets for anything. I didn't see anything wrong in that – just enjoyed myself among lively, engaging young people who clearly liked me and whatever fame my name gave me.

Of course, I reciprocated Steve's generosity by inviting him to London and taking him to various East End nightspots and The Guv'ner's pub, run by twin brothers George and Andrew Wadman, who had become known to Reggie through their boxing achievements. For the next two years, Steve and I went to various charity events, not only in Newcastle, where I was always made so welcome, but all over London, and we always enjoyed each other's company.

If Steve was shocked that I was pale, grey-haired and had lost a lot of weight since he'd last seen me, in court, he didn't show it; he just started chatting in that lively way of his, as though we'd seen each other only yesterday. Obviously, he wanted to know what I thought about the case, and I told him I was clearly a victim of entrapment, but didn't know why I'd been set up. He said he had no idea either.

I said the only reason that made sense was that the authorities had been shocked by the hero-worship for Reggie at Ronnie's funeral, and wanted to quash any chances of his parole by locking me away as an evil drug dealer. Treating me as a hardened criminal by transporting me here in paper overalls seemed to endorse this thinking. Like me, Steve was disgusted by that; for some reason, they were out to humiliate me, he said.

Eventually, we moved on to happier topics, reflecting on the enjoyable times we'd shared together, in London and the North-East, and before he left I asked him if he'd mind letting various people know where I was – particularly Big Albert – and to arrange transport for Diana and Les Martin. Steve was a good bloke; he said he'd deal with it.

I'd never felt one hundred per cent since developing that chill. The pains in my chest had been getting worse and, in the last week of July, I collapsed in the prison's health centre, barely able to breathe. I was rushed to the city's Dryburn Hospital, and, a few days later, the *Sun* ran a story by a reporter named Mike Sullivan, stating 'Charlie Kray is fighting for his life after suffering a suspected heart attack'. The word 'suspected' was crucial: with the hospital unwilling to release patients' details, Sullivan didn't know for sure whether I'd had a heart attack or not. The prison source he quoted as saying 'Charlie hasn't been well for some time' was spot on, however – although very understated. I'd been feeling terrible, and my mood wasn't helped after finally being allowed the updated edition of *Me and*

430

My Brothers. Reading all I'd said about my Gary's tragic death, and how the undercover police had used his funeral to get into me, knocked me bandy and there were days when I couldn't stop crying. My God, how I missed my lovely, lovely boy. It was at distressing times like this that I did wonder, with my appeals now lost, whether life was worth living; whether I should end it all and be with Gary.

It turned out that I hadn't had a heart attack; but the bit about fighting for my life was true. Apparently, I had pneumonia – brought on, I was in no doubt, by freezing in those paper overalls.

I was moved back to the prison, feeling more like my old self, and felt even better towards the end of August when I was told I was being transferred to Parkhurst, on the Isle of Wight. Although it would mean a longer journey for Big Albert, it would mean I'd be able to see more of Diana, Laurie O'Leary, Joey Pyle, hopefully Freddie Foreman – and, more particularly, Wilf Pine, who had health problems of his own and had been unable to travel to Long Lartin and Frankland. Wilf and his wife, Ros, were now living on the South Coast, at Christchurch, and while it was still a couple of hours – by car and ferry – to the Isle of Wight, the journey was certainly shorter and far more pleasant than it was to that 'forbidding fortress' in the far north.

I was so looking forward to seeing Wilf again. We'd been great pals since the summer of 1975, shortly after I'd been reunited with Diana, and were having trouble finding a place to live. Wilf heard about this from Laurie O'Leary and, over afternoon tea at the Dorchester Hotel, in Park Lane, told me that Diana and I were welcome to use his house in Minnis Bay, on the Kent coast: Wilf was now part of a record company managing rock groups and spent most of his time out of the country, and he had a flat in London anyway.

A few friends had clubbed together and given me a couple of grand on my release from prison, but, by the end of that summer, most of it had gone and Diana and I were virtually skint. One day we decided to have a tot up to see just how broke we were, and emptied all the money we could find on the dining table. I counted all the change and notes, then looked at Diana, the love of my life and soulmate, and grinned: 'Darling. I love you twenty-two quid.'

She gave me a warm smile and hugged me. 'And I love you, too, Charlie Kray.'

After that, 'I love you twenty-two quid' became our secret code – a reminder of when we were so in love that nothing, not even the shortage of cash, could spoil our happiness.

Les Martin wasn't giving up. Still fuming that my appeal against sentence had been turned down, he wrote to the European Court of Human Rights asking if it was against the law in England to sentence anyone over seventy to twelve years. He also asked for the Court's view on such a person being released with an electronic tag, given that the UK prison population is the highest in Western Europe. And, just for good measure, Les added a PS to his fax, saying that, as we are all European now, a law should be introduced making entrapment acceptable as a defence in the UK, as it is in Europe.

I had to hand it to Les. After my sentence he'd told anyone who cared to listen that he was going to battle to clear my name, or at least make life easier for me. And he was proving true to his word, bless him.

Chapter Twenty-eight

Shortly after arriving at Parkhurst, my address book was returned to me and I quickly started contacting all the friends I'd neglected during my illness at Frankland. I wrote to Robin to thank him for sending me a copy of Ken Follett's novel *The Key to Rebecca*, which had gone to No. 1 in the American bestsellers' list. Before becoming a multi-millionaire novelist, Ken had worked for Robin's publishing company, Everest Books, and, noticing that *Rebecca* was dedicated to Robin, I reminded him of the time, in 1975, that Ken and I had a pub lunch to discuss the first edition of *Me and My Brothers*, which Everest was publishing. I had a few quid in my pocket and, as Ken was such a lovely guy, I happily paid for our lunch, which, in the light of what has happened to each of us, has always struck me as amusing and ironic. Here I am in prison, skint, and Ken's rolling in it, with homes in London and the Caribbean. But good luck to him: he's a talented writer and deserves all his success.

I'd only been on the island a few weeks when Big Albert was cleared to visit me – and even though he lived two hundred or so miles away, he was soon visiting me twice a month. He would lock up The Elbow Room in the early hours – sometimes as late as 5 A.M. – grab a few hours' sleep, then drive to Portsmouth to catch the Isle of Wight ferry. After a light lunch, he would drive to the prison and was never, ever a minute late for the visit. In times of trouble, you find out who your true friends are, and Albert proved himself to be one of the firmest, most loyal I could have wished to have.

Sometimes he came with a mutual friend, Keith Smart, formerly the drummer with the Rockin' Berries pop group, now their manager, and we had a laugh one day after I found Keith on his own in the visiting hall.

'Where's Big Albert?' I asked, disappointed that the big man wasn't there.

'He's being strip-searched,' Keith said.

'WHAT?' I said, shocked. 'Why?'

'To check him out for drugs,' Keith said.

I couldn't believe it. Albert being daft enough to try to smuggle drugs in to me was too ridiculous for words.

'When we were going through security, one of the police dogs was all over him,' Keith said. 'So they took him away.'

Albert didn't emerge until half an hour later. Apparently they had him starkers but for his underpants, seriously believing he was hiding something. Having driven so far, Albert wasn't too happy about the hassle, and having half an hour lopped off his visiting time, but, typically, he quickly made a joke of it. Next time, he promised, he'd put a Bonio in his pocket to give the dog something to find. We had a chuckle about that, and it gave me something else to think about for a while.

That November, I was thrilled to hear that Wilf and Joey had been given Visiting Orders to see me. If they, too, were shocked that I looked gaunt and haggard, and the long, flowing barnet that had always amused people had been cut short, they didn't show it. They did their best to lift my spirits, but I was so worried that my legs had swollen and I was having even more trouble breathing that I found it hard to respond.

When they asked what was wrong with me, all I could say was: 'I don't know. I suppose it must be old age.' Deep down, though, I feared there was more to it than that and, three months later, I was proved right when my legs ballooned even more and I was transferred to nearby St Mary's Hospital for tests.

I had no idea anyone on the outside knew I was there, but, the next day, Wilf turned up unexpectedly. He said someone had contacted Reggie, in Wayland Prison, in Norfolk, and Reggie had rung him, asking him to check on me. I was surprised. Reggie was still writing letters, slagging me off about this and that, and I didn't think he was bothered about me, one way or the other.

Wilf took one look at the long chain linking me at the wrist with a prison officer sitting beside the bed and said, as politely as he could: 'Is that really necessary for someone as old and sick as Charlie?'

'I don't like it either,' the officer replied. 'But it's laid down in the regulations. There's nothing I can do.'

However, the chain was several feet long and, without being asked, the officer moved out of earshot, so that Wilf and I could have a few private moments.

'I'm in real trouble, Wilf,' I said. 'The doctors say they don't know what's wrong, but have a look at this.' I pulled back the sheets and showed him my legs and feet, which were now so swollen I could barely walk.

Seeing me in such a state must have hurt Wilf: he knew I'd always kept myself in trim – never more than eleven stone – and was proud of my slim figure. We chatted for an hour or so, about nothing in particular, then Wilf left, promising to come back the next day. I appreciated that more than you can imagine: I was so lonely and worried that I desperately wanted the comfort of such a good friend.

When Wilf arrived the following afternoon, I almost broke down. 'The doctors have told me they can treat whatever I've got with medication,' I said. 'They've recommended I go back to the nick later today.'

Typically, Wilf tried to see the positive in that. 'Well, at least you've got something they can cure,' he said. 'Keep your chin up – you'll be feeling better soon.' I wasn't so sure and, again, my suspicions proved right because, a week later, I was back in hospital, having yet more tests. Reggie got word and, again, rang Wilf, asking him to check on me.

When he arrived, I was propped up in bed, feeling relaxed – and looking it, according to Wilf. We chatted for a bit, then he made an excuse to leave. 'I've got to go somewhere for an hour or so,' he said. 'Anything you want while I'm out?'

'You know what, Wilf,' I said, 'I'd love some prawn sandwiches – brown bread. I've been dreaming about them.'

When Wilf hadn't returned after two hours, I started to get anxious, fearing the visit had proved too much for him and he'd gone home. But then in he walked, carrying not just a massive selection of seafood sandwiches but two pairs of smart, blue pyjamas, matching dressing gown and a pair of slippers, big enough to fit my enormous feet. I didn't know what to say, I was so touched. I hadn't given a thought to my grey prison pyjamas, but Wilf obviously felt I'd feel better in something more in keeping with the smart image I'd always maintained on the outside.

Fifteen minutes or so later, a doctor came in and talked to me about the results of the tests. I'm sure he explained everything as well as he could, but, to be truthful, I was so confused I didn't understand most of what he said. He mentioned septicaemia, emphysema, pneumonia, pleurisy but I had no idea how serious they were and, in the end, asked him to tell Wilf everything about my condition.

Over the next few weeks Wilf convinced me I would get better; I only needed a heart bypass operation, he said. But then one of the doctors shocked me by saying he was going to try to get me a compassionate release, on the grounds that I was terminally ill. I was gutted and hurt that Wilf had conned me. 'Why did you lie to me, Wilf?' I asked.

'Listen, Charlie,' he said. 'Use your brains. There's no way, at your age, that the authorities are going to pay out thousands for you to have a bypass. But once we get you out on compassionate grounds I'll arrange for our friends to hold benefit nights all over the country to raise money to get you the best surgeon in the land to operate privately.'

I believed him; desperately wanted to. 'I'm sorry to have doubted you, mate,' I said. 'Just get me out of here and get me that operation.'

In their wisdom, the authorities decided that Reggie no longer posed a threat to anyone and, over the next two weeks, he was brought to Parkhurst every other day. Someone somewhere obviously had a brain, because, suddenly, he was allowed to stay permanently in my vacant prison cell, to save him, and accompanying prison officers, the 400-mile round trip. That was the good news; the bad news was that, rules being rules, Reggie had to be handcuffed, and his legs chained together at the ankles, before he left the jail. Shuffling through the hospital, in front of gawking patients and staff, was unnecessarily humiliating, and it upset both of us.

But, then, nothing changes, does it? Reggie Kray was still viewed as a monster and needed to be treated as such.

I was allowed as many visitors as I liked, and Wilf wrote down the people I wanted to see most, in addition to Ronnie's childhood friend, Laurie O'Leary, who had been visiting regularly since I'd arrived on the island. Top of my list was Diana, of course, but she was working at the Ideal Home Exhibition in London, as she'd done every year since I'd come out of prison in 1975.

Wilf contacted our mutual friends, Joey Pyle, Big Albert and Keith Smart, and all responded immediately. Soon, Big Albert was making that ten-hour round trip, not once, but three times a week. The first time he arrived – again with Keith – my feet were so swollen I was unable to walk and had to use a wheelchair. As I was wheeled in to meet them, Keith, who has a fast wit, joked: 'Now, come on, Charlie, don't let them push you around!' That got us off to a bright start and we had a good visit, talking about everything, it seemed, except what was wrong with me.

When I needed to go to the loo, Albert offered to take me, and as he helped me out of the wheelchair I remembered what I'd told Flanagan in Belmarsh.

'They won't let me out of prison until I can't walk,' I'd said.

I was not a free man, but I *was* out of prison. Being proved right was no consolation at all.

Another person I was desperate to see was my dear old mate Freddie Foreman. But there was a problem, now that Reggie was visiting every day. The two of them hadn't spoken for about four years since Fred went on TV, revealing information about the Frank Mitchell killing that Reggie thought mugged him off badly. He was furious, and ever since had blanked all efforts at a reconciliation. Even now, he refused to be in the same room as Fred, which upset me. Life's too short to harbour grudges, isn't it?

Fred decided to come to the hospital anyway and it was a lovely surprise when he walked in with Diana. I was looking the best I could, in my new pjyamas, dressing gown and ridiculously large slippers, but I knew I was unrecognizable as the man Fred knew. He failed to hide his shock. Leaning down, he took my hand and said: 'My pal, it breaks my heart to see you like this.'

'You know what breaks *my* heart, Fred?'

He shook his head.

'That I ever introduced you to those twins of mine. Look at all the trouble they've caused you.'

Fred shook his head again. 'No, Charlie, no. You've got it wrong. You don't understand.'

And I didn't.

'I was with *you*, Charlie,' he said. 'Always you. I was *never* with the twins.'

I felt my eyes filling up: at the lowest ebb of my life, it

438

was what I needed to hear, and when they left I felt calmer and happier than I had done for weeks.

We'd always got on, Fred and me, and I wasn't at all surprised he chose *Respect* for the title of his autobiography, because he, more than anyone else in the London under-world, commanded it.

Me and the twins had grown up with that word, respect. Mum drummed it into me as a small boy that it was the greatest word in the English language: if you gave respect to people, she'd say, you nearly always got it back. I felt it my duty to drum it into the twins, too, and now, thinking back, I wondered whether I went over the top. For the word became all-important in their lives and, as they grew into young men, it became part of their everyday language; they were almost obsessive about it. As respectful people them-selves they demanded respect from others and, if they didn't get it, they were physically equipped to do something about it. Which they did quite often.

What made the twins so fearsome that they became legends in their own time? If anyone's to blame, it's prob-ably me. I was the one who made them aware their fists were lethal weapons. I was the one who bought them their first boxing gloves and taught them how to take care of themselves. I was the one who told them how good they were and took them, at just ten, to a boxing club. I was the one who persuaded them to turn pro and trained and sparred with them and sat in their corners, advising, encouraging, convincing them they were uniquely outstanding, with the potential to become champions.

I was the one who made them believe they were invincible.

Certainly no one can blame our mother for how the twins turned out. She did her best for them, as she did for me. When Ronnie and Reggie got in trouble as kids, she'd tell them: 'You mustn't argue with people – it's not right.' But they'd make light of it, telling her this or that person had done something bad and they had to sort it out. They loved the violence even then.

When they had flare-ups indoors Mum always cut them short. But how could she control them when they were away from the house? She tried her best to guide them, to discourage them from arguing and fighting, but, as they grew into teenagers and young men, she couldn't be with them twenty-four hours a day – any more than I could.

Lots of people, I know, find it impossible to accept that our mother didn't know what the twins were up to. Well, I can assure you she didn't. She was terribly naive; all the family were, believe it or not. And she never asked questions. Obviously, she got to hear the rumours of the heavy violence and the Cornell killing, but the twins merely glossed over it. 'It's just talk, Mum,' they'd say. 'Just people in the clubs.' And Mum always accepted it. Once, she was asked on TV if stories of the twins' violent exploits were true and she replied, simply: 'I don't know.' And she didn't, believe me.

I've often wondered whether, deep down, Mum *did* know they had an evil streak, but turned a blind eye because she couldn't face the truth.

Certainly she was always on my back, asking me to look after Ronnie and Reggie. Even when they were grown up, she'd worry about them and say to me: 'Oh, Charlie, those twins.' I knew it would ease her mind if I was watching out for them, so I did. Over the years, I must have saved dozens of lives by stepping in and talking Ronnie out of whatever vengeance he was planning when he was 'on one'. Usually I was able to sit him down and make him see sense, but if he was in one of his moods I'd go the other way and agree with him. 'You know what, Ron – you're right,' I'd say. 'You should do this geezer. Publicly execute him.'

That would do the trick. 'What! Are you mad?' Ronnie would say.

'No, I'm not mad. You're right and I'm wrong. Get hold of the dirty bastard. Go down Shoreditch High Road and put one in the nut. That's what he deserves!'

Ronnie would stare at me, horrified. 'You *are* mad,' he'd say. 'I'm having nothing more to do with you. Forget it.'

I did. And so did he – until the next time!

Now, confined to a wheelchair, unable to walk, but with plenty of time to think, I found myself wondering if the twins' lives would have turned out differently if I'd taught them a different sport; bought them football boots, not boxing gloves, and encouraged them to vent whatever anger and frustration they felt by running across a field, not slugging another human being.

I knew much more about boxing, though: it has always been an honourable sport, and I believed it offered the twins – two academically unqualified young men – the best chance to make something of themselves; to become the sort of people who would warrant the respect they wanted.

I always tried to do my best for my brothers, but, unfortunately, they rarely saw it that way. I never got any credit for anything, only the blame when things didn't turn out to their liking. I was their scapegoat, their human punchbag who would never hit back, no matter how much punishment I took. At no time did they show any understanding, let alone sympathy, for the selfish way they destroyed my life. At times they even gave me the impression that they thought it was my fault they were in prison.

My fault! All along I'd warned them that certain members of their so-called Firm would grass them up if the police got lively. But they took no notice; they didn't respect my judgement, never had. And, of course, I was proved right. When the going got tough, Ronnie Hart, Albert Donaghue and Scotch Jack Dickson went straight to Nipper Read and his team. Hart and Donaghue, particularly, loved the violence – and the money it brought in – but as tough guys they proved themselves cowards. Donaghue was one of the most vicious villains around and carried out much of the violence the twins were accused of. Yet he was allowed to walk away and begin a new life.

I would have loved the twins to have shown me some gratitude – or even just some recognition – for the warnings I gave, problems I sorted out, and for helping arrogant, ungrateful idiots the twins befriended behind bars. But Ronnie and Reggie were not made that way. The only time I remember feeling really close to them was that day in August 1982, when our mother died and I comforted them – Ronnie in Broadmoor, Reggie in Maidstone Prison. They were at their lowest ebb and maybe seeing things as they really were, for the one and only time in their lives. Both said they were proud of me. And they thanked me for all I was doing.

Sadly, their memories proved short. Older brother Charlie, good old reliable Charlie, was just a bit too soft, too easy-going, for their liking. They never said as much, but I'm sure my brothers viewed me as a huge disappointment.

Certainly respect was something they never once showed me.

Chapter Twenty-nine

With Charlie fading so fast, and unable to talk to me as his co-writer, I had to produce the following chapters without him – something I could never have done without a dear mutual friend of ours, Wilf Pine.

During the last three weeks of March, Charlie started going downhill, and by the first Sunday in April, Wilf decided to stay at the hospital, sleeping overnight in a bedside chair. By Tuesday, Charlie was drifting in and out of consciousness, but, in a wide-awake moment, suddenly brought up his funeral.

'You know I've never been a gangster, Wilf,' he said. 'And I don't want to be remembered as one, because of the twins. I was never like them, and I don't want people thinking I *was* – even when I'm dead. I spent my life trying to distance myself from their way of life, and a gangster's funeral would associate me with all they stood for, which wouldn't be right.'

Charlie told Wilf that he wanted his body taken to Diana's flat near Crystal Palace, with a few friends, stay there overnight, then be buried quietly, with no fuss, at Chingford Cemetery, beside his son, Gary. Charlie felt this would be a fitting way for him to say goodbye, for, although he liked lots of parties, he also enjoyed the quiet life.

Despite the differences they had had throughout their lives, Charlie felt sure Reg would respect his wishes.

A few hours later, that same Tuesday, Reg was brought from the prison to be with his brother. As next of kin, he was asked by a senior nurse whether he wanted Charlie resuscitated.

After a brief discussion, Reg decided against it. He was then asked which religion Charlie believed in and if Reg wanted a priest present when Charlie passed away.

'No priests, no vicars,' Reg replied. 'Nothing religious.'

Later, Reg sat down with Wilf and said: 'We must be realistic. What do you think we should do about Charlie's funeral?'

Wilf told him what Charlie had said that morning and Reg looked surprised. Then, after thinking about it for a few seconds, he said: 'All right. If that's what he wants, that's what he'll have.'

By mid-afternoon, Wilf had contacted Diana, still working at the Ideal Home Exhibition in central London, and she was on her way to the island. Charlie was now fading fast, but seemed to be aware the end was near because he told Wilf: 'I must hold on for my Di.'

At six-thirty, Charlie was fading so quickly that Reg was brought to the hospital again to say goodbye. But a raging storm had caused the ferry bringing Diana to be diverted from Ryde to Fishbourne, three miles away, and it was touch and go whether she would make it in time to say her own goodbye. She finally arrived, soaking wet from the torrential rain, and held Charlie in her arms. He appeared to be unconscious, but as soon as he heard Diana say: 'Charlie, I'm here', he opened his eyes.

'How much do you love me, Charlie Kray?' she asked softly.

'Twenty-two quid,' Charlie replied, in a feeble whisper.

An hour or so later, he died in Diana's arms.

Chapter Thirty

As Charlie Kray said himself, he was not a gangster and didn't want a highly publicized gangster's funeral that would, in the eyes of millions, link him to his violent brothers.

But he got one anyway. Reggie saw to that. Reggie had revelled in the misguided adulation of those cheering, chanting hordes at Ronnie's funeral and wanted more of it. But that was not the only betrayal of a man who Charlie, in moments of brutal, drink-enhanced honesty, referred to as 'an animal'.

Shortly after Charlie's death, Diana phoned my wife, Sue, and asked her if she would speak on her, and her family's, behalf at the funeral. Charlie had insisted on Sue representing him at Ronnie's and Gary's funerals and Diana was sure he would want her to speak at his, because they liked each other so much.

Of course, Sue agreed, and they spent half an hour or so discussing which poems would be appropriate and what Diana wanted Sue to say on her behalf. The next day, Sue rang the flat in Upper Norwood and Diana put the phone on loudspeaker, so that her daughter, Claudine – who was staying with her – could hear how Sue had put Diana's thoughts into words.

Everything, it seemed, was going smoothly. But the following afternoon Diana phoned our home in Kent, steaming.

'That bastard Reg,' she fumed. 'Can you believe it? He's told me that Charlie can't be buried at Chingford. There are only two spaces left in the family plot and he wants them for himself, and Bradley Allardyce.' Bradley was a young prisoner who Reggie called his 'adopted son'.

Diana was disgusted that Reggie could be so disrespectful to his older brother, but was not surprised: she had seen Charlie hurt many times by Reggie's outbursts, which is why she'd always had as little to do with him as possible. There was no love lost between them.

Claudine came on the phone, sobbing. Her voice breaking, she told Sue she loved Charlie dearly. To her, he was Dad, always had been, and he'd even given her away on her wedding day. She never wanted him buried with the twins; she wanted him cremated and his ashes scattered around a tree she planned to plant beside South Norwood lake, which she could see from the balcony of the flat, in Cantley Gardens. Often, sitting next to her on the balcony taking the sun, Charlie had said to her what a lovely, peaceful spot it was, and Claudine could think of no resting place more fitting for a man she loved and respected so much – someone who had never let her down. She wanted to be able to take her daughter, Georgia May, to the place where Charlie was at rest, whenever she needed to talk something over with him.

The problem was that Charlie had always said he wanted to be buried beside Gary. To deny him that was unthinkable, so Diana started to consider having Gary's body exhumed and reburied, with Charlie, in the cemetery of the local church, where Claudine had married.

In the end it didn't come to that: Reggie had a change of heart and gave Charlie priority over his young prison buddy. He told Diana he would be taking over the arrangements for the funeral, and, to avoid further upset, Diana left him to it.

Having had no contact with Reggie over the funeral, and not wanting to fuel possible tension, Sue said she'd understand if Diana changed her mind about her speaking.

Diana was horrified and said that was one area where Reggie would not have his way: Charlie might not be getting the quiet funeral he wished for, but all those who came to mourn his passing would, most certainly, hear the voice he liked so much.

Charlie would have been embarrassed – mortified, perhaps – by the show his brother put on for his farewell. True, it was not as ostentatious as the hyperbolic affair Reggie orchestrated for Ronnie: no black-plumed horses clip-clopped in front of a glass-sided hearse; only eighteen limousines, not twenty-nine, ferried family and friends; considerably fewer menacing minders patrolled outside English's funeral parlour, and St Matthew's Church, further along Bethnal Green Road; and a mere 5,000 or so curious onlookers thronged the streets outside the church and along the funeral route to Chingford Cemetery. But for such a courteous, engaging and dignified gentleman, who had made it clear he wanted a low-key farewell, with the minimum of fuss, the occasion of that sunny Wednesday 19 April was a disgrace. And an insult to Charlie's memory.

That he ignored his older brother's dying wish, thus affording him the lack of respect and love he had all his life, says more about Reggie Kray's self-obsessed, selfish and arrogant manner than anything I can.

Thankfully, and ironically, the saving grace was that in staging such a public funeral, albeit for his own glorification, Reggie did provide an opportunity for those who knew Charlie to pay their last respects. The streets and high office windows may have been crammed with gawpers and wannabe gangsters who had thrilled to the Kray legend, but inside St Matthew's 300 people generated a warmth that, I'm sure, could only have come from those who genuinely knew and liked Charlie.

That warmth clearly did not exist between Reggie and

Diana. The animosity between them, fuelled by Reggie's outrageous behaviour over the burial plot, was symbolized by the seating arrangements, handled on the day by Flanagan but carefully planned by Reggie: Diana was in the front row, to the right of Charlie's coffin, with Claudine and her son, Dean, and his family; Reggie was on the other side, handcuffed to a Wayland Prison officer, but clinging to his wife, Roberta, like a kid in the back row of the pictures. The gulf was only a matter of feet, but Charlie's soulmate and his brother were worlds apart, as they had been for twenty-five years. They barely glanced at each other throughout the fifty-minute ceremony.

That Charlie was by far the most popular of the three brothers became evident when Freddie Foreman's son, Jamie, stepped up to the lectern to read out messages from Charlie's friends and acquaintances. Jamie, an accomplished TV and movie actor, is experienced in delivering written lines under testing conditions, but the emotion of the occasion and his love for Charlie got to him that day. Poor Jamie's voice frequently cracked, and the loud sniffing among many of the congregation showed that he was not alone in being touched by such an enormous demonstration of affection.

Stepping down from the lectern, near to tears, Jamie said: 'Charlie's smile will be ingrained on my heart.'

After the hymn 'Fight The Good Fight', Sue stepped up to read her own tribute to Charlie. Few, if any, of the congregation, I suspect, would have expected to hear Shakespeare recited at his funeral, but that's how my wife started her address.

> And when he shall die, take him,
> And cut him out in tiny stars,
> And he shall make the heavens so bright
> That all the world will be in love with night.

To Sue, those beautiful words, from *Romeo and Juliet*, seemed to sum up Charlie perfectly, because she went on to say: 'My friend Charlie's bright smile lit up any room . . .'

To a hushed church, she read her own tribute:

> '*I have very clear images of Charlie all over our home – sharing dinner in the dining room, drinking coffee in the kitchen, partying in our lounge – but most clearly I can see him sitting in our garden, when he and my husband, Robin, were working on his book.*
>
> *Charlie was a delight to work with. Of course, he always looked the business. Smart and clean and smelling sweet, he'd arrive, on time, with that wonderful smile to greet me. He would work hard with us, but, more important, I can still hear his wonderful laughter when recalling some of the great times he'd enjoyed with friends.*
>
> *Many of you here will have your own memories of those stories: time spent with Charlie, your friend.*
>
> *But, of course, he was far more than a friend to dear Diana.*
>
> *Her memories span more than thirty years, from that wonderful moment when Charlie tracked her down and they were reunited, seven years after their chance meeting in Leicester.*'

And then Sue read out the words she had written for Diana:

> '*Charlie and I were a partnership. Like all relationships, it had its highs and lows. We shared a wonderful life that spun us in all directions. We had a superb time which we enjoyed to the full. There was lots of laughter and joy and the occasional sadness. There were so many good times shared with friends from all walks of life – most of you are here today. We all adored Charlie's laughter and his wit. Something, I know, each and every one of us will always treasure.*
>
> *I know, too, he has taken with him a small piece of each*

449

*and every one of you here today. We have all lost someone
very special.*

*It is a comfort to me that on the wet and windy night at the
end, Charlie was sitting waiting for me. He said he knew
I would come. I am so grateful I shared that time with him.*

*I will especially miss Charlie's wonderful big blue, blue
eyes. A picture of his enchanting smile will remain forever
in my heart, until the day when I also walk into the light
and am reunited with my Charlie.*

Charlie, I just want to tell you how much I love you.
I love you twenty-two quid.'

Sue went on to read 'Stop All the Clocks', by W. H. Auden,
on Diana's behalf, then the beautiful words about
fatherhood, written by Tony Holland, the creator of *East-
Enders*, for Claudine and Dean. She finished her tribute
with the poem by an anonymous writer, 'Weep Not For
Me'.

Not to be outdone, Reggie had recorded himself reciting
the poem 'Do Not Stand at My Grave and Weep', and his
feeble voice echoed through the church on loudspeakers,
leaving most, if not all, of the congregation bemused.

Five years before, Dave Courtney had talked Reggie out
of playing his own recorded tribute at Ronnie's funeral, and
it was lamentable that Reggie didn't have anyone with the
guts to give him the same advice this time. Reggie deserves
praise for wanting to make a personal contribution, but,
quite honestly, his voice did not have the gravitas to make
his reading anything but embarrassing for everyone who
heard it. But, then, in his later years, Reggie always felt he
knew best. And, judging by his reaction to the noisy crowds
after the service, I'm sure he felt it was as much his day as
Charlie's. As the oak casket was carried from the church,
to Shirley Bassey singing 'As Long As He Needs Me', and
Reggie emerged into the bright sunshine, he gave a regal

wave to the crowds, enthusiastically responding to Frankie Fraser's call for 'Three cheers for Reggie'.

'As Long As He Needs Me'? In all my experience, Reggie was *never* there when Charlie needed him.

The Reggie Kray 'Roadshow' continued, as it had done at Ronnie's funeral, with crowds lining the route to Chingford Cemetery and what has become known as 'Kray Corner' – the plot where Reggie's parents, brother, nephew and wife are buried.

He paid his respects at each grave, then, with Roberta beside him, looked on stoically as Charlie's coffin was lowered into the ground next to his beloved Gary. Who knows whether Reggie gave a thought to the unimaginable hurt he'd caused Diana and Claudine by planning to deny Charlie the right to slip into eternity with the son he adored so much?

As Reg was hugged and kissed by mourners, Diana said: 'Charlie would have loved this sunshine.' But her words were drowned by more cries of 'Three cheers for Reg', and 'Take the cuffs off', as Reggie was taken from the graveside to the blue people carrier waiting to take him back to Norfolk.

We had all come to bury Charlie, the Gentleman, but thousands had come to hail Reggie, the Gangster.

And that's just the way he'd planned it.

A Personal View

As *Me and My Brothers* is an autobiography, one would expect Charlie to come out of it as a good guy; a very likeable, non-violent, law-abiding individual who paid a dreadful price for his brothers' murderous ways. But that *is* the truth. And if this book does nothing else but convince people that Charlie was not a gangster, then I'm happy. And I know Charlie would have been, too.

I didn't know him as well as some people – Wilf Pine and Albert Chapman and, of course, Diana, for example – but, as Charlie's first publisher, then his ghostwriter, I spent hundreds of hours over many months getting close to him and unquestionably saw the man behind the myth, understood, as much as one could, the anger, bitterness and downright frustration he felt.

After his conviction in the McVitie case, it was open season for the media where Charlie was concerned. To newspapers and TV alike, he *was* an accessory to murder, *was* a willing party in all the madness and mayhem the twins brought to sixties London. And, on his release from prison, in 1975, journalists still believed he *was* the twins' mouthpiece, *was* the brain behind their businesses that supposedly capitalized on their infamy.

I have personal experience of how that wrongful conviction earned Charlie his shameful reputation.

In 1987, when I was collaborating with Charlie for a rewrite of the first edition of *Me and My Brothers*, I was a sub-editor on the *Daily Express*, working in the late afternoon and night. One of my colleagues, Bill Montgomery, knew I was ghosting Charlie's story, but knew nothing of how we were doing it. When I told him I'd spent the morning taping Charlie in my garden, he was horrified.

'You allow that man *in your house*?'

'Of course I do,' I said. 'Why shouldn't I?'

'Because he's one of the Krays,' Bill said. 'They murdered people, for God's sake.'

'Charlie didn't murder anyone,' I told him quietly.

'He may not have wielded the knife that killed McVitie, but he did his brothers' dirty work. Got rid of a dead body.'

'No he didn't,' I said. 'Charlie had nothing to do with the murder. He was stitched up by the police.'

Bill scoffed. 'How can you be sure he's telling the truth?'

'How can you be so sure he's not,' I said. 'You've never even met the man.'

'And I don't want to.'

'Because he's a Kray?'

'Yeah, if you want to put it that way. They're all gangsters.'

'Charlie wasn't a gangster, Bill,' I said. 'The twins were the gangsters.'

'They were all the same, Robbie,' he said. 'All the same.'

I didn't want a row, so I forced a smile. 'Let's agree to disagree, Bill. Let's leave it there.'

And we did. We never spoke about Charlie, or his book, again – even when it was published the following September and I took a copy into the office. But that conversation played on my mind and brought into sharp focus the enormity of the problem the Kray name gave Charlie. If a seasoned sub-editor, responsible for writing headlines and editing reporters' copy in a national newspaper, believed it to be true, what price the millions of readers? If a journalist with forty years' experience detested the Kray name so much what hope did that give Charlie?

I can understand why Charlie decided not to fight to clear

his name. But, given the way his life panned out, I'm not sure that well-intentioned advice of Ronnie's psychiatrist was right. On his release from prison, Charlie was so distressed and humiliated by people's reaction to him that his happy-go-lucky personality changed and he had no self-confidence.

What he so needed was a platform to give his side of what, for him, was a desperately tragic story. The Press and TV weren't going to give it to him, but the Court of Human Rights in Strasbourg might have. After all, in 1975 he had a very strong case to put before it, because, shortly after his conviction, the prosecution's main witness, Ronald Hart, made a statement on oath stating he had lied about Charlie's involvement in the McVitie case. Then, later, both Tony and Chris Lambrianou confessed that they, with Ronnie Bender, had taken McVitie's body from Evering Road.

We'll never know whether Charlie would have been allowed to win such an action; probably not, since it would have meant reopening the whole case and that would have brought into the open the reason Charlie had been convicted for a crime he didn't commit. But, at the very least, the fact that the Kray twins' elder brother was challenging his conviction, and had compelling new evidence to support him, would have made headlines and provided the platform Charlie needed; given him the chance to tell the world he did not do what he'd been imprisoned for.

And that would have given him a purpose in life.

As it was, he drifted rather aimlessly, wanting so much to get involved in some legitimate venture but not having the wherewithal to pull anything together. Much has been said – in the papers and on the internet – about Charlie being the brains behind the twins' so-called empire, but that's rubbish. Successful businessmen have vision – and Charlie had none. If you outlined a scheme that would earn him, say, £100,000 over two years and then gave him an alternative of five grand in his hand now, Charlie would take the second option, no question.

Whether it was because he'd been robbed of precious years of his life and wanted to make up for lost time, I don't know, but Charlie always looked to today, not tomorrow. If ever anyone epitomized the old adage 'A bird in the hand is worth two in the bush', it was him.

That's why I knew, sitting in Redbridge Magistrates' Court two days after Charlie's arrest, that all the headlines of him masterminding a £78 million two-year drugs deal were ludicrous. Such an elaborate operation would require careful planning and attention to detail – not Charlie's strengths at all.

Like Charlie and all his friends, I'm at a loss to know why he was targeted. For, make no mistake, he *was* targeted. And, despite the prosecution arguing to the contrary, he *was* entrapped. Some people have said that Charlie was in the wrong place at the wrong time, unwittingly mingling with known drug dealers, who were under police surveillance. But this doesn't add up; no one but Charlie and his two co-defendants were arrested. More likely is the theory of one of the leading barristers in the case: that Jack and his undercover team had run up enormous expenses in a drug operation which, after several months' surveillance, had produced no results. Under pressure to make arrests, they met the likeable, but woefully naive, Patsy Manning, who boasted of his long friendship with Charlie. Now, who better than the last of the Krays to get the police off the hook? What a career boost that would be for Jack. But after the introductions were made, Charlie did not keep in touch with Jack; the undercover man kept ringing *him*. If Jack had not made contact, that would have been the end of it. But the Geordies were determined to lure Charlie into their carefully spun web and, sadly, he was so gullible, so trusting – and so broke – that he was a pathetically easy victim. Having said that, I was intrigued to learn at the trial that, although the police had dozens of hours of Charlie on tape, only a few were used in evidence. The majority of the recordings were either of such poor sound quality, or so banal, that they proved nothing – except, perhaps, that the police had to tape Charlie for many hours before they got him to say what they wanted. Knowing how much he giggled and ran off at the mouth when he was having 'a good drink', I'm sure he proved very frustrating.

Lest anyone doubts Charlie's poor financial state at that time, I can vouch that he *was* broke. Penniless, in fact. As I told the court, I rang Charlie at Judy's home shortly after we'd been to David Bailey's studios for a photo shoot for a *Sunday Telegraph* magazine feature I'd set up. When I asked how he was, Charlie was typically chirpy, but then said: 'To be truthful, Rob, I'm not too clever. I can't even afford a packet of fags.'

I told him I could advance him his share of the *Sunday Telegraph*'s £150 fee and drove to Sanderstead with it. I remember Charlie being excited at having met 'some lovely guys in Newcastle who had bundles of money'. At that time, I don't believe Charlie had any idea what his new-found friends were going to put to him.

What I find nauseating, given the tragic outcome, is that those 'lovely guys' would have known within minutes of meeting Charlie that he was not – unquestionably *not* – a conniving drug baron, capable of all they later claimed he was. They would have seen the man as he genuinely was – amiable and likeable, but ineffectual and without two ha'pennies to rub together. Yet they pursued him, preyed on his vulnerability at a traumatic time in his life, to get themselves a result.

Like all Charlie's friends, I found the charges outrageous – incredible – but that he'd been arrested for *something* was not really a surprise. I knew from experience that it didn't take much for the police to show interest in Charlie Kray. Driving home after a party at my house, one of my wife's distant relatives was involved in a drunken domestic row. Police were called and the young woman boasted that she'd been at a party with Charlie Kray. Three TV stars and a national newspaper editor were also there – among a hundred guests – but she mentioned only Charlie, and, shortly after 3 A.M., two officers arrived at the house wanting to know if he was there. I found it interesting that the young woman omitted to mention anyone else at the party, and wondered whether the police would have found it necessary to turn up if she had.

I don't know what purpose those boys in blue thought their visit served, but it was a clear indication that, more than twenty years on, the name Kray still sparked police interest. And if further proof was needed, I got it in 1993, when a financier named Donald Urquhart was murdered by a motorcycle hitman outside his home in Marylebone. Charlie did not know Urquhart and certainly had no idea why he was gunned down. But he was arrested and questioned for several hours anyway. And, of course, KRAY BROTHER QUIZZED IN MURDER PROBE made striking – and legally safe – headlines.

It was grossly unfair, of course, and the next morning Charlie came to see Sue and I to ask if there was anything we could do about it. There was: we had to get some positive publicity. Fast. I rang the *London Tonight* TV programme, offering them an exclusive live interview that evening. They jumped at it and, shortly before 7 P.M., Charlie was interviewed by Alistair Stewart, who was clearly delighted at being handed a scoop on a story that had made all that day's newspapers.

Charlie was excellent in that interview, very focused on making the point that, again, the Kray name was causing him problems. But, two days later, the soft, insecure side of his nature let him down after I set up an interview on the *Richard & Judy* morning TV chat show, which had a national audience.

We were flown to the Liverpool studios and all the way there – and in the hospitality room before he went on camera – I coached Charlie on how to handle the interview; urged him not to allow himself to be side-tracked, but to stick to the point – which was the curse of the Kray name. I could have saved my breath. The first question Richard Madeley asked was: 'What was it like with the twins in the East End in the sixties?' and Charlie was off, naively reliving all the oft-told nonsense again. I was furious and gave him a hard time afterwards for blowing a perfect opportunity to get his feelings across to millions of viewers. But that was Charlie. Whereas Alistair Stewart led him on the hard news angle, Richard and Judy wanted only the usual rubbish that had been in the papers on and off for thirty years, and Charlie did not have the hard-nosed confidence to steer the conversation his way.

It was this lack of arrogance and self-importance that made him so different from the twins. They were forceful personalities who always wanted things their own way, but Charlie was gentle-natured, easy-going, and never forced himself on anyone. While the twins would be quick to use violence if they felt wronged, Charlie would make his point with passion, not aggression. Like the twins, he was good with his fists, but never used them outside the boxing ring. His brothers wanted him to be part of the violence, but Charlie did not want to know and, much to their annoyance, tried to distance himself by moving away from Bethnal Green with his wife, Dolly. He preferred to stay at home with her, but, one evening – after much persuasion – Charlie agreed to go to a meeting with the twins and their Firm. After listening to their violent plans, Charlie went to walk out, prompting Ronnie to make fun of him 'running back

458

to his wife'. It was one of the few times Charlie lost his temper, as he told the twins what he really thought of their so-called friends. He tried to convince them to end the violence, but, of course, the twins never listened to him. What did their soft-hearted brother know?

If all the newspaper talk about Charlie being a feared gangster hadn't been so serious, he would have found it funny. The twins had a reputation for 'demanding with menaces', but Charlie always had difficulty *asking* for money – even if it was rightfully due. When he was short of cash, he'd even get me to ring HarperCollins to ask about his royalty cheque, because he did not want anyone thinking he was pushy!

Charlie was well mannered and courteous, too, and, despite all that had happened to him, loved to laugh. It was this, as much as his effortless charm, that endeared him to women. Barbara Windsor, for one, thought the world of Charlie in the sixties – and still did when I arranged a reunion backstage at one of her theatre performances. She always talked about his 'Steve McQueen good looks' and, while I was collaborating with her for her autobiography, she confessed to being bitterly disappointed that he had not left Dolly to live with her. Naturally, I felt that readers of his own story would want details of his relationship with Barbara, but Charlie was so discreet and gentlemanly, in an old-fashioned way, that he declined to reveal anything that would embarrass her.

If you get the impression I liked Charlie Kray, you're right. Indeed, I've never met anyone who didn't like him. There was nothing *to* dislike; nothing at all. That's why those Chelmsford Prison guards shook his hand so warmly, after delivering him to Albany Prison. That's why Prison Officer Jenkins wrote such a glowing testimonial. And that's why so many people from all walks of life, and from all over the country, were quick to go to court to speak up for him. He was a genuinely nice bloke, a decent, warm human being, who appreciated even the smallest kindness, rarely spoke badly of anyone and always showed respect, often to people who didn't deserve it.

Sadly for Charlie, the positive side of his personality was not an image the media was prepared to portray. And, again, I have personal experience to prove the point. When the *Sunday Telegraph* sent a journalist, Justine Picardie, to interview Charlie two months after Gary's death, I met her beforehand to ask what line she was proposing to take with the piece. She wanted to know the real man, she said, so I told her she was in for a pleasant surprise that would be good for her article: the person she was about to meet was nothing like the one she had read about, and she had the chance to get information he had never told any journalist before. Ms Picardie, all coy smiles and compliments, seemed most keen on writing something fresh and original on Charlie. On the basis of what she wrote it was clear she had her own agenda.

What appeared in the magazine was a sarcastic, shabby piece that, in my opinion, matched the writer and, more significantly, missed the point spectacularly. I'd explained that Charlie was broke and in deep grief over his son's death, but Ms Picardie portrayed him, unjustly, as a cash-conscious opportunist, making a mint out of his brothers' notoriety. She claimed he was marketing Kray twins' T-shirts, using David Bailey's iconic photo. He was not; he had never even seen one. She claimed he had a 'practical involvement' in the selling of the Kray name and was protecting it from 'unwelcome outsiders, muscling in on the act'. He did not, and was not. In fact, at this time, Charlie was out of favour with Reg, over some imagined slight, and was not in contact with either him or Ronnie. Often, the first Charlie knew of what the twins were up to was when he read it in the papers.

460

The article bore little resemblance to what I'd seen and heard at the interview and I wrote to Ms Picardie pointing out her inaccuracies and the unfairness of her piece. Unsurprisingly, she did not reply.

I was angry and embarrassed at making a serious error of judgement on Charlie's behalf, but he was typically philosophical: after all, he'd been living with a negative press since his release from prison. And with such cynical journalists continuing to put the knife in, he was stuck with it for ever.

How sadly ironic that the name Charlie bore with pride for so long should cause him such misery and shame.

How tragic that a name synonymous with violence should cut short the life of someone so gentle.

To everyone who knew him, he was Champagne Charlie – a true gentleman who would throw a party, but never a punch.

And that's how I'll remember him.

Also available

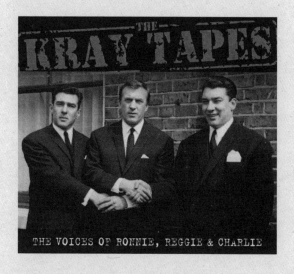

3 x CD Audio Box Set
Also available at www.rightrecordings.com